T0402382

LBGTQ+ Crime and Victimization

This book provides research and analysis on an understudied topic: the LBGTQ+ community as victims and offenders. Most publications focus on LBGTQ+ history and the community's movement towards equality and acceptance in society and law. A focus on how the criminal justice system victimizes and marginalizes LBGTQ+ persons is needed. Consequently, this work includes chapters on members of the LBGTQ+ community who work in the criminal justice system, forced sexual orientation efforts, transgender legal concerns, LBGTQ+ persons who are arrested and imprisoned, and online dating hate crimes. International scholars provide their individual stories about being gay, bisexual, or lesbian and working as a police or correctional officer. Other international contributors explain their research on crime and how the law and criminal justice community does not provide LBGTQ+ persons with protection or support as offenders or victims. This book will be of interest to researchers and advanced students of Criminology, Sociology, Law, and Gender Studies. It was originally published as a special issue of the journal *Women & Criminal Justice*.

Frances P. Bernat (JD, PhD) is a Texas A&M System and Arizona State University Regents Professor and Emerita at Arizona State University, Tempe, USA. She is nationally and internationally known for her scholarship, which involves the interplay between law and criminal justice: immigration, criminal law and procedure, cybercrime, human sex trafficking, and youth deviance and resilience.

LBGTQ+ Crime and Victimization

Edited by
Frances P. Bernat

Routledge
Taylor & Francis Group

LONDON AND NEW YORK

First published 2023
by Routledge
4 Park Square, Milton Park, Abingdon, Oxon, OX14 4RN

and by Routledge
605 Third Avenue, New York, NY 10158

Routledge is an imprint of the Taylor & Francis Group, an informa business

Chapters 1,3–6 and 8–10 © 2023 Taylor & Francis
Chapter 2 © 2021 Rachel Keighley. Originally published as Open Access.
Chapter 7 © 2021 Gloriana Rodriguez Alvarez and Alejandro Fernandez Munoz. Originally published as Open Access.
Chapter 11 © 2021 W. Carsten Andresen. Originally published as Open Access.

With the exception of Chapters 2,7 and 11 no part of this book may be reprinted or reproduced or utilised in any form or by any electronic, mechanical, or other means, now known or hereafter invented, including photocopying and recording, or in any information storage or retrieval system, without permission in writing from the publishers. For details on the rights for Chapters 2,7 and 11, please see the chapters' Open Access footnotes.

Trademark notice: Product or corporate names may be trademarks or registered trademarks, and are used only for identification and explanation without intent to infringe.

British Library Cataloguing-in-Publication Data
A catalogue record for this book is available from the British Library

ISBN13: 978-1-032-45378-1 (hbk)
ISBN13: 978-1-032-45379-8 (pbk)
ISBN13: 978-1-003-37668-2 (ebk)

DOI: 10.4324/9781003376682

Typeset in Minion Pro
by codeMantra

Publisher's Note
The publisher accepts responsibility for any inconsistencies that may have arisen during the conversion of this book from journal articles to book chapters, namely the inclusion of journal terminology.

Disclaimer
Every effort has been made to contact copyright holders for their permission to reprint material in this book. The publishers would be grateful to hear from any copyright holder who is not here acknowledged and will undertake to rectify any errors or omissions in future editions of this book.

Contents

Citation Information

The chapters in this book were originally published in the journal *Women & Criminal Justice*, volume 32, issue 1–2 (2022). When citing this material, please use the original page numbering for each article, as follows:

Chapter 1
Confronting Oppression: Reframing Need and Advancing Responsivity for LGBTQ+ Youth and Young Adults
Krystal Roig-Palmer and Faith E. Lutze
Women & Criminal Justice, volume 32, issue 1–2 (2022) pp. 2–28

Chapter 2
Hate Hurts: Exploring the Impact of Online Hate on LGBTQ+ Young People
Rachel Keighley
Women & Criminal Justice, volume 32, issue 1–2 (2022) pp. 29–48

Chapter 3
Gay Dating Platforms, Crimes, and Harms in India: New Directions for Research and Theory
Rahul Sinha-Roy and Matthew Ball
Women & Criminal Justice, volume 32, issue 1–2 (2022) pp. 49–65

Chapter 4
"Missing and Missed": Failures of the Bruce McArthur Investigation and the Ongoing Victimization of Toronto's Rainbow Streets
V. Bragagnolo
Women & Criminal Justice, volume 32, issue 1–2 (2022) pp. 66–92

Chapter 5
Workplace Experiences of Lesbian and Bisexual Female Police Officers in the Royal Newfoundland Constabulary
Sulaimon Giwa, Roddrick A. Colvin, Rosemary Ricciardelli, and Amanda P. Warren
Women & Criminal Justice, volume 32, issue 1–2 (2022) pp. 93–110

Chapter 6
Surviving the Landings: An Autoethnographic Account of Being a Gay Female Prison Officer (in an Adult Male Prison in England)
Sarah Nixon
Women & Criminal Justice, volume 32, issue 1–2 (2022) pp. 111–130

For any permission-related enquiries please visit:
http://www.tandfonline.com/page/help/permissions

Notes on Contributors

W. Carsten Andresen, Criminal Justice, St. Edward's University, Austin, USA.

Matthew Ball, School of Justice, Queensland University of Technology—Gardens Point Campus, Brisbane, Australia.

Frances P. Bernat, Texas A&M System and Arizona State University, Tempe, USA.

Sonia Boulos, International Relations and Law, Universidad Antonio de Nebrija, Madrid, Spain.

V. Bragagnolo, School of Gender, Sexuality and Women's Studies, York University, Toronto, Canada.

Roddrick A. Colvin, School of Public Affairs, San Diego State University, USA.

Courtney A. Crittenden, Department of Social, Cultural, and Justice Studies, University of Tennessee at Chattanooga, USA.

Alejandro Fernandez Muñoz, Universidad Estatala Distancia, San Jose, Costa Rica.

Hannah C. Gateley, Department of Social, Cultural, and Justice Studies, University of Tennessee at Chattanooga, USA.

Sulaimon Giwa, School of Social Work, Memorial University of Newfoundland, St. John's, Canada.

César González-Cantón, Management and Organizations, CUNEF Universidad, Madrid, Spain.

Rachel Keighley, School of Criminology, University of Leicester, UK.

Faith E. Lutze, Department of Criminal Justice and Criminology, Washington State University, Pullman, USA.

Karen McGuffee, Department of Social, Cultural, and Justice Studies, University of Tennessee at Chattanooga, USA.

Sarah Nixon, Natural and Social Sciences, University of Gloucestershire, UK.

Claire Nolasco Braaten, Department of Social Sciences, Criminology Program, Texas A&M University-San Antonio, One University Way, USA.

Christina N. Policastro, Department of Social, Cultural, and Justice Studies, University of Tennessee at Chattanooga, USA.

Rosemary Ricciardelli, Department of Sociology, Police Studies, Memorial University of Newfoundland, St. John's, Canada.

Gloriana Rodriguez Alvarez, King's College London, United Kingdom of Great Britain and Northern Ireland.

Krystal Roig-Palmer, Department of Criminal Justice and Criminology, Washington State University, Pullman, USA.

Rahul Sinha-Roy, School of Justice, Queensland University of Technology—Gardens Point Campus, Brisbane, Australia.

Michael S. Vaughn, Department of Criminal Justice and Criminology, Institute for Legal Studies in Criminal Justice, College of Criminal Justice, Sam Houston State University, Huntsville, USA.

Amanda P. Warren, School of Social Work, Memorial University of Newfoundland, St. John's, Canada.

The LBGTQ+ Community and Criminal Justice

This book is devoted to LBGTQ+ research on crime and victimization. Discrimination against members of a minority community is a problem that exists worldwide. In the 21st century, members of the LBGTQ+ community have experienced some gains: gay rights, marriage equality, and the abolishment of various discriminatory laws in some nations around the world. However, the LBGTQ+ community has also experienced hate crime violence, marginalization, cultural hostility, and other actions that reinforce their social and legal exclusion. In 2020, for example, although hate crimes against gay persons in the United States decreased, hate crimes against transgender persons increased (Yurcaba, 2021a). In addition, in 2021, the State of Texas had the most anti-transgender bills (40) proposed in 2021 (Freedom for All Americans, 2021a). In November 2021, President Biden participated in a Day of Remembrance for the 45 persons killed by anti-transgender violence in the United States (Judd, 2021). These deaths disproportionately fall on Black transgender individuals, many of who live in the southern United States (Yurcaba, 2021b). According to Freedom for All Americans (2021b), there are 29 states which do not fully protect the LBGTQ+ community from discrimination. To understand the nature and extent of discrimination against the LBGTQ+ community, this volume addresses crime and victimization, discriminatory laws and criminal justice policies, and the impact of discrimination on the LBGTQ+ community. This book also includes chapters on LBGTQ+ offenders and persons working in the criminal justice system. I hope that you find the following chapters to be insightful, and provocative about what the criminal justice system can and should do to respond to the needs of the LBGTQ+ community.

References

Freedom for All Americans. (2021a). *Legislative tracker: Anti-transgender legislation*. Retrieved from https://freedomforallamericans.org/legislative-tracker/anti-transgender-legislation/

Freedom for All Americans. (2021b). *How we are winning LGBTQ nondiscrimination nationwide*. Retrieved from https://freedomforallamericans.org/how-were-winning/

Judd, D. (2021, November 20). Biden marks 'deadliest year on record for transgender Americans' on day of remembrance. *CNN Politics*. Retrieved from https://www.cnn.com/2021/11/20/politics/joe-biden-transgender-day-of-remembrance/index.html

Yurcaba, J. (2021a, September 1). Anti-gay hate crimes fell slightly in 2020 while anti-trans crimes rose, FBI says. *NBC News*. Retrieved from https://www.nbcnews.com/nbc-out/out-news/anti-gay-hate-crimes-fell-slightly-2020-anti-trans-crimes-rose-fbi-say-rcna1846

Yurcaba, J. (2021b, November 19). Transgender people in 'survival mode' as violence rises, anti-trans bills become law. Retrieved from https://www.nbcnews.com/nbc-out/out-news/transgender-people-survival-mode-violence-rises-anti-trans-bills-becom-rcna6053

Frances P. Bernat

Confronting Oppression: Reframing Need and Advancing Responsivity for LGBTQ+ Youth and Young Adults

Krystal Roig-Palmer and Faith E. Lutze

ABSTRACT
Research in juvenile and criminal justice concerning how to assess and target interventions to LGBTQ+ youth and young adults is insufficient. With the proliferation of the *Risk-Need-Responsivity Model* (RNR), risk/need assessment tools have become evidence-based practice providing guidance to determining risk, identifying need, and the importance of targeting interventions to advance prosocial behavior. Critics have noted that during implementation of the *RNR Model*, the focus is too often on the risk principle at the expense of the need and responsivity principles. This study provides evidence from an intensive case study, and process evaluation of the *Lambert House: LGBTQ+ Youth Community Center*, that responsivity needs to be prominent when serving LGBTQ+ youth and young adults. Based on an analysis of 60 semi-structured interviews with program participants, staff, and community advocates, we argue that risk/need assessment tools driven by the RNR model be inclusive and responsive to LGBTQ+ youth and young adults.

INTRODUCTION

Sexual and gender minority youth and young adults live in a heteronormative society that does not consistently provide access to comprehensive services essential for healthy adolescent developmental experiences. Settings such as schools, recreational programs, health clinics, homeless shelters, juvenile detention centers, probation, and other related institutions are not necessarily equipped to facilitate culturally competent services that are responsive and comprehensive to the needs of LGBTQ+ youth. Although contemporary social movements and legal decisions have brought greater acceptance, LGBTQ+ youth and young adults often remain marginalized and underserved in mainstream society (Glaister, 2008; Irvine, 2010; Majd et al., 2009; Mogul et al., 2011).

The dynamics of sexual orientation and/or gender identity formation specific to LGBTQ+ youth and young adults can be perplexing and overwhelming to some practitioners in professional settings where they may receive minimal or only superficial training to improve their cultural competency of the LGBTQ+ population. Nonetheless, forward thinking practitioners in youth-rearing environments want to know how they can orient their practice to provide comprehensive services to sexual and gender minority youth. Without specific guidance about how to assess and treat LGBTQ+ individuals, practitioners often rely on existing "off the shelf," evidence-based, assessment tools originally designed using heteronormative, primarily male, justice involved populations to inform their decisions (see Duwe & Rocque, 2017; Hamilton et al., 2020, 2021). Thus, justice professionals have broadly adopted assessment tools informed by the Risk-

Need-Responsivity Model (RNR). The RNR Model provides the foundational framework for the assessment of both adults and juveniles who are justice involved (Bonta & Andrews, 2010).

Assessment tools provide actuarial methods to predict who is most likely to persist in anti-social and criminal behavior. Although extensive reviews have shown that these tools are statistically more reliable than clinician-based subjective assessments (Drake, 2014; Duwe & Rocque, 2017; Hamilton et al., 2021; Picard-Fritsche et al., 2017), they have been criticized for being developed based solely on official record data that may be biased against BIPOC due to increased surveillance and sanctioning by the justice system (see Kurlychek & Johnson, 2019; Picard-Fritsche et al., 2017) and for failing to be gender responsive to the unique risks and needs of girls and women (Salisbury et al., 2009; Van Voorhis, 2012). In spite of these meaningful critiques, both advocates and critics of risk assessment tools have been essentially silent on the salient issue of contextualizing LGBTQ+ experiences to inform assessments, decision-making, and most importantly to develop responsive programs with the integrity to competently serve the needs of LGBTQ+ youth.[1]

The current study builds upon prior research by contextualizing the experiences and perspectives of LGBTQ+ youth as related to each of the RNR domains included within most contemporary, actuarial, risk assessment tools used to assess both adults and juveniles. We base our analyses on interviews conducted with adult advocates, youth, and young adults voluntarily participating in a LGBTQ+ youth community center. We argue that LGBTQ+ youth who are vulnerable to becoming justice involved are likely to be low risk and high need due to experiences complicated by enduring social stigma, marginalization, and the associated emotional and physical trauma perpetrated against them that may last over the life course. We provide support for the argument that risk/need assessment tools driven by the RNR model be inclusive and responsive to LGBTQ+ youth and adults. We emphasize that programs should be prevention oriented, provide social support, and be trauma informed to proactively reduce the risks and to address the unique needs of LGBTQ+ youth. Finally, we argue that failing to be responsive to the risks and needs of LGBTQ+ youth who are, or may become, justice involved fails to take responsibility for justice by merely defaulting to heteronormative gendered and patriarchal systems of oppression embedded within existing evidence-based juvenile and criminal justice practice (Adams et al., 2009; Brechin, 2000; Chesney-Lind & Eliason, 2006)

Reframing Risk, Addressing Need, and Advancing Responsivity for LGBTQ+ Youth

The Risk-Need-Responsivity (RNR) Model has become a driving force in assessing "what works" to change the criminogenic behavior and attitudes of justice involved individuals (Andrews & Bonta, 2010). Most research inclusive of the RNR Model heavily focuses on the *risk principle* and the likelihood a person will reoffend and on the *need principle* that identifies the underlying dynamic factors that may be changed through correctional intervention and treatment. The *responsivity principle*, the least studied component of the RNR Model, refers to designing interventions based on the most effective way to engage individuals in programs using strategies aligned with their learning styles and cultural identities. These cognitive-behavioral strategies include the *relationship principle* that is based on "establishing warm, respectful and collaborative working alliances with the client" and the *structuring principle* that advances change through "appropriate modeling, reinforcement, problem solving" and other organized activities that reinforce prosocial behavior (Bonta & Andrews, 2007).

---

[1] See Harvell et al. (2018) for mention of LGBTQ+ in a review of screening, assessment, and structured decision making with justice involved juveniles. Although LGBTQ+ youth are mentioned, gender/sex nonconforming youth are consistently grouped together with gender and girls and not as an independent group worthy of unique screening or assessment.

The RNR Model has become an essential component of the *Principles of Effective Interventions* (PEI) (National Institute of Corrections, 2013, 2016). Meta-analyses show that rehabilitation programs and intervention strategies that target high risk individuals and their criminogenic needs with cognitive-behavioral treatment (CBT) programs are generally successful in significantly reducing recidivism (see Andrews & Bonta, 2010; Feucht & Holt, 2016; Wanner, 2018). The PEI also advances the use of programs that are responsive to the needs of clients by understanding their life experiences and responding via a professional lens of cultural competence. CBT programs that are culturally competent are shown to significantly enhance positive outcomes (Horrell, 2008).

Ultimately, risk assessment tools are used by systems to predict the future behavior of individuals who are currently justice involved, govern their treatment needs, and gauge the level of control and surveillance necessary to prevent future harm to the community. Thus, the decisions based on these tools have powerful consequences for the justice involved related to their access to treatment, the type of treatment received, and the level of control and surveillance by which they will be subjected to over time (Lutze, 2021; Van Voorhis, 2012). Therefore, concerns have been raised about potential bias and the likelihood of adverse effects resulting in greater control and surveillance of BIPOC as well as girls and women. Criticisms of risk assessments as they apply to race, ethnicity, and gender are applicable to understanding how such tools may also have limitations in assessing LGBTQ+ populations.

Racial/Ethnic bias, especially for Black Americans, is a critical concern due to the use of official record data generated solely by criminal justice agencies to construct and validate risk assessment tools. Although actuarial tools have been found to reduce racial/ethnic bias at the individual decision-making level within jurisdictions (see Hamilton et al., 2019; Picard-Fritsche et al., 2017), the primary concern is related to macro-level inputs resulting in biased outcomes for marginalized and vulnerable populations (Kurlychek & Johnson, 2019; Lutze, 2021; Picard-Fritsche et al., 2017). BIPOC across communities and people who live in poor communities with higher levels of cumulative disadvantage (i.e., mental illness, poverty, unemployment, violent crime, etc.) are significantly more likely to encounter the police, and be stopped, searched, arrested, jailed, convicted, and incarcerated (see Alexander, 2012; Browning & Arrigo, 2021; Clear, 2007; Edelman, 2017; Mogul et al., 2011; Natapoff, 2018; Ritchie, 2017; Van Cleve, 2016; Williams & Battle, 2017; Zielinski et al., 2020). Thus, BIPOC and poor people are likely to be assessed as higher risk because they have accumulated more criminal history events within the official record data due to greater surveillance and exposure to criminal justice processing when compared to other races/ethnicities.

Gender bias is another critical concern about risk/need assessment tools that are constructed and validated using majority male samples and then extrapolated to the assessment of girls and women. Corrections practitioners as well as gender and justice scholars have expressed concern that these tools ignore many of the risk factors and needs that are most relevant to women such as relationships, depression, parenting issues, self-esteem, self-efficacy, trauma, and victimization (see Van Voorhis et al., 2010, p. 262). Ongoing research shows mixed results with some studies finding the tools valid for use with women, and others showing conflicting results advancing a practical and scientific need for further refinement (see Van Voorhis et al., 2010 for a review).

Thus, it is only recently that gender specific domains were designed to understand girls and women's unique experiences and how assessment may be used to inform culturally competent program designs that are responsive to their needs (see Covington & Bloom, 2007; Salisbury et al., 2009; Van Voorhis, 2012; Van Voorhis et al., 2010; Wright et al., 2012). Van Voorhis (2012, p. 118) points out, "In sum, women's issues do not become the focus of policy and innovation because the science that would foster such change devotes limited attention to them, and what is not observed is not attended to." She continues by observing, "…the evidence-based mandate places women and minorities, who have been understudied, at a distinct disadvantage" (Van Voorhis, 2012, p. 118).

We believe the LGBTQ+ population has also received limited attention and therefore have not been attended to scientifically and are consequently disadvantaged in contemporary evidence-based mandates to fund and implement "what works." Although racial and gender bias have been identified as critical concerns due to coercive and oppressive systems that introduce bias into race-neutral and gender-neutral assessments, little concern has been expressed about how LGBTQ+ individuals may be impacted by heteronormative-neutral assessments that, similar to race and gender, appear neutral, but instead leave LGBTQ+ individuals invisible, unattended, and disadvantaged. As will be discussed in more detail below, it is reasonable to believe that the policing of gender-conformity (see Mogul et al., 2011; Ritchie, 2017), places sexual and gender minority youth at an increased exposure to justice involvement and overrepresentation within official record data, thus skewing the assessment toward higher risk.

In addition, LGBTQ+ youth and young adult's experiences are too often narrowly defined or made invisible by conveniently extrapolating definitions of conventional, cis-gender conforming, heteronormative, life experiences to sexual and gender minority youth. Narrowly defining or defaulting to heteronormative conforming categories for LGBTQ+ youth, makes invisible the stressful emotional labor involved in consistently having to navigate hostile spaces and/or toxic relationships producing emotional, psychological and physical violence and trauma. Thus, attempts to carefully navigate and escape harm are subject to justice professionals' mis-specifying genuine survival strategies as criminogenic, anti-social attitudes or behaviors on the part of LGBTQ+ youth and young adults. This is likely to result in over assessing risk, underestimating need, and failing to assign LGBTQ+ individuals to safe, supportive, and responsive programs that do not perpetuate ongoing harm. To successfully create responsive interventions and accurately assess risk and need, it is critical to understand the intersectional pathways that adversely affect the sexual and gender minority population on an individual, institutional and social/cultural level.

Intersectionality Theory and the Marginalization of Sexual and Gender Minority Youth

Since the 1980s, intersectionality has "exposed how single axis thinking undermines legal thinking, disciplinary knowledge production, and struggles for social justice" (Cho et al., 2013, p. 787). Intersectionality theory defines differences in individual oppression as structured by a multi-faceted web of social inequalities, emphasizing the breadth of social relationships connected within assorted dimensions of circumstance and identities (Jeppesen, 2010; Mattias de Vries, 2012; McCall, 2005; Stone, 2009). This theoretical approach points to the necessity of an inter-active or intersectional understanding of various forms of oppression including patriarchal sex and gender oppression, white supremacy, capitalism, and ableism (Johnson, 2005; Kendall, 2020; Richie, 2012; Ward, 2008; Young, 1990, 2011). For example, someone who is physically disabled, is a person of color, *and* identifies as Trans* cannot be understood simply in terms of being disabled, a person of color, *or* as Trans* independently. Instead, one must account for the combination of these factors to truly understand the situational oppression of that individual.

Social institutions such as school, work, home, and neighborhoods are responsible for perpetuating many of these systems of oppression because they conventionally define what is deviant or abnormal (Fedders, 2006; Russell & Horn, 2017; Spade, 2015). The cultivated shape of oppression results, not as an "articulated theory" or "legal guideline," but instead as "habits of thought" and "routine styles of reasoning that are embedded in the precedents and practices of the institution" (Garland, 2001, p. 188). Ultimately, "intersectional prisms excavate and expose multilayered structures of power and domination by adopting a grounded praxis approach; they also engage the conditions that shape and influence the interpretive lenses through which knowledge is produced and disseminated" (Cho et al., 2013, p. 804). Shahani (2005) explains, "reparative responses to institutionalized oppressions are not only attuned to the material circumstances that shape queer lives, but are also invested in mapping ways to actually make these lives better" (p. 187). In essence, through a "reparative thinking" lens (Sedgwick, 1997) it is only then possible to see the engrained intersectional oppressions sexual and gender minority youth face.

Studies respective to sexual and gender minority youth over recent decades have predominately focused on factors of deficit pertaining to identity development, public health (physical and mental), commitment and achievement in primary education, and how victimization is relative to these risk elements. Succinctly, this particular scope of research entails the disproportionate risks sexual and gender minority youth face in comparison to non-sexual and gender minority youth regarding suicide ideation and attempts (D'Augelli et al., 2001; Eliason, 2011), substance use (Fish, 2012; Marshal et al., 2008), sexually transmitted diseases and infections (Santelli et al., 2006), the various types of harassment and victimization (verbal, emotional, and physical) that take place in different school environments (Heck et al., 2011; Kosciw et al., 2016; Kosciw et al., 2012; Kosciw et al., 2018), and the survival choices made that involve sex work and sex trafficking (Abramovich, 2012; Katz, 2014; Kidd, 2003). In other words, most of the research thus far across disciplines considering the sexual and gender minority youth population has been centered around identifying this population as "at-risk," correspondingly revealing the plausible negative outcomes they frequently confront (Horn et al., 2009; Robertson, 2014).

Our current knowledgebase of sexual and gender minority youth is commanding, but more research is needed to better understand how we can build and apply an interconnectedness of preventative structural systems of social and functional support within our communities that can help decrease the likelihood of sexual and gender minority youth facing the risk factors that will increase their likelihood of encountering public systems such as the juvenile and criminal justice system (Diaz & Kosciw, 2012; Fish, 2012; Himmelstein & Bruckner, 2011; Katz, 2014; Kosciw et al., 2015; Ramon & Warrener, 2015; Robertson, 2014; Talburt, 2004). The personal experience of marginalization within society often starts at a very young age and has the capacity to influence lifestyle, and eventually one's legacy in becoming another criminal justice statistic (Chesney-Lind & Shelden, 2014; Mogul et al., 2011).

The current delineation of at-risk elements comprehensive to sexual and gender minority youth and young adults within social service programming is practically non-existent in comparison to the literature supporting heteronormative positive youth development. Therefore, it is important to consider all of the informal and formal "social domains" a young adult will either involuntarily or voluntarily be exposed to, or be involved with during adolescence (Catalano et al., 2004). Adolescents can be exposed to an array of pro-social support systems that are found in social domains including family, school, church, workplace, and community (Bailey & Brake, 1975; Butler, 2010; Catalano et al., 2004; Lerner et al., 2006, 2009; Lerner & Steinberg, 2009; Seidler, 2010). The reality behind these social domains, as they pertain to sexual and gender minority youth, is that these domains are typically void of comprehensive networks of support to foster positive youth developmental experiences for this much understudied population. The current study addresses this gap in the literature by examining the importance of culturally competent, safe, and responsive strategies to address the risks and needs of LGBTQ+ youth and young adults.

METHODOLOGY

The findings reported here are part of a larger qualitative, intensive, case study that sought to evaluate the theoretical structure and program integrity of a community-based youth center purposefully designed to serve LGBTQ+ youth and young adults. We first describe the research setting and then give a brief overview of why the larger study was initiated and its importance to setting the stage for these deeper analyses describing the potential risks, needs, and responsive approaches most relevant to LGBTQ+ youth and young adults. Second, we describe the sample and the analytic strategy. Finally, we structure the findings in relation to each of the domains identified to bring attention to the necessity for culturally competent interpretations by professionals of risks and needs as they may apply to LGBTQ+ youth and young adults.

Research Setting

The current study is based on *Lambert House: LGBTQ+ Youth Community Center* located in Seattle, Washington. *Lambert House* is a longstanding community youth center serving the needs of LGBTQ+ youth and young adults. It is 1 of only 27 similar programs (stand-alone; brick-and-mortar) in the United States. It began during the 1970s, when Dr. Robert Deisher was the director of the *Child Development and Mental Retardation Center* at the University of Washington and took particular notice of his sexual and gender minority youth clientele who frequently visited his medical practice (K. Schulman, personal communication, October 31, 2017). More specifically, he witnessed a multitude of negative health outcomes the youth exhibited, and he felt this was mainly due to the extreme social isolation they were all experiencing. Dr. Deisher felt these clients could benefit from meeting one another and established with his colleagues the Association of Gay and Lesbian Youth Advocates (AGLYA) in 1981.[2] In 1991, AGLYA leased a house establishing for the first time a dedicated space for social service provision exclusive to sexual and gender minority youth. In 1993, the organization was renamed *Lambert House: LGBTQ+ Youth Community Center*.[3] Today, *Lambert House* provides a multitude of preventative social support services in its very own dedicated physical space and has a national reputation as one of the leading organizations of LGBTQ+ peer community building in the Pacific Northwest.

The philosophy of *Lambert House* is structured around its ability to foster, maintain, and sustain peer community building amongst sexual and gender minority youth. The program stakeholders believe this aspect of socialization in a safe social setting is the most effective strategy for tackling the risks and needs that sexual and gender minority youth disproportionately face throughout their life course such as psychological and social isolation, family conflict, homelessness, alcohol and drug use, HIV/STD's/STI's, truancy, survival sex, suicide, and other such factors of marginality.

Lambert House is open for drop-in, Monday through Friday (4:00pm–9:30pm PST). This center is for youth to have a safe social space to frequent and make friendships with other youth (11 to 22 years of age) and adult volunteers. The center also coordinates various enrichment activities that take place outside of program drop-in hours intended to expose youth to new pro-social experiences with their peers and adult volunteers. *Lambert House* serves approximately 1,150 individual youth each year (2018–2020). There are 5 fulltime permanent paid regular staff and 75 adult volunteer advocates who work in a variety of roles on a weekly and/or monthly basis at the youth center. These adult volunteers play crucial roles as informal role models and mentors to the program participants. Some of the socialization opportunities *Lambert House* plans and facilitates for its youth are evening dinners, support groups three times a week (i.e., Trans* Night, Boys Who Like Boys, and Ultra Violet [formerly known as: Queer Young Females]), outdoor recreational hikes, chaperoning cultural events in the region, art nights, and LGBTQ+ movie nights.

---

[2]To the best of the first author's knowledge, AGLYA was the first LGBTQ+ young adult organization to apply for and receive 501(c)(3) status, and to provide prevention-focused services for sexual and gender minority youth in the world outside of a college campus.

[3]*Lambert House* is named in memory of Gray Lambert, who was one of the founding youth advocates for the program.

Integrated Program Theory Development

Developed by Krystal Roig-Palmer
05/24/2018

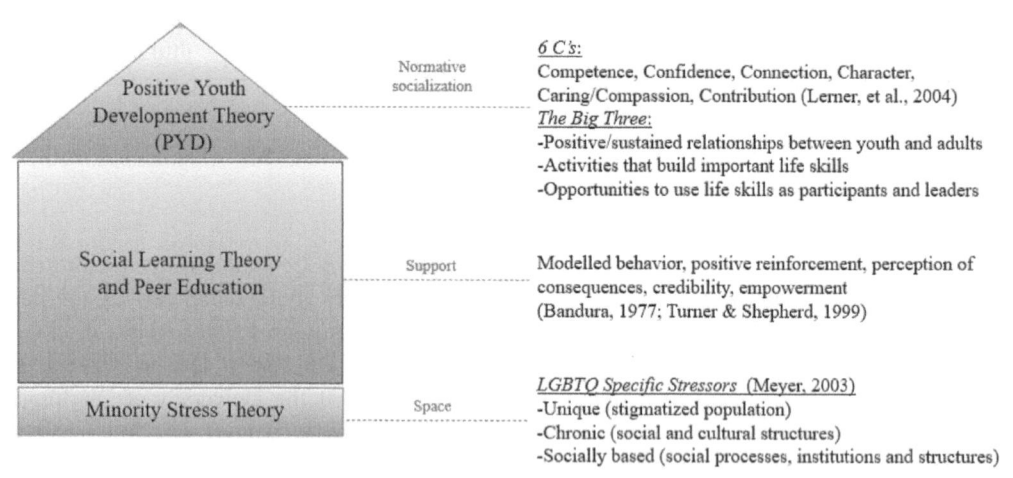

Figure 1. Lambert House Theory to Practice Model (LH TIP).

Also, there are many events *Lambert House* hosts that are solely youth-driven that entail dances, performance events, and other types of social gatherings geared toward peer community building.

Purpose of the Larger Study

Practitioners and community leaders contend that community-based organizations such as *Lambert House* play a significant role in supporting the LGBTQ+ youth and advancing positive outcomes for individuals and the community at large (Daley et al., 2007; Diaz & Kosciw, 2012; DiFulvio, 2011; Fish et al., 2019). It is important for program administrators to show evidence of their program's integrity in producing positive outcomes in order to raise the public and private funds necessary to sustain financial viability and stability. Empirical studies of these community-based organizations, however, are extremely limited, because they lack a theoretical foundation and the structure necessary to identify cohorts of participants, identify comparison groups, and the ability to isolate the potential effects of the program's social activities, life skills programs, or treatment interventions. Thus, for the larger study, Roig-Palmer (2020) began the research process by first qualitatively establishing a theoretical model underlying the intentions of the *Lambert House* approach followed by the development of a logic model to describe the process of implementation and how the program theory and structure aligned with the *Principles of Effective Interventions* (PEI) (see Roig-Palmer, 2020).

A rigorous community-based participatory research framework[4] was used to include the *Lambert House* staff in the theory building and process evaluation research procedure. This analysis involved three separate phases and lasted for a duration of almost four years. The results of the larger study, using grounded theory, produced the *Lambert House Theory Into Practice Model* [*LH TIP Model*] (Roig-Palmer, 2020). This model is an integrated theory using: 1) Minority

---

[4]When the Principle Investigator Roig-Palmer approached the Administrator of Lambert House to conduct research, he made clear that gaining access would require a commitment to the organization and the youth for one year as an adult volunteer in the program space. A traditional "colonial" research approach that extracted data from an oppressed population without serving the greater needs of the organization or the youth would not be acceptable. He would only allow a research project originating from a Community-Participatory Research Methodology (see Stoecker, 2013) in which the key stakeholders inspired the research questions in which the results, either positive or negative, would best serve the needs of the community being studied.

Stress Theory, 2) Social Learning Theory, and 3) Positive Youth Development Theory (see Figure 1).

Most relevant to the study presented here, and the foundational layer of the *LH TIP Model*, is the Minority Stress Theory (Meyer, 2003). This theory explains how LGBTQ+ individuals have exclusive experiences of stigma in the form of societal structural barriers which adversely affect them in multiple ways. Goodman (2015) discusses how these invisible social systems of marginalization can be found in our heteronormative society on the structural levels of individual, institutional, and social/cultural. This theory also gives specific explanations as to the harassment, victimization (e.g., emotional, physical, sexual) and violence the LGBTQ+ population may endure over a life course (Fish et al., 2019; Meyer, 2003; Toomey et al., 2018). Additionally, Minority Stress Theory describes how the program participants experience discourse on an intersectional level, and that they do not only identify as LGBTQ+ (e.g., have different gender identities and sexual orientations), but also as people of color, and have specific preferences on personal pronouns.

Aim of the Current Study

When this *LH TIP Model* was aligned with the *Principles of Effective Interventions* (i.e., evidence-based practice framework) (see Roig-Palmer, 2020), important findings were revealed that are foundational to the RNR Model and to the current in-depth analyses providing support for reassessing the importance of risk, need, and, most importantly, responsivity for LGBTQ+ youth. The larger study showed that the foundation of the program is theoretically rooted in responsivity (i.e., Minority Stress Theory). Second, LGBTQ+ youth and young adults need access to a safe, dedicated, physical space (i.e., *Lambert House*) providing culturally competent and comprehensive social support that is directly related to each of the domains outlined in actuarial risks/needs assessment tools. Third, the larger study established the necessity to advance the professional education of justice professionals to employ informed syntax when assessing risks/needs through a culturally competent, trauma-informed lens exclusive to the LGBTQ+ community versus a purely criminogenic lens (i.e., survival crimes vs. antisocial behavior/attitudes). In essence, just because a program offers interventions to an "at-risk" population does not mean participation and authentic engagement will ensue. The likelihood of retaining LGBTQ+ participation is unlikely if a youth/young adult does not feel safe, welcome, that they belong, or cannot directly identify with what a program has to offer. Lastly, the *LH TIP Model* revealed a critical finding in "how" and "what" preventative justice and social service provisions should be modeled for LGBTQ+ individuals thus informing a critique of the RNR Model's application to LGBTQ+ youth and young adults.

Research Procedure

Throughout the duration of the larger study, Roig-Palmer (2020) completed approximately 600 h of direct service through volunteering with *Lambert House*. During this time, she served as an adult volunteer, conducted informal individual/group counseling sessions, cooked dinners, and facilitated many other activities with the program participants. Thus, the Principle Investigator (PI) was known by many of the youth and their guardians, was trusted, and had an established rapport with the staff, youth, and advocates.

Three specific groups were recruited for participation in the research: (1) paid program staff and volunteers, (2) youth and young adult program participants, and (3) community advocates.[5] Interviews were conducted in three phases. The first phase focused on the program staff and

---

[5]Community advocates included adults living in the community who advocate or support LH. This group included people such as a legal parent/guardian, teacher, probation officer, police officer, case manager, mentor, etc.

volunteers and the second and third phases focused on the youth participants and the community advocates. Each group was first notified about the study by the Program Directory via an email listserv maintained by the center. The email provided a recruitment script describing the study and the researcher's contact information so study participants could contact the PI directly without *Lambert House* staff knowing who participated in the study and thus providing confidentiality. In addition, while staffing the front desk where people check into the center, the PI recruited youth, staff, and volunteers by providing a copy of the recruitment script and contact information for consideration to participate at a later date.

Those who volunteered were asked to participate in a semi-structured interview in a private office at *Lambert House* or in a place convenient to the participant's work or home (adult participants only). Before conducting each interview, informed written consent was obtained. Interviews ranged from 30 min to two hours. During the final data collection phase of this study, *Lambert House* was closed to in-person activities due to the COVID-19 pandemic. The final interviews followed the same procedure described above, but were conducted via Zoom instead of in-person. The interview schedule aligned with the Gugiu and Rodríguez-Campos (2007) protocol designed to capture narrative that is specific to youth programming from various types of stakeholders and included a series of open-ended questions that focused on participant characteristics, someone's general understanding of the program, and the interviewees' participation/experiences with the program. Interviews were audio recorded, transcribed into text, and coded by the first author using a series of qualitative bracketing methods (Dey, 1993; Hennick et al., 2011). The technique Thematic Network Analysis (TNA) was utilized throughout the data triangulation process to effectively examine the links between emergent themes and organize the networks of data sources between all themes identified. Iterative coding strategies (inductive and deductive) were employed for all initial and focused coding processes as it was critical to include concepts of the research literature this study focused on as well as the actual words from the study participants (Charmaz & Mitchell, 2001; Corbin & Strauss, 1990). Lastly, the computer software *NVivo* was employed to support a more rigorous analytic process in maintaining proper organization of both inductive and deductive codes (Attride-Stirling, 2001).

In addition to interviews, program documents, policy manuals, and descriptive organizational data were reviewed and field observation notes were recorded. Each of these sources of data were crucial for strengthening the validity of conclusions for this analysis, and each were very useful to triangulate with one another to ensure interpretations converged (Bekhet & Zauszniewski, 2012; Denzin & Lincoln, 2000; Fusch & Ness, 2015; Schensul et al., 1999).

Research Sample

The target sample was 10–15 research participants from the paid and volunteer staff and the community advocates. The target sample for youth participants was 10–15 youth participants ages 11–17, and 10–15 young adult participants ages 18–22. It was originally estimated that 10–15 research participants from each group would be adequate to reach saturation, yet remain flexible enough in allowing the inductive process to determine "actual saturation" (Hennick et al., 2011). The final sample included 60 semi-structured interviews. The demographic characteristics of the final sample are summarized in Table 1.

FINDINGS

Risk, Needs, and Responsivity for LGBTQ+ Youth and Young Adults

The focus of this analysis is on the dynamic needs of the LGBTQ+ youth and young adult population that are necessary to informing professionals about the intersectional pathways that increase the risk of LGBTQ+ youth to become justice involved. In addition, the findings have

Table 1. Demographic characteristics of the sample.

	Phase 1 study participants Volunteers and administrators ($N = 10$)	Phase 2 study participants	
		Program participants ($N = 20$)	Adult advocates ($N = 30$)
Gender identity			
Male	4	1	9
Female	4	3	14
Trans	1	11	3
Non-binary	–	4	3
Questioning	–	1	–
Other	1	–	1
Sexual orientation			
Lesbian	2	4	4
Gay	4	1	9
Bisexual	–	3	2
Demi-Bisexual	–	1	–
Pansexual	1	7	–
Asexual	–	2	2
Queer	1	1	2
Other	–	–	2
Heterosexual	2	1	9
Age			
11–17	–	9	–
18–22	–	9	–
23–39	7	2	14
40–55	2	–	9
56+	1	–	7
Preferred personal pronouns			
she/her/hers	4	10	17
he/him/his	5	3	9
they/them/theirs	1	6	3
No preference	–	1	1
Race			
White	10	14	29
Non-White	–	6	1
Ethnicity			
None stated	9	12	25
Latin X or Hispanic	–	4	1
Non Latin X and Non Hispanic	1	4	4
Years of volunteer service			
1–3 years	4	–	–
4–7 years	3	–	–
8–10 years	1	–	–
Years of attending as a Program Participant			
Less than a year	–	9	–
1–5 years	–	9	–
5–10 years	–	2	–

utility in establishing the need for accurate assessments and the design and implementation of interventions responsive to the needs of LGBTQ+ youth. Thus, the findings will be structured in relation to the domains identified in the Prosocial Achievement Change Tool (PACT). The PACT is grounded in the RNR Model and is focused on risk and protective factors present in a young person's life that greatly influence an individual's propensity toward justice involvement.

The analyses reveal how risk and need may be contextualized within an understanding of a non-heteronormative experience and "how" programs, such as *Lambert House*, may model responsivity in addressing the exclusive needs of its program participants by providing support, trauma informed practice, and specifically targeted interventions in a safe and comprehensive space. Lastly, the PACT domains will not be described in a traditional numerical order and will instead be integrated with the study findings in a logical order based on youth development. Through an intersectional lens it quickly becomes clear that the risk and protective factors, and even the static factor of sex, may significantly vary for LGBTQ+ youth.

Demographics and the Fluidity of Sex and Gender

Youth risk-need assessments consider demographic characteristics such as age, race/ethnicity, and gender (Durso & Gates, 2012; Heck et al., 2011; Hunt & Moodie-Mills, 2012; Majd et al., 2009). These characteristics in the demographic domain are considered static as they cannot be changed through specific interventions and therefore it is common for software programs to auto-populate these fields, and the gender field specifically, into a binary category of either female or male. These categories default to heteronormative social/cultural interpretations of sex/gender and the associated sex roles and behavioral expectations attached to each (see Johnson, 2005; Mogul et al., 2011; Ritchie, 2017). In the case of sexual and gender minority youth and young adults, it is critical that gender identity be viewed as fluid on a spectrum opposed to a binary category. Defaulting to a heteronormative binary categorization that appears innocuous, can be detrimental to understanding the needs of heterosexual youth (i.e., default to male as norm, gender nonresponsive, gender stereotypes/toxic masculinity, etc.), but may be especially detrimental to non-heteronormative youth. Professionals may over rely on interpreting youth behavior through narrowly defined traditional gender roles and assign youth to programs unable to meet the needs or mitigate the risk of LGBTQ+ youth and young adults.

Binary and/or heteronormative assignments to programs is likely to undermine success for both staff and the LGBTQ+ youth and young adult participants. Several *Lambert House* advocates and participants spoke to the nuanced differences that are managed through advancing beyond traditional binary assignment. It is important to highlight that if the program interventions provided by *Lambert House* were not responsive to the specific needs of LGBTQ+ youth and young adults, the program would more than likely not be in operation. Without embracing the fluid gender/sex spectrum, these same kids would instead seek out the preventative social service provisions elsewhere from local churches, recreational centers, or after-school programs. Adult Advocate # 11 explains this point quite simply:

> I think it's a careful marriage of the activities and those providing the activities. ... If the kiddos are not having a good time, and enjoying that time and feeling safe and supported, they're not going to be there. But if you don't have the adults that can provide the right kind of support, that's going to be able to keep the place safe and supported and available, then you can't do that either. So, there's a fine line there I think in terms of what motivates youth to attend the Lambert House program.

Adult Advocate #14 explained the difference in having an informed and dedicated space for LGBTQ+ youth and young adults to have access to in comparison to Gay Straight Alliance (GSA) clubs found at schools that are open-minded enough to have such a club:

> When I think about a GSA program, it's unrelated to Lambert House. Like you're still in a predominantly heteronormative, heterosexist environment, in a publicly run school for the most part. Just because you have a classroom with a rainbow flag on it doesn't mean that the kids have a sense of ownership with their experience as being 'othered.' So, to have a brick-and-mortar location where you can be you and others get you, and to have that feeling of ownership in a physical space is very important.

Program Participant #14 stressed the importance of having a place like Lambert House that allows you the "freedom to just be you" and to learn more about who you are and what it means to be LGBTQ+ with others who you can trust and depend on:

> So basically, it's like gay school after school. And it's pretty great because like you don't really get to see people who look like you or act like you outside of Lambert House all the time ... or meet people who

have the same experience as what you see in the media or you just feel underrepresented and you are just confused about what you're going through.

In broader context, programs that are culturally competent for heteronormative girls/women or boys/men fail to be responsive to the complex gender and social identities of nonconforming youth. Thus, professionals, heteronormative youth participants, and families may unintentionally place LGBTQ+ youth at emotional and physical risk by focusing on their behavior while ignoring their true gender identity and preferred personal pronouns (Ansara & Hegarty, 2014; Grant et al., 2011).

As the next section will show, the conflict and stress experienced by LGBTQ+ youth within families may go beyond parents and guardians' frustration with anti-social or criminal *behavior* as is the case with heteronormative youth, and instead, target a LGBTQ+ youth's core identity of who they feel they are internally related to their *"true gender self"* (Ehrensaft, 2011). Being viewed as inherently flawed as a person versus being judged just for one's delinquent behavior creates additional emotional and psychological trauma for LGBTQ+ youth that must be recognized and treated by justice professionals.

Family Relationships and Housing Instability

The family domain focuses on the interpersonal relationships one has with parents and/or caregivers, and the expectations a family unit has in terms of social rules and behaviors that are acceptable. The strength of the relationship youth may have with their family is often considered a protective factor. Even within a heteronormative stable family, however, LGBTQ+ youth may experience additional stressors. Sexual and gender minority youth and young adults do not always have a family unit to model what is socially acceptable beyond a heteronormative example. Additionally, if a young person's gender identity and sexual orientation are not accepted first in the home (e.g., biological parental/guardian home) a youth/young adult is severely impacted, placing them in other unstable living circumstances that may be equally stigmatizing and hostile (e.g., run away youth shelter, foster care, correctional facility, or homeless). Thus, there may be no safe place to live for LGBTQ+ youth.

Many of the youth and advocates at *Lambert House* expressed the importance of having a safe place surrounded by others who fully accept their true gender identity and sexual orientation. Program participants expressed how they have found their own sense of "family" at the *Lambert House* program. Program Participant #6 explained how they now have a "chosen family" that is different from their biological family:

> Well, I mostly live with my mother and my father doesn't give a shit. Well as long as I'm not being hurt he's okay with it. But living with my mom, she is doing better and I love her to death but she is a conservative woman that's lived… well she's a baby boomer and stuff like that, so I just kind of like don't fit into her conservative views. Me trying to fit in with her minority views of my community is so difficult. So, it's like Lambert House is more my speed, and she knows that I essentially have a family here where the conservative views don't hold me back.

Program Participant #7 compared their biological family to the family/community they found at Lambert House:

> But yeah, here, there is a sense of community which goes hand-in-hand with being a family. I grew up going to church every week and I come from an extremely religious family with very helicopter parents. So, when I was younger I was only allowed to hang out with people that I went to church with. So, throughout the time that I was in high school I really hadn't made any significant friends because personally I wasn't allowed to have people over if my parents did not know their parents and if they did not go to church. And so, at school, I tended to flock more towards things like drama club and theater and things like that because those spaces are more stereotypically LGBTQ+. So after having left the house from where I grew up, and never having heard about this place before… despite not living too far away from it… when I found out about this place I was like overjoyed.

Program Participant #4 shared how they are in good relations with their biological parent, but also chose to highlight the importance of "family" they found at Lambert House:

> I really liked going to see the adults and talking to them about things going on. A lot of them often have very good advice whether it's related to identity or if it's just something about growing up it's been really nice to have someone to talk to you about that. I do feel like I've kind of always had a weekly family that I choose I could always depend on.

Ultimately, family relationships are considered a "primary context for adolescent development," yet very few studies have undertaken the importance of familial acceptance roles for sexual and gender minority youth (Ryan et al., 2010, p. 205). Parents and guardians may be overwhelmed by the stigma of raising a LGBTQ+ youth, and pressure heteronormative conformity which creates a toxic environment and more often than not, an outright rejection of a LGBTQ+ youth/young adult that ultimately forces them out of the house.

In turn, a very large portion of LGBTQ+ youth and young adults face homelessness at a much higher rate than heteronormative youth and young adults (Abramovich, 2012; Corliss et al., 2002; Durso & Gates, 2012; Feinstein et al., 2001; Katz, 2014; Kosciw et al., 2018; Majd et al., 2009; Palmer et al., 2016; Ray, 2006; Snyder et al., 2016). Homelessness can include "living in temporary shelters, living with friends, or acquaintances for short periods of time, or living in low-cost hotels located in high risk communities" (see Lutze et al., 2014, p. 472; Lutze & Lau, 2017). Homelessness amongst adolescents, regardless of whether or not they are *gender conforming*, can result from abuse/neglect they endure at home/shelter. For sexual and gender minority youth and young adults, many risk being kicked out of their home for simply being who they are which is oftentimes mistaken for a young person making a "choice" to be LGBTQ+. Therefore, making a "choice" places them in a category that is socially unacceptable to the family, church, friends of family, and other members of their social circle. Program Participant #20 highlighted this point:

> Well, Lambert House is also for like hooking up people with services or like you know housing, and like food and stuff that they might need. Because I think a lot of homeless people are queer. And we are really at risk of being homeless because our families may not approve of our identities or whatever.

Thus, too often LGBTQ+ youth and young adults are deprived of the unconditional, relational and functional support from parents critical to positive youth development. Regardless of gender and sexual orientation, most youth consider home as a refuge from external stressors serving as a protective factor. When home is not safe, many youths find respite in school from the stressors at home. Yet, for LGBTQ+ youth, school can also be a place where stigma and marginalization present additional challenges preventing them from instinctively looking toward their peers and adult mentors in school settings. In the following, we show how the social institution of "school" is actually a critical gateway to other stigmatizations LGBTQ+ experience which further limits accessibility to protective factors such as building positive relationships with peers and adults outside of one's family.

School, Peer Relationships, Employment, Use of Free Time & Skills

The *school* domain centers around how schools generally serve as formal institutions that guide social and *skill development*, as well as *employment development*, that provide students with opportunities to model and build healthy *peer relationships*. Yet, school may not serve as a protective factor for LGBTQ+ students as it may for heteronormative students. A foundation of research over the past two decades has confirmed school environments are not always supportive of the sexual and gender minority students (Daley et al., 2007; Feinstein et al., 2001; Heck et al., 2011; Himmelstein & Bruckner, 2011; Kosciw et al., 2018; Majd et al., 2009; Mottet, 2013; Sears, 2005). According to the *2017 National School Climate Survey* of 23,001 students (ages 13–21), over half (59.5%) of sexual and gender minority students reported feeling unsafe and over one third (34.9%) missed at least one entire day of school in the past month because they felt unsafe or uncomfortable with respect to their sexual orientation or gender expression (Kosciw et al., 2018). Feeling unsafe was even greater for Trans* (Transgender) youth with nearly all (90%) reporting feeling unsafe while attending school (Katz, 2014). An unfortunate reality is that sexual and gender minority students typically avoid school spaces that are more gender segregated (bathrooms and locker rooms) as well as school functions (75.4%) and extracurricular activities to some extent (70.5%) (Kosciw et al., 2018).

A majority of LGBTQ+ youth also report experiencing discrimination at the institutional level (62.2%) due to discriminatory policies or practices by the school (Kosciw et al., 2018). Discriminatory policies included sexual and gender minority students not being allowed to attend school dances with a same gender partner, prevention of students writing about or facilitating school functions including sexual and gender minority topics, and Trans* youth being told they cannot wear clothes unsuitable to their legal sex. Even more distressing, almost half (42.1%) of LGBTQ+ students had been prevented from using their chosen name or pronoun (Kosciw et al., 2018).

Lambert House participants spoke directly to the importance of participating in conventional school activities that fully accepted and engaged their gender identity and sexual orientation. For example, one Adult Advocate shared how *Lambert House* provides a safe/comprehensive space for LGBTQ+ youth and young adults in their *free time* that they do not have access to at their schools:

> But the middle schoolers in one of the groups I facilitate, I remember them being so excited about the queer dances we host every year because in their schools they don't get to experience this. Schools typically have it to where they cannot dance with the person they want to dance with, or take to the dance who they want or dress the way they want. One of the transmasculine youth I have goes to an all-girls school, and he really would not be allowed to be himself at a school dance because it's a religious all-girls school. He probably would not even be allowed to wear the suit he wants to wear. So, he was all like 'oh my gosh it's going to be Halloween so I get to dress up however I want to dress up?' And then they got off on this whole costume tangent but just seeing them be super excited that they get to dance with who they want to dance with is very different from a school dance. Plus, they get to meet other people from other schools who are of the LGBTQ+ community, so this opportunity to socialize kind of expands too. For example, they might say 'oh well I don't really want to dance with anyone because I don't like anyone at my school.'

One of the program participants gave a general description of certain activities they have participated in over the years at *Lambert House* that they have not had accessibility to for most of their life in school, at home, or other social settings:

> So, it's a drop-in youth center where people can pop in and hang out. They have food every weekday at the center, and family style dinners. We have the clothing bank, library, computers to use for homework, art supplies, a pool table, lots of different music ... oh and then there are outside events. An outside event would be, well for example the art one that we just recently went on. It was an art museum to see the LGBTQ+ exhibition. Then there's also hiking trips that are lots of fun. I've also gone to see the Gay Men's Choir with Lambert House before in Seattle. One time we went to a concert for a local queer artist at Lambert House and they had speakers at the event to speak about Lambert House. I was one of the speakers at the event along with my boyfriend. Also, Lambert House also does holiday parties and dances for different type of special events. We usually do these events for the winter holiday, Valentine's Day, and PRIDE and other events like that.

Adult Advocate #6 explained how important *Lambert House* is for their child since it has been the only setting her child has been able to experience socialization and an opportunity to build pro-social relationships with others at:

> She has been committed to going on a regular basis. It's helped her develop social connections with people her age and people older. She's actually made friendships with older teens who have jobs and have different experiences from her.

The opportunity to be surrounded by role models and engage in positive peer relationships without having to guard one's true gender identity and sexual orientation creates the space for the personal growth essential to building a successful future. Schools may not always provide a safe learning or social environment that allow sexual and gender minority students to "fit in" and to build the soft skills necessary to easily transition into adult work settings and retain stable employment after high school.

Having strong interpersonal connections with coworkers at a place of *employment* is an important factor to consider and can lead to future goal setting for a career. Program Participant #2 shared how appreciative they are for *Lambert House* and the fact that they can still have adolescent/young adulthood experiences in what they typically do not have access to in other settings outside of *Lambert House*:

> And as you go up in age, and get to 22 before you age out of the program, I think that number is really nice because a lot of places that I know only cover up to 18 for some stuff like how to get a job, or what to prepare for after high school. It's kind of unfortunate because high school is really chaotic and we don't really fit in, and even after high school, it's very chaotic. So, to go from this experience that you're used to being in high school for 4 years or however long, and then right into adulthood with no support like we have at Lambert House … it's a lot. As long as you have the experience that you have here at the drop-in and knowing you can still come here after high school and start easing into adulthood is nice.

Program Participant #3 stated how excited and useful the *Lambert House* job skills class was to framing how to pursue employment:

> I used the rainbow connections for jobs today and that was very helpful and useful. Thefacilitator convinced me to apply for jobs I'm not exactly qualified for just for the funof it, and so we'll see how that goes. I learned a lot.

A Program Participant explained how much they learned from participating in a youth planning committee (for a large community event) in their spare time through the *Lambert House*. They further explained how this experience also taught them *skills* they now use today in their current job:

> Participating as a paid intern with Lambert House in planning large community events helped me tremendously because it gave me more of a professional and career aspect of things. These were paid internships too. So, I put that on a resume when it came time to apply for a job outside of Lambert House. Lambert House really helped me develop so many skills that I find I'm using quite a lot in my current job. Right now, it's kind of my first more professional job. And so, a lot of what I do in communicating with other people like via email or phone calls and planning things like creating appointments and whatnot and recording things … a lot of these things are skills that I first started to develop in these internships through Lambert House.

Lambert House shows how social support and culturally centered responsive contexts for LGBTQ+ youth provides a means to subsidize the conventional heteronormative environment experienced at school. These stark experiential differences give insight into how schools may inadvertently create a pipeline to early justice involvement especially when gender-conformity is policed and nonconformity is stigmatized and sanctioned.

Pathways from School to Early Justice Involvement

The PACT domain *criminal history* considers diversion, detention and other referrals a young adult may encounter. Currently, research clearly delineates the increased propensity of early justice involvement LGBTQ+ youth and young adults face in schools. For instance, sexual and gender minority youth are subjected to school sanctioning at a much higher rate than gender-conforming youth (Carter et al., 2014; Feinstein et al., 2001; Himmelstein & Bruckner, 2011; Knight & Wilson, 2016; Majd et al., 2009; Palmer et al., 2016).

Being disciplined for behaviors associated with violating school rules used to police compliance with heteronormative expectations may have a cumulative effect creating multiple forces pushing

LGBTQ+ students out of school. For example, Kosciw et al. (2018) found that 92% of LGBTQ+ youth who left high school reported mental health concerns, such as depression, anxiety, or stress, as the primary reasons for leaving high school. Not surprising, academic concerns (70.1%), including poor grades, high number of absences, or not having enough credits to graduate, and a hostile school climate (59.8%) were also contributing factors in their decision or doubts about finishing high school.

The increased risk of sexual and gender minority youth receiving sanctioning of any kind in their schools links them to an increased likelihood to be pushed closer to the juvenile justice system (Himmelstein & Bruckner, 2011; Katz, 2014; Kosciw et al., 2018; Majd et al., 2009; McNamara & Burns, 2018; Meiners, 2015; Palmer et al., 2016; Rocque & Paternoster, 2011). Justification for punishment or victimization often ensues once a school and/or its personnel proscribe a young adult as "incorrigible" or as a "problem youth." Thus, the sexual and gender minority youth community are a significant sub-population of the school-to-prison pipeline group and are over-represented in juvenile detention facilities (ACLU, 2008; Snapp et al., 2015).

Ultimately, after becoming justice involved in some capacity, there are a sundry of reasons as to why sexual and gender minority youth find themselves in a state of instability. Feelings of isolation, anger, confusion, suicide ideation, helplessness and many other emotions transform what may have been low risk/low need into high risk/high need circumstances for LGBTQ+ youth and young adults. In the following, other high need PACT domains are highlighted in alignment with the responsive target interventions the *Lambert House* program provides its program participants. *Lambert House* provides an intentional preventative example of how LGBTQ+ programming may disrupt the school to justice system pipeline for sexual and gender minority youth and young adults.

Mental Health, Attitudes/Behaviors, Aggression, Alcohol and Drugs and Skills

The PACT *mental health* domain considers past and current forms of neglect and abuse a youth has encountered in their life course. The PACT *attitudes/behaviors domain* is centered around the structure of values, beliefs and rationalizations a person has which strongly connect with personal identity. This domain is also concerned with cognitions that include irritability, impulsivity, and feeling resentful or defiant. The PACT *aggression* domain is reliant on one's tolerance for frustration, hostile interpretations of the intentions/actions of others, and general use of violence toward others. Finally, the PACT *alcohol and drug* domain is centered on substance use/abuse that can essentially be the juncture point for youth/young adults to participate in actual criminal activity.

The succeeding sections will further explain why the domains described above often result from the chronic stigmatizations this population faces in multiple social settings and how *Lambert House* provides preventative social service provisions to develop, foster and maintain the *skills* domain needed to overcome such marginalization. Understanding how mental health concerns such as anxiety, depression, low self-esteem, suicide (ideations, attempts, completions), and other relative factors are all interconnected in some way to social stigmatizations makes it very difficult for young sexual and gender minority adults to develop a healthy identity true to themselves (Marshal et al., 2008). It is important for professionals to note that addressing general and mental health complications using professional counseling or medical practice relative to such stressors are not exactly easy for young sexual and gender minority adults either (Abramovich, 2012; Horn et al., 2009; Katz, 2014; Kosciw et al., 2018; Marshal et al., 2008). If young LGBTQ+ youth/young adults have not "come out" to their family or peers, they may not feel they can approach a professional to help them work through mental health needs or to receive sex-positive comprehensive information.

Lambert House provides an outlet, and support systems that foster the development of skills needed to build resiliency toward intersectional systems of oppression that adversely impact their mental health. For instance, Adult Advocate #22 discussed observational experiences they encountered over the years in terms of how program participants would start to generally feel better about themselves in identifying with the LGBTQ+ community:

> I mean, at Lambert House, the youth finally have a social group instead of being an outcast which they more commonly experience in society than most are aware of. You definitely see some psychological improvement, irrespective of what their original condition is, just from having others like them in this space. So, you have kids that come in with PTSD from always being marginalized and cast off from what they would consider their social group because they have a secret, or maybe they are 'out,' or for whatever reason they are cast aside. And when you find a niche it doesn't just benefit a youth, it benefits everyone, and it's definitely something that gives them more confidence. It's basic psychology of Maslow's hierarchy of needs. Once you fulfill the physical needs you start climbing up with the social needs and things are much more fulfilled in terms of needs being met. You start self-actualizing when you're able to when you're not in crisis anymore. When you have your physical needs met, then you can start looking at some other matters such as identity issues because you are safe to do so.

Reporting victimization of any kind is generally not a comfortable or simple decision, and it is even more difficult to do so as an individual who is unwillingly categorized as being part of a marginalized population. Kosciw et al. (2018, p. 28) explained that of the students surveyed "(55.3%) never reported incidents of victimization to school staff" because these young adults were not confident there would be an effective intervention. Furthermore, 60.4% of the surveyed students claimed that when they did report such incidents of victimization, school personnel "did nothing and/or told the reporting student to ignore the victimization" (Kosciw et al., 2018, p. 31). More specifically, 21.4% of the surveyed students who reported victimization were told by school staff "to change their behavior (e.g., to not act 'so gay' or not to dress a certain way)" (Kosciw et al., 2018, p. 31).

Unfortunately, disruption due to marginalization in the life areas of education, family, relationships with others, and physical/mental health can result in substance abuse of drugs and/or alcohol for an individual. The rate of substance abuse is extremely high for the sexual and gender minority population (Barnaby et al., 2010). Program Participant #15 shared details about someone they met at *Lambert House* who battled substance use/abuse:

> We had a friend who we all met there, so he overdosed on Fentanyl accidentally. And so yeah, that was a really new experience for a lot of us because we have never known anyone who died from an incident of using drugs. We did not know that he was using Fentanyl and we knew that he smoked pot but. So, when he died it was definitely a unique experience but because we had that close community at Lambert House, we were all really bonded by it and we were all like you know … this is really upsetting but we're not going to forget him and we're going to remember him. … but we're all definitely awake now on the issue and we've become very conscious about drugs. We had a lot of adults support us at Lambert House too when that happened to our friend, and teach us how serious of a risk it is within our community. So yeah, if you do anything, any hard drugs, we will immediately respond with, 'you know what, cut it out you're getting sober and we're taking you to rehab and we will do something to prevent you from dying because we're not having someone else die.'

Adult Advocate #9 claimed, "I'm absolutely certain that Lambert House during the time that I was there, saved at least five different people from suicide and at least 15 from dying from drugs."

Program Participant #6 explained how the support groups at *Lambert House* were a lifeline for them when they were younger and were first starting the program. They further explained how the exposure to these support groups was the only reasons they eventually felt comfortable in seeking individual counseling for other matters they wanted to work through as they got older that involved manic depression from years of bullying and other sources of harassment:

> Well the minute I turned 19 is when I kind of stopped going to the Lambert House support groups, and it's not because there was anything wrong, but I started going to like legit therapy. Because I was going really just for my mental state, but sometimes what I needed most of all was like more one-on-one therapy. So, it's nice to go to a group therapy session but for me I needed the one-on-one as I got older and then realized that I wanted that sort of experience. Also, I am one of the older individuals here, sometimes I

don't really relate to a lot of the youths' problems in comparison to mine just because I'm an adult now and my problems are a little bit more on the adult side I guess.

Program Participant #4 highlighted the importance of accessibility to support groups for LGBTQ+ youth and young adults who do not have professional adults in their schools, doctors' offices, or other related social settings they can talk with and receive comprehensive support from:

Yeah, I mean I think it's really important to have an even more private setting where you can talk to someone more experienced and knowledgeable about being any certain type of way and if you have questions about whether its medical, or social or mental like … it's important to be able to talk about these things. People don't want to do that out in the open. So, it's important to have those little groups where people can really get in a smaller room and be with someone who's trustworthy that they can talk to you about these things because you really just can't do that with your parents necessarily unless you're out to your parent, or if you even have the comfort to do that. But most parents don't have the same experience as you do after you come out in terms of what you're going through.

Program Participant #17 makes another distinct point on this matter by explaining:

A lot of people at Lambert seem to have some sort of forces pushing on them and it's kind of like a constraint. But yeah, people in our community battle depression and anxiety, and all these mental illnesses that are constantly there. There are anxieties they face in being who they are and at Lambert House you can kind of see them pushing back against those forces and really opening up. The school that I go to is very competitive and there is not a lot of room for sexualization. So being at Lambert really helps me with my mental health as sort of escaping from that competitive arena and actually being with human beings and being able to have tough conversations with that I can also learn from with others like me.

Finally, part of unstable general health entails the higher risk sexual and gender minority youth face in contracting sexually transmitted infections and sexually transmitted diseases (STI's & STD's) (Grossman et al., 2005; Santelli et al., 2006). Sex-positive, sex education is not always taught in school settings and if it is covered, it is often discriminatory and supported by derogatory beliefs sustained by religion or formalized through restrictive government policy amongst other cultural stigmas (Kosciw et al., 2016; Kosciw et al., 2018). Moralistic approaches too often result in faith-based efforts to "pray the gay away" instead of providing general health/wellness information for sexual and gender minority youth (Katz, 2014, p. 14). This leaves LGBTQ+ youth vulnerable to victimization in unhealthy and too often violent relationships.

For example, Adult Advocate #9 shared how crucial *Lambert House* was for them when they used to be a program participant who was experiencing homelessness at the time, and battling severe aggression while caught in the cycle of domestic violence while living on the streets. They explained how if they would not have found the community they did at *Lambert House*, they would have never had access to the resources they did to help them meet basic means of life to survive such as food, clothing, safe homeless shelter referrals, and counseling to address their PTSD which resulted from the sexual assault amongst other traumas they encountered while living on the streets as a kid. Adult Advocate #9 stated:

At Lambert House, for me, it was about survival. Community is absolutely necessary. At Lambert House, I found people that I could be around who became part of my pack while I was on the streets. There were other kids there like me who were homeless and had no place to go. So, like that means as a pack on the streets, we would move together as groups for safety. As a person who was born with a vagina, safety is important when it comes to being on the streets because I faced a much higher likelihood to be raped. Out of the five encounters I had while I was homeless on the streets as a kid, I was only raped once though. I was lucky compared to others.

Relatedly, Adult Advocate #14 talked about some of the youth they encountered in their career working with at-risk LGBTQ+ youth who need a safe place like *Lambert House* to seek refuge and resources that are specific to the high needs of this population:

> Lambert House has such an open-door policy, you do get all comers. You got kids that are like trauma survivors who have been through the foster care system, suffered through sexual and physical abuse, and they have every reason to be upset and angry. Sometimes they go through things and at times a volunteer has to step in and help manage an occasional crisis. This is where the youth know they can come to be safe and to get support and connected to the appropriate resources.

Ultimately, being at higher risk of contracting STI's or STD's amongst other physical health related risks, matters are further compounded in terms of sexual and gender minority youth being forced to make survival choices related to various types of sexual exploitation, elevated drug and alcohol use, drug sales, theft, and non-school based victimization that is physical and sexual in nature (DiFulvio, 2011; Grossman et al., 2005; Katz, 2014; Knight & Wilson, 2016; Mayer et al., 2008). Ultimately, it becomes clear that what may be interpreted as "antisocial" or "criminogenic" for many LGBTQ+ youth could likely be the legitimate and normal responses to surviving the stigma, marginalization, victimization, and trauma of living within a relentless heteronormative oppressive system.

Criminal History Viewed through a Responsive Lens

The conventional RNR framework of assessing youth/young adult static risks (*criminal history domain*) and dynamic needs are dismantled when applying a non-binary lens to what is considered criminogenic, non-criminogenic, and defining what has the capacity to "change" versus that which does not. No program participant openly disclosed they had a criminal history, however, Interviewee #10 further explained how the sexual and gender minority youth population does face an increased propensity to become justice involved:

> Our population faces marginalization, discrimination, and lack of access to preventative services and it puts our community in a difficult position. In the eyes of LGBTQ+ folks, what they see as legitimate acts or behaviors is defined by the system as crimes. For our kids and young adults here, sometimes they get caught up in doing what they feel they need to do in order to survive. Literally survive.

Adult Advocate #11 (criminal justice practitioner) more specifically focused on explaining misconceptions of the label "crime" versus "survival crime:"

> So yeah, you sometimes have to consider the practical side of things by realizing where people are at in life. I encountered some youth at Lambert House who were … what you and I would say in our line of work in the criminal justice system working with at risk youth, who were being sexually exploited. So, when I would see them, I would first do a quick check in and have a conversation with them as part of doing your due diligence as an adult mentor to them. And so, after three years of working with this person, it was just kind of like … things changed in their behavior and that's when I found out they were doing which was unfortunately being sexually exploited with someone who they saw as their partner. Was there a crime being committed? They were of consenting age, and they were over 18 and the other party was over 18. So, this young adult consented to this because their exploiter was saying, "hey you don't have to worry about rent and you can just live here with me. I'll take care of that for you." I mean what's the crime you know? But from another point of view, the young adult saw the relationship as something that was mutual, and that was wanted. In reality, it was the only way they were going to have housing. So, now we're talking about a completely different scenario involving a criminal though. In my perspective the criminal is not the person who I'm thinking of that I used to mentor at the program who was doing it to survive. Instead, it's the person who is exploiting it because they know it's the only way the other person can survive is by trading sex for a basic need, and in the case of this young person it was shelter, food and what they thought was a safe place to sleep. And I don't think the criminal justice system looks at it that way, but as a provider in the field working with youth, it's always one of those things to navigate that is hard for sure. Unless I would have worked with the LGBTQ+ community and tried to teach others, I don't think my colleagues in the field would have had a lot of experience and understanding about this sort of stuff when it comes to that.

Adult Advocate #22 who has extensive experience working with homeless youth and young adults shared their experiences witnessing youth live a "life of crime" (e.g., truancy, theft) and how *Lambert House* navigates this circumstance:

We have to know what shelters are friendly when we get calls from outreach who pick up a kid and they are trying to get them to a short-term shelter and they find out the kid is also LGBTQ. If you are not careful, and you send a kid to the wrong type of shelter, it's a quick route for a kid into the criminal justice system. … But you see youth that are in some homeless shelters who get by with literally living a life of crime to be honest. Their main profession other than skipping school as you know, with truancy is, 'Okay, let's go to this neighborhood and you know see if anybody's here during the day' … So yeah, there are a lot of kids that participate in crimes with people they are identifying as their community. … and they're looking for connection no matter where it comes from, they are going to take it. And certain shelters have gang violence and gang affiliations and so they may get jumped into a gang a year from now or whenever. … It's all a matter of time though really, because a community of youth who are homeless and participating in crimes to survive … they're always looking to recruit. So, having adult mentors at Lambert House, to kind of guide them, they can see a path that is not criminal and have a chance to live a different life. It's even just seeing that path that I think makes the biggest difference because they can talk to people their own age who happen to not be on that path and they're on a different path.

These observations by adult advocates show that for LGBTQ+ youth and young adults, risk and need is often associated with other's responses to their true gender self and sexual orientation, and when unattended to in meaningful and supportive ways may have dire consequences. Thus, responses by those responsible for the care of sexual and gender minority youth and young adults can quickly aggravate or mitigate the circumstances and conditions influencing life-long outcomes.

Unfortunately, living within heteronormative and patriarchal systems of oppression too often means sanctions may be levied for just existing in the space of one's true gender self and sexual orientation or for acting upon the frustration, anger, and helplessness caused by having to fight to survive emotionally, psychologically, and physically within heteronormative dominated spaces. Fortunately, the freedom to exist joyfully and confidently as an LGBTQ+ youth/young adult can be achieved within spaces that are responsive to the needs of this specific population. The content of the interviews reported in this study clearly show the relational support, functional support, and trauma informed care necessary to be responsive to LGBTQ+ youths' unique challenges, concerns, and desire to live unencumbered by society's heteronormative and patriarchal expectations. Maybe even more importantly, however, the interviews show how it is possible to be responsive to the strengths, prosocial attitudes, and desires to achieve the social justice necessary to live free from hate. Therefore, the results of this study have utility in informing future policy and practice to better serve sexual and gender minority youth and young adults.

Policy Implications and Conclusion

The current study brings attention to the importance of considering how current science-based practices still need to be critically assessed in their generalizability to LGBTQ+ youth and young adults. Too often studies are conducted without consideration of the systems of oppression and the broader social influences in which research is embedded (Lutze, 2021). As Van Voorhis (2012, p. 118) revealed about girls and women, "what is not observed is not attended to," is also true for sexual and gender minority youth and young adults at risk of becoming justice involved. The current study is useful to reframing the narrative for bringing LGBTQ+ youth and young adults into the vision of scholars and practitioners responsible for advancing "what works" in juvenile justice and youth development. It is no longer acceptable for leading approaches relied upon to inform the care, treatment, sanctioning, and the surveillance of others to be void of cultural competency and a fully developed understanding of responsivity. Professionals steeped in cultural competency and programs designed purposefully to meet the needs of others is achievable for LGBTQ+ youth and young adults. The findings of this study lead to four key recommendations to advance the responsivity principle for LGBTQ+ youth and young adults.

First, systems of oppression must be acknowledged and how they directly impact marginalized and vulnerable youth and young adults. Without first exposing the invisible structures dictating the intense pressure on LGBTQ+ youth and young adults to conform to heteronormative, cisgender expectations, it is impossible to appropriately understand and therefore measure the critical contexts driving the risk, need, or responsivity of this population. Thus, theoretical advancement beyond traditional criminological and psychological approaches is necessary to inform the formal responses to marginalized at risk youth. Understanding intersectionality, structured oppression, and the persistence of historical trauma through Minority Stress Theory (Meyer, 2003; Roig-Palmer, 2020) allows for theory to be translated into effective practice (see *LH TIP Model* by Roig-Palmer, 2020) and potentially working to strengthen existing translations of theory into practice such as that broadly implemented through the *RNR Model* (see Andrews & Bonta, 2015). Existing risk assessment tools must be calibrated accordingly or revised so they do not place LGBTQ+ youth and young adults at a distinct disadvantage in the promotion of evidence-based mandates directly tied to policy, practice, and funding. Thus, understanding and embracing intersectionality and cultural competency is critical to advancing meaningful approaches and interventions that are responsive to the needs of sexual and gender minority youth and young adults.

Second, social and functional support are critical components of responsivity. Systems of oppression and exclusion experienced by LGBTQ+ youth and young adults often create circumstances that place stress on personal relationships and create periods of severe deprivation that can have a cumulative impact over time. Social and functional support are critical to enhancing positive outcomes (see Cohen, 2012; Lin et al., 1986). Thus, responsivity must be steeped in social support inclusive of "establishing warm, respectful and collaborative working alliances" (Bonta & Andrews, 2007) within an understanding of meeting sexual and gender minority youth and young adults where they are within the context of their lived experience. In addition, often embedded within the withdrawal of social support by those responsible for the wellbeing of LGBTQ+ youth and young adults, functional support is also withdrawn leading to housing and food instability, poverty, and the inability to meet basic needs. Thus, functional support is critical to responsivity and must be linked to prosocial relational support to advert the risk of having to rely on dysfunctional and violent relationships in order to assure physical and emotional survival.

Third, trauma informed care within trauma informed agencies and systems must be used to provide the foundation for responsive programs addressing the risks and needs of LGBTQ+ youth and young adults. There is a clear relationship between trauma (historical and immediate) and negative outcomes related to health, education, employment, homelessness, family violence, mental illness, chemical dependency, and justice involvement (see SAMHSA, 2014). Although these outcomes are also true for other marginalized and vulnerable populations with histories of trauma, sexual and gender minority youth and young adults often exist within a crosscurrent of emotional, psychological, and physical trauma that is inseparable from their core identity. Thus, professionals must possess culturally competent understandings and the enhanced skills necessary to be fully responsive to and effective in treating LGBTQ+ youth and young adults.

Finally, responsivity must be steeped in flexibility with direct conduits to structured activities and programs with treatment integrity. Too often, community programs addressing the risks and needs of youth are superficial and lack the structural fidelity to effectively serve the needs of those most amenable to seeking and receiving much needed help. Likewise, many evidence-based programs are fully structured, restricted, and narrowly serve those coerced into participation or those who are ready to acquiesce to full compliance no matter the fit. Although both are acceptable along a full continuum of care, making visible the needs of LGBTQ+ youth and young adults provides an opportunity to be innovative in attending to and advancing the responsivity principle as related to the LGBTQ+ population.

LGBTQ+ youth and young adults expressed the benefit of fluid access to a holistic emotionally, psychologically, and physically safe space that immediately, without question, accepts them for who they are. This space, *Lambert House*, became a powerful conduit to professionals, advocates, and peers capable of providing functional support, but most profoundly providing informal prosocial, meaningful, relationships that created the space to seek formal, professional and structured treatment designed to meet the specific and oftentimes unique needs of LGBTQ+ youth and young adults. Importantly, youth were allowed to simultaneously fail and succeed as they navigated the process of maturing into their true identities/orientations without fear of being expelled from the space, programs, and community. Thus, innovations in responsivity must embrace change as a process and provide flexible opportunities for professionals and youth to recalibrate levels and types of engagement without fear of abandonment.

Undoubtedly LGBTQ+ youth and young adults are confronted with a series of ongoing challenges generated by the pressures of living in a heteronormative society that oppresses, stigmatizes, and marginalizes those who are perceived as different. The pressure to conform often permeates informal social institutions such as families, churches, and social networks as well as formal institutions such as school, work, socials services, and the justice system. These pressures are woven into and layered upon the everyday efforts of youth and young adults who are already navigating the process of finding one's connection and independence within both informal and formal networks. To address the risk and needs of LGBTQ+ youth and young adults requires new and innovative programs purposefully designed to be responsive to participants' strengths as well as to the deficits inflicted by an oppressive, stigmatizing, society and its institutions. Templates such as *Lambert House: LGBTQ+ Youth Community Center* already exist to provide a clear example of how policy and innovation may be achieved when time and attention is devoted to first understanding and then serving the needs of LGBTQ+ youth and young adults.

REFERENCES

Abramovich, I. A. (2012). No safe place to go-LGBTQ youth homelessness in Canada: Reviewing the literature. *Canadian Journal of Family and Youth / Le Journal Canadien de Famille et de la Jeunesse, 4*(1), 29–51. https://doi.org/10.29173/cjfy16579

Adams, R., Dominelli, L., & Payne, M. (Eds.). (2009). *Critical practice in social work*. Palgrave Macmillan.

Alexander, M. (2012). *The new Jim Crow: Mass incarceration in the age of colorblindness*. The New Press.

American Civil Liberties Union (ACLU). (2008). *What is the school-to-prison pipeline?*. ACLU. https://www.aclu.org/racial-justice/what-school-prison-pipeline.

Andrews, D. A., & Bonta, J. (2015). *The psychology of criminal conduct*. Routledge.

Andrews, D., & Bonta, J. (2010). *The psychology of criminal conduct* (5th ed.). Anderson Publishing Company.

Ansara, Y. G., & Hegarty, P. (2014). Methodologies of misgendering: Recommendations for reducing cisgenderism in psychological research. *Feminism & Psychology, 24*(2), 259–270. https://doi.org/10.1177/0959353514526217

Attride-Stirling, J. (2001). Thematic networks: an analytic tool for qualitative research. *Qualitative Research, 1*(3), 385–405.

Bailey, R., & Brake, M. (Eds.). (1975). *Radical social work*. Arnold.

Barnaby, L., Penn, R., & Erickson, P. G. (2010). Drugs, homelessness & health: Homeless youth speak out about harm reduction. *The Shout Clinic Harm Reduction Report [PowerPoint slides]*. https://youthrex.com/report/drugs-homelessness-health-homeless-youth-speak-out-about-harm-reduction/

Bekhet, A. K., & Zauszniewski, J. A. (2012). Methodological triangulation: An approach to understanding data. *Nurse Researcher, 20*(2), 40–43. https://doi.org/10.7748/nr2012.11.20.2.40.c9442

Bonta, J., & Andrews, D. A. (2007). Risk-need-responsivity model for offender assessment and rehabilitation. *Rehabilitation, 6*(1), 1–22.

Bonta, J., & Andrews, D. A. (2010). Viewing offender assessment and rehabilitation through the lens of the risk-needresponsivity model. Offender supervision: New directions in theory, research and practice (pp. 19–40).

Brechin, A. (2000). Introducing critical practice. *Critical Practice in Health and Social Care*, 25–47.

Browning, M., & Arrigo, B. (2021). Stop and risk: Policing, data, and the digital age of discrimination. *American Journal of Criminal Justice, 46*(2), 298–316. https://doi.org/10.1007/s12103-020-09557-x

Butler, A. (2010). Adolescent identity development: Who we are *[PowerPoint slides]*. http://actforyouth.net/adolescence/toolkit/identity.cfm.

Carter, P., Fine, M., & Russell, S. T. (2014). *Discipline disparities series: An overview*. The Equity Project.

Catalano, R. F., Berglund, M. L., Ryan, J. A., Lonczak, H. S., & Hawkins, J. D. (2004). Positive youth development in the United States: Research findings on evaluations of positive youth development programs. *The Annals of the American Academy of Political and Social Science, 591*(1), 98–124. https://doi.org/10.1177/0002716203260102

Charmaz, K., & Mitchell, R. G. (2001). Grounded theory in ethnography. *Handbook of Ethnography, 160*, 174.

Chesney-Lind, M., & Eliason, M. (2006). From invisible to incorrigible: The demonization of marginalized women and girls. *Crime, Media, Culture: An International Journal, 2*(1), 29–47. https://doi.org/10.1177/1741659006061709

Chesney-Lind, M., & Shelden, R. G. (2014). *Girls, delinquency, and juvenile justice*. Wiley & Sons, Inc.

Cho, S., Crenshaw, K. W., & McCall, L. (2013). Toward a field of intersectionality studies: Theory, applications, and praxis. Signs: *Journal of Women in Culture and Society, (38)* (4), 785–810. https://doi.org/10.1086/669608

Clear, T. R. (2007). *Imprisoning communities: How mass incarceration makes disadvantaged neighborhoods worse*. Oxford University Press.

Cohen, B. D. (2012). Reimagining gender through policy development: The case of a 'single- sex' educational organisation. *Gender & Education, 24*(7), 689–705.

Corbin, J. M., & Strauss, A. (1990). Grounded theory research: Procedures, canons, and evaluative criteria. *Qualitative Sociology, 13*(1), 3–21. https://doi.org/10.1007/BF00988593

Corliss, H. L., Cochran, S. D., & Mays, V. M. (2002). Reports of parental maltreatment during childhood in a United States population-based survey of homosexual, bisexual and heterosexual adults. *Child Abuse & Neglect, 26*(11), 1165–1178. https://doi.org/10.1016/S0145-2134(02)00385-X

Covington, S. S., & Bloom, B. E. (2007). Gender responsive treatment and services in correctional settings. *Women & Therapy, 29*(3–4), 9–33. https://doi.org/10.1300/J015v29n03_02

D'Augelli, A. R., Hershberger, S. L., & Pilkington, N. W. (2001). Suicidality patterns and sexual orientation-related factors among lesbian, gay, and bisexual youths. *Suicide and Life-Threatening Behavior, 31*(3), 250–264. https://doi.org/10.1521/suli.31.3.250.24246

Daley, A., Solomon, S., Newman, P. A., & Mishna, F. (2007). Traversing the margins: Intersectionalities in the bullying of lesbian, gay, bisexual and transgender youth. *Journal of Gay & Lesbian Social Services, 19*(3–4), 9–29. https://doi.org/10.1080/10538720802161474

Denzin, N. K., & Lincoln, Y. S. (2000). Strategies of inquiry. *Handbook of Qualitative Research, 2*, 367–378.

Dey, I. (1993). *Qualitative data analysis: A user-friendly guide for social scientists*. Routledge.

Diaz, E. M., & Kosciw, J. G. (2012). Jump-starting youth community leadership: An evaluation of a leadership development program for lesbian, gay, bisexual, transgender & ally youth. *Journal of Youth Development, 7*(1), 125–136. https://doi.org/10.5195/JYD.2012.157

DiFulvio, G. T. (2011). Sexual minority youth, social connection and resilience: From personal struggle to collective identity. *Social Science & Medicine, 72*(10), 1611–1617. https://doi.org/10.1016/j.socscimed.2011.02.045

Drake, E. (2014). *Predicting criminal recidivism: A systematic review of offender risk assessments in Washington State* (Doc. No. 14-02-1901; pp. 579–613). Washington State Institute for Public Policy. https://www.wsipp.wa.gov/ReportFile/1554/Wsipp_Predicting-Criminal-Recidivism-A-Systematic-Review-of-Offender-Risk-Assessments-in-Washington-State_Report.pdf

Durso, L. E., & Gates, G. J. (2012). *Serving our youth: Findings from a national survey of services providers working with lesbian, gay, bisexual and transgender youth who are homeless or at risk of becoming homeless*. The Williams Institute with True Colors Fund and The Palette Fund.

Duwe, G., & Rocque, M. (2017). Effects of automating recidivism risk assessment on reliability. *Criminology & Public Policy, 16*(1), 235–269. https://doi.org/10.1111/1745-9133.12270

Edelman, P. (2017). *Not a crime to be poor: The criminalization of poverty in America*. The New Press.

Ehrensaft, D. (2011). *Gender born, gender made: Raising healthy gender-nonconforming children*. Workman Publishing Inc.

Eliason, M. (2011). Introduction to special issue on suicide, mental health, and youth development. *Journal of Homosexuality, 58*(1), 4–9. https://doi.org/10.1080/00918369.2011.533622

Fedders, B. (2006). Coming out for kids: Recognizing, respecting, and representing LGBTQ youth. *Nevada Law Journal, 6*, 101–134.

Feinstein, R., Greenblatt, A., Hass, L., Kohn, S., & Rana, J. (2001). *Justice for all? A report on lesbian, gay, bisexual and transgendered youth in the New York Juvenile Justice System* (pp. 1–69). Lesbian and Gay Youth Project Urban Justice Center: Educational Resources Information Center.

Feucht, T., Holt, T. (2016). *Does cognitive behavioral therapy work in criminal justice? A new analysis from crimesolutions.gov* (NCJ 249825; pp. 10–17). National Institute of Justice. http://nij.gov/journals/277/Pages/crimesolutions-cbt.aspx

Fish, J. (2012). *Social work and lesbian, gay, bisexual and trans people: Making a difference*. The Policy Press.

Fish, J. N., Moody, R. L., Grossman, A. H., & Russell, S. T. (2019). LGBTQ youth-serving community-based organizations: Who participates and what difference does it make? *Journal of Youth and Adolescence, 48*(12), 2418–2431. https://doi.org/10.1007/s10964-019-01129-5

Fusch, P. I., & Ness, L. R. (2015). Are we there yet? Data saturation in qualitative research. *The Qualitative Report, 20*(9), 1408.

Garland, D. (2001). *The culture of control: Crime and social order in contemporary society*. Chicago University Press.

Glaister, A. (2008). Introducing critical practice. In The *critical practitioner in social work and health care* (pp. 8–26). The Open University.

Goodman, D. J. (2015). Oppression and privilege: Two sides of the same coin. *Journal of Intercultural Communication, 18*, 1–14.

Grant, J. M., Mottet, L. A., Tanis, J., Harrison, J., Herman, J. L., & Keisling, M. (2011). *Injustice at every turn: A report of the National Transgender Discrimination Survey*. National Center for Transgender Equality and National Gay and Lesbian Task Force.

Grossman, A. H., D'Augelli, A. R., Howell, T. J., & Hubbard, S. (2005). Parents' reactions to transgender youth' gender nonconforming expression and identity. *Journal of Gay & Lesbian Social Services, 18*(1), 3–16. https://doi.org/10.1300/J041v18n01_02

Gugiu, P. C., & Rodríguez-Campos, L. (2007). Semi-structured interview protocol for constructing logic models. *Evaluation and Program Planning, 30*(4), 339–350. https://doi.org/10.1016/j.evalprogplan.2007.08.004

Hamilton, Z., Kigerl, A., & Kowalski, M. (2021). Prediction is local: The benefits of risk assessment optimization. *Justice Quarterly*, 1–23. https://doi.org/https://doi.org/10.1080/07418825.2021.1894215

Hamilton, Z., Kowalski, M. A., Kigerl, A., & Routh, D. (2019). Optimizing youth risk assessment performance: Development of the modified positive achievement change tool in Washington State. *Criminal Justice and Behavior, 46*(8), 1106–1127. https://doi.org/10.1177/0093854819857108

Hamilton, Z., Kowalski, M. A., Schaefer, R., & Kigerl, A. (2020). Recrafting youth risk assessment: Developing the modified positive achievement change tool for Iowa. *Deviant Behavior, 41*(10), 1268–1289. https://doi.org/10.1080/01639625.2019.1609302

Harvell, S., Love, H., Pelletier, E., & Warnberg, C. (2018). *Bridging research and practice in juvenile probation: Rethinking strategies to promote long-term change* (p. 86). Urban Institute.

Heck, N. C., Flentje, A., & Cochran, B. N. (2011). Offsetting risks: High school gay-straight alliances and Lesbian, Gay, Bisexual, and Transgender (LGBT) Youth. *School Psychology Quarterly, 26*(2), 161–174. https://doi.org/10.1037/a0023226

Hennick, M., Hutter, I., & Bailey, A. (2011). *Qualitative research methods*. Sage Publications Ltd.

Himmelstein, K. E. W., & Bruckner, H. (2011). Criminal justice and school sanctions against non-heterosexual youth: A national longitudinal study. *Pediatrics, 127*(1), 49–57. https://doi.org/10.1542/peds.2009-2306

Horn, S. S., Kosciw, J. G., & Russell, S. T. (2009). Special issue introduction: New research on lesbian, gay, bisexual, and transgender youth: Studying lives in context. *Journal of Youth and Adolescence, 38*(7), 863–866. https://doi.org/10.1007/s10964-009-9420-1

Horrell, S. C. V. (2008). Effectiveness of cognitive-behavioral therapy with adult ethnic minority clients: A review. *Professional Psychology: Research and Practice, 39*(2), 160–168. https://doi.org/10.1037/0735-7028.39.2.160

Hunt, J., & Moodie-Mills, A. (2012). The unfair criminalization of gay and transgender youth: An overview of the experiences of LGBT youth in the juvenile justice system. *Center for American Progress, 29*, 1–12.

Irvine, A. (2010). We've had three of them: Addressing the invisibility of lesbian, gay, bisexual, and gender nonconforming youths in the juvenile justice system. *Columbia Journal of Gender and Law, 19*, 675.

Jeppesen, S. (2010). Queer anarchist autonomous zone and publics: Direct action vomiting against homonormative consumerism. *Sexualities, 13*(4), 463–478. https://doi.org/10.1177/1363460710370652

Johnson, A. (2005). *The gender knot: Unraveling our patriarchal legacy* (Revised and Updated). Temple University Press.

Katz, A. B. (2014). LGBT youth in the juvenile justice system: Overrepresented yet unheard. *Law School Student Scholarship, 503*, 1–28.

Kendall, M. (2020). *Hood feminism: Notes from the women that a movement forgot*. Viking.

Kidd, S. (2003). Street youth: Coping and interventions. *Child and Adolescent Social Work Journal, 20*(4), 235–261. https://doi.org/10.1023/A:1024552808179

Knight, C., & Wilson, K. (2016). *Lesbian, Gay, Bisexual and Trans people (LGBT) and the criminal justice system*. Palgrave Macmillan.

Kosciw, J. G., Greytak, E. A., Bartkiewicz, M. J., Boesen, M. J., & Palmer, N. A. (2012). *The 2011 National School Climate Survey: The experiences of lesbian, gay, bisexual and transgender youth in our nation's schools*. GLSEN.

Kosciw, J. G., Greytak, E. A., Giga, N. M., Villenas, C., & Danischewski, D. J. (2016). *The 2015 national school climate survey: The experiences of Lesbian, Gay, Bisexual, Transgender, and Queer youth in our nation's schools*. GLSEN.

Kosciw, J. G., Greytak, E. A., Zongrone, A. D., Clark, C. M., & Truong, N. L. (2018). *The 2017 national school climate survey: The experiences of Lesbian, Gay, Bisexual, Transgender, and Queer youth in our nation's schools*. GLSEN.

Kosciw, J., Palmer, N., & Kull, R. (2015). Reflecting resiliency: Openness about sexual orientation and/or gender identity and its relationship to well-being and educational outcomes for LGBT students . *American Journal of Community Psychology*, 55(1–2), 167–178. https://doi.org/10.1007/s10464-014-9642-6

Kurlychek, M. C., & Johnson, B. D. (2019). Cumulative disadvantage in the American criminal justice system. *Annual Review of Criminology*, 2(1), 291–319. https://doi.org/10.1146/annurev-criminol-011518-024815

Lerner, R. M., Lerner, J. V., Almerigi, J., Theokas, C., Phelps, E., & Naudeau, S. (2006). Towards a new vision and vocabulary about adolescence: Theoretical, empirical, and applied bases of a "positive youth development" perspective. In L. Balter & C. Tamis-LeMonda (Eds.), *Child psychology: A handbook of contemporary issues* (pp. 1–66). Psychology Press/Taylor & Francis.

Lerner, J. V., Phelps, E., Forman, Y., & Bowers, E. P. (2009). Positive youth development. In R. M. Lerner, L. Steinberg, R. M. Lerner, L. Steinberg (Eds.), *Handbook of adolescent psychology, Vol 1: Individual bases of adolescent development* (3rd ed., 524–558). John Wiley & Sons Inc.

Lerner, R. M., & Steinberg, L. (Eds.). (2009). *Handbook of adolescent psychology, volume 1: Individual bases of adolescent development* (Vol. 1). John Wiley & Sons.

Lin, N., & Dumin, M. (1986). Access to occupations through social ties. *Social Networks*, 8(4), 365–385.

Lutze, F. E. (2021). ACJS 2019 presidential address taking responsibility for justice: transforming criminal justice at the intersection of human rights and activism. *Justice Quarterly*, 38(1), 1–21. https://doi.org/10.1080/07418825.2020.1849361

Lutze, F. E., & Lau, J. L. (2017). Centering women's reentry within safe, secure, and affordable housing. In L. Carter & C. Marcum (Eds.), *Female offenders and reentry: pathways and barriers to returning to society*. SAGE.

Lutze, F. E., Rosky, J. W., & Hamilton, Z. K. (2014). Homelessness and reentry: A multisite outcome evaluation of Washington State's reentry housing program for high risk offenders. *Criminal Justice and Behavior*, 41(4), 471–491. https://doi.org/10.1177/0093854813510164

Majd, K., Marksamer, J., & Reyes, C. (2009). Hidden injustice: Lesbian, Gay, Bisexual, Transgender youth in juvenile courts. *The Equity Project: NJDC*, 1–164.

Marshal, M. P., Friedman, M. S., Stall, R., King, K. M., Miles, J., Gold, M. A., Bukstein, O., & Morse, J. Q. (2008). Sexual orientation and adolescent substance use: A meta-analysis and methodological review. *Addiction (Abingdon, England)*, 103(4), 546–556. https://doi.org/10.1111/j.1360-0443.2008.02149.x

Vries, K. M. (2012). Intersectional identities and conceptions of the self: The experience of transgender people. *Symbolic Interaction*, 35(1), 49–67. https://doi.org/10.1002/symb.2

Mayer, K. H., Bradford, J. B., Makadon, H. J., Stall, R., Goldhammer, H., & Landers, S. (2008). Sexual and gender minority health: What we know and what needs to be done. *American Journal of Public Health*, 98(6), 989–995. https://doi.org/10.2105/AJPH.2007.127811

McCall, L. (2005). The complexity of intersectionality. *Signs: Journal of Women in Culture and Society*, 30(3), 1771–1800. https://doi.org/10.1086/426800

McNamara, R. H., & Burns, R. G. (2018). *Multiculturalism, crime, and criminal justice*. Oxford University Press.

Meiners, E. R. (2015). Project muse: Offending children, registering sex. *WSQ: Women's Studies Quarterly*, 43(1–2), 246–263. https://doi.org/10.1353/wsq.2015.0021

Meyer, I. H. (2003). Prejudice, social stress, and mental health in lesbian, gay, and bisexual populations: Conceptual issues and research evidence. *Psychological Bulletin*, 129(5), 674–697. https://doi.org/10.1037/0033-2909.129.5.674

Mogul, J., Ritchie, A., & Whitlock, K. (2011). *Queer (in)justice: The criminalization of LGBT people in the United States*. Beacon Press.

Mottet, L. (2013). Modernizing state vital statistics statutes and policies to ensure accurate gender markers on birth certificates: A good government approach to recognizing the lives of transgender people. *Michigan Journal of Gender and Law*, 19(2), 373–470.

Natapoff, A. (2018). *Punishment without crime: How our massive misdemeanor system traps the innocent and makes America more unequal*. Basic Books.

National Institute of Corrections. (2013). *Evidence-based practices in the criminal justice system*. United States Department of Justice.

National Institute of Corrections. (2016). *The principles of effective interventions*. United States Department of Justice. http://nicic.gov/theprinciplesofeffectiveinterventions

Palmer, N. A., Greytak, E. A., & Kosciw, J. (2016). *Educational exclusion: Drop out, push out, and the school-to-prison pipeline among LGBTQ youth*. GLSEN.

Picard-Fritsche, S., Rempel, M., Tallon, J., Adler, J., & Reyes, N. (2017). *Demystifying risk assessment: Key principles and controversies*. Center for Court Innovation.

Ramon, S., & Warrener, J. (2015). Evaluating the project empowering young LGBT adults: Methodology and key findings of a European action research. *Romanian Journal of Experimental Applied Psychology*, 6(2), 37–55.

Ray, N. (2006). *An epidemic of homelessness. National, Gay and Lesbian Task Force Policy Institute, National Coalition for the Homeless*. http://graphics8.nytimes.com/packages/pdf/national/20070307HomelessYouth.pdf.

Richie, B. (2012). *Arrested justice: Black women, violence, and America's prison nation*. New York University Press.

Ritchie, A. (2017). *Invisible no more: Police violence against black women and women of color*. Beacon Press.

Robertson, M. A. (2014). *Coming out and coming up: LGBT-identified youth and the queering of adolescence* [Sociology Graduate Theses & Dissertations, University of Colorado at Boulder]. 33.

Rocque, M., & Paternoster, R. (2011). Understanding the antecedents of the school-to-jail link: The relationship between race and school discipline. *Journal of Criminal Law and Criminology, 101*, 633–666.

Roig-Palmer. (2020). *Survival to support: Prevention programs for LGBTQ + youth and young adults* [Dissertation]. Department of Criminal Justice and Criminology.

Ryan, C., Russell, S. T., Huebner, D., Diaz, R., & Sanchez, J. (2010). Family acceptance in adolescence and the health of LGBT young adults. *Journal of Child and Adolescent Psychiatric Nursing, 23*(4), 205–213. https://doi.org/10.1111/j.1744-6171.2010.00246.x

Russell, S. T., & Horn, S. S. (2017). *Sexual orientation, gender identity, and schooling: The nexus of research, practice, and policy*. Oxford University Press.

Salisbury, E. J., Van Voorhis, P., & Spiropoulos, G. V. (2009). The predictive validity of a gender-responsive needs assessment: An exploratory study. *Crime & Delinquency, 55*(4), 550–585. https://doi.org/10.1177/0011128707308102

Santelli, J., Ott, M. A., Lyon, M., Rogers, J., Summers, D., & Schleifer, R. (2006). Abstinence and abstinence-only education: A review of US policies and programs. *Journal of Adolescent Health, 38*(1), 72–81. https://doi.org/10.1016/j.jadohealth.2005.10.006

Schensul, S. L., Schensul, J. J., & LeCompte, M. D. (1999). *Essential ethnographic methods: Observations, interviews, and questionnaires*. AltaMira Press.

Schulman, K. (2017). *Executive Director, Lambert House: LGBTQ + Youth Community Center, Seattle, WA*. Personal communication.

Sears, J. (2005). *Gay, lesbian, and transgender issues in education programs, policies and practices*. Harrington Park Press.

Sedgwick, E. K. (1997). Paranoid reading and reparative reading, or, you're so paranoid, you probably think this introduction is about you. In E. K. Sedgwick (Eds.), *Novel gazing: Queer readings in fiction* (pp. 1–37). Duke University Press.

Seidler, V. (2010). *Embodying identities: Culture, differences and social theory*. The Policy Press.

Shahani, N. G. (2005). Pedagogical practices and the reparative performance of failure, or, "what does [Queer] knowledge do? *JAC, 25*(1), 185–207.

Snapp, S. D., Hoenig, J. M., Fields, A., & Russell, S. T. (2015). Messy, butch, and queer: LGBTQ youth and the school-to-prison pipeline. *Journal of Adolescent Research, 30*(1), 57–82. https://doi.org/10.1177/0743558414557625

Snyder, S. M., Hartinger-Saunders, R., Brezina, T., Beck, E., Wright, E. R., Forge, N., & Bride, B. E. (2016). Homeless youth, strain, and justice system involvement: An application of general strain theory. *Children and Youth Services Review, 62*, 90–96. https://doi.org/10.1016/j.childyouth.2016.02.002

Spade, D. (2015). *Normal life: Administrative violence, critical trans politics, and the limits of law*. Duke University Press.

Stoecker, R. (2013). *Research methods for community change: A project-based approach* (2nd ed.). SAGE.

Stone, A. L. (2009). More than adding a T: American Lesbian and Gay activisits' attitudes towards Transgender inclusion. *Sexualities, 12*(3), 334–354.

Substance Abuse and Mental Health Services Administration [SAMHSA]. (2014). *Trauma-informed care in behavioral health services*. Treatment Improvement Protocol (TIP) Series, 57. HHS Publication No. (SMA), 13–4801.

Talburt, S. (2004). Constructions of LGBT youth: Opening up subject positions. *Theory into Practice, 43*(2), 116–121. https://doi.org/10.1207/s15430421tip4302_4

Toomey, R. B., Ryan, C., Diaz, R. M., & Russell, S. T. (2018). Coping with sexual orientation-related minority stress. *Journal of Homosexuality, 65*(4), 484–500. https://doi.org/10.1080/00918369.2017.1321888

Van Cleve, N. (2016). *Crook county: Racism and injustice in America's largest criminal court*. Stanford Law Books.

Van Voorhis, P. (2012). On behalf of women offenders: Women's place in the science of evidence-based practice. *Criminology & Public Policy, 11*(2), 111–145. https://doi.org/10.1111/j.1745-9133.2012.00793.x

Van Voorhis, P., Wright, E. M., Salisbury, E., & Bauman, A. (2010). Women's risk factors and their contributions to existing risk/needs assessment: The current status of a gender-responsive supplement. *Criminal Justice and Behavior, 37*(3), 261–288. https://doi.org/10.1177/0093854809357442

Ward, J. (2008). *Respectably queer: Diversity culture in LGBT activist organizations*. Vanderbilt University Press.

Wanner, P. (2018). *Inventory of evidence-based, research-based, and promising programs for adult corrections* (No. 18-02-1901; pp. 1–16). Washington State Institute for Public Policy. https://www.wsipp.wa.gov/ReportFile/1681/Wsipp_Inventory-of-Evidence-Based-Research-Based-and-Promising-Programs-for-Adult-Corrections_Report.pdf

Williams, J. M., & Battle, N. T. (2017). African Americans and punishment for crime: A critique of mainstream and neoliberal discourses. *Journal of Offender Rehabilitation*, *56*(8), 552–566. https://doi.org/10.1080/10509674.2017.1363116

Wright, E. M., Van Voorhis, P., Salisbury, E. J., & Bauman, A. (2012). Gender-responsive lessons learned and policy implications for women in prison: A review. *Criminal Justice and Behavior*, *39*(12), 1612–1632. https://doi.org/10.1177/0093854812451088

Young, M. (1990). *Justice and the politics of difference*. Princeton University Press.

Young, M. (2011). *Responsibility for justice*. Oxford University Press.

Zielinski, M. J., Allison, M. K., Brinkley-Rubinstein, L., Curran, G., Zaller, N. D., & Kirchner, J. A. E. (2020). Making change happen in criminal justice settings: Leveraging implementation science to improve mental health care. *Health & Justice*, *8*(1), 21 https://doi.org/10.1186/s40352-020-00122-6

🔓 OPEN ACCESS

Hate Hurts: Exploring the Impact of Online Hate on LGBTQ+ Young People

Rachel Keighley 🆔

ABSTRACT
Research has demonstrated how LGBTQ+ hate is widespread on the internet. The nature of the online world is such that the permanence and desistance of hate is greater than its offline counterpart. However, comparatively little attention has been paid to the impacts of this type of behavior. Drawing on the findings of a survey involving 175 LGBTQ+ respondents aged 13–25, and 15 follow-up interviews, this paper addresses this gap by exploring the range of significant impacts that LGBTQ+ young people experience on their well-being and relationships with others. Given the ubiquitous nature of online abuse, this paper demonstrates the need for a targeted criminal justice response. Consequently, this paper discusses the implications of the findings with respect to future research.

INTRODUCTION

The rise of the internet as an online community space represents a symbol of technological ingenuity and a new era of social interactions (Wall, 2001). In particular, LGBTQ+ youth establish online safe spaces to explore their gender and sexuality, whilst building authentic peer connections (De Ridder & Van Bauwel, 2015). However, there is a darker side of internet use, with LGBTQ+ young people becoming increasingly vulnerable to online hate (Marston, 2019).

Online hate as a concept is not new, however we are seeing increasing levels of awareness within policy and scholarship domains. Prior to this, hate crime discussions have precluded any meaningful understanding of microaggressions and "every day" hate, by largely focusing on acts of violence and discrimination that are deemed liable for criminal justice responses (Chakraborti, 2018). However, online hate speech, including incidents that do not meet the threshold of "crime," are now being considered as a problem in their own right. Described as an "endemic" (Bachmann & Gooch, 2017: p4) research demonstrates that LGBTQ+ people are more vulnerable to online hate than their heterosexual, cisgender peers (Powell et al., 2020; Marston, 2019). Yet current criminal justice models fail to appropriately engage with the nature and harms of this novel form of online hate.

Previous research into LGBTQ+ online hate has not considered the full spectrum of targeted abuse, and therefore our attempts to understand this pernicious social problem are lacking context (Williams, 2019). Moreover, where current literature demonstrates the varied impacts of offline hate, comparatively little attention has been paid to the impacts of online hate on

This is an Open Access article distributed under the terms of the Creative Commons Attribution-NonCommercial-NoDerivatives License (http://creativecommons.org/licenses/by-nc-nd/4.0/), which permits non-commercial re-use, distribution, and reproduction in any medium, provided the original work is properly cited, and is not altered, transformed, or built upon in any way.

LGBTQ+ youth. As such, research has overlooked how the permanence and desistance of online hate amplifies both the direct and bystander effects experienced by LGBTQ+ youth (Williams, 2019). Our understanding of the extreme impacts of offline hate, including increased rates of depression, anxiety, self-harm and suicide (Cooper & Blumenfeld, 2012; McDermott, 2015; Williams, 2019) demonstrate the importance of understanding the impacts of online hate on LGBTQ+ youth.

This paper seeks to address the gap in current understandings of LGBTQ+ online hate. Drawing on findings from a survey involving 175 LGBTQ+ respondents aged 13-25, and 15 follow-up semi-structured interviews, this paper details a range of significant impacts that LGBTQ+ young people experience, showcasing how online hate is damaging and a cause for concern (Keighley, 2022). Consequently, this paper demonstrates the importance of a harms focused approach to criminal justice. In order to judiciously present this argument, the first section of this paper provides a summary of key literature, including problems defining LGBTQ+ online hate within the legal sphere, and attempts to quantify incidence rates of LGBTQ+ targeted hate. Second, the methodology is reported, including details of the sample and participant recruitment process. Finally, this paper presents some key findings with respect to the impacts of LGBTQ+ online hate on young people. By developing our understanding of the ubiquitous nature of this novel form of hate, this paper suggests a need for prioritizing meaningful responses to support LGBTQ+ young people within and beyond criminal justice avenues. Most notably, this paper demonstrates a need to transform criminal justice policy to be inclusive of the harms of online hate. Such a reformation of criminal justice frameworks together with a coalition of multilateral efforts will be most effective in reducing the harm caused by hate online (Banks, 2010).

LGBTQ+ ONLINE HATE

Defining LGBTQ+ Online Hate

Online hate is neither clearly, nor consistently defined in legal and academic research circles and there are important distinctions made between hate crime and hate speech. Within the matrix of defining what constitutes online hate, criminal justice institutions are interested in the criminal aspects only. The Council of Europe, alongside the Committee of Ministers, is the first and only international intergovernmental organization to have adopted an official definition of hate speech. Recommendation (97)20 defines hate speech as, "covering all forms of expression which spread, incite, promote or justify racial hatred, xenophobia, anti-Semitism or other forms of hatred based on intolerance" (Council of Europe, 1997, p. 107). This was refined in 2008 by the European Union following a consultation to include,

> all conduct publicly inciting to violence or hatred directed against a group of persons or a member of such a group defined by reference to race, colour, religion, descent or national or ethnic origin (Framework Decision 2008/913/JHA)

Whilst certainly a clearer definition in scope, by solely focusing on public incitements to violence of hatred, private incidents are excluded. Moreover, it remains unclear whether sexuality and/or gender identity are protected characteristics as no mention is given anywhere in the legal summary.

However well-intentioned these legal definitions may be, difficulties arise when deciding at what point speech crosses the line from an expression of opinion to an illegal act (CPS (Crown Prosecution Service),), 2019). In most countries, the law makes a distinction between a hate crime (liable for criminal sanction), a hate incident (non-criminal offence) and hate speech (which may or may not constitute a criminal offence). To use the UK as an example, as a country who meticulously records hate crime incidents at a higher rate than comparable countries (FRA, 2018), the police are obliged to record all hate crimes and hate incidents (UK Council for

Internet Safety (UKCIS), 2019). Hate speech, which commonly occurs online, is often left out of hate crime and hate incident reports. Thus, a problem arises when policing online hate from a merely legal standpoint. Failing to include online hate speech in a legal definition, is to underestimate the tangible harms and negative outcomes on LGBTQ+ people experiencing online hate. Currently, our legal understanding of hate online sits apart from contextual facts, such as the causes and consequences of these acts (Siegel, 2020). This is despite the extensive literature detailing the harms of wider identity targeted hate online (Sellars, 2016). This is none more pronounced than when offensive and controversial hate speech falls under Article 10 of the European Convention on Human Rights (Council of Europe, 2020). Article 10 allows for certain protections for freedom of speech that includes the freedom to offend others. Furthermore, the geographic indeterminacy of the internet has meant that States with diverging hate and free speech laws have clashed over jurisdictional rights when attempting to prosecute hate cases (Banks, 2010). There are inherent difficulties in both policing online hate according to geographical demarcations, but also by seeking to extend jurisdictional powers when enforcing content and regulation laws in States that do not concur. Thus, our understandings of online hate are clouded by a judgment on criminal culpability and freedom of speech.

Online hate beyond what is considered a crime is the object of intense scrutiny by academic scholarship. There are again problems with consistency in terms, which is likely affecting understandings of LGBTQ+ online hate. "Hate," "harassment" and "abuse" are often used interchangeably in the academic literature when referring to online hate (Hardy & Chakraborti, 2020). Yet these are typically not motivating factors in the commission of an online hate incident and certain acts are not protected under such so-called umbrella concepts (Chakraborti, 2018). Thus, despite the important contributions academic definitions have made, a lack of common understanding has garnered a reputation for responding to online hate that is rather permeable (Chakraborti & Hardy, 2017; Powell & Henry, 2017).

Where both legal and academic definitions of hate speech typically focus on the physical manifestations of the act and the geographical relevancy to State criminal justice agencies, they fail to understand that harm is an important factor to be considered (Banks, 2010). A universal definition of hate speech that is inclusive of harms is one which understands that an important facet of the law is to protect its citizens from injury. The European Union's attempts to harmonize European National Laws marks an important step in effectively responding to hate online within criminal justice spheres (Framework Decision 2008/913/JHA). However, it still fails to engage with hate speech that could be subsumed under freedom of speech protections (Banks, 2010). Current criminal justice efforts are limited in their ability to effectively respond to LGBTQ+ online hate. Consequently, online hate is growing exponentially in an online world that is increasingly viewed as lawless.

Prevalence of LGBTQ+ Online Hate

Hate crime, both online and offline, is reportedly on the rise worldwide, with the UK recording a 19% increase in anti-LGB hate crimes from 13,314 incidents per year in 2018/19 to 15,835 per year in 2019/20 and a 16% increase in transgender hate crimes from 2,183 incidents to 2,540 incidents (Home Office, 2020). Similar increases have been reported to ODIHR, in which 1272 sexuality and gender-identity motivated bias crimes were recorded across 35 States (ODIHR, 2019), an increase from 840 reports across 29 States in 2018 (ODIHR, 2018). In the USA, the FBI reported 1393 hate crimes targeting a person's sexual orientation and/or gender identity (FBI, 2019). Whilst hate crime is now firmly under the lens of an international audience, much of this official research fails to include online hate within its scope.

Currently, as a rule, the police do not record online hate crimes to the same extent as their offline equivalents. Therefore, it is important to identify the small, but nonetheless notable body of academic research within the field whose contributions have estimated the high levels of LGBTQ+ online hate. In a recent study by Galop, 96% of UK based LGBTQ+ respondents had experienced more than one incident of online hate in the last five years alone (Hubbard, 2020). This is supported by similar figures in the Sussex Hate Crime Project (Paterson et al., 2018), in which 83% of 116 LGBTQ+ participants had experienced at least one incident of online hate and 86% had been indirectly victimized online at least once. On a larger scale, Ditch the Label and Brandwatch analyzed 10 million online posts over a three-and-a-half-year period to explore transphobic attitudes in the USA and UK (Brandwatch & Ditch the Label, 2019). They found 1.5 million transphobic comments amid wider conversations around trans people and gender identity. In a similar study, Brandwatch and Ditch the Label analyzed 19 million tweets over four years and found 390,296 to include homophobic insults and 19,003 to include transphobic insults (Brandwatch & Ditch the Label, 2016).

The aforementioned research has made some noteworthy contributions to our understanding of the insidious nature of LGBTQ+ online hate. Yet the empirical literature fails to account for the role age plays in victimization experiences. This is despite current understandings that young people are among the earliest adopters and most avid users of social media sites (Keipi et al., 2016; Ofcom, 2018a, 2018b). In tangent reports suggest young people are at greater risk of exposure to hate content (Jones et al., 2013; Ofcom, 2019a, 2019b). A small number of studies have found higher rates of online hate targeting LGBTQ+ youth as compared to older demographics. Research by GLSEN and partners in the USA found that one in four (26%) out of 1960 LGBTQ+ youth surveyed, reported being bullied online specifically because of their sexual orientation or gender identity in the past year, and one in five (18%) said they had experienced bullying and harassment via text message (GLSEN et al., 2013). In a UK based study, 1 in 20 of 2,544 LGB + people had been the target of homophobic abuse online in the last 12 months. The highest rates of abuse were experienced by the younger cohorts, with 7% being 18 to 24-year-olds (Guasp et al., 2013). Similarly, the same study found that 28% of LGB + participants observed online abuse directed at someone else, with the highest proportion being observed by 18 to 24-year-olds (45%). A final study by Myers et al. (2017) collected data from 1,182 young people aged 13–25 from 75 different countries. Their findings suggest bisexual, pansexual and queer participants report higher rates of exposure to cyberbullying than their heterosexual, gay, or lesbian peers.

Taken together, the above empirical research suggests concerning rates of victimization for LGBTQ+ youth and young people globally, with perpetrators and victims of online hate not necessarily residing in the same country (Yar & Steinmetz, 2019). However, there is a skepticism toward the concept of online hate, including a general disbelief that it is a problem and an ignorance around the harms associated with it at an individual and community level (Hardy & Chakraborti, 2020). Therefore, this article explores the limited research into the effects of LGBTQ+ online hate.

THE IMPACTS OF LGBTQ+ ONLINE HATE

When developing our understanding of LGBTQ+ online hate, we must challenge the assumption that what occurs online is neither harmful, nor inconsequential to a person's life offline (Hardy & Chakraborti, 2020). Williams (2019) argues online hate has the potential to cause greater harms than offline hate due to some unique factors of the internet. The perception or potential for anonymity online means perpetrators of online hate are more likely to offend, and these offenses can be more serious due to the disinhibition effect (Williams, 2019). Galop recorded a range of emotional and behavioral responses, similar to those found in the well-documented effects of offline hate (Stray, 2017; Williams, 2019). Anger, sadness and anxiety were the most highly reported effects (76, 70, and 67% respectively). Respondents also reported a deterioration in mental and physical well-being, including feelings of depression, shame and paranoia.

Moreover, Awan and Zempi (2016) identified blurred boundaries between the online and off-line world. Thus, there is a continuity of hate in both the virtual and physical world. It can be difficult to isolate online threats from the possibility of their materializing in the "real world." Research suggests this leads to withdrawal, social isolation and self-blame for being targeted (Hubbard, 2020). Furthermore, levels of internalized homophobia, either by downplaying the experiences or invalidating your own identity can increase, which Stray (2017) suggests is as a result of growing up in a heteronormative society. The Sussex Hate Crime Project found instances of online hate were linked to particular emotional and behavioral responses (Paterson et al., 2018). Viewing hate online can generate feelings of anger and anxiety, which produces either help-seeking responses (e.g. discussing and reporting online abuse) or avoidant behaviors (e.g. ignoring the abuse, social withdrawal) (Paterson et al., 2018). This is supported by Galop's research in which some respondents reported an increased determination to engage in activism (Hubbard, 2020).

There exists very little research looking specifically at the effects of LGBTQ+ online hate on young people, despite an understanding that LGBTQ+ youth are exposed to more hate, and that young people typically experience more adverse effects than older cohorts (Keipi et al., 2016; UK Council for Child Internet Safety (UKCCIS),), 2017). General research has demonstrated that LGBTQ+ youth have an elevated risk for suicide and self-harm and mental health problems (McDermott, 2015). Cooper and Blumenfeld (2012) carried out a small US study on LGBTQ+ online hate with 250 participants. 56% of participants had experienced depression and 35% had suicidal thoughts as a result of their experiences of LGBTQ+ online hate. Most experienced a range of behavioral responses, altering their appearance and their day-to-day interactions with their peers. Consequently, research suggests that young people have a preclusion to a wide variety of coping mechanisms, ranging from emotional and behavioral reactions, which impact their mental health both positively and negatively.

The scholarship available demonstrates the illocutionary power of LGBTQ+ online hate to cause widespread harms (Williams, 2019). However, the majority of research is quantitative in nature and misses the lived experiences of those being exposed to hate content online. When distinguishing between hate speech and hate crime, we fail to see that the impacts of LGBTQ+ online hate do not differ according to the criminal severity of the act. This paper therefore seeks to engage with LGBTQ+ youth regarding their experiences of all forms of online hate. This paper showcases how online hate is damaging and addresses the gaps in the literature that fail to understand the range of significant impacts that LGBTQ+ young people experience. Consequently, this paper demonstrates the need for criminal justice changes that effectively widens the scope of State responsibility to respond to the LGBTQ+ online hate endemic.

METHODOLOGY

Recruitment and Participants

This research collected data from 175 LGBTQ+ individuals aged 13–25 using a survey, followed by 15 semi-structured interviews with 16- to 25-year-olds, as part of a wider doctoral study looking at LGBTQ+ online hate experiences, impacts, and expectations and experiences with support services. Survey data was collected between February and September 2020, via *onlinesurveys.ac.uk*. Interviews were carried out exclusively via zoom or phone call between April and June 2020. Participants were recruited predominantly from the UK ($n = 155$), owing to the CoVID-19 pandemic and global shutdown of many infrastructural access points. However, six other countries are represented: France (6.9%), USA (1.7%), Italy (0.6%), Germany (0.6%), Canada (1.2%) and Hong Kong (0.6%). Table 1 displays the demographic analysis for the sample with regards to age, gender and sexual orientation.

Table 1. Participant demographics.

Variable		$N = 175$	Percentage (%)
Age	13–15	61	34.90
	16–17	40	22.90
	18–21	38	21.70
	22–25	38	20.60
Gender (can check all that apply)	Agender	7	4
	Demi-boy	1	0.60
	Demi-girl	2	1.10
	Female	110	62.90
	Non-binary	14	8
	Gender-fluid	14	8
	Male	37	21.10
	Prefer not to say	2	1.10
Is your gender the same as the sex you were registered with at birth?	Yes	127	72.60
	No	43	24.60
	Prefer not to say	5	2.90
Sexual orientation (can check all that apply)	Aromantic	1	0.60
	Asexual	13	7.40
	Bisexual	63	36
	Fluid-sexuality	8	4.60
	Gay	31	17.70
	Lesbian	42	24
	Pansexual	38	21.70
	Queer	34	19.40
	Questioning	14	8

Columns one and two contains the variable demographics for participants, third column details the number of participants within that variable and column four shows this as a percentage of total participants.

Participants were recruited through a number of avenues. The LGBTQ+ population are considered hidden and when accessing hidden populations there is a lack of clear sampling frames (Sulaiman-Hill & Thompson, 2011). Snowball sampling offered the best method to locate participants, and to enrich data quality. Subsequently, the primary pool of participants referred the research to their LGBTQ+ peers, either through word of mouth, or by sharing the survey link across their social media platforms, creating a snowball effect as they proposed other participants whose experiences and characteristics were relevant to this research (Bryman, 2016). As predicted by Kosinski et al. (2015) this positive feedback loop led to a self-sustaining recruitment process, with a rapid growth in sample size.

This research also engaged with new and emerging recruitment methods. Social media platform advertisements have become widely regarded as useful tools for participant recruitment in social science research (see: Wozney et al., 2019; McRobert et al., 2018; Kosinski et al., 2015). This body of research informed this study's use of social media advertisements, by adding a useful way to target hard to reach populations. The Facebook and Instagram Ads tool allows you to selectively recruit participants based on targeted demographic information, social interactions and user behaviors (Kosinski et al., 2015). Facebook and Instagram Ads were utilized specifically given that Facebook is used by over two and a half billion people globally every month (Omnicoreagency.com, 2020a) and Instagram is accessed by one billion users a month (Omnicoreagency.com, 2020b). Furthermore, 72% of teenagers use Instagram, whilst 30% of global Instagram audiences were aged between 18 and 24 years (Omnicoreagency.com, 2020b). Meanwhile, Facebook is accessed by 88% of online users aged 18–29 (Omnicoreagency.com, 2020a). A recent blog by Kemp (2019), a chief analyst for DataReportal, estimated that the potential reach for advertising on Facebook is 113.3 million 13 to 17-year-olds, and 52.9 million on Instagram. This speaks to the success of using social media ads and is certainly reflected in their use for this research project, which saw an increase of 97 further survey responses over a four-week ad campaign.

The survey and follow-up interviews explored the nature and impact of LGBTQ+ young people's experiences of online hate, and their experiences and expectations of support services, including, but not limited to criminal justice and social media platform responsibilities. In both instances questions were predominantly open ended, to allow LGBTQ+ voices to be centered. The survey and interviews were comprised of 3 sections - A: nature of LGBTQ+ online hate; B: experiences of support services; C: expectations of support services. This article focuses on a sub-section of findings from Section A, detailing the relative harms of LGBTQ+ online hate on young people. It is not within the remit of this paper to discuss ongoing difficulties in defining and measuring online hate. Indeed, it is for this very reason that online hate was not defined to allow participants a free narrative to describe their experiences. To define online hate is to strategically or accidentally omit key victimization experiences (Powell et al., 2020). The interplay and overlap between what ought to be considered a spectrum of hate experiences highlights how research which treats such concepts as mutually exclusive has failed to provide an all-encompassing understanding of the true nature of online hate. By clearly demarcating LGBTQ+ online hate as a subjective concept, the contributions this paper will make to the field are clear in terms of understanding the lived realities and impacts of LGBTQ+ online hate and thus, the need for a more nuanced, meaningful response with respect to support, policy and prevention.

The data was analyzed using Braun and Clarke's thematic analysis (Clarke et al., 2015). When exploring emotions and lived experiences there is no objective truth, therefore an inductive approach to thematic analysis was used (Terry et al., 2017). It was important that this stage of data analysis was inductive, as the themes needed to arise from participant experiences, opinions, behavior and practices, rather than preexisting assumptions regarding LGBTQ+ online hate (Clarke et al., 2015; Terry et al., 2017). A highly useful approach to data analysis, this centered the lived experiences and opinions of the LGBTQ+ community in defining the parameters of hate online, and to truly understand the impacts of online hate, and how they interact within their social worlds as a result. This presented an opportunity to acknowledge the discrete incidents individuals experience based on their relative socio-demographic circumstances and the norms and influences of the societies in which they live (Takács & Szalma, 2020). By using such a participatory research approach (Kindon et al., 2007; Bagnoli & Clark, 2010) this study allowed for an equitable collaboration process. This is reflected in the data analysis, and the achievement of a more "relevant," morally aware, and nonhierarchical piece of research (Fuller & Kitchen, 2004; Pain, 2004).

DISCUSSION

The results of this study indicate that LGBTQ+ young people are negatively affected by experiences of online hate in ways similar to research detailing the impacts of offline hate (Stray, 2017; Williams, 2019). The strength of the qualitative data procured from this study highlights some key impacts, brought to life by respondents' own narratives, as their experiences are predominantly directed by free-text responses. 110 people described how their experiences of LGBTQ+ online hate made them feel, and a further 47 went into further detail after being prompted by an exemplar list of common impacts, based upon current literature (Stray, 2017; Williams, 2019). 120 participants engaged with the multiple-choice question detailing the effects of LGBTQ+ online hate (Figure 1). However, the rates at which LGBTQ+ young people experience harms as a result of their experiences of online hate is compounded by unique identity factors. Before proceeding with the qualitative data exploring the impacts of online hate, it is important to recognize the prominence of the intersectionality of identity and double-edged hate directed toward LGBTQ+ people. An important finding from this research suggests a person's

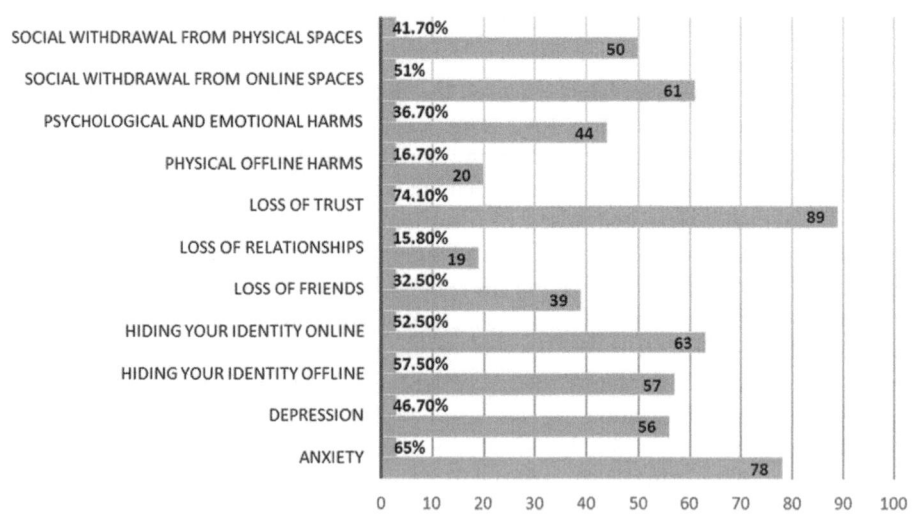

Figure 1. Shows the effects of LGBTQ + online hate and the number of participants reporting each effect.

Table 2. Crosstabulation and chi-square test analysis of gender and anxiety.

	Anxiety		
	Not anxiety	Anxiety	Total
Gender			
Male			
Count	11	9	20
Expected count	11.1	8.9	20.0
% Within gender	55.0%	45.0%	100.0%
Female			
Count	67	38	105
Expected Count	58.2	46.8	105.0
% Within gender	63.8%	36.2%	100.0%
Trans			
Count	19	31	50
Expected count	27.7	22.3	50.0
% Within Gender	38.0%	62.0%	100.0%
Total			
Count	97	78	175
Expected count	97.0	78.0	175.0
% Within gender	55.4%	44.6%	100.0%

Pearson Chi-Square Test: χ^2 (2, $N = 175$)=0.01, $p < .05$.

gender compounds with their sexuality on rates of reported impacts following experiences of online hate. The following Tables 2–4 compare the rates at which cisgender males, cisgender females and transgender participants reported rates of anxiety, loss of trust and feelings of safety (consequently resulting in person's hiding their identity both on and offline), as the most commonly reported impacts in Figure 1.

The observed rates of anxiety for female and trans participants in Table 2 were different to what we would have expected by chance. This demonstrates that females are over-represented in the not anxious category and trans participants are over-represented in anxious category. This finding contradicts what we usually expect to find, where rates of anxiety in LGBTQ+ females is typically higher (for example see Gillig & Bighash, 2021). The chi-square tests were run to explore the differences between what was observed and expected. They confirm the difference between the expected and observed rates is statistically significant ($\chi^2 = 9.134$, $df = 2$, $p=.010$). Similar statistically significant results were found for experiences of trust (or lack thereof) and experiences of

Table 3. Crosstabulation and chi-square test analysis of gender and loss of trust.

	Loss of trust		
	Trusting	Loss of trust	Total
Gender			
Male			
Count	8	12	20
Expected count	9.9	10.1	20.0
% Within gender	40.0%	60.0%	100.0%
Female			
Count	61	44	105
Expected count	52.2	52.8	105.0
% Within gender	58.1%	41.9%	100.0%
Trans			
Count	18	32	50
Expected count	24.9	25.1	50.0
% Within gender	36.0%	64.0%	100.0%
Total			
Count	87	88	175
Expected count	87.0	88.0	175.0
% Within gender	49.7%	50.3%	100.0%

Pearson Chi-Square Test: χ^2 (2, $N = 175$)=0.024, $p < .05$.

Table 4. Crosstabulation and chi-square test analysis of gender and hiding identity online and offline.

	Hiding identity		Total
	Not hiding identity	Hiding identity	
Gender			
Male			
Count	9	11	20
Expected count	10.9	9.1	20.0
% Within gender	45.0%	55.0%	100.0%
Female			
Count	65	40	105
Expected count	57.0	48.0	105.0
% Within gender	61.9%	38.1%	100.0%
Trans			
Count	21	29	50
Expected count	27.1	22.9	50.0
% Within gender	42.0%	58.0%	100.0%
Total			
Count	95	80	175
Expected count	95.0	80.0	175.0
% Within gender	54.3%	45.7%	100.0%

Pearson Chi-Square Test: χ^2 (2, $N = 175$)=0.045, $p < .05$.

hiding identity online and offline beyond what is expected by chance (Tables 3 and 4). According to the data presented in Table 3, once again, the observed and expected counts for female and trans participants differ by a considerable amount. This demonstrates that females are over-represented in the no loss of trust category and trans participants are over-represented in the loss of trust category. The observed and expected counts of males roughly approximate each other, which demonstrates that males are more or less equally represented in retaining trust and experiencing loss of trust as a result of experiences of online hate. The chi-square tests also confirm the difference between the variables is statistically significant ($\chi^2 = 7.467$, $df = 2$, $p=.024$). Finally, according to the data in Table 4, the observed and expected counts of the data for females and trans participants differ by a considerable amount. This demonstrates that females are over-represented in the not hiding their identity category and trans participants are over-represented in the hiding their identity category. The chi-square tests also confirm the difference between the variables is statistically significant ($\chi^2 = 6.192$, $df = 2$, $p=.045$). Therefore, the null-hypothesis is rejected; thus, there is a statistically significant difference between the rates at which different genders experience anxiety, loss of trust and a need to hide their identity following experiences of LGBTQ+ online hate. Consequently, the research suggests when we are exploring the impacts of LGBTQ+ online hate, a recognition of a person's gender identity is also necessary to understand the ways aspects of our identity intersect to contribute to experiences of effects as a result of LGBTQ+ online hate. This point ought to be considered and adjusted for during quantitative and qualitative analysis.

Having established the differing rates at which LGBTQ+ young people experience adverse effects as a result of LGBTQ+ online hate, this paper now focuses on expanding our qualitative knowledge of the impacts. The qualitative efforts within this research highlight two important points. First, clearly in evidence are a wide range of impacts that transcended the severity or frequency of hate incidents experienced. Second, whilst a large number of individuals shared their experiences freely, the disparity between rates of effects reported within Figure 1 and subsequent qualitative excerpts shows a disconnect between our quantifiable understandings of the impacts of LGBTQ+ online hate, and the raw, lived experiences required to truly understand these effects. This disconnect ought to be kept in mind when working with vulnerable populations and the emotional labor needed to engage in research such as this. Also, to proceed with caution when merely looking at LGBTQ+ online hate from either solely a quantitative or qualitative viewpoint. With these points in mind, the qualitative findings from the survey and interviews are broadly categorized into some key topical effects: well-being effects, and relationships and social interactions.

Well-Being Effects

The first theme to be discussed are the negative effects on well-being reported by research participants. When describing how their experiences and observations of LGBTQ+ online hate made them feel, LGBTQ+ young people reported feeling a range of emotions, often comorbidly, including but not limited to sadness and depression, shame, inferiority, and behavioral responses such as social withdrawal.

Sadness and Depression

One of the most common emotions expressed were feelings of sadness and depression. 39 individuals reported varying levels of dejection within their free-text responses. Responses including words such as "upset," "sad," "hurt" and "depressed" were extremely common. Multiple studies have recorded elevated rates of depression in LGBTQ+ individuals, with a potential motivating factor being experiences of marginalization and discrimination (Cooper & Blumenfeld, 2012; Stray, 2017). These elevated levels of depression were self-disclosed by a number of participants,

> The impact on the depressive state, I can confidently say, is absolutely evident. It has contributed to the isolated feeling and extremely low self-worth that accompanies that in a very specific and targeted way

> Respondent #64, asexual, trans male, 22–25

> While I do not believe that LGBTQ+ online harassment was the primary cause of any of my difficulties or diagnoses. I can definitely state that online hate based on my sexual orientation has affected my mental state, to the point that my psychiatrist started me on antidepressants

> Respondent #73, pansexual, male, 18–21

Thus, experiences of online hate have a profound impact on one's mental health. These examples illustrate how experiences of poor mental health already evidenced in young people, can be exacerbated by identity-targeted discrimination. Other participants expressed sadness that hate motivated by a person's sexuality or gender identity still exists in today's societies,

> [I was] upset that people actually think that, I guess I'd thought maybe people weren't as bad until I started getting comments saying that being gay is wrong

Respondent #95, asexual, queer, agender, non-binary, 13–15

Broader underlying systems of oppression and marginalization within the fabric of society have long been recorded as motivating factors for bias and hate (Alorainy et al., 2019; Leets, 2002; Perry, 2001). Power relations play a marked role in experiences of LGBTQ+ online hate, as the ingroup-outgroup dynamics of society breed the idea of status and a hierarchy of "normative" and "non-normative" sexualities and genders (Leets, 2002), despite desires to diversify understandings that all sexualities and genders are natural. An awareness of difference, and the tension created by dominant understandings of normal, universal identity categories (Welzer-Lang, 2008), has pervaded LGBTQ+ young people's perceptions of how gender and sexuality should look. This point will be returned to in greater detail when we explore feelings of inferiority and invalidity.

Shame and Self-Blame

Participants reported an evolving sense of shame and self-blame, born out of experiences of depression and sadness. This followed a period of forced introspection in which the object of blame was their own identity, rather than any fault lying with the perpetrators,

It has somewhat reinforced some of the initial feelings I had prior to discovering that asexuality was "a thing" in thinking that I am broken

Respondent #64, asexual, trans male, 22–25

This shame and self-blame is palpable through the majority of young people's responses. Between the ages of 13 and 25 we know individuals undergo a critical time of self-exploration, as they navigate understanding their identities and how they fit into the social world around them (De Ridder & Van Bauwel, 2015). When social cues from this world are invalidating their sense of identity, impressionable and unsure young people can internalize this.

It has caused negative feelings towards myself, where I feel ashamed or upset for being myself, where I have felt like I have to hide or change my identity. Where I have specifically tried to come across as straight or "straight passing" in order to avoid confrontation

Respondent #73, pansexual, male, 18–21

This sense of shame develops into a marked sense of inferiority, in which hierarchies of identity are reinforced by those being marginalized.

Feelings of Inferiority and Invalid Identities

One of the motivations behind hate crimes are to reinforce this hierarchy of identity, in which the most marginalized remain oppressed and ostracized (Perry, 2001). Reports of inferiority and expressions that their identity is invalid speaks to the so-called success and power of LGBTQ+ online hate perpetration. We can see the role social dominance theory plays in rules on identity (Sidanius & Pratto, 2001) and LGBTQ+ young people's awareness of this,

It wasn't until I got to school, puberty and there was all that social pressure and expectations from other people that and I thought 'hang on am I not normal, am I supposed to be a girlygirl and go with boys', so for me it was a wakeup call and a bit of a shock that people aren't just going to accept me as I am, and I'm maybe not safe at this school, in this small village where nobody else is like me

Interviewee RT, pansexual, trans male, 22–25

LGBTQ+ young people feel an inordinate amount of pressure to assimilate to the dominant identity categories within society, rather than meeting their own needs for self-expression. All these experiences continue to reinforce the social hierarchy boundaries already in place. Self-blame and feelings of inferiority were often intertwined, affecting an individual's understanding of gender and sexuality, thus creating a sense that there's a right or wrong way to be. The power and privilege afforded to dominant groups is displayed in LGBTQ+ young people's desires to conform, rather than embrace their difference (Sidanius & Pratto, 2001).

> Like I was a terrible person and that I was disgusting, and I didn't know how to think of myself anymore and I considered just "acting straight" to avoid it all
>
> Respondent #115, pansexual, female, 13–15

> Made me feel like being LGBT + was wrong morally & spiritually and that I should hide that part of myself if I want to feel accepted
>
> Respondent #67, gay, queer, male, 22–25

Feeling like there is something immoral regarding your own identity is bound to have a marked effect on your mental well-being as evidenced by respondents reporting an increase in depression and anxiety alongside these feelings of shame and inferiority. The effects on LGBTQ+ young people's mental well-being then, is far more complex than categorizing according to depression, sadness, and anxiety on its own. An understanding of the power structures and hierarchical systems that make up society are critical to understand how an individual develops their sense of self and as a result navigates the social world (Leets, 2002). This is the next theme to be discussed in terms of the behavioral changes implemented by LGBTQ+ young people to mitigate mental well-being effects and minimize future victimization.

Relationships and Social Interactions

The second and most consistent theme to arise from the data were the profound effects LGBTQ+ online hate had on young people's relationships and social interactions. Respondents reported a marked change in how they navigated their social worlds, with an overwhelming need to hide their identity both online and offline. These changes in behavior are used to mitigate and protect from future victimization experiences. Respondents reported a heightened lack of safety and loss of trust in both friends and strangers, thereby causing increased rates of isolation and withdrawal from both online and offline spaces. Thus, experiences of online hate drastically impacts both the emotional and physical well-being of an individual, as well as their liberty and rights to occupy certain social spaces (Perry & Alvi, 2012). As highlighted in the previous section, LGBTQ+ online hate has a profound impact on an individual's sense of self-worth, and by withdrawing from both geographical and virtual spaces, reinforces the marginalization and otherness of LGBTQ+ young people.

Fear and Lack of Safety
Through repeated exposure to LGBTQ+ online hate, participants reported heightened levels of fear. 21 participants used the terms "fear," "scared," "terrified" or "frightened" to describe their experiences in some way. Fear is reported to be one of the main intentions of hate (Awan & Zempi, 2016; Perry & Alvi, 2012), and this research is the first detailed report of fear manifesting in LGBTQ+ youth as a result of online hate. The anonymity of the online world amplified the fear effect in respondents, who were often unable to identify the perpetrators of hate. This manifested in feeling helpless and paralyzed,

> [I have a] fear of online hate comments every time I post something now
>
> Respondent #56, queer, pansexual, female, 18–21

Continually respondents demonstrated that the effects of LGBTQ+ online hate do not stay isolated to the online world, but filter into all aspects of a person's life. Respondents reported fear for their physical well-being, and the physical well-being of their LGBTQ+ peers. As identified within the literature, such is the nature of hate as a message crime, targeting LGBTQ+ identity as a whole and anyone who belongs to the identity group (Paterson et al., 2018). One respondent described this experience as,

> From incidents I have witnessed I feel angry and upset and also scared. I feel safe because I am a bisexual woman who is in a heterosexual relationship and is not openly out as bi so I do not feel like I will be targeted but I feel angry and upset and scared for the people who don't fly under the radar like me
>
> Respondent #5, bisexual, female, 22–25

Thus, visible difference is correlated with perceived vulnerability to hate as well as empathy toward other potential victims. The care and comradery felt by LGBTQ+ young people show how acutely aware they are that their gender and sexuality is the object of hate, discrimination and marginalization. We see this expressed in perceptions of how conformity to the norm of cisgender and heterosexuality offers certain levels of protection from hate, as suggested by the data in which trans participants are over-represented in hiding their identity as a result of hate experiences. The safety experienced within conformism is a powerful influencer on LGBTQ+ young people wishing to avoid hate. Overall patterns in the data show LGBTQ+ young people report that feelings of fear led to feeling unsafe in expressing their true identity to others.

> I really feel like I lack any form of trust with others, I can easily detach now. I don't like spending much time with other people nor do I actively try to promote myself as LGBT+. If I do tell someone, they end up judging me (from my pov)
>
> Respondent #113, bisexual, pansexual, female, gender-fluid, 16–17

This lack of trust is deeply embedded in the majority of respondents' associations with others. Perceptions of a hierarchy of identity amplified difference as a vulnerability to be hidden. Moreover, the lack of trust expressed by participants manifested as a skepticism of the safety of society as a whole. A combined mistrust of social players and social leaders highlights a power play embedded within the fabric of society as a contributing factor responsible for upholding hierarchical identities,

> It honestly proves the view that we have not progressed in any way as a civilization or a people, people are still horrible, and this is not a safe world to be in if you are different. It does make you more cynical overall
>
> Respondent #22, gay, male, 22–25

> It's rarely dealt with, even when reported. So, you start to realize that online there are no protections for queers or non cis people. Our only protection there is our own community
>
> Respondent #8, lesbian, gay, queer, female, 22–25

Questioning how society fails to eradicate online hate and the continued marginalization of LGBTQ+ people deepened the sense of hopelessness accompanying respondents' fear to take up space in mainstream society. This sentiment is encapsulated in a question of "if society will not protect you, who will?" Thus, the emotional impacts of sadness, shame and fear develop into behavioral changes that limits the liberty and mobility of LGBTQ+ young people in both online and physical spaces; the next theme to be discussed within this study's findings.

Isolation and Withdrawal from Online/Offline Spaces

Perhaps due to heightened feelings of fear and losing trust in the availability of safe spaces, many participants reported an overwhelming sense of isolation. Consequently, faced with the possibility of having to constantly safeguard in potentially threatening environments, LGBTQ+ young people chose to withdraw from the online and offline world. This supports findings from Perry and Alvi (2012) that in order to avoid future experiences of hate, LGBTQ+ young people develop strategies to negotiate their safety. Many respondents described these behavioral changes as necessary; such were the dangers of occupying certain spaces as openly LGBTQ+. These changes in routine activities and expressions of identity are shared in some of the most detailed responses,

> It made me not want to talk to anyone online. My mental health deteriorated, and I didn't trust anyone (whether online or offline) enough to talk to them about it. I now get anxiety talking to other people online and I usually hide my sexual orientation and gender identity for as long as I can

> Respondent #130, fluid-sexuality, trans male, 16–17

> The experience of continually having to "hide" my queerness online is a constant feeling of looking behind my shoulder in a sense and being overly careful online. I often do not go on Facebook because of this, and use other sites such as Twitter to share my true self

Respondent #44, queer, female, 22–25

Reports of behavioral changes are often comorbid with reports in deterioration of mental well-being. The emotional harms of LGBTQ+ online hate, and the relative unsafety and lack of LGBTQ+ friendly spaces, limit the choice of viable coping mechanisms. The question of safety is ongoing, as respondents reported a continual change to their behavior online and offline. The use of avoidant behaviors offline shows how the impacts of LGBTQ+ online hate does not stay within the confines of the online platform in which it occurred. The perception of danger and fear of further victimization is such that most respondents reported a blanket withdrawal from all social spaces, as opposed to just those where the hate experiences occurred,

> I left social media and spent most of my time alone

> Respondent #34, gay, male, 22–25

> I couldn't tell my parents what was happening because I wasn't out to them because they're very LGBT-phobic. I'd stay in my room for days binging Netflix and sleeping. My friends would try to contact me, but I would decline their calls or ignore their messages. And I wouldn't come downstairs for days at a time

> Respondent #79, questioning, non-binary, 13–15

The impacts of LGBTQ+ online hate are neither isolated, nor short term, but permeate into a person's whole life, even when their sexuality is not contextually relevant. An incident of online hate targeting your sexuality or gender identity has the illocutionary power to affect your perceptions of how the entire world will view you (Williams, 2019). With something so personal, caution, fear and mistrust of repeat episodes of rejection are enough to amplify the negative mental health effects. Thus, creating a vicious cycle between fear of safety, loss of trust and social withdrawal. Moreover, there were no significant differences in reports of behavioral changes between participants who were the direct target of an online hate incident and those who observed online hate.

> I've been diagnosed with social anxiety for a while but receiving and observing hate online made me anxious to come out and be honest about who I am. I've also wanted to avoid social media because of the hate against LGBT people I see even when it isn't directed at me

> Respondent #138, lesbian, female, 13–15

The near constant exposure to anti-LGBTQ+ sentiment and subsequent withdrawal from spaces which continue to host this hate reinforces the "us versus them" binary reported in anti-Muslim hate crime research (Awan & Zempi, 2016). By strengthening the idea of the "other" and preventing interactions between different identities and communities, we see how behavioral changes as a result of online hate can harbor a system of resentment, fear and ostracism between both the LGBTQ+ community and the cisgender, heterosexual community.

LIMITATIONS AND FUTURE RESEARCH

This study contains some limitations which should be considered alongside an understanding of the findings. First, as highlighted within the methods section, the sample largely comes from the United Kingdom, therefore it is unclear if experiences of LGBTQ+ online hate differs depending on the home State of the person. However, as the internet is a world without borders (Yar & Steinmetz, 2019), research suggests the reach of online hate is far greater than its offline counterpart. Moreover, as discussed, it is the responsibility of criminal justice agencies to develop multilateral responses to online hate. Given the geographic indeterminacy of the internet, it is reasonable to argue that the physical location of a person is more relevant to problems of jurisdictional rights as opposed to likelihood of being victimized (Banks, 2010). Additionally, as a qualitative piece of research, each person's experiences of LGBTQ+ online hate are simultaneously considered to be true and valid. Whilst this is a strength of this research in understanding the complex and multi-faceted nature of experiences of online hate, one must take caution in trying to apply a universal framework to this study. As discussed, there are limits to these frameworks themselves, given a lack of universal understanding of online hate. But nonetheless an objective framework would be useful to investigate the potential differing rates at which LGBTQ+ individuals of diverse genders, sexualities and ages experience online hate. Therefore, further quantitative research is needed to explore experiences of online hate within an international sample.

On the point of sample size, this study attempted to recruit participants using snowball sampling. No study is entirely free from bias, and whilst this research achieved a diverse sample in terms of gender, sexualities and age, participants were predominantly UK based and from white backgrounds. The lack of ethnic and racial diversity within the sample is likely due to the restricted conditions through which the data collection was carried out. As previously mentioned, the research was solely carried out through the first few months of the Coronavirus Pandemic and international lockdowns. A lot of infrastructural access point were closed, therefore the sample pool was very much restricted in its reach. Every piece of research into identity must consider how identity is intersectional.

Furthermore, this research attempted to understand the intersections between a person's gender and sexuality on impacts of LGBTQ+ online hate. It is important to recognize that gender is a fluid concept, and therefore a number of participants identify with more than one gender label (e.g. female and genderfluid). When carrying out statistical tests, to analyze the full cohort of participants, gender has to be treated as nominal. Within each potential gender category, there existed unstable cells due to small participant numbers. Thus, to run the tests, overarching categories were created between genders (cisgender female, cisgender male and trans participants). This resulted in an overhaul of the nuance of gender and may undermine the true relationship between gender and sexuality. Moreover, there was a much lower proportion of participants identifying as male than female and transgender, which is unexpected given population frequencies (Antjoule, 2016; Office for National Statistics, 2020). Therefore, this could induce possible biases in the data. To further understand the relationship between the intersections of identity, a larger sample size is needed to successfully run the statistical tests between every possible gender category. Therefore, future research is needed to determine how the intersections of gender, race, religion, ethnicity, and other aspects of a young person's identity intersect to contribute or exacerbate their marginalization experiences.

CONCLUSION

This paper explored how LGBTQ+ online hate impacts young people beyond what we currently know from quantitative research. This study revealed that online hate is damaging, producing a range of significant emotional and behavioral responses in LGBTQ+ young people, in particular reports of sadness, shame, and feelings of inferiority. LGBTQ+ young people develop an internalized sense of blame for their victimization and seek to assimilate to the dominant identity categories within society, unable to safely express their own gender or sexuality. This perceived lack of safety permeates through most participants' responses, producing long-term behavioral changes. LGBTQ+ young people have developed coping strategies for navigating the social world which largely consists of opting out of participating in society altogether. Respondents reported how their withdrawal limited opportunities for identity-building and peer development. As critical aspects of a young person's development, and the importance of the online world as a vehicle for this, we can see how online hate has a profound impact, affecting a person's life online, offline, as well their relationships with themselves and with others (De Ridder & Van Bauwel, 2015).

It is clear from this research, that given the multifaceted, complex effects of online hate, responses similarly need to be multidimensional. Currently, our focus in responding to online hate lies solely within criminal justice pathways. Whilst responses to combatting online hate need to go beyond the punitive aspects of criminal law, the law has a significant role to play in responding to such conduct (Barker & Jurasz, 2018). However, this paper demonstrates that a failure to provide provisions for a comprehensive understanding of hate speech in any legal definition, precludes our ability to appropriately respond to online hate. This paper's findings clearly demonstrate that online hate has tangible impacts that restrict liberty, causes isolation, and is detrimental to LGBTQ+ young people's mental health and physical well-being. Moreover, when experienced during childhood and critical periods of youth development, they can increase the likelihood of school dropout, chemical dependency and abuse, homelessness, and other types of instability during adulthood (Ecker et al., 2020; Keuroghlian et al., 2014; Subhrajit, 2014; Gwadz et al., 2004). Thus, the full spectrum of online hate should be taken more seriously through legal definitions and by criminal justice agencies to avoid future reliance on and relationships between criminal justice agencies and LGBTQ+ young people.

A harms approach to online hate recognizes the role of criminal law within the social world. LGBTQ+ people are entitled to rights and justice, not just symbolic protections (Perry, 2008). An understanding of the tangible impacts on LGBTQ+ people's lives can shape the law into a cohesive framework to successfully protect its citizens from the complex nature of online hate. Where currently the law is failing to appropriately respond to online hate lies within its failure to recognize that the harms of hate are a problem for social and legal justice (Siegel, 2020). This paper recommends that a legal definition of hate speech that is inclusive of harm serves to afford LGBTQ+ people the respect and rights of equal citizenship, but also expands our understandings of hate motivation and online hate to target all forms of discrimination within society (Perry, 2008). Consequently, as Perry (2008) argues, such a reformation of criminal justice frameworks demonstrates the perceived cultural value of a marginalized group as both the target of and remedy for oppression. This has a redistributive effect to transform cultural attitudes as the law shapes behaviors and understandings of sexuality and gender identity (Wigerfelt et al., 2015).

This paper recognizes that not all instances of hate will require a criminal justice response. Further input from support agencies, online platforms, and other institutions responsible for the well-being of children and young adults are also needed to develop a holistic approach to supporting LGBTQ+ young people. Banks argues that such a coalition of multilateral efforts will be most effective in reducing the harm caused by hate online (Banks, 2010). As we have seen, online hate that does not amount to a crime still has a profound impact on the lives of LGBTQ+ young people. With such extreme emotional, psychological, and physical adverse effects, there is convincing evidence of the need for services to offer support to victims of all forms of online hate. Therefore, criminal justice agency responsibility is twofold (Barker & Jurasz, 2018). Primarily, criminal justice agencies need to widen the scope of which online hate incidents are considered criminal offenses. However, they are also responsible for increasing regulation and greater liability for online platforms hosting this hate. Therefore, where an incident of does not reach the threshold for criminal culpability, online service providers ought to be made more accountable for maintaining safe online environments free from hate and harm. Yet, research suggests that inconsistent responses from the law, social media platforms, internet providers and support services convey the impression that hate that is not criminal in nature is not serious enough to warrant a response (Hardy & Chakraborti, 2020). A shift toward a more cohesive, relative understanding of online hate, alongside a rejection of the assumption that what occurs online is neither harmful, nor serious in nature, would begin to mend the mistrust between the LGBTQ+ community, authorities, and wider communities. Therefore, this study acts as a stepping stone and a justification for future research to explore a targeted response to all forms of online hate with respect to social support, policy changes and prevention.

ACKNOWLEDGEMENTS

Many thanks to the research participants for their time and honesty when talking about such an emotional topic. Also, thanks to Professor Neil Chakraborti and Professor Teela Sanders, whose support and comments on earlier drafts proved invaluable. This research received no specific grant from any funding agency in the public, commercial, or not-for-profit sectors.

DISCLOSURE STATEMENT

No potential conflict of interest was reported by the author(s).

ORCID

Rachel Keighley ⓘD http://orcid.org/0000-0001-5245-933X

DATA AVAILABILITY STATEMENT

The data that support the findings of this study are available on request from the corresponding author, Rachel Keighley. The data is not publicly available due to the thesis being ongoing and their containing information that could compromise the privacy of research participants.

REFERENCES

Alorainy, W., Burnap, P., Liu, H., & Williams, M. (2019). The enemy among us: Detecting hate speech with threats based 'othering' language embeddings. *ACM Transactions on the Web, 13*(3), 1–26. https://doi.org/10.1145/3324997

Antjoule, N. (2016). The hate crime report 2016 [online]. *Galop*, pp. 1–35. Retrieved September 01, 2021, from http://www.galop.org.uk/wp-content/uploads/2016/10/The-Hate-Crime-Report-2016.pdf.

Awan, I., & Zempi, I. (2016). The affinity between online and offline anti-Muslim hate crime: Dynamics and impacts. *Aggression and Violent Behavior, 27*, 1–8. https://doi.org/10.1016/j.avb.2016.02.001

Bachmann, C., & Gooch, B. (2017). *LGBT in Britain: Hate Crime and Discrimination*. Stonewall.

Bagnoli, A., & Clark, A. (2010). Focus groups with young people: a participatory approach to research planning. *Journal of Youth Studies, 13*(1), 101–119. https://doi.org/10.1080/13676260903173504

Banks, J. (2010). Regulating hate speech online. *International Review of Law, Computers & Technology, 24*(3), 233–239. https://doi.org/10.1080/13600869.2010.522323

Barker, K., & Jurasz, O. (2018). Online violence against women: The limits & possibilities of law. Stirling Law School & Open University Law School. http://oro.open.ac.uk/53637/1/OVAW%20-%20The%20Limits%20%26%20Possibilities%20of%20Law%20%282018%29.pdf

Brandwatch and Ditch the Label. (2016). *Cyberbullying and hate speech*. Brandwatch.

Brandwatch and Ditch the Label. (2019). *Transphobia report 2019*. Brandwatch.

Bryman, A. (2016). *Social research methods*. Oxford University Press.

Chakraborti, N. (2018). Responding to hate crime: Escalating problems, continued failings. *Criminology & Criminal Justice*, 18(4), 387–404. https://doi.org/10.1177/1748895817736096

Chakraborti, N., & Hardy, S. J. (2017). Beyond empty promises? A reality check for hate crime scholarship and policy. *Safer Communities*, 16(4), 148–154. https://doi.org/10.1108/SC-06-2017-0023

Clarke, V., Braun, V., & Hayfield, N. (2015). Thematic analysis. *Qualitative Psychology: A Practical Guide to Research Methods*, (3rd ed.), pp. 222–248.

Cooper, R. M., & Blumenfeld, W. J. (2012). Responses to cyberbullying: A descriptive analysis of the frequency of and impact on LGBT and allied youth. *Journal of LGBT Youth*, 9(2), 153–177. https://doi.org/10.1080/19361653.2011.649616

Council of Europe. (1997). Recommendation, No. R., (97) 20 of the committee of ministers to member states on "hate speech. *Council of Europe* [online]. Retrieved August 03, 2021, from https://rm.coe.int/1680505d5b.

Council of Europe. (2020). *Freedom of expression: Guide on Article 10 of the European Convention on Human Rights*, August 2020, ECHR. [online]. Retrieved May 21, 2021, from https://www.echr.coe.int/Documents/Guide_Art_10_ENG.pdf.

CPS (Crown Prosecution Service). (2019). *Hate crime annual report 2018–19*. Crown Prosecution Service [online]. Retrieved August 07, 2021, from https://www.cps.gov.uk/sites/default/files/documents/publications/CPS-Hate-Crime-Annual-Report-2018-2019.PDF.

De Ridder, S., & Van Bauwel, S. (2015). The discursive construction of gay teenagers in times of mediatization: youth's reflections on intimate storytelling, queer shame and realness in popular social media places. *Journal of Youth Studies*, 18(6), 777–793. https://doi.org/10.1080/13676261.2014.992306

Ecker, J., Aubry, T., & Sylvestre, J. (2020). Pathways into homelessness among LGBTQ2S adults. *Journal of Homosexuality*, 67(11), 1625–1643. https://doi.org/10.1080/00918369.2019.1600902

FBI. (2019). *Hate crime statistics 2019*. US Department of Justice.

FRA. (2018). *Hate crime recording and data collection practice across the EU*. European Union Agency for Fundamental Human Rights.

Framework Decision 2008/913/JHA. *Framework decision on combating certain forms and expressions of racism and xenophobia by means of criminal law*. (2008), OJ L 328 of 6.12.2008. EU Lex [online] https://eur-lex.europa.eu/legal-content/EN/TXT/?uri=LEGISSUM:l33178.

Fuller, D., & Kitchen, R. (2004). Radical theory/critical praxis: academic geography beyond in the academy? In D. Fuller and R. Kitchen (Eds.), *Radical theory/critical praxis: Making a difference beyond the academy?* (pp.1–20). Praxis (e)Press.

Gillig, T. K., & Bighash, L. (2021). Network and proximity effects on LGBTQ youth's psychological outcomes during a camp intervention. *Health Communication*, 1–7. https://doi.org/10.1080/10410236.2021.1958983

GLSEN, CiPHR, and CCRC. (2013). Out online: The experiences of Lesbian. *Gay, bisexual and transgender youth on the internet*. GLSEN.

Guasp, A., Gammon, A., & Ellison, G. (2013). *Homophobic hate crime: The gay British crime survey 2013* (pp.1–32). Stonewall.

Gwadz, M. V., Clatts, M. C., Leonard, N. R., & Goldsamt, L. (2004). Attachment style, childhood adversity, and behavioral risk among young men who have sex with men. *The Journal of Adolescent Health*, 34(5), 402–413. https://doi.org/10.1016/S1054-139X(03)00329-X

Hardy, S. J., & Chakraborti, N. (2020). *Blood, threats and fears: The hidden worlds of hate crime victims*. Springer Nature.

Home Office. (2020). *Hate crime, England and Wales, 2019/20*. Home Office, Crime and Policing Statistics.

Hubbard, L. (2020). Online hate crime report 2020 [online]. Retrieved August 04, 2021, from *Galop*. http://www.galop.org.uk/wp-content/uploads/Online-Crime-2020_0.pdf.

Jones, L. M., Mitchell, K. J., & Finkelhor, D. (2013). Online harassment in context: Trends from three youth internet safety surveys (2000, 2005, 2010). *Psychology of Violence*, 3(1), 53–69. https://doi.org/10.1037/a0030309

Keighley, R. (2022). *The dark side of social media: Exploring the nature, extent, and routinisation of LGB + online hate* [Unpublished doctoral thesis]. University of Leicester.

Keipi, T., Näsi, M., Oksanen, A., & Räsänen, P. (2016). *Online hate and harmful content: Cross-national perspectives*. Routledge.

Kemp, S. (2019). Over 3.5 billion people are on social media; Facebook still biggest with teens; Esports on the rise. *Podium*. Retrieved May 14, 2021, from https://thenextweb.com/podium/2019/07/17/over-3-5-billion-people-are-on-social-media-facebook-still-biggest-with-teens-esports-on-the-rise/>

Keuroghlian, A. S., Shtasel, D., & Bassuk, E. L. (2014). Out on the street: a public health and policy agenda for lesbian, gay, bisexual, and transgender youth who are homeless. *The American Journal of Orthopsychiatry*, 84(1), 66–72. https://doi.org/10.1037/h0098852

Kindon, S., Pain, R. and Kesby, M., eds., (2007). *Participatory action research approaches and methods: Connecting people, participation and place*. Routledge.

Kosinski, M., Matz, S. C., Gosling, S. D., Popov, V., & Stillwell, D. (2015). Facebook as a research tool for the social sciences: Opportunities, challenges, ethical considerations, and practical guidelines. *The American Psychologist, 70*(6), 543–585. https://doi.org/10.1037/a0039210

Leets, L. (2002). Experiencing hate speech: Perceptions and responses to anti-semitism and antigay speech. *Journal of Social Issues, 58*(2), 341–361. https://doi.org/10.1111/1540-4560.00264

Marston, K. (2019). Researching LGBT + youth intimacies and social media: The strengths and limitations of participant-led visual methods. *Qualitative Inquiry, 25*(3), 278–288. https://doi.org/10.1177/1077800418806598

McDermott, E. (2015). Asking for help online: Lesbian, gay, bisexual and trans youth, self-harm and articulating the 'failed' self. *Health, 19*(6), 561–577. https://doi.org/10.1177/1363459314557967

McRobert, C. J., Hill, J. C., Smale, T., Hay, E. M., & van der Windt, D. A. (2018). A multi-modal recruitment strategy using social media and internet-mediated methods to recruit a multidisciplinary, international sample of clinicians to an online research study. *PLOS One, 13*(7), e0200184–11. https://doi.org/10.1371/journal.pone.0200184

Myers, Z. R., Swearer, S. M., Martin, M. J., & Palacios, R. (2017). Cyberbullying and traditional bullying: The experiences of poly-victimization among diverse youth. *International Journal of Technoethics, 8*(2), 42–60. https://doi.org/10.4018/IJT.2017070104

ODIHR. (2018). 2018 Hate crime data key findings. *OCSE/ODIHR* [online]. Retrieved May 21, 2021, from https://hatecrime.osce.org/sites/default/files/documents/Website/Infographics/2018-key-findin_updated%20Feb%202020.pdf.

ODIHR. (2019). 2019 Hate crime data key findings. *OCSE/ODIHR* [online]. Retrieved May 21, 2021, from https://hatecrime.osce.org/sites/default/files/documents/Website/Infographics/2019/2019%20Key%20Findings%20UPDATED%20JAN%202021_PDF.pdf.

Ofcom. (2018a). *Adults' media use and attitudes report* [online]. Retrieved May 21, 2021, from https://www.ofcom.org.uk/__data/assets/pdf_file/0011/113222/Adults-Media-Use-and-Attitudes-Report-2018.pdf.

Ofcom. (2018b). *Children and parents: media use and attitudes report 2018* [online]. https://www.ofcom.org.uk/research-and-data/media-literacy-research/childrens/children-and-parents-media-use-and-attitudes-report-2018. Accessed 21 May 2021.

Ofcom. (2019a). Adults: Media use and attitudes report 2019 [online]. Retrieved May 01, 2021, from *Ofcom.* https://www.ofcom.org.uk/__data/assets/pdf_file/0021/149124/adults-media-use-and-attitudes-report.pdf.

Ofcom. (2019b). *Children and Parents: Media use and attitudes report 2019.* [online] London: Ofcom. Retrieved May 01, 2021, from <https://www.ofcom.org.uk/__data/assets/pdf_file/0023/190616/children-media-use-attitudes-2019-report.pdf>

Office for National Statistics. (2020). *Population estimates.* Office for National Statistics.

Omnicoreagency.com. (2020a). *Facebook by the numbers (2020): Stats, demographics & fun facts* [online]. Retrieved May 21, 2021, from https://www.omnicoreagency.com/facebook-statistics/.

Omnicoreagency.com. (2020b). *Instagram by the numbers (2020): Stats, demographics & fun facts* [online]. Retrieved May 21, 2021, from https://www.omnicoreagency.com/instagram-statistics/.

Pain, R. (2004). Social geography: Participatory research. *Progress in Human Geography, 28*(5), 652–663. https://doi.org/10.1191/0309132504ph511pr

Paterson, J., Walters, M. A., Brown, R., & Fearn, H. (2018). *The Sussex hate crime project* (pp. 1–53). Sussex.

Powell, A., & Henry, N. (2017). *Sexual violence in a digital age.* Palgrave Macmillan.

Powell, A., Scott, A. J., & Henry, N. (2020). Digital harassment and abuse: Experiences of sexuality and gender minorities. *European Journal of Criminology, 17*(2), 199–223. https://doi.org/10.1177/1477370818788006

Perry, B. (2001). *In the name of hate: Understanding hate crimes.* Routledge.

Perry, J. (2008). The 'perils' of an identity politics approach to the legal recognition of harm. *Liverpool Law Review, 29*(1), 19–36. https://doi.org/10.1007/s10991-008-9034-9

Perry, B., & Alvi, S. (2012). We are all vulnerable' The in terrorem effects of hate crimes. *International Review of Victimology, 18*(1), 57–71. https://doi.org/10.1177/0269758011422475

Sellars, A. (2016). *Defining hate speech* (pp.16–48). Berkman Klein Center Research Publication.

Sidanius, J., & Pratto, F. (2001). *Social dominance: An intergroup theory of social hierarchy and oppression.* Cambridge University Press.

Siegel, A. A. (2020). Online hate speech. In N. Persily & J. Tucker (Eds.), *Social Media and Democracy: The State of the Field, Prospects for Reform* (1st ed., pp. 56–88). Cambridge University Press.

Stray, M. (2017). Online hate crime report 2017 [online]. *Galop,* pp. 1–27. Retrieved May 26, 2021, from http://www.galop.org.uk/wp-content/uploads/2017/08/Online-hate-report.pdf.

Subhrajit, C. (2014). Problems faced by LGBT people in the mainstream society: Some recommendations. *International Journal of Interdisciplinary and Multidisciplinary Studies, 1*(5), 317–331.

Sulaiman-Hill, C. M., & Thompson, S. C. (2011). Sampling challenges in a study examining refugee resettlement. *BMC International Health and Human Rights, 11*(1), 2–10. https://doi.org/10.1186/1472-698X-11-2

Takács, J., & Szalma, I. (2020). Democracy deficit and homophobic divergence in 21st century Europe. *Gender, Place & Culture, 27*(4), 459–478. https://doi.org/10.1080/0966369X.2018.1563523

Terry, G., Hayfield, N., Clarke, V., & Braun, V. (2017). Thematic analysis. In: C. Willig & W. Stainton Rogers (Eds.), *The Sage Handbook of Qualitative Research in Psychology*. (2nd ed., pp. 17–37).

UK Council for Child Internet Safety (UKCCIS). (2017). *Children's online activities, risks and safety a literature review by the UKCCIS Evidence Group* [online]. UKCCIS, pp. 1–106. Retrieved August 10, 2021, from https://assets.publishing.service.gov.uk/government/uploads/system/uploads/attachment_data/file/759005/Literature_Review_Final_October_2017.pdf.

UK Council for Internet Safety (UKCIS). (2019). *Adult online hate, harassment and abuse: A rapid evidence assessment* [online]. Gov.uk, pp. 1–131. Retrieved August 10, 2021, from https://assets.publishing.service.gov.uk/government/uploads/system/uploads/attachment_data/file/811450/Adult_Online_Harms_Report_2019.pdf.

Wall, D. ed., (2001). *Crime and the Internet*. Routledge.

Welzer-Lang, D. (2008). Speaking out loud about bisexuality: Biphobia in the gay and lesbian community. *Journal of Bisexuality, 8*(1–2), 81–95. https://doi.org/10.1080/15299710802142259

Wigerfelt, A. S., Wigerfelt, B., & Dahlstrand, K. (2015). Online hate crime: Social norms and the legal system. *Quaestio Iuris, 8*(3), 1859–1878.

Williams, M. (2019). *Hatred behind the screens: A report on the rise of online hate speech*. Hate Lab.

Wozney, L., Turner, K., Rose-Davis, B., & McGrath, P. J. (2019). Facebook ads to the rescue? Recruiting a hard to reach population into an Internet-based behavioral health intervention trial. *Internet Interventions, 17*(100246), 100246–100246. https://doi.org/10.1016/j.invent.2019.100246

Yar, M., & Steinmetz, K. F. (2019). *Cybercrime and society*. SAGE Publications Limited.

Gay Dating Platforms, Crimes, and Harms in India: New Directions for Research and Theory

Rahul Sinha-Roy ⓘ and Matthew Ball

ABSTRACT
This paper argues that gay dating platform-facilitated crimes and abuses in India are produced and perpetuated by structural queerphobia and sex-negativity in Indian society. We illustrate how sex-negativity and queerphobia are embedded in Indian families, neighborhoods, criminal law, and the criminal justice system, which help produce/exacerbate these crimes. We offer some recommendations as to how these can be changed and posit that future empirical studies should focus on reforming societal structures producing/exacerbating these crimes. We also suggest that framing safe dating advice in a more sex-positive light will reduce self-blame and better address these issues. Overall, we contend that a sex-positive queer-criminological theoretical lens will offer more effective approaches on which to base preventative measures and assist in supporting those experiencing such crimes.

INTRODUCTION

In recent years, gay dating platform-facilitated crimes have received considerable media attention in India (see Ansar, 2018; Bhattacharya, 2018; Orinam, 2014; Times News Network, 2014). Typically, cases involve blackmailing, extortion, physical and sexual assault, image-based sexual abuse, robbery, or theft, perpetrated by an individual met via a gay dating platform. Some of these crimes, like image-based sexual abuse or blackmail, involve abuse that continues beyond the initial encounter. NGOs, community groups, and people who experience such incidents have taken to social media to highlight the existence of these victimizations (see, for example, Harmless Hugs, 2019; Queer Friendly Lawyers Network-West Bengal, 2020; Queerythm, 2019; Yes We Exist, 2019a, 2019b). Recently, there have been arrests of small gangs of people involved in victimizing users of gay dating platforms (see Jaiswal, 2019; Singh, 2019; Times News Network, 2019). People who experience these crimes are often reluctant to report the incidents or seek help owing to the social stigmas around casual sex (see Shivanand et al., 2019) and queer sexualities (Boyce, 2006) in India.

Despite the seriousness and frequency of these crimes, and their impacts on the users of these platforms, to date, there is a dearth of empirical research on this issue in the Indian context. Moreover, there are no official statistics on these crimes, perhaps owing to the diverse nature of harms and abuses involved, and that no separate class of offenses exists for them. A mixed-methods study involving MSM (men who have sex with men), transgender women, and hijras in India confirmed what we have outlined before—that sexual partners met online were often the perpetrators of a range of victimization, including asking for money after sex, theft, physical assault, forced sex, extortion, and blackmail (Li et al., 2017). Another qualitative study with 35 MSM around Mumbai, India reiterated multiple risks and challenges on gay dating platforms, including information security and identification by others and blackmail (Birnholtz et al., 2020). Beyond this, though, little is known about these issues.

This paper responds to this lack of research, setting out the empirical and theoretical parameters within which research on this issue ought to proceed. We suggest that these crimes are produced and perpetuated by the structural queerphobia and sex-negativity in Indian society, and argue that it is important that these factors are considered in future research and theorizing in this context. Our paper is positioned in relation to multiple bodies of thought in criminology. It contributes to Queer Criminology, which explores the role that an individual's sexuality or gender identity plays in victimization and offending (Dalton, 2016). It also adopts a "sex-positive" approach (Wodda & Panfil, 2020), which suggests that, in the context of crime and victimization involving sex and sexuality, criminological studies need to shift from a moralizing understanding of sex that sees it as a site of danger and vulnerability, toward one that recognizes sex as pleasurable and as a right (Wodda & Panfil, 2020). We situate our discussion in the socio-legal context of India and illustrate how the crimes can be understood as produced, perpetuated, and sustained by systemic queerphobia and sex-negativity in that specific context. In so doing, we argue that future research and theorization on these experiences should be clearly positioned within these theoretical and contextual coordinates. Such a focus will increase criminological understandings of these crimes and contribute to developing prevention strategies and support programs, thereby improving queer individuals' overall experiences with the criminal justice system in India.

We begin by providing a broad overview of gay dating platforms and other queer online spaces in India and outline the socio-cultural context of India within which these platforms operate. We then discuss a range of abusive practices and crimes perpetrated through or enabled by, gay dating platforms in India, throughout which we show how structural queerphobia and sex-negativity underpin these crimes and the variety of responses to them. We suggest that safe dating advice in this context is largely sex-negative and could be framed more clearly in a sex-positive framework. Throughout, we highlight the need for more research on these issues in the Indian context, establish the importance of focusing on the systemic factors that perpetuate such harms.

TERMINOLOGY IN THE INDIAN CONTEXT

Before we begin, a note on terminology is in order. Throughout this paper, we use the term "gay dating platforms" to include a range of mobile applications and web-based platforms that are marketed as providing a range of services, including dating, social networking, and chats for the gay community. Such platforms act as spaces for social networking, dating, or arranging sexual encounters (Dasgupta, 2017, pp. 8–9) and are used by not only gay, bisexual, transgender, or queer-identifying people, but also by straight identifying men looking primarily for casual sex (see Rhoton et al., 2016). While we recognize the diverse users of these platforms, we adopt the term "gay" when sometimes referring to these platforms because this is the dominant way these platforms are referred to in academic research,[1] and popular media (Bhattacharya, 2018; Salaria, 2020). Many of these platforms also market themselves as gay-oriented, by making their gay target audience clear in their homepages by using phrases like "gay dating that goes deeper" (PlanetRomeo, n.da), "one world, one social gay app" (Blued, n.d) and "gay social network" (Hornet, n.d). Although other platforms market themselves in more inclusive ways (Grindr, n.da; Taimi, n.d), the platforms mostly reproduce a form of visibility and identity which aligns more

---

[1] These platforms are variedly referred to in the literature as gay male social networking applications (Tziallas, 2015), geosocial networking (GSN) apps (Rhoton et al., 2016) and sometimes, also as gay hookup apps (Ahlm, 2017).

with gay tropes than anything else. Example gay tropes include fields for sexual positions (top, bottom, versatile) or dick size or circumcision details in profiles. In this sense, these platforms are markedly different from other platforms catering to women seeking women (regardless of gender identity).

We use the term "people who have faced crimes/abuses" throughout this paper to refer to those who have experienced victimization or abuse through these platforms. We acknowledge that people who face crimes or trauma can self-identify with a range of labels, including victim, survivor, thriver, overcomer, and these identities can change across one's lifetime (Ben-David, 2020). For the purposes of this paper, we do not use any of these specific labels unless citing from a source that specifically uses one of these labels.

Finally, we use the term "queer" to refer to the multitude of non-heterosexual sexualities and non-conforming gender identities in India. We acknowledge that this is a contentious term and that it might not resonate with all those we are seeking to include here. Many non-heterosexual and/or transgender people in India might not identify with labels like queer or gay or bisexual (for sexual orientation) or transgender (for gender identity). The usage of "queer" in the Indian context has particularly been criticized for being elite and foreign or Western (Tellis, 2012). Individuals might identify with more local labels like *kothi*, *panthi*, double-deckers, *jogappa*, *hijras*, or might not self-identify with any label at all (Boyce, 2007). However, some have critiqued these terms themselves as essentializing (Boyce, 2007). To address this, some have used the term MSM (Asthana & Oostvogels, 2001; Mimiaga et al., 2015) or same-sex attracted (Vanita & Kidwai, 2000) to refer to the wide variety of sexualities in India. However, there are also problems with those terms, as "MSM" risks excluding people who do not identify as men (transgender women, *hijra*, or *jogappa* communities, for example) and hence, are unlikely to be "same-sex" attracted. The word "queer" has already been used in the Indian context to refer to a diverse set of sexualities and gender identities (Narrain & Bhan, 2005, p. 4) and, in line with that, we use "queer" to capture both concrete sexual and gender identities (like gay, bisexual, *kothi*, *panthi*, trans-woman, or genderqueer), as well as non-heterosexual desires and behavior which do not come with labels. This challenge highlights a limitation of language that perhaps no single term would adequately reflect the multitude of sexual desires, sexual behaviors, and sexual identities (or lack thereof) in India. The word "queer," in its ambiguity and fluidity, might just be able to encompass the varied sexualities and sexual behaviors lying outside the purview of heterosexuality in this context.

GAY DATING PLATFORMS, QUEERPHOBIA, AND SEX-NEGATIVITY IN INDIAN SOCIETIES

To begin the discussion on crimes and harms enabled by gay dating platforms, one of the key aspects to discuss is the techno-social context in which the crimes happen. In this section, we begin by discussing the platforms themselves: their history, popularity, and the stigma around their use in India. Before gay dating platforms existed in app form, digital queer dating in India consisted of chatrooms (yahoo or MSN) and messaging services on social media platforms like Orkut, Facebook, or Hi5 (Chakraborty, 2012; Das, 2019a; Tellis, 2007). PlanetRomeo, a popular web-based dating platform aimed at gay men, dominated the Indian market from the early 2000s. Around 2011, gay dating apps like Grindr and Scruff expanded to India (Das, 2019a). These apps are applications on mobile handheld devices that use Global Position Systems to identify other app users based on locational proximity, and to facilitate "satellite dating" or "location based dating" (Quiroz, 2013). More recently, Blued, a Chinese-made app, entered the Indian market, with a number of features claiming to ensure the safety of its users (Sharma, 2019). Similarly, Delta, an Indian-made app for LGBT+ dating which launched recently promises to be more inclusive than other app companies (Das, 2019b; Mahale, 2018). Although official statistics are not readily available to the public, India reportedly had 1.3 million PlanetRomeo users in 2015 and 11,000 Grindr users in 2013 (Dasgupta, 2017, pp. 8–9). Contemporary India, thus, features several dating platforms, both mobile and web-based; some exclusively catering to the queer population, and others, like Tinder, not catering exclusively to one community.

Gay dating platforms are popular around the world for several reasons. One of the main reasons that queer people use such community-focused dating platforms is because they may experience isolation from society and the platforms afford a connection with one's community while maintaining significant anonymity (Narin, 2018). Other reasons for their popularity include difficulty in identifying queer people in the physical world, fear of rejection, and the possibility of queerphobic backlash (Fox, 2014). These dating platforms free people from not only these limitations, but also the locational confines of conventional queer venues like bars (Blackwell et al., 2015; Brubaker et al., 2016). The simplicity, privacy, and anonymity afforded by the platforms are especially welcomed in the Indian context as there is considerable social stigma and taboo around queer identities and sexual behavior, and because conventional queer venues are almost non-existent (Dasgupta, 2017). Gay dating platforms are also particularly popular as they are visually driven consumerist spaces. Hence, conventionally attractive bodies, sometimes represented in the form of self-made pornographic images (Phillips, 2015, p. 72), make up most of the user interface on many of the platforms. Such sexually attractive images on user profiles act as both the "narcissistic gaze of the subject" and "the voyeuristic gaze of the other" (Mowlabocus, 2010, p. 94) and add to the popularity of the platforms. To retain people's interest for a longer time, the platforms use the gaming logic of rewards and punishments (Tziallas, 2015, p. 761). Here, receiving an intimate image, being asked on a date, or continuing chats are seen as gifts or rewards, while being ignored or blocked are seen as punishments (Phillips, 2015; Tziallas, 2015).

The dominant public perception is that gay dating platforms are primarily used to find partners for casual sex or hooking up: a "distinctive type of social encounter, a quick sexual encounter between strangers based on location awareness" (Licoppe et al., 2016, p. 2555), sometimes referred to in the literature as "digital cruising" (see Mowlabocus, 2010). This perception is evidenced both through research with users of these platforms in the US and France (Ahlm, 2017, p. 368; Sam Chan, 2018, p. 2572), as well as popular culture discourses around such platforms, including those in India (see for example Duffy, 2019; Singh, 2018). However, research indicates that people use gay dating platforms for a variety of goals and objectives, like arranging immediate sexual encounters, finding romantic partners or friends (Corriero & Tong, 2016) or just chatting (Blackwell et al., 2015), and, indeed, not all identify as gay (see, for example, Rhoton et al., 2016). Some users use them for merely killing time (see Rice et al., 2012). These goals and motivations for using dating platforms are often overlapping, fluid, temporally inconsistent, and ambiguous (see Fitzpatrick & Birnholtz, 2018; Sam Chan, 2018). This is because users aim to maximize the potential of dating platforms, and are "open to" a far greater number of possibilities than the specific goals mentioned on their profiles (Sam Chan, 2018).

The limited research that has occurred in India supports this research that there is a diverse array of reasons that people use these platforms. Dasgupta's study of the politics of digital queer male sexualities indicates that dating platform users use them to form a variety of "virtual and physical intimacies" like sexting, posting in semipublic groups, chatting with other people on these platforms, and, specifically, hooking up (Dasgupta, 2017, pp. 41, 45, 52, 73). A Mumbai-based study reported that queer individuals use multiple gay dating platforms to search for potential partners for sex (Rhoton et al., 2016). However, despite the diverse ways in which these platforms are used, there is an overarching perception in India that those using these platforms are engaging in "digital cruising" for sex. The perception of "digital cruising" sometimes causes moral judgment from society, as using a gay dating platform is seen as an active attempt to act out one's queerness. This is perceived to be more socially transgressive as it involves queer people expressing themselves sexually and seeking out sexual pleasure as opposed to "benign" queer desire. For example, Ranade et al. (2020, p. 158) observe that parents often discuss their children's same-sex partners but have "severe hesitation" when thinking about them having a sexual relationship. This needs to be understood in light of homonormative, queerphobic, and sex-negative traditions in India.

Like other neoliberal economies, in India, media representations (Das, 2018), activism (Ghosh, 2015), as well as the Supreme Court judgment that decriminalized "gay sex" (Kumar, 2020) privilege homonormativity—that is, a de-politicized queer community that privileges certain practices like domesticity, monogamy, marriage, and sexual restraint (Duggan, 2002). This consequently brackets other practices like polygamy, or casual, anonymous, or public sex as "bad" or less desirable (Peterson & Panfil, 2014, p. 549). Seeking anonymous sexual encounters on gay dating platforms is not seen as "respectable." This homonormative framework overlaps with Rubin's hierarchization of sexual relations in society. Rubin contends that sex taking place within the limits of a "charmed circle" that is marked *inter alia* by monogamy and privacy is good or respectable sex, whereas other types of sexual activity that lie outside of this charmed circle are less respectable or good (Rubin, 2012) and hence, stigmatized. Applying this framework to the context of gay dating platforms helps illustrate the stigma that surrounds users who are perceived as being promiscuous and hence, less respectable. It has been reported that users of gay dating platforms manage respectability in this context by employing a variety of techniques, such as blocking familiar people (like colleagues or neighbors) or not displaying their face in their profile picture (Ahlm, 2017).

The stigma around queer sexualities and sexual behavior are not unique to India, but the Indian context produces specific factors that make it acute. Family honor and reputation hold important positions in Indian societies. The literature on inter-faith or inter-caste relations and honor killings in India (Baxi et al., 2006; Gupta, 2010) offers ample evidence toward this. Most Indian families maintain close ties with their relatives, sometimes despite the geographical distance (Mullatti, 1995). This leads to a unique control being exerted by family members, resulting in the heavy policing of social norms. Social stigma is also more pronounced, with any socially transgressive behavior being met with ridicule and disapproval from the extended family, family friends, and neighbors. Anthropologists refer to this as the "shame culture" in Indian societies (Vanita & Kidwai, 2000, p. 198). Hence, individuals and families in India are more sensitive to circumstances that can lead to losing their "reputation" in society (Srivastava & Singh, 2015). Indian societies are also considerably sex-negative. Any sexual behavior taking place outside of a family-approved marriage has a considerable social stigma attached to it (Shivanand et al., 2019; Singh et al., 2020). Unsurprisingly, "carnal intercourse against the course of nature," which was a crime in India until September 2018, carries an enormous amount of social and familial stigma and shame (Mimiaga et al., 2015; Srivastava & Singh, 2015; Thompson et al., 2013). Hence, the power regimes within family structures try their best to promote compulsory heterosexuality (HT correspondent, 2020; Sinha Roy, 2016, p. 291).

In addition to the family, the State, social institutions, and the media also perpetuate prejudice against queer individuals in India. While decriminalization of "carnal intercourse against the course of nature" has meant that penetrative queer sex in private now avoids the formal scrutiny of the state, other facets of sexual being and expression continue to be scrutinized and proscribed by the State and society. There are many examples that illustrate blatant discrimination and atrocities against queer individuals, which suggest a broadly queerphobic culture in India, despite recent legal changes. Notable examples include "femme" gay men recently being arrested by the police on alleged suspicion of being sex workers (Bhattacharjee, 2020), a gay teenager being driven to commit suicide because of bullying (India Today Web Desk, 2019), queer people being forced to undergo "conversion therapies" by family (HT correspondent, 2020), and popular social media influencers blatantly promoting hate speech against queer individuals (Singh, 2020). It is in this queerphobic social environment that gay dating platform-related crimes and abuses take place.

ABUSIVE PRACTICES AND CRIMES ENABLED BY GAY DATING PLATFORMS: a PRODUCT OF STRUCTURAL SEX NEGATIVITY AND QUEERPHOBIA

As highlighted in the introduction, gay dating platforms facilitate abusive practices and crimes. One recognizable reason for these is that these platforms seemingly afford unique pathways for the commission of crimes. These affordances can arise from the easy identification of queer individuals (Knight & Wilson, 2016, p. 67), user anonymity, and easy access to someone's house gained through the pretext of a hookup. These affordances, coupled with the stigma that surrounds queer sexual identity or behavior in India, make users of gay dating platforms in India particularly vulnerable to crimes and abusive practices. This section discusses some of these crimes and the queerphobia and sex-negativity that produce or perpetuate this. Importantly, many of these crimes cannot always be identified as existing or occurring distinctly online (cybercrime/cyber-violence) or distinctly offline (physical crimes) (see Bluett-Boyd et al., 2013). What is of specific interest here, though, is the way that these platforms have enabled or enhanced the commission of these crimes. The following sections discuss a few of these crimes and abuses and illustrate their link to systemic queerphobia and sex-negativity.

Image-Based Sexual Abuse

Image-based sexual abuse, especially sexual extortion, is one such crime that often features as a prominent form of gay dating platform-enabled crime and exists both online and offline (see, for example, Press Trust of India, 2017). Image-based sexual abuse has been defined as a continuum of abusive practices that usually involve the non-consensual creation and/or threats of/actual distribution of private sexual images (Mcglynn & Rackley, 2017, p. 536; McGlynn et al., 2017). One form of image-based sexual abuse is sexual extortion (McGlynn et al., 2017, p. 34). Defined as the practice of threatening to distribute someone's private sexual images to make them do something or exact revenge (Wolak & Finkelhor, 2016), sexual extortion features prominently as a form of gay dating platform-related victimization in India. Typically, perpetrators threaten to distribute private sexual images, sometimes created without the knowledge of those whose images are used and demand monetary or sexual favors (see for example Press Trust of India, 2017). Empirical studies based in other countries have also shown that non-heterosexual adults are at a higher risk of facing image-based sexual abuse than heterosexual adults (see Gámez-Guadix et al., 2015; Priebe & Svedin, 2012). Gay dating platform users mitigate the risk of image-based sexual abuse by typically cropping out identifying features from an intimate photo, sending intimate images after the recipient has shared theirs, or by chatting with a prospective recipient for some time to build trust before sharing intimate images (Waldman, 2019). Yet image-based sexual abuse continues to happen in India to those using these platforms.

In the Indian context, the problem is exacerbated because even the consensual sending of "obscene images" is illegal under the literal interpretation of section 67 of The Information Technology Act (2000). Although there is no available precedent for such prosecution, the question remains whether people who encounter image-based sexual abuse would be prosecuted or stigmatized if they had voluntarily shared the images with anyone (a sexual partner, for instance). This also highlights the structural sex-negativity of the law itself. The law, especially section 67 of the IT Act (The Information Technology Act, 2000), has been criticized for being used to morally police and ban all forms of sexual expression through technology (Datta et al., 2017, p. 46). This is especially because there is no mention of consent in the language of the section. Lack of consent, or violation of sexual autonomy, is at the heart of the crime of image-based sexual abuse

(Mcglynn & Rackley, 2017). The Indian law overlooks this in its focus on responding to obscenity (Datta et al., 2017, pp. 44–47). This inherent sex-negativity of the law, along with the social stigma linked to any form of sexual expression (Singh et al., 2020) including sexting, make it challenging for people to seek redress through the criminal justice system. To address this, it is important that the law creates a distinction between non-consensual and consensual sharing of private sexual images. This will help the law to move away from its current abstinence-focused approach to a model that endorses affirmative consent and recognizes sexting as a valid form of sexual expression and media production (Henry et al., 2020, pp. 161–165). While this is important, it is only a small step, as queer people must also contend with additional stigma grounded in queerphobia when reporting image-based sexual abuse (discussed further next).

Misuse of Photos and Other Identifying Information

Gay dating platforms enable another type of abusive practice which is not unique to India but whose effects are exacerbated by the cultural context of queerphobia: misuse of photos and other identifying information. Photos voluntarily displayed on gay dating platform profiles are routinely used to commit a variety of offenses beyond image-based sexual abuse in India, including impersonation, blackmail, and extortion (Birnholtz et al., 2020). Perpetrators have threatened to "out" users to their family, as GPS functionality of the platforms sometimes allow people to pinpoint someone's residence (Birnholtz et al., 2020). Similarly, users who furnish social media information on their profiles have been threatened with "outing" on social media (Birnholtz et al., 2020). Profile photos have also been used in the past to commit gross violations of privacy.

A pertinent example is the infamous 2011 TV9 sting operation, where a Hyderabad-based news channel aired a sensational news segment laden with moral panic around "rampant gay culture" in Hyderabad. This segment aired profile pictures of users of PlanetRomeo on live TV along with recorded excerpts from telephone conversations with users arranging hookups (Osserman, 2019). Although this generated huge outrage and opposition, resulting in the TV company having to air a public apology and pay a hefty fine (Singh, 2018), the incident goes a long way to illustrate the moral panic around queer sexualities and sexual behavior in India. Firstly, the broadcaster was catering to the queerphobic apprehensions of society (Osserman, 2019). This is clear from the usage of headings like "gay culture rampant in Hyderabad" or "boys chasing boys has become a new fashion in Hyderabad" (Osserman, 2019, pp. 179, 180). Secondly, the playing of telephonic conversation recordings where a TV9 investigator and a PlanetRomeo user were arranging a hookup (Singh, 2018) sought to cater to the sex-negativity and moral panic around sex in Indian society. This example shows that the culture of hypervisibility and/or surveillance on gay dating platforms, coupled with queerphobia in Indian society, exposes queer people to a range of abuses and crimes.

Romance Frauds

Another more direct abusive practice prevalent on dating platforms that cannot always be identified as distinctly online or offline is romance fraud. For users of gay dating platforms in India, this is again of unique concern. In recent times, the incidence of romance frauds through gay dating apps has increased manyfold in India (Chandran, 2021). Romance frauds/scams in the context of heterosexual dating platforms have been conceptualized as incidents where a person is defrauded through a perceived genuine romantic relationship (Cross et al., 2018). There are a number of ways in which these are operationalized (Rege, 2009), but studies based in the UK have reported that most typically romance frauds follow a few recurrent patterns (Gillespie, 2017; Whitty, 2013). In India, known incidences typically involve developing a relationship with a person (supposedly located in another country) over a period of time who plans to visit the person being defrauded. The perpetrator is supposedly detained at the airport by Customs and requires a significant amount of money from the person being defrauded to be released (Chandran, 2021). Once the person pays the money to those posing as "custom officers," the perpetrator blocks the person being defrauded on all communication platforms (Chandran, 2021). Although not much research on romance scams exists in India, research conducted in Australia and the UK on heterosexual populations have reported that most romance frauds involve psychological abuse (Cross et al., 2018) and significantly affect the well-being of victims/survivors (Buchanan & Whitty, 2014).

These frauds are a cause for unique concern for queer people. Although romance frauds are not overtly queerphobic, anxieties around sex-negativity and queerphobia underpin the experiences of those being defrauded, especially when it comes to their seeking help. This is not just because formal reporting of these incidents will require disclosure of someone's sexual identity/ preferences, running the risk of them being outed to family. Sex negativity and queerphobia also make it difficult to find queer affirmative support services, like counselors, bankers, or lawyers, whose services might be crucial to a person defrauded (see Chandran, 2021). More research focused on gay dating platform enabled romance frauds in India will elucidate the unique experiences and challenges that queer individuals face in India.

Assault, Robbery, and Criminal Intimidation

Direct abusive practices facilitated by gay dating platforms include criminal intimidation, robbery, physical and sexual assault perpetrated by individuals met via these platforms. News articles and community discussions on these crimes make it clear that these often occur in hookup situations (for example, see Bhattacharya, 2018; Mehta, 2018; Times News Network, 2019). A typical scenario involves a user arranging a hookup through a gay dating platform and, upon reaching the sexual partner's house, being accosted by four or five people threatening to "out" or assault them if they do not hand over their valuables (see Bhattacharya, 2018; Queer Friendly Lawyers Network & Varta Trust, 2018; Salaria, 2020). Notably, such crimes (particularly blackmail and extortion) existed in India prior to the emergence of gay dating platforms (Gupta, 2011). Often, such crimes occur in popular cruising spots, and sometimes the perpetrators are police constables themselves, entrapping queer individuals (Cohen, 2009; Elouard & Essén, 2013).

What is unique about these crimes is their connection to queerphobia and sex-negativity. Perpetrators use queerphobia embedded in a variety of social structures: family or neighborhoods (by threatening to out to family or property owners), workplace (by threatening to out at workplace), or the criminal justice system (by threatening to call the police). In addition to queerphobia, perpetrators use sex-negativity and shame associated with casual sexual activities in Indian society to their advantage. Property owners and neighborhoods are known to be hostile to both queer individuals (Bhaskaran, 2004, p. 125; International Commission of Jurists, 2019, pp. 8–9) and casual/non-marital sexual behavior (Bernroider, 2018). They are reportedly extremely hostile to casual sex, with property owners and neighborhoods undertaking strict surveillance of unmarried renters, especially women (see Bernroider, 2018). Disclosure of someone's involvement in casual sex or hookup, especially if they are queer, can lead to judgment, ridicule, or even eviction (Bernroider, 2018, p. 765). Hence, sex negativity becomes as relevant as queerphobia (if not more relevant) in producing and perpetuating these crimes in Indian society.

As heteronormativity and sex-negativity are ingrained in so many societal structures, a starting point for addressing this can be an inclusive educational curriculum in schools. Although the Draft New Education Policy 2019 of the Government of India mentioned sex education in schools (Ministry of Human Resource Development, Government of India, 2019), the final National Education Policy 2020 did not adopt it (Ministry of Human Resource Development, Government of India, 2020). Neither of these policies mentions the incorporation of sexual and gender diversity in school curricula, although they do mention the inclusion of transgender students in schools. Some research has demonstrated a fair amount of public support for the implementation of comprehensive sexual education in Indian schools (see Das, 2014; O'Sullivan et al., 2019). Similarly, advertising campaigns by local government bodies and companies can help unsettle societal heteronormativity and bring about acceptance for diverse sexualities (Ayoub & Garretson, 2017; Chauhan & Shukla, 2016).

While these crimes or abuses are not unique to the Indian context, the issues of queerphobia and sex-negativity in the Indian context, coupled with the slow pace of cultural change after legal change has occurred combine here to create conditions that impact uniquely on the experience of these crimes, the ability of those involved to seek help, and their experience when they do so. Yet, while research on these issues has been undertaken elsewhere, only relatively few studies have been undertaken in the Indian context. This means that more empirical research in the Indian context considering the above factors of queerphobia and sex-negativity is required if a fuller and more accurate understanding of these issues is to be developed.

REPORTING AND HELP-SEEKING BARRIERS FOR GAY DATING PLATFORM RELATED CRIMES

Queerphobia and sex-negativity not only impact the experience of gay dating platform-related crime but also directly limits help-seeking and the reporting of such crimes. International literature on queerphobic crimes generally shows that their rates of reporting are low (Miles-Johnson, 2013; Robinson & Berman, 2010) because, when it comes to reporting queerphobic crimes, individuals face several unique barriers like fear of queerphobia that are grounded "within a broader social and political context" (Peel, 1999, p. 165). Such barriers have been referred to in the literature as a form of secondary victimization: additional victimization that victims/survivors of queerphobic crimes face at the hands of family, friends, workplace, and the State when reporting them (Berrill & Herek, 1990, pp. 401–402). Those victimized by crimes on or enabled by gay dating platforms run the risk of such secondary victimization as formal reporting would require one to disclose their sexual identity and interest in queer sexual behavior (which follows directly from their presence on a gay dating platform or arranging a hookup). Given the queerphobic and sex-negative socio-cultural context of India, this leads to severe stigma and ridicule at the hands of family, friends, relatives, workplaces, and the police themselves (Mimiaga et al., 2015; Srivastava & Singh, 2015; Thompson et al., 2013). So, it is likely that people are reluctant to report such incidents. This deprives people of an important mechanism for responding to victimization. The literature on queerphobic hate crimes finds that reporting is an important coping mechanism for victims/survivors, as it feels like an effective next step and seemingly a service to the queer community at large (Feddes & Jonas, 2016, p. 63). It can also be a necessary pathway to achieving formal justice.

Studies in different countries have identified several reasons behind the non-reporting of queerphobic crimes. Findings from such studies in the US indicate that police officers themselves believe that the police do not take queer individuals seriously and did not treat them equally to heterosexual individuals (Bernstein & Kostelac, 2002, pp. 317, 323; Culotta, 2005). Practicality, safety, self-blame (Peel, 1999), shame, and fear of prejudice (Knight & Wilson, 2016, p. 67) are additional reasons for non-reporting. In South Africa, Wells and Polders found that fear of not being taken seriously, perceived/actual ineffectiveness of the police, friends' unpleasant experience with the police, fear of being abused by the police, "outing," and embarrassment were common factors for non-reporting among LGB people (Wells & Polders, 2006, p. 26). In Australia, studies have found that the reasons for non-reporting included unfair treatment, fear of discrimination and being "outed," procedural confusion, previous negative experiences and perceived police homophobia (see Miles-Johnson, 2013, p. 11; Robinson & Berman, 2010). In the UK, similar findings were reported and included downplaying/normalizing the victimization experience, and a lack of awareness and clarity around the procedures and outcomes of reporting (Chakraborti & Hardy, 2015, p. 24). Likewise, in the Netherlands, a mixed-methods study found similar reasons for the non-reporting of crimes and found that a fear of further backlash from the perpetrators and a desire to leave the experience behind (Feddes & Jonas, 2016).

A recurrent theme amongst the barriers identified above is the belief or apprehension about prejudice and homophobia in the criminal justice system. This has been argued as a vestige of the complicated and violent history of policing queer individuals (see Wolff & Cokely, 2007; Dwyer, 2014). This applies to India very well as India has its own sparsely documented similar history of policing queer individuals. This is especially so because of section 377 of the Indian Penal Code (1860): the provision often dubbed the anti-sodomy law of India. Since its enactment in 1860, this infamous law (along with several others) gave the police the authority to harass and assault queer individuals (Rege, 1996) until its repeal in 2018. The actual number of reported judgments where section 377 has been used to prosecute people is seemingly low, given that only thirty cases were reported involving section 377 from the period between 1860–1992 (PUCL-Karnataka, 2001, p. 12). However, the police had routinely weaponized it to entrap, harass, blackmail, and extort money from queer individuals who cruised in public spaces (Li et al., 2017; Misra, 2009). The police have also illegally detained, abused, and sometimes "outed" queer individuals to their families (for some documented instances, see PUCL-Karnataka, 2001, pp. 13–14). These have been extensively documented in books (Narrain & Bhan, 2005; Shahani, 2021), journal articles (Dutta et al., 2019; Li et al., 2017), civil society reports (Bhandari et al., 1991; PUCL-Karnataka, 2001), newspaper columns, and queer periodicals (Bharat, 2014). Although the law criminalizing homosexual acts has been read down, the police continue to harass and commit atrocities against queer individuals in India (for some documented instances of recent police atrocities, see Bhattacharjee, 2020). This structural queerphobia of the criminal justice system deters queer individuals from approaching criminal justice agents in India, resulting in skewed or limited understanding of crimes affecting queer people in India.

This police culture makes the crimes unique in India to the extent that the perpetrators can exploit or take significant advantage of the vulnerability, shame, and social stigma around reporting crimes by queer people. Research in other countries have shown that strategies like respectful and appropriate engagement with queer people, creating liaison positions within the police force (Goldberg et al., 2019), third party reporting centers (Chakraborti & Hardy, 2015), increased queer representation in the police force and queer-friendly identity markers (like rainbow badges) (Robinson & Berman, 2010) would make queer people more comfortable in reporting hate crimes. Although not much literature exists in the Indian context, open discussions between community-based organizations and the police and sensitization of the police force have been shown to work quite well (see, for example, Times News Network, 2020) so far. More research focusing on police culture and recommendations around changing this culture of hostility and stigma will help devise strategies to improve crime reporting experiences for queer people in India.

SEX-NEGATIVE FRAMING OF SAFE DATING ADVICE AND DISCOURSE

An important pathway to respond to these issues beyond the criminal justice system is through the platforms themselves. Dating platforms have acknowledged and taken steps to address crimes and abusive practices on their platforms. They generally do this by making users aware of safer dating practices by publishing "safe dating advice" on their websites (see for example Grindr, n.db; PlanetRomeo, n.db) or by continually adding new safety features to their platforms. For example, Tinder, a popular dating app (although not exclusively designed for queer people), recently started providing an optional photo verification feature, where all user-uploaded photos are verified with a selfie that users need to take through the app (Tinder, n.d). In India, Blued, a gay dating app, has launched an "anti-cyberbullying" campaign and partnered with LGBTQIA + organizations to provide helpline numbers to people who have faced "crises" (Blued, 2019). Similarly, promising to be safer than other platforms, Delta, an Indian-made queer dating app, offers a verification measure where users receive a trust score based on a number of disclosures, like identity documents, social media information, or selfies taken via the app (Das, 2019b). In addition to dating app companies, in India, civil society groups, NGOs, and online support groups have also worked hard to create more awareness around the issue by continually publishing flyers, pamphlets, and digital bulletins disseminating information on safe dating practices (see Brindaalakshmi, 2017; Good as You Bangalore, 2018; Queer Friendly Lawyers Network-West Bengal, 2020; Queer Friendly Lawyers Network & Varta Trust, 2018; Vasudevan, 2011).

While these moves offer a potential alternative to a criminal justice response, we suggest that much of this advice pivots around users self-regulating their desires and actions. Because of this focus on the "self," we argue that these self-regulatory measures can easily feed into the stigma around casual sex and crime victimization, potentially leading to self-blame. This, we suggest, limits help-seeking, and impacts on how effectively these abuses can be prevented and the extent to which their impacts can be mitigated. For example, advice phrased as "Don't rush into things" (Grindr, n.da) or "Keep your eyes open and stay safe" (PlanetRomeo, n.da) frame "rushed" and anonymous sex as dangerous, and subtly shift the responsibility for safety onto those who choose to partake in this "dangerous activity." This shifting of responsibility opens a possibility of self-blame in the event of victimization and contributes to the barriers surrounding help-seeking and reporting. We do not suggest that such advice around self-regulation is not helpful or necessary, but that it is predominantly sex-negative. Such advice can be clearly contrasted to prevention advice and recommendations around crimes and abuses that happen to those positioned within Rubin's charmed circle, like those who are married. For example, recommendations around prevention of domestic violence within heterosexual families in India include disrupting the acceptability of violence as a feature of marital homes and strengthening the ability of community groups to respond positively to the disclosure of such violence (International Center for Research on Women & The Centre for Development & Population Activities, 2000). Such advice focuses on changing structures like patriarchy or stigma around disclosure. They do not frame relationships or marriages as inherently dangerous, do not stigmatize those engaging in marriage, and nor do they urge people to "keep their eyes open" while entering a marriage or a relationship.

Advice around gay dating platform-related crime prevention needs more explicit acknowledgment of sexual pleasure as a right and sex in anonymous contexts as "good" as in other contexts. This can be done by foregrounding and normalizing help-seeking, irrespective of the amount of risk someone has taken or irrespective of how many safety precautions they have or have not followed. There are multiple ways that this can be furthered. To begin with, safe-dating advice columns/webpages can start with statements assuring users of non-judgmental support, irrespective of the risk that someone took, followed by helpline numbers and other contact details of support workers. Such strategies can begin to reduce self-blame and encourage more people to seek support.

CONCLUSION

In this paper, we have highlighted gay dating platform-related crimes and abuses in India, and the increased attention they are receiving. We detailed what is currently known about those crimes and practices, and highlighted the need for more academic engagement with the systemic factors producing and perpetuating these crimes and abuses, specifically sex-negativity and queerphobia. Building on sex-positive criminology, we argued that social structures in India, including the family, neighborhoods, criminal law, and the police perpetuate queerphobia and sex-negativity, which facilitate the commission of these abuses and crimes and structure the experience of the crime or abuse. We also noted the points at which queerphobic and sex-negative cultures deter people from reporting these experiences to the police or seeking help, depriving them of access to formal justice mechanisms. We also showed how sex-negative framing of safe dating advice can lead to self-blame, and suggested that such advice be reframed in a sex-positive light. To develop these arguments, we have drawn from the extant literature, most of which has not, to this point, specifically focused on the Indian context. This paper serves not only to draw academic attention in queer criminology and related fields to these issues in the Indian context but also to highlight the need for further empirical research. Studies squarely positioned within queer and sex-positive criminology would provide insights that are more reflective of the Indian context. They would also uncover new approaches to preventing these abuses and providing support, thereby contributing to greater access to social and legal justice for those impacted by these abuses and crimes.

ORCID

Rahul Sinha-Roy (iD) http://orcid.org/0000-0002-9403-9728

REFERENCES

Ansar, S. (2018, June 30). Behind Grindr India lies a world of sexual assualt, rape, and blackmail. *The Print.* https://theprint.in/featured/behind-grindr-india-lies-a-world-of-sexual-assualt-rape-and-blackmail/76538/

Asthana, S., & Oostvogels, R. (2001). The social construction of male "homosexuality" in India: Implications for HIV transmission and prevention. *Social Science & Medicine, 52*(5), 707–721. https://doi.org/10.1016/S0277-9536(00)00167-2

Ayoub, P. M., & Garretson, J. (2017). Getting the message out: Media context and global changes in attitudes toward homosexuality. *Comparative Political Studies, 50*(8), 1055–1085. https://doi.org/10.1177/0010414016666836

Baxi, P., Rai, S., & Ali, S. (2006). Legacies of common law: 'Crimes of honour' in India and Pakistan. *Third World Quarterly, 27*(7), 1239–1253. https://doi.org/10.1080/01436590600933404

Ben-David, S. (2020). From victim to survivor to overcomer. In J. Joseph & S. Jergenson (Eds.), *An international perspective on contemporary developments in victimology: A festschrift in honor of Marc Groenhuijsen* (pp. 21–30). Springer.

Bernroider, L. (2018). Single female tenants in South Delhi–Gender, class and morality in a globalizing city. *Gender, Place and Culture, 25*(5), 758–774. https://doi.org/10.1080/0966369X.2018.1428535

Bernstein, M., & Kostelac, C. (2002). Lavender and blue: Attitudes about homosexuality and behavior toward lesbians and gay men among police officers. *Journal of Contemporary Criminal Justice, 18*(3), 302–328. https://doi.org/10.1177/1043986202018003006

Berrill, K. T., & Herek, G. M. (1990). Primary and secondary victimization in anti-gay hate crimes: Official response and public policy. *Journal of Interpersonal Violence, 5*(3), 401–413. https://doi.org/10.1177/088626090005003012

Bhandari, A., Sahni, P. S., Jain, J. P., Shalini, S. C. N., Bhardwaje, J., Gautam, S., & Lalitha, S. A. (1991). *Less Than Gay: A Citizens' Report on the Status of Homosexuality in India.* AIDS Anti-Discrimination Movement. https://s3.amazonaws.com/s3.documentcloud.org/documents/1585664/less-than-gay-a-citizens-report-on-the-status-of.pdf

Bharat. (2014, June 20). Section 377 To Be Filed Against Gay Doctor Who Is A Victim Of Blackmail. *Gaylaxy Magazine.* http://www.gaylaxymag.com/latest-news/section-377-to-be-filed-against-gay-doctor-who-is-a-victim-of-blackmail/?fbclid=IwAR3I3tANkMnW4_99y0qE4Id2jbSpwcLlrQzzXIzVpOk1bNZaI632zwuwVrw#gs.m8535e

Bhaskaran, S. (2004). *Made in India: Decolonizations, queer sexualities, trans/national projects.* Palgrave Macmillan.

Bhattacharjee, P. (2020, July 30). Police violence against LGTBQIA + people in Kolkata highlights need for sensitisation. *The Wire.* https://thewire.in/lgbtqia/police-violence-against-lgtbqia-people-in-kolkata-highlights-need-for-sensitisation

Bhattacharya, A. (2018, June 22). In India, gay dating apps are both a safe haven and a target. *Quartz India.* https://qz.com/india/1268931/for-lgbtq-indians-dating-apps-like-grindr-and-planet-romeo-both-help-and-hurt/

Birnholtz, J., Rawat, S., Vashista, R., Baruah, D., Dange, A., & Boyer, A. M. (2020). Layers of marginality: An exploration of visibility, impressions, and cultural context on geospatial apps for men who have sex with men in Mumbai. *Social Media + Society, 6*(2), 205630512091399. https://doi.org/10.1177/2056305120913995

Blackwell, C., Birnholtz, J., & Abbott, C. (2015). Seeing and being seen: Co-situation and impression formation using Grindr, a location-aware gay dating app. *New Media & Society, 17*(7), 1117–1136. https://doi.org/10.1177/1461444814521595

Blued. (n.d). *Homepage*. https://www.blued.com/en/index.html

Blued. (2019, Jul 10). *Anti Cyber Bully Campaign - #BluedAgainstCyberBully LGBTQ Voices* [Video]. YouTube. https://www.youtube.com/watch?v=3jt4pjio2Rs&ab_channel=Blued

Bluett-Boyd, N., Fileborn, B., Quadara, A., & Moore, S. (2013). *The role of emerging communication technologies in experiences of sexual violence: A new legal frontier?* (Issue Research Report No. 23). Australian Institute of Family.

Boyce, P. (2006). Moral ambivalence and irregular practices: Contextualizing male-to-male sexualities. *Feminist Review, 83*(1), 79–98. https://doi.org/10.1057/palgrave.fr.9400282

Boyce, P. (2007). 'Conceiving kothis': Men who have sex with men in India and the cultural subject of HIV prevention. *Medical Anthropology, 26*(2), 175–203. https://doi.org/10.1080/01459740701285582

Brindaalakshmi K. (2017). *Chennai Pride's guide to handle online harassment for the LGBTQIA+*. Hidden Pockets. https://hidden-pockets.com/chennai-prides-guide-to-handle-online-harassment-for-lgbtqia/

Brubaker, J. R., Ananny, M., & Crawford, K. (2016). Departing glances: A sociotechnical account of 'leaving' Grindr. *New Media & Society, 18*(3), 373–390. https://doi.org/10.1177/1461444814542311

Buchanan, T., & Whitty, M. T. (2014). The online dating romance scam: Causes and consequences of victimhood. *Psychology, Crime & Law, 20*(3), 261–283. https://doi.org/10.1080/1068316X.2013.772180

Chakraborti, N., & Hardy, S.-J. (2015). *LGB&T hate crime reporting: Identifying barriers and solutions*. Equality and Human Rights Commission. https://www.equalityhumanrights.com/sites/default/files/research-lgbt-hate-crime-reporting-identifying-barriers-and-solutions.pdf

Chakraborty, K. (2012). Virtual mate-seeking in the urban slums of Kolkata. *South Asian Popular Culture, 10*(2), 197–216. https://doi.org/10.1080/14746689.2012.682871

Chandran, B. V. (2021). *My boyfriend is a scam*. Our Voices. http://orinam.net/my-boyfriend-is-a-scam/

Chauhan, G. S., & Shukla, T. (2016). Social media advertising and public awareness: Touching the LGBT chord! *Journal of International Women's Studies, 18*(1), 145–155. https://vc.bridgew.edu/jiws/vol18/iss1/11

Cohen, L. (2009). Lucknow noir. In D. A. B. Murray (Ed.), *Homophobias: Lust and loathing across time and space* (pp. 162–184). Duke University Press.

Corriero, E. F., & Tong, S. T. (2016). Managing uncertainty in mobile dating applications: Goals, concerns of use, and information seeking in Grindr. *Mobile Media & Communication, 4*(1), 121–141. https://doi.org/10.1177/2050157915614872

Cross, C., Dragiewicz, M., & Richards, K. (2018). Understanding romance fraud: Insights from domestic violence research. *The British Journal of Criminology, 58*(6), 1303–1322. https://doi.org/10.1093/bjc/azy005

Culotta, K. (2005). Why victims hate to report: Factors affecting victim reporting in hate crime cases in Chicago. *Kriminologija & Socijalna Integracija, 13*(2), 15–28.

Dalton, D. (2016). Reflections on the emergence, efficacy, and value of queer criminology. In A. Dwyer, M. Ball, & T. Crofts (Eds.), *Queering Criminology* (pp. 15–35). Palgrave Macmillan UK.

Das, A. (2014). Sexuality education in India: examining the rhetoric, rethinking the future. *Sex Education, 14*(2), 210–224. https://doi.org/10.1080/14681811.2013.866546

Das, S. (2018). The politics of representation and visibility: A sociological engagement with an Indian queer webzine. *ISS e-Journal, 2*(1), 107–127.

Das, V. (2019a). Dating applications, intimacy, and cosmopolitan desire in India. In A. Punathambekar & S. Mohan (Eds.), *Global digital cultures perspectives from South Asia* (pp. 125–141). University of Michigan Press.

Das, V. (2019b). Designing queer connection: An ethnography of dating app production in urban India. *Ethnographic Praxis in Industry Conference Proceedings, 2019*(1), 384–397. https://doi.org/10.1111/1559-8918.2019.01295

Dasgupta, R. K. (2017). *Digital queer cultures in India*. Routledge India.

Datta, B., Vanniyar, S., George, J. L., Mathews, N., Bali, R., Nepal, Z. A. I., Maskay, J., Karmacharya, S., Kirven, S., Deshapriya, P. M., Wijewardene, J. M. M. S., Wijesiriwardena, S., & Vale, H. (2017). *EROTICS South Asia exploratory research: Sex, rights and the internet*. https://www.apc.org/sites/default/files/Erotics_1_FIND.pdf

Duffy, N. (2019, May 28). Grindr outlawed in Lebanon. *Pink News*. https://www.pinknews.co.uk/2019/05/28/grindr-outlawed-lebanon/

Duggan, L. (2002). The new homonormativity: The sexual politics of neoliberalism. In R. Castronovo & D. D. Nelson (Eds.), *Materializing Democracy: Toward a Revitalized Cultural Politics*. (pp. 175–194)Duke University Press.

Dutta, S., Khan, S., & Lorway, R. (2019). Following the divine: an ethnographic study of structural violence among transgender jogappas in South India. *Culture, Health & Sexuality, 21*(11), 1240–1256. https://doi.org/10.1080/13691058.2018.1555718

Dwyer, A. (2014). Pleasures, perversities, and partnerships: The historical emergence of LGBT-police relationships BT. In D. Peterson & V. R. Panfil (Eds.), *Handbook of LGBT Communities, Crime, and Justice* (pp. 149–164). Springer.

Elouard, Y., & Essén, B. (2013). Psychological violence experienced by men who have sex with men in Puducherry, India: A qualitative study. *Journal of Homosexuality*, 60(11), 1581–1601. https://doi.org/10.1080/00918369.2013. 824325

Feddes, A. R., & Jonas, K. J. (2016). *LGBT hate crime, psychological well-being, and reporting behaviour: LGBT community and police perspectives.* https://psychologievansociaalgedrag.nl/wp-content/uploads/sites/262/2018/01/Feddes_Reporting_LGBT_HateCrime.pdf

Fitzpatrick, C., & Birnholtz, J. (2018). "I Shut the Door": Interactions, tensions, and negotiations from a location-based social app. *New Media & Society*, 20(7), 2469–2488. https://doi.org/10.1177/1461444817725064

Fox, M. (2014). Grindr ' s lonely crowd. *The Gay & Lesbian Review Worldwide*, 21(5), 19–22.

Gámez-Guadix, M., Almendros, C., Borrajo, E., & Calvete, E. (2015). Prevalence and association of sexting and online sexual victimization among Spanish adults. *Sexuality Research and Social Policy*, 12(2), 145–154. https://doi.org/10.1007/s13178-015-0186-9

Ghosh, A. (2015). LGBTQ activist organizations as "respectably queer" in India: Contesting a western view. *Gender, Work & Organization*, 22(1), 51–66. https://doi.org/10.1111/gwao.12068

Gillespie, A. (2017). The electronic Spanish prisoner: Romance frauds on the internet. *The Journal of Criminal Law*, 81(3), 217–231. https://doi.org/10.1177/0022018317702803

Goldberg, N. G., Mallory, C., Hasenbush, A., Stemple, L., & Meyer, I. H. (2019). *Police and the criminalization of LGBT people.* UCLA School of Law. https://williamsinstitute.law.ucla.edu/publications/police-criminalization-lgbt/

Good as You Bangalore. (2018, June 19). DOs & DON'Ts of instant dating. *Good as You Bangalore.* https://goodasyoublr.blogspot.com/2015/09/dos-donts-of-instant-dating.html?fbclid=IwAR3XFs2qrDxNMkEJUNLQBaqmDXkSoDZHTBFFQ0mT4fP8tIIeUkcDSaOF_n4

Grindr. (n.da). *Homepage.* https://www.grindr.com/

Grindr. (n.db). *Safety tips.* https://help.grindr.com/hc/en-us/articles/217955357-Safety-Tips

Gupta, A. (2011). The moral order of blackmail. In A. Narrain & A. Gupta (Eds.), *Law like love: Queer perspectives on law* (pp. 483–509). Yoda Press.

Gupta, D. (2010). Tyranny of cousins. *India International Centre Quarterly*, 37(2), 46–56.

Harmless Hugs [harmlesshugs] (2019, April 8). Harmless Hugs conducted a meeting yesterday to discuss safe dating practices for the LGBT+ community. [Facebook status update]. https://www.facebook.com/harmlesshugs/posts/2368970196467612

Henry, N., McGlynn, C., Flynn, A., Johnson, K., Powell, A., & Scott, A. J. (2020). *Image-based sexual abuse: A study on the causes and consequences of non-consensual nude or sexual imagery.* Routledge.

Hornet. (n.d). *Homepage.* https://hornet.com/

HT correspondent. (2020, May 18). Kerala student's suicide puts focus on dubious 'conversion therapy.' *Hindustan Times.* https://www.hindustantimes.com/india-news/kerala-student-s-suicide-puts-focus-on-dubious-conversion-therapy/story-fmgMhK8nFVUuddV97xvDXN.html

India Today Web Desk. (2019, July 9). Not my fault I was born gay: 19-year-old commits suicide over homophobia. *India Today.* https://www.indiatoday.in/india/story/gay-man-suicide-homophobia-lgbt-helplines-1565041-2019-07-09

International Center for Research on Women & The Centre for Development and Population Activities. (2000). *Domestic violence in India: A summary report of a multi-site household survey.* https://www.icrw.org/wp-content/uploads/2016/10/Domestic-Violence-in-India-3-A-Summary-Report-of-a-Multi-Site-Household-Survey.pdf

International Commission of Jurists. (2019). *Living with dignity sexual orientation and gender identity-based human rights violations in housing, work, and public spaces in India.* https://www.icj.org/wp-content/uploads/2019/06/India-Living-with-dignity-Publications-Reports-thematic-report-2019-ENG.pdf

Jaiswal, A. (2019, September 16). Gang befriends boy on LGBT app, kidnaps him in Mathura. *The Times of India.* https://timesofindia.indiatimes.com/city/agra/gang-befriends-boy-on-lgbt-app-kidnaps-him-in-mathura/articleshow/71140793.cms

Knight, C., & Wilson, K. (2016). *Lesbian, gay, bisexual and trans people (LGBT) and the criminal justice system.* Palgrave Macmillan.

Kumar, P. (2020). Mapping queer "celebratory moment" in India: Necropolitics or substantive democracy? *Community Development Journal*, 55(1), 159–176. https://doi.org/10.1093/cdj/bsz031

Li, D. H., Rawat, S., Rhoton, J., Patankar, P., Ekstrand, M. L., Rosser, B. R. S., & Wilkerson, J. M. (2017). Harassment and violence among men who have sex with men (MSM) and hijras after reinstatement of "Sodomy Law". *Sexuality Research & Social Policy*, 14(3), 324–330. https://doi.org/10.1007/s13178-016-0270-9

Licoppe, C., Rivière, C. A., & Morel, J. (2016). Grindr casual hook-ups as interactional achievements. *New Media & Society*, 18(11), 2540–2558. https://doi.org/10.1177/1461444815589702

Mahale, A. (2018, October 21). The Guysexual's brutally honest review of delta. *Firstpost*. http://www.firstpost.com/weekend-specials/the-guysexuals-brutally-honest-review-of-delta-5415741.html

Mcglynn, C., & Rackley, E. (2017). Image-based sexual abuse. *Oxford Journal of Legal Studies, 37*(3), 534–561. https://doi.org/10.1093/ojls/gqw033

McGlynn, C., Rackley, E., & Houghton, R. (2017). Beyond 'revenge porn': The continuum of image-based sexual abuse. *Feminist Legal Studies, 25*(1), 25–46. https://doi.org/10.1007/s10691-017-9343-2

Mehta, G. (2018, September 27). Gay men in India reveal terrifying tales of rapes and extortion on dating app Grindr. *News18*. https://www.news18.com/news/buzz/gay-men-in-india-reveal-terrifying-tales-of-rapes-and-extortion-on-dating-app-grindr-1884845.html

Miles-Johnson, T. (2013). LGBTI variations in crime reporting: How sexual identity influences decisions to call the Cops. *SAGE Open, 3*(2), 215824401349070. https://doi.org/10.1177/2158244013490707

Mimiaga, M. J., Closson, E. F., Thomas, B., Mayer, K. H., Betancourt, T., Menon, S., & Safren, S. A. (2015). Garnering an in-depth understanding of men who have sex with men in Chennai, India: A qualitative analysis of sexual minority status and psychological distress. *Archives of Sexual Behavior, 44*(7), 2077–2086. https://doi.org/10.1007/s10508-014-0369-0

Ministry of Human Resource Development, Government of India. (2019). *Draft National Education Policy 2019*. https://www.education.gov.in/sites/upload_files/mhrd/files/Draft_NEP_2019_EN_Revised.pdf

Ministry of Human Resource Development, Government of India. (2020). *National Education Policy 2020*. https://www.education.gov.in/sites/upload_files/mhrd/files/NEP_Final_English_0.pdf

Misra, G. (2009). Decriminalising homosexuality in India. *Reproductive Health Matters, 17*(34), 20–28. https://www.jstor.org/stable/40647442 https://doi.org/10.1016/S0968-8080(09)34478-X

Mowlabocus, S. (2010). *Gaydar culture: Gay men, technology and embodiment in the digital age* (1st ed.). Ashgate Publishing.

Mullatti, L. (1995). Families in India: Beliefs and realities. *Journal of Comparative Family Studies, 26*(1), 11–25.

Narin, B. (2018). A netnography study about Wapa as a mobile dating application: An existence struggle from Turkey. *Moment Journal, 5*(2), 343–367. https://doi.org/10.17572/mj2018.2.343367

Narrain, A., & Bhan, G. (2005). *Because i have a voice: Queer politics in India* (1st ed.). Yoda Press.

O'Sullivan, L. F., Byers, E. S., & Mitra, K. (2019). Sexual and reproductive health education attitudes and experience in India: How much support is there for comprehensive sex education? Findings from an Internet survey. *Sex Education, 19*(2), 145–161. https://doi.org/10.1080/14681811.2018.1506915

Orinam. (2014, March 4). Gay man from India bravely handles blackmailers he met on a dating website. *The Orinam Blog*. http://orinam.net/gay-man-bravely-handles-blackmailers-dating-website/

Osserman, J. (2019). 'Gay culture rampant in Hyderabad': Analysing the political and libidinal economy of homophobia. In S. Frosh (Ed.), *New voices in psychosocial studies. Studies in the psychosocial* (pp. 179–193). Palgrave Macmillan.

Peel, E. (1999). Violence against lesbians and gay men: Decision-making in reporting and not reporting crime. *Feminism & Psychology, 9*(2), 161–167. https://doi.org/10.1177/0959353599009002008

Peterson, D., & Panfil, V. R. (2014). Handbook of LGBT communities, crime, and justice. In D. Peterson, & V. R. Panfil (Eds.), *Handbook of LGBT communities, crime, and justice*. Springer.

Phillips, C. (2015). Self-pornographic representations with Grindr. *Journal of Visual and Media Anthropology, 1*(1), 65–79. https://www.visual-anthropology.fu-berlin.de/journal/Vol_1_1_2015/PHILLIPS.pdf

PlanetRomeo. (n.da). *Homepage*. https://www.planetromeo.com/auth/login

PlanetRomeo. (n.db). *Romeo safety*. https://www.planetromeo.com/en/care/safety/

Press Trust of India. (2017, July 16). Five 'gay club' members held for extorting Rs 2 lakh from man. *Outlook*. https://www.outlookindia.com/newsscroll/five-gay-club-members-held-for-extorting-rs-2-lakh-from-man/1100587

Priebe, G., & Svedin, C. G. (2012). Online or off-line victimisation and psychological well-being: A comparison of sexual-minority and heterosexual youth. *European Child & Adolescent Psychiatry, 21*(10), 569–582. https://doi.org/10.1007/s00787-012-0294-5

PUCL-Karnataka. (2001). *Human rights violations against sexuality minorities in India: A study of kothi and hijra sex workers in Bangalore, India*. https://archive.nyu.edu/bitstream/2451/33911/2/sexualminorities.pdf

Queer Friendly Lawyers Network & Varta Trust. (2018). *Blackmailer … .* https://vartagensex.org/advice-rights-and-laws/2017/01/blackmailer/

Queer Friendly Lawyers Network-West Bengal. (2020). *Better mental health for safer dating?* https://vartagensex.org/advice-mind-body-family/2020/09/better-mental-health-for-safer-dating/

Queerythm [queerythm]. (2019, May 28). It is, with our pride to share our association with one of the world's largest dating platform Blued to fight queer bullying and issues. Queerythm's prestigious 24x7 helpline is now in association with Blued for this cause PAN India. [Facebook status update]. https://www.facebook.com/queerythm/photos/a.220559891774399/598735033956881/?type=3&theater

Quiroz, P. A. (2013). From finding the perfect love online to satellite dating and "loving-the-one-you're near": A look at Grindr, Skout, Plenty of Fish, Meet Moi, Zoosk and Assisted Serendipity. *Humanity & Society*, *37*(2), 181–185. https://doi.org/10.1177/0160597613481727

Ranade, K., Shah, C., & Chatterji, S. (2020). Making sense: Familial journeys towards acceptance of gay and lesbian family members in India. In B. D. Prasad, S. Juvva, & M. Nayar (Eds.), *The contemporary Indian family: Transitions and Diversity* (pp. 144–166). Routledge.

Rege, A. (2009). What's love got to do with it? Exploring online dating scams and identity fraud. *International Journal of Cyber Criminology*, *3*(2), 494–512.

Rege, S. (1996). Homophobia in the name of Marxism. *Economic and Political Weekly*, *31*(22), 1359–1360. https://www.epw.in/journal/1996/22/discussion/homophobia-name-marxism.html

Rhoton, J., Wilkerson, J. M., Mengle, S., Patankar, P., Rosser, B. S., & Ekstrand, M. L. (2016). Sexual preferences and presentation on geosocial networking apps by Indian men who have sex with men in Maharashtra. *JMIR mHealth and uHealth*, *4*(4), e120. https://doi.org/10.2196/mhealth.5600

Rice, E., Holloway, I., Winetrobe, H., Rhoades, H., Barman-Adhikari, A., Gibbs, J., Carranza, A., Dent, D., & Dunlap, S. (2012). Sex risk among young men who have sex with men who use Grindr, a smartphone geosocial networking application. *Journal of AIDS and Clinical Research*, *3*(S4), 1–8. https://doi.org/10.4172/2155-6113.S4-005

Robinson, S., & Berman, A. (2010). *Speaking out: Stopping homophobic and transphobic abuse in Queensland*. Australian Academic Press.

Rubin, G. S. (2012). Thinking sex: Notes for a radical theory of the politics of sexuality. In G. S. Rubin (Ed.), *Deviations: A Gayle Rubin reader*. Duke University Press.

Salaria, S. (2020, March 3). Noida: Executives trapped on gay dating app, robbed. *The Times of India*. https://timesofindia.indiatimes.com/city/noida/execs-trapped-on-gay-dating-app-robbed/articleshow/74448730.cms

Sam Chan, L. (2018). Ambivalence in networked intimacy: Observations from gay men using mobile dating apps. *New Media & Society*, *20*(7), 2566–2581. https://doi.org/10.1177/1461444817727156

Shahani, P. (2021). *Gay bombay: Globalization, love and (be)longing in contemporary India* (Issue 2020). SAGE Publications.

Sharma, S. (2019, February 20). Love is love: How blued is making finding love online easier for same-sex couples. *Hindustan Times*. https://www.hindustantimes.com/sex-and-relationships/love-is-love-how-blued-is-making-finding-love-online-easier-for-same-sex-couples/story-y7STFBIzNnkj9X9vPGinUK.html

Shivanand, M. J., Solunke, H., Reddy, K. S., Raman, R., Kalra, G., & Tandon, A. (2019). Sexual disorders in Asians. *Journal of Psychosexual Health*, *1*(3–4), 222–226. https://doi.org/10.1177/2631831819862890

Singh, S. R. (2020, June). CarryMinati, Queerphobia *and other masculine stereotypes on social media*. Feminism in India. https://feminisminindia.com/2020/06/02/queerphobia-masculine-stereotypes-social-media/#

Singh, S. K., Vishwakarma, D., & Sharma, S. K. (2020). An epidemiology of premarital sexual behaviour in India: Exploring gender differences. *Journal of Health Management*, *22*(3), 389–412. https://doi.org/10.1177/0972063420937938

Singh, P. (2018). The TV9 sting operation on PlanetRomeo: Absent subjects, digital privacy and LGBTQ activism. In D. Dasgupta, R. K. Dasgupta (Eds.), *Queering digital India*. Edinburgh University Press.

Singh, S. (2018, July 7). Tired of gay dating apps like Grindr and PR? Blued is the gay social app you have been waiting for. *Gaylaxy Magazine*. http://www.gaylaxymag.com/articles/lifestyle/tired-of-gay-dating-apps-like-grindr-and-pr-blued-is-the-gay-social-app-you-have-been-waiting/#gs.6wpqic

Singh, S. (2019, September 16). Noida police bust gang trapping and looting gay people through Grindr, arrest 3. *Gaylaxy Magazine*. http://www.gaylaxymag.com/latest-news/noida-police-bust-gang-trapping-and-looting-gay-people-through-grindr-arrest-3/#gs.irom75

Sinha Roy, M. (2016). Intimate spaces of struggle: Rethinking family and marriage in contemporary India. In K. A. Jacobsen (Ed.), *Routledge handbook of contemporary India* (pp. 283–296). Routledge.

Srivastava, S., & Singh, P. (2015). Psychosocial roots of stigma of homosexuality and its impact on the lives of sexual minorities in India. *Open Journal of Social Sciences*, *3*(8), 128–136. https://doi.org/10.4236/jss.2015.38015

Taimi. (n.d). *Homepage*. https://taimi.com/

Tellis, A. (2007). Cyberpatriarchy: Chat rooms and the construction of "man to man" relations in urban India. In C. Kwok-bun, J. W. Walls, & D. Hayward (Eds.), *East-West identities: Globalization, localization, and hybridization* (pp. 361–372). Brill.

Tellis, A. (2012). Disrupting the dinner table: Re-thinking the 'queer movement' in contemporary India. *Jindal Global Law Review*, *4*(1), 142–156.

The Indian Penal Code 1860. s. 377 (India) https://www.indiacode.nic.in/show-data?actid=AC_CEN_5_23_00037_186045_1523266765688&sectionId=46160&sectionno=377&orderno=434

The Information Technology Act 2000. s. 67 (India) https://www.indiacode.nic.in/show-data?actid=AC_CEN_45_76_00001_200021_1517807324077&orderno=83#13092

Thompson, L. H., Khan, S., Du Plessis, E., Lazarus, L., Reza-Paul, S., Hafeez Ur Rahman, S., Pasha, A., & Lorway, R. (2013). Beyond internalised stigma: Daily moralities and subjectivity among self-identified kothis in Karnataka, South India. In *Culture, Health and Sexuality* (Vol. 15, Issue 10, pp. 1237–1251). Taylor & Francis.

Times News Network. (2014, April 13). Gay extortion cases up in Mumbai after ruling on Section 377. *The Times of India*. https://timesofindia.indiatimes.com/india/Gay-extortion-cases-up-in-Mumbai-after-ruling-on-Section-377/articleshowprint/33677592.cms

Times News Network. (2019, September 16). Robbers posing as gay escorts arrested in Ahmedabad. *The Times of India*. https://timesofindia.indiatimes.com/city/ahmedabad/robbers-posing-as-gay-escorts-arrested/articleshow/71141711.cms

Times News Network. (2020, September 16). Police to sensitise personnel to deal with LGBTQ people. *The Times of India*. https://timesofindia.indiatimes.com/city/kolkata/police-to-sensitise-personnel-to-deal-with-lgbtq-people/articleshow/78137194.cms

Tinder. (n.d.). *What is photo verification?* https://www.help.tinder.com/hc/en-us/articles/360034941812-What-is-Photo-Verification-

Tziallas, E. (2015). Gamified eroticism: Gay male "'social networking'" applications and self-pornography. *Sexuality & Culture, 19*(4), 759–775. https://doi.org/10.1007/s12119-015-9288-z

Vanita, R., & Kidwai, S. (2000). *Same-sex love in India.* Palgrave Macmillan US.

Vasudevan, A. (2011). *Dealing with extortion.* Orinam.

Waldman, A. E. (2019). Law, privacy, and online dating: Revenge porn in gay online communities. *Law & Social Inquiry, 44*(04), 987–1018. https://doi.org/10.1017/lsi.2018.29

Wells, H., & Polders, L. (2006). Anti-gay hate crimes in South Africa: Prevalence, reporting practices, and experiences of the police. *Agenda, 20*(67), 20–28. https://doi.org/10.1080/10130950.2006.9674694

Whitty, M. T. (2013). The scammers persuasive techniques model: Development of a stage model to explain the online dating romance scam. *The British Journal of Criminology, 53*(4), 665–684. https://doi.org/10.1093/bjc/azt009

Wodda, A., & Panfil, V. R. (2020). Introduction. In A. Wodda & V. R. Panfil (Eds.), *Sex-positive criminology* (pp. 1–16). Routledge.

Wolak, J., & Finkelhor, D. (2016). *Sextortion: Findings from a survey of 1,631 victims.* Thorn. www.wearethorn.org

Wolff, K. B., & Cokely, C. L. (2007). "To protect and to serve?": An exploration of police conduct in relation to the gay, lesbian, bisexual, and transgender community. *Sexuality and Culture, 11*(2), 1–23. https://doi.org/10.1007/s12119-007-9000-z

Yes We Exist [YesWeExistIndia]. (2019a, May 27). Beware! The rise of dating scams and fraud in India. [Facebook status update]. https://www.facebook.com/YesWeExistIndia/photos/a.201725747195107/342991043068576/?type=3&theater

Yes We Exist [YesWeExistIndia]. (2019b, June 5). The dating scams and sexual assaults continue. [Facebook status update]. https://www.facebook.com/YesWeExistIndia/photos/a.201725747195107/347307979303549/?type=3&theater

"Missing and Missed": Failures of the Bruce McArthur Investigation and the Ongoing Victimization of Toronto's Rainbow Streets

V. Bragagnolo

ABSTRACT

This article analyzes "Missing and Missed: Report of The Independent Civilian Review into Missing Person Investigations," a review of Toronto Police's conduct during "missing persons" investigations. Analyzing the Bruce McArthur investigation and police's failed efforts to solve some of his victims' "missing persons" cases, questions if overt bias or intentional discrimination influenced police procedure are answered. Critical of blanket statements that pardon police wrongdoing, this article explores the report's recommendations and concludes with a suggestion of a crime prevention model to be considered by Toronto Police who are expected to release a plan of implementation in or before April 2022.

Within Toronto's downtown core is a rainbow strip consisting of bars, cafes, drag performances, bookshops, and trivia nights (*Home: The Village*, n.d.; *Neighbourhood: The Gay Village*, n.d.; Teitel, 2017). Surrounding the intersections of Church and Wellesley Streets, Toronto's Gay Village (the Village) has housed and hosted many members of the LGBTQ2S+ community (*Home: The Village*, n.d.; Leong, 2011; Levinson-King, 2019; Neighbourhood: The Gay Village, n.d.; Teitel, 2017). However, although the Village is well-known for being the city's designated safe haven, queer[1] folk have long shared experiences of violence and victimization that have occurred amongst Toronto's Rainbow Streets (Daro, 2017; Dunn, 2017; Hasham et al., 2019; Zamon, 2017).

VIOLENCE in THE 1970S AND 1980S: FROM MULTIPLE HOMICIDES TO BATHHOUSE RAIDS

In the early 1970s, Toronto saw queer folk from across Canada migrate to the Village, which at that time, only made up the "small stretch of Yonge Street between College and Wellesley streets" (Mayor et al., 2018). With same-sex relations being decriminalized in Canada in 1969, members of the LGBTQ2S+ community believed that they could build a new life in the Village; an authentic one where they no longer had to hide who they were (Mayor et al., 2018). However, what became of the Village, a space that was supposed to garner a sense of safety and security, was a site of violence.

---

[1] This paper will use LGBTQ2S+ and queer interchangeably when referring to folks that retain the affiliation.

14 Homicides in 3 ¹/₂ Years

Between 1975 and 1978, fourteen men that lived in or frequented the Village were murdered (Mayor et al., 2018). Eerily, the facts of many of the fourteen reported homicide cases were similar. All the victims were members of the LGBTQ2S+ community and five of the fourteen men were reported as "last seen leaving the St. Charles Tavern at the south end" (Mayor et al., 2018) of the Village strip. Many of the victims were also found dead in their homes with stabbing, asphyxiation, or blunt-force trauma identified as the cause of death; 'overkill' being listed in many police reports (Mayor et al., 2018). Due to the similarities amongst the homicide cases, members of the Village community pleaded with Toronto Police to investigate the possibility of a serial killer. However, the Toronto Police did not support this speculation (Mayor et al., 2018). To date, seven of the homicide cases have been solved with listed motives of robbery, overdue payments, and violent assault, while the remaining seven cases have gone cold (Isai, 2018; Mayor et al., 2018).

The Bathhouse Raids

As some members of the Toronto Police were tasked with solving the open homicide cases from the 1970s, others were conducting raids across the city. Due to little improvement in provincial and federal human rights coverage for members of the LGBTQ2S+ community in the early 1980s, unlawful raids were constantly conducted on minimally protected queer establishments (Bradburn, 2013; Guidotto, 2006, p. 3, 37, 39). The 1981 Toronto bathhouse raids, far from "an isolated incident"[2] but historically well-known due to the violently charged practices used by Toronto Police during the raids, consisted of 151 Toronto Police officers storming four of the city's most popular bathhouses. During the raids, more than 300 men were arrested by Toronto Police from the Richmond Street Health Emporium, the Barracks, the Club Baths, and the Romans II Health and Recreation Spa, charged with being found ins or keepers of a bawdy house (Bradburn, 2013; Guidotto, 2006, p. 3, 39). Using physical force, such as punching and choking, Toronto Police wanted to not only harm queer folk found in the bathhouses, but they aimed to publicly humiliate them as well. Whether it be through using pens to carve the room numbers that the men were found in into their hands or using homophobic language to make the men feel lesser than, the motivation behind the raids was emotionally and physically harming members of the queer community (Guidotto, 2006, p. 45, 89; Nangwaya, 2016). The violence experienced by queer folk at the hands of Toronto Police during the raids, paired with the slow police response to solving the 1970s homicide cases, heightened levels of distrust between police and the LGBTQ2S+ community. Decades later, this relationship "would only worsen" as more queer folk from the Village would disappear, becoming victims of ongoing violence, while Toronto Police would again dismiss the possibility of a serial killer targeting members of the LGBTQ2S+ community (Mayor et al., 2018).

The 2000s: 8 Homicides in 7 Years

On January 29th, 2003, Bruce McArthur, a white man and a recently separated father from Oshawa, Ontario, pleaded guilty to one count of assault with a weapon and assault causing bodily harm (Brockbank, 2019; Hardwick, 2019). After using a lead pipe to attack a man in his Village home, McArthur had voluntarily turned himself in to Toronto Police (Brockbank, 2019; Epstein, 2021, p. 14; Hardwick, 2019). The medical report cited no reasoning or mental health issues

---

[2] In Canada, numerous raids were conducted on queer establishments, such as bathhouses, leading up to the Toronto bathhouse raids. Even after the violent Toronto raids, police across the country continued to conduct these ambushes. For example, The Warehouse in Hamilton was raided in 2004 (Guidotto, 2006, p. 3).

acting as contributors, and regardless of the violent nature of McArthur's actions, the psychiatrist assigned to the case claimed he was minimal risk; unlikely to reoffend (Brockbank, 2019; Epstein, 2021, p. 14). As his sentence, McArthur received probation, but with restrictions. He was not allowed to go to the Village or engage with male sex workers, and he was banned from using weapons for ten years. He was also given a court order to seek counseling for his anger issues and to provide a DNA sample to be kept on file (Brockbank, 2019).

After McArthur's first documented assault and conviction, he remained dormant. However, on September 6th, 2010, Skandaraj Navaratnam disappeared over the Labor Day long-weekend. He was "last seen leaving Zipperz nightclub" (Brockbank, 2019; Epstein, 2021, p. 15). Almost four months after Navaratnam's disappearance, on December 29th, 2010, Abdulbasir Faizi disappeared after visiting Steamworks, a bathhouse in the Village (Brockbank, 2019; Epstein, 2021, p. 16). Both cases remained open for almost two years when on October 14th, 2012, Majeed Kayhan also disappeared from around Yonge and Alexander Streets, close to where both Navaratnam and Faizi disappeared (Brockbank, 2019; Epstein, 2021, p. 17). Again, the cases of the now three queer men of color remained open. By January of 2016, McArthur had killed two other men. Soroush Mahmudi, who was reported missing after he did not 'clock in' for his work shift on August 15th, 2015, and Kirushna Kumar Kanagaratnam who had disappeared on January 9th, 2016, but was not reported missing (Brockbank, 2019). Thus, by March of 2016, Toronto Police were tasked with solving four reported and open "missing persons" cases. However, in April of 2016, McArthur's sixth victim, Dean Lisowick, disappeared after being discharged from the Scott Mission on Spadina Avenue. Like Kanagaratnam, he was also not reported missing at the time of his disappearance (Brockbank, 2019). Two months later, McArthur struck again and attempted to strangle a man, referred to as Mr. AD, in the back of his van while having a sexual encounter (Brockbank, 2019; Epstein, 2021, p. 30). Mr. AD escaped and reported the attack to police, resulting in McArthur's arrest. However, after providing a statement framed by confusion of whether consent to being choked was given during their sexual encounter, McArthur was unconditionally released; records indicating that his statement was deemed credible (Epstein, 2021, p. 30–31). After being released, McArthur remained dormant for almost a full year until April 30th, 2017, when Selim Esen was reported missing from the area of Yonge and Bloor Streets (Brockbank, 2019; News Staff, 2019). It would be the day after Toronto's annual Pride Parade that McArthur would kill for the reported last time. On June 26th, 2017, Andrew Kinsman got into McArthur's maroon Dodge Caravan (Brockbank, 2019; Epstein, 2021, p. 37). This would be the last time he was seen (Brockbank, 2019).

4 Decades of a Serial Killer 'on the Loose' in Toronto's Gay Village?

Four decades after the 1970s string of murders, 66-year-old white[3] serial killer,[4] McArthur, was convicted on January 29th, 2019, of eight counts of first-degree murder and sentenced to life in prison for each of the eight counts. He will be eligible for parole at the age of 91 after he serves

---

[3]Further exploration of white violence and aggression against people of color, specifically the romanticization of the white, male serial killer, which is demonstrated when glorified in media, is necessary in order to further research in the field of serial murder but was not possible in the confines of this paper.

[4]What constitutes a serial killer varies as there is "no universally agreed upon" definition (White et al., 2010, p. 18). However, understandings of the serial killer consider some of the following factors: (1) two or more victims, (2) the serial killer's relationship to the victims, (3) the serial killer's motive or motivation, (4) the number of separate instances, (5) if there was a cooling period between victims, and 6) if several of the serial killer's victims were murdered (White et al., 2010, p. 18). Combining the FBI's 2008 definition and the work of White et al. (2010), this paper defines a serial killer as a person that kills two or more people in independent instances that are separated by a cooling off period where "the killer resumes his/her daily routine, such as going to work, going home, and being with his/her family" (White et al., 2010, p. 18 and 19). Reports of McArthur's romantic relationships with some of his victims, his overall number of victims, and the cooling periods that occurred between victims where McArthur would return to his family-life and job are what classify McArthur a serial killer (Epstein, 2021).

twenty-five years in prison (Westoll, 2019). When comparing the details of the murders that McArthur was convicted of with those of the cold cases from the 1970s, suspicion that McArthur may have begun killing in his twenties is formulated (Mayor et al., 2018). Like the men killed in the 1970s, McArthur's victims were all members of the LGBTQ2S+ community that frequented venues in the Village. McArthur's victims' causes of death were also similar to the deaths of many of the men in the 1970s; pointing to asphyxiation or blunt force trauma, with extreme force noted in police reports (Isai, 2018; Mayor et al., 2018). In addition, existent research on age of onset of serial killers further suggests that McArthur likely began killing decades before his 2019 conviction.

Age of Onset of Serial Killers

In his *Characteristic Study of White Male Serial Killers*, Welch (2011) argues that when comparing the case studies of known and convicted serial killers, specific variables can be detected and strategically used "to identify and limit the scope of research in serial murder" (p. 5). After considering six cases of convicted serial killers from both the United States and Canada, Welch (2011) found that specific components present themselves in many cases of serial murder, such as a desire to harm animals, substance and alcohol abuse, a volatile family or home environment, and little commitment to work and personal life (p. 5). However, although Welch (2011) dismisses research focused on age variables due to a lack of available statistical information, which resulted in juvenile serial killers not being included in the study, the small sample of case studies that he does provide point to a trend in known and convicted adult serial killers (p. 6). Of the six case studies, Welch (2011) records that each adult serial killer began killing between the ages of twenty-three and 44, resulting in twenty-eight years of age being the average age of onset (p. 7). In fact, of the total six case studies included, 50% of the men began killing in their twenties (Welch, 2011, p. 7).

Furthermore, using the *Radford Serial Killer Database*, Aamodt et al. (2008) argue that there is difficulty in predicting age, however, their data still suggests that when concerning the age distribution of known serial killers in the United States, Canada, and worldwide, almost half (45.3%) began killing in their twenties and the likelihood of serial killers beginning their sprees in their 50s, although possible, is statistically uncommon (p. 1, 6). In addition, Aamodt et al.'s (2008) work only includes serial killers with three or more victims and does not account for serial killers that were arrested after killing two times but would have continued killing if they were not apprehended (p. 2). Thus, it would be fair to suggest that an inclusion of these individuals could increase the overall percentage of serial killers that began killing in their twenties. Combined, both Welch (2011) and Aamodt et al. (2008) provide evidence that known serial killers worldwide overwhelmingly have began killing in their twenties, and when the 1970s string of murders were committed, McArthur, who at the time was working in downtown Toronto, would have been in his twenties (Mayor et al., 2018). Thus, after pairing the available research on age of onset of serial killers with the noted similarities amongst the homicides McArthur was convicted of and those still open from the 1970s, suspicion that McArthur is to blame for the murders that took place in the Village four decades ago is not only reasonable but is a likely probability.

METHOD

This paper emerged from the news of the completion of "Missing and Missed: Report of The Independent Civilian Review into Missing Person Investigations" (the "Review"), which was released in April 2021 after a 31-month long investigation (Woods, 2021). Acting as a document analysis, this paper analyzes the "Review." In combination with the "Review," a thorough, systematic examination of existing qualitative studies, which theorize violence against marginalized communities and detail the history of queer experiences of violence, is conducted. This review of documentation was done in order to better understand and explore the ways in which blanket statements made in systemic reviews can excuse police wrongdoing and create a falsified version of events in the archive. The following begins by objectively examining police procedure, providing the step-by-step process taken when reporting "missing persons" and how said cases can develop into homicide investigations. Following the same structure of the "Review," this paper separately examines the police efforts when tasked with solving McArthur's six reported victim's "missing persons" cases. However, by positioning an analysis of the "Review's" conclusions within an intersectional feminist perspective, this paper questions Epstein's claim that there was no overt bias or intentional discrimination during the McArthur investigation (Epstein, 2021, p. 3, 61). Such an approach differs from that taken on by Epstein in the "Review." To conclude, this paper draws from two existing community initiatives in the United States, Mothers/Men Against Senseless Killings (MASK) and the Dallas Domestic Violence Task Force (DDVTF), in order to suggest a hybrid model of crime prevention to be considered by Toronto Police as they prepare to release their implementation plan in or before April 2022 (Woods, 2021).

Understanding "Missing Persons" Investigations in Canada

Community Safety

The International Association of Chiefs of Police (IACP) provides trainings and programs, hosts educational conferences, and keeps units from across the globe informed of new policing ideas and initiatives brought forth by experts in the field. As indicated on the association's main page, the IACP also provides resources to guide the profession's corresponding procedure and practices worldwide (About IACP, n.d.). Similarly, but with a specific focus on the police practices and leadership in Ontario, the Ontario Association of Chiefs of Police (OACP) acts as "a channel for police officers to share [their experiences and] ideas ... [so they can] create solutions ... [for] challenges" (Home, n.d.) in policing in the province (*Home*, n.d.). Crime prevention resources released by both governing organizations, which have likely been reviewed by and incorporated into practice by Toronto Police, emphasize the importance of community safety. Both governing associations appear to support recognizing suspicious or criminal activity, and "stop[ping] crime before it occurs" (Crime prevention 2019: You are crime prevention, 2019), which lowers rates of victimization (Crime prevention 2019: You are crime prevention, 2019). What this means is that maintaining a safe environment and having communal connections or ties acts as a deterrent when preventing small and large-scale crime, such as theft and abduction (Crime prevention 2019: You are crime prevention, 2019).

Reporting A "Missing Person"

Community safety is compromised when a member of the community becomes a "missing person." A "missing person" is someone whose "whereabouts are unknown and unexplainable for a period of time that is regarded by knowledgeable parties as highly unusual or suspicious in consideration of the subject's behaviour patterns, plans or routines" (Buckley, 2012, p. 5). A "missing persons" report is initiated when a complainant contacts the Toronto Police (Missing persons unit, n.d.). During this initial stage of the reporting process, complainants are expected to aid the complaint taker and the initial responding officer in their collection of information regarding the "missing person" (Buckley, 2012, p. 8). Initially, they are asked "to provide a complete description of the missing person and details regarding [the] last time they were seen including the date, time and location" (Missing persons unit, n.d.). The attending officer is then dispatched to the residence of the complainant. However, the complainant must complete a "missing person" questionnaire prior to the attending officer's arrival and give said officer a copy once they arrive at the residence (Missing persons unit, n.d.). While at the residence, the attending officer will also collect and record the details of any physical evidence that may assist in solving the "missing persons" case. In addition, the complainant will be tasked with answering additional questions about the "missing person," information that is expected to be well-documented by the attending officer (Missing persons unit, n.d.). These questions include descriptions of their physical appearance, their mental and physical health, and their emotional well-being (Missing persons unit, n.d.). The complainant will also be asked for a picture of the "missing person." This will "assist in the investigation … [because it] can be used in a News Release, Social Media posts and shared with the Media" (Missing persons unit, n.d.). Sharing the "missing person's" identifying information will "bring attention to the case and generate leads" (Missing persons unit, n.d.) in the community that will be pursued or followed up on. Follow ups can, for example, include a background check. Other questions regarding "cell phone numbers, … carrier/service providers, email addresses, social media accounts, banking information, … driver's licence, … friends/family and their contact information, and places where they frequent" (Missing persons unit, n.d.) will also be asked "as a part of the standard investigative procedure" (Missing persons unit, n.d.) and is shared to other forces in the surrounding area using databases or through direct contact by phone (Missing persons unit, n.d.). In addition, as per Ontario's set adequacy standards, if an individual is reported missing and there is 1) officer suspicion that foul play was involved or 2) no trace of the individual for 30 plus days following the initiation of the "missing persons" report, the case is to be given 'major case status', marking the solving of said case a priority for officers (Epstein, 2021, p. 29).

Homicide Investigations

When a "missing person" is suspected or found as a victim of a homicide or foul play, police are obligated to initiate or treat the case as a homicide investigation (Missing persons unit, n.d.; Understanding the criminal justice system, n.d.). Although homicide investigations are conducted within and by different departments, investigative processes follow similar procedure. The initial responding officer is the first at the scene of a homicide. When they first arrive on the scene, their role is to gauge whether the scene is safe, address, if any, existing "dangerous situations", detain, if any, suspects, call for medical or police assistance, such as rescue and homicide investigators, and pinpoint witnesses (Howell, 1999, p. 1). They will then examine any physical objects or belongings at the scene that appear tampered with and take note of these discrepancies. The formal recordings the initial responding officer collects, such as inconsistencies noted in the physical setting of the scene of the crime, form the basis of solving the investigation[5] and are turned over to homicide investigators once they arrive to the scene (Howell, 1999, p. 5, 8). In addition to the initial responding officer's formal recordings, the homicide investigators create their own notes, such as crime scene sketches and photographs collected during their secondary search of the crime scene, and gather evidence found at the scene. Investigators are also responsible for interviews and interrogations to be conducted with witnesses and suspects once returning to the station or in the days to follow, and processing the physical and trace evidence, such as fibers, blood, and other fluids (Howell, 1999, p. 15, 16, 18). After the homicide investigators conduct their initial investigative work, the Chief Coroner will determine "the identity of the deceased and the facts as to how, when, where and by what means [the] death occurred" (Understanding the criminal justice system, n.d.). These details will aid investigators in formulating a timeline to help gain a greater understanding of the events that led up to the victim's death. In many instances, an autopsy, which is a medical examination of a deceased body, follows the Chief Coroner's

---

[5]In all investigations, police and investigators are expected to prioritize the documentation process. Included in all documentation should be what was done by those on the scene and what officers saw, heard, smelled, etc. (Howell, 1999, p. 1).

initial examination and can be ordered by warrant for possession without the consent of family if it will aid in solving the homicide case (Death investigations, n.d.a,b). When the initial investigation, the Chief Coroner's investigation statement, and the autopsy report are completed, investigators hold hope that combined, they will clearly point to the accused whom criminal charges can be laid against. To lay charges against an accused, "the police must have strong evidence, including witness statements and various reports, including police, medical or incidental" (Saini law, 2020).

Concerns Regarding Investigative Practices

The existing frameworks, outlining the processes officers are expected to follow, leave room for personal judgment or consideration.[6] For example, when initiating a "missing persons" investigation, "the priorities [the officers on the scene] set and the action they take will depend on the situation as they find it" (Understanding the criminal justice system, n.d.). Meaning, officers determine which cases are priority "and require immediate action, and which cases are less critical" (Buckley, 2012, p. 2). When leaving room for Toronto Police to make choices based on personal judgment or consideration instead of having a clear standardized operating procedure, there is the potential for a lack of consistency, response-wise, across investigations; reasonings for judgements possibly being influenced by social understandings and arrangements (Buckley, 2012, p. 13). And although there is an ongoing rebuttal to the suggestion of a standardized operating procedure, which argues that as cases vary, investigative processes may also change alongside said investigations to meet the nature of those specific cases, the solution to the concern of existing variances amongst investigation practices appears to be that communities should just blindly trust officers. However, to ask communities, such as the LGBTQ2S+ community, that has been historically victimized by Toronto Police, to have confidence in the decisions of officers on the force is absurd, especially when examples of recent investigations within the city, such as the McArthur case, demonstrate how police continue to fail queer folk and leave them exposed to violence (Kur, 2021).

FINDINGS: POLICE FAILURES IN THE MCARTHUR INVESTIGATION

Skandaraj Navaratnam. Abdulbasir Faizi. Majeed Kayhan.
All loved. All deserving of thorough and prioritized investigations into their disappearances. All failed by Toronto Police.

From the onset of the Navaratnam "missing persons" case and well into the final stages of the Project Houston investigation, Toronto Police had no intention of reaching out to the LGBTQ2S+ community or its connected Police Service resources, no desire to conduct coordinated investigations (consisting of formal recordings), and in general, they had no plan on how to approach the "missing persons" cases of the three queer men of color (Epstein, 2021, p. 23–24).

Skandaraj Navaratnam

Skandaraj Navaratnam was McArthur's first victim after his 2003 assault conviction. He was reported missing ten days after he disappeared in September of 2010 (Brockbank, 2019). What

---

[6]When police are brought forth a report of a "missing person", "key considerations the police take into account when responding to a missing persons report [include]: the well-being of the missing person; respect for the right of an individual to go missing; compassionate treatment of the relatives and friends of the missing person; likelihood that the person missing may have been the victim of a serious crime; preservation and management of evidence in suspicious cases; and appropriate level of resources for each individual report" (Buckley, 2012, p. 1).

was concerning about the Toronto Police's investigation, or lack thereof, into Navaratnam's disappearance was their failure to pursue potential leads. For example, during the initial stages of the investigation, Navaratnam's file was passed amongst a number of investigators. However, none of these investigators saw the importance in contacting the Police Service's LGBTQ2S+ liaison officer to put them in touch with leaders and organizations in the Village community (Epstein, 2021, p. 15). Navaratnam was a queer man of color who frequented the Village. In fact, he was last seen in the area prior to his disappearance (Brockbank, 2019). It would appear that speaking to members of the Village community would have been the best option for Toronto Police assigned to the case when searching for leads. In fact, using the Police Service's connections to organizations or leaders in the LGBTQ2S+ community would have "ensure[d] that the right people were spoken with and that existing barriers to providing information to the police [such as mistrust and fear] were reduced" (Epstein, 2021, p. 15). The Toronto Police's failure to seek help from the Village community in the initial stages of the Navaratnam case can take partial blame for why the case went cold. However, in addition to searching for leads through the use of community outreach, investigators can also turn to physical evidence collected at the scene.

At the time of Navaratnam's disappearance, his computer was seized by Toronto Police (Epstein, 2021, p. 15). Not only did the computer provide information about the dating websites that Navaratnam was participating on or a member of, but it also contained detailed correspondences between Navaratnam and McArthur, known as *silverfoxtoronto* (Epstein, 2021, p. 15). However, the computer was not examined until 2012, two years after Navaratnam's disappearance, and the correspondences on said computer would not be uncovered until 2017. Thus, questions arise regarding why Toronto Police failed to examine the contents of the computer (Epstein, 2021, p. 15). Without warning, Navaratnam had vanished and left behind loved ones, but also a dog that he had tasked no one to care for (Epstein, 2021, p. 15). Such a disappearance would suggest the involvement of foul play. Any suggestion of foul play in the disappearance of any individual, let alone one that is part of a marginalized community, should result in giving said case 'major case status' regardless of understandings that "strong "possibility" falls [just] short of reasonable and probable grounds to believe" (Epstein, 2021, p. 16). Knowing the evidence pointed to foul play, Toronto Police should have followed both routes to uncover leads, but they did not (Epstein, 2021, p. 16). They failed Navaratnam and, shortly after, they would fail Abdulbasir Faizi.

Abdulbasir Faizi

Abdulbasir Faizi was reported missing in December of 2010 (Brockbank, 2019). However, although Faizi, like Navaratnam, frequented the Village, he lived in Peel Region (Epstein, 2021, p. 16). Thus, Peel Police initially investigated his disappearance. When comparing the investigation that the Peel Police conducted into the Faizi disappearance to the efforts put forth by the Toronto Police in solving the Navaratnam case, the "Review" notes that the Peel Police put forth a "superior" investigation, contacting members of the queer community and the Salaam Queer Muslim Community Center (Epstein, 2021, p. 16). Although the purpose of this paper is not to examine how Peel Police handle "missing persons" cases, acknowledging their efforts, which resulted in successful findings that linked both the Navaratnam and Faizi cases, and their passing of said information to Toronto Police, which would later be ignored, demonstrates how uncoordinated the Toronto Police's response was to these two men's cases (Epstein, 2021, p. 17).

In January of 2011, two members of the Peel Police engaged in a conversation. In this conversation, the officer looking into the Faizi disappearance was informed of the Navaratnam case, which was still an open "missing persons" case at the time. After Navaratnam's disappearance, Peel Police were not informed by Toronto Police of the open "missing persons" case (Epstein,

2021, p. 16, 17). Although concerning in its own right as not informing surrounding regional services of existing open cases would make drawing connections between similar cases in nearby areas difficult, what is also problematic is that after finding links between the two missing men's cases, the Peel officer tasked with solving the Faizi case reached out to Toronto Police and was met with a failed response (Epstein, 2021, p. 17). After contacting the Toronto Police three times—twice being ignored, not even receiving a phone call back, and once being acknowledged and informed the link would be looked into—the "Review" notes there was no evidence proving any action was taken on the end of the Toronto Police to investigate the ties between the cases. In fact, it took Toronto Police two years to look into the possible links between the Navaratnam and Faizi cases; an opportunity only available because Peel Police immediately put Faizi's case on PowerCase, an online database used to store investigation information (Epstein, 2021, p. 17, 21-22). Gathered from the Toronto Police's handlings of the Faizi case and its ties to the Navaratnam case is the evident failure to perform a coordinated investigation that prioritized the disappearances of two men whose similar identities and frequenting of the same area suggested a link between their disappearances. Not only did Toronto police fail to follow up on a tip provided by Peel Police, but they also did not formally document their procedures—waiting until late 2012 to upload the Navaratnam case to PowerCase (Epstein, 2021, p. 16, 17). Again, for the second time, Toronto Police failed a member of the LGBTQ2S+ community. It would be almost two years following the disappearance of Faizi, that Majeed Kayhan's disappearance would be handled with the same lack of prioritization (Brockbank, 2019).

Majeed Kayhan

Majeed Kayhan was reported missing by his family in October of 2012. Like Navaratnam and Faizi, Kayhan was last seen in the Village community (Brockbank, 2019). However, Toronto Police were not aware of his ties with the LGBTQ2S+ community until a month after his disappearance (Epstein, 2021, p. 17). For the third and last time prior to the launch of the Project Houston investigation, another queer man of color disappeared, and his case was met with no clear police plan of action. Similar to Navaratnam's case, Kayhan's "missing persons" case was labeled low priority. In fact, the investigator on the case even put the investigation on hold while they took a two-week vacation in November (Epstein, 2021, p. 18). With no Missing Persons Unit in the Toronto Police force at the time, and no plan of action on how to proceed with "missing persons" investigations—often being passed from investigator to investigator—no connections with the two other open cases of queer men of color that had disappeared from the Village community were made (Epstein, 2021, p. 18, 19).

Project Houston

By the time of the Project Houston launch in 2012, three queer men of color were missing—all known to have frequented the same area and all leaving behind loved ones (Brockbank, 2019). In the initial stages of their investigations, Toronto Police failed to exhaust their resources and thoroughly investigate these men's cases. Navaratnam, Faizi, and Kayhan deserved more. And it has been believed since the launch of Project Houston that this understanding is what trailblazed the taskforce. However, the "Review" states that the Project Houston investigation was only initiated due to a Swiss informant tip, suggesting that a possible cannibalism ring could have been the cause for Navaratnam's disappearance (Brockbank, 2019; Epstein, 2021, p. 19). Without said tip, it can be argued that this taskforce would have never been created and these cases would have continued to be labeled as low priority; possibly to have never been solved.

Project Houston was an 18-month long investigation where police obtained around 40 warrants and interviewed a number of individuals who had known or encountered Navaratnam,

Faizi or Kayhan, including McArthur (Brockbank, 2019). In November of 2013, McArthur was interviewed by investigators, but later labeled a witness and released, not being questioned further about the disappearances of the men in the Village for another three years (Epstein, 2021, p. 14). The "Review" points to a number of failures in police procedure, most notably, a lack of coordinated and consistent investigations, during Project Houston (Epstein, 2021, p. 23). First, prior to McArthur's interview, there was no "meaningful examination of … [McArthur's] history, including his previous criminal conduct" (Epstein, 2021, p. 14). The officer who interviewed McArthur failed to conduct a Legacy Search, which 'pulls up' historical records, because they believed that any past violent activity would be "irrelevant to McArthur's credibility" (Epstein, 2021, p. 14). The failure to conduct a Legacy Search prior to McArthur's interview as a part of the Project Houston investigation demonstrates what would appear as a failure at the hands of Toronto Police to prioritize these men's cases. In addition, and even more alarming, is that McArthur was released after his interview during the Project Houston investigation even though, at this time, Toronto Police were aware of evidence that linked McArthur to Navaratnam, Faizi, and Kayhan (Epstein, 2021, p. 14). For example, in September of 2013, Toronto Police found the username *silverfoxx51* on a notepad belonging to Faizi (Epstein, 2021, p. 21).

Secondly, not only did the uncoordinated investigation lack necessary preparation and briefing, but it also failed to formally record details, such as recording interviews and uploading evidence and information collected to PowerCase. For example, Toronto Police did not upload McArthur's interview during the Project Houston investigation into PowerCase (Epstein, 2021, p. 22). In addition, Toronto Police once again did not inform other reginal services of the evidence that they had gathered during the Project Houston investigation, such as links between McArthur and the three missing men (Epstein, 2021, p. 21–22). Instead of following proper protocol, the "Review" states that the Project Houston investigation heavily relied on the investigators' memory and the passing along of verbally assigned tasks, which in itself is a flawed approach to service work due to difficulty in remembering every detail of a case (Epstein, 2021, p. 12, 22). Ultimately, regardless of the evidence collected that pointed to McArthur as a person of interest, in April of 2014, Project Houston was scaled back due to what police claimed was a lack of criminal evidence (Brockbank, 2019; Epstein, 2021, p. 26). However, this paper argues that the taskforce was not successful because of the flawed police work conducted during the investigation. There was no plan and no coordinated investigation—suggesting a lack of desire to solve the open "missing persons" cases of three queer men of color (Epstein, 2021, p. 23–24).

PROJECT PRISM

Soroush Mahmudi. Selim Esen. Andrew Kinsman.
All loved. All deserving of thorough and prioritized investigations into their disappearances. Only some failed by Toronto Police.

Soroush Mahmudi

Following the scaling back of Project Houston, Soroush Mahmudi disappeared from the Village community in August of 2015 (Brockbank, 2019; Epstein, 2021, p. 29). The "Review" stated that there was difficulty in making a connection between Mahmudi and the other missing men due to Mahmudi living in Scarborough at the time of his disappearance (Epstein, 2021, p. 29). Similar to Kayhan, Mahmudi's ties to the LGBTQ2S+ community were unknown to Toronto Police during the initial stages of the investigation into his disappearance. In addition, similar to the cases of the other three queer men of color that had disappeared, Mahmudi's case was not given a 'major case status' (Epstein, 2021, p. 29-30). The low priority status Mahmudi's "missing persons" case received, the same status that Navaratnam, Faizi and Kayhan's cases were also labeled with, demonstrates a decision Toronto Police made that goes against provincially set adequacy standards (Epstein, 2021, p. 11, 29-30). Mahmudi, Navaratnam, Faizi and Kayhan's cases should have been given and labeled high priority.

Selim Esen

In August of 2017, Toronto Police launched its second task force, Project Prism. The investigation was launched after Selim Esen disappeared in April of 2017 (Brockbank, 2019). The "Review" acknowledged that further action was taken during the investigation of the Esen case compared to the efforts made to solve the cases of the previous four queer men of color that had disappeared (Epstein, 2021, p. 33). Practices that differed in the Esen case included the use of social media platforms, community involvement, and inquiring from external police units (Epstein, 2021, p. 33). The officer assigned with Esen's case not only reached out to members of the LGBTQ2S+ community, but they also "tweeted" about the open case using the social media platform, *Twitter*. In addition, the Cyber Crimes Unit was tasked with further examining Esen's movements on social media platforms and his use of the *web* (Epstein, 2021, p. 33). However, it is important to note that any connections made between Project Prism and Project Houston were uncovered by luck. Due to Toronto Police failures during the Project Houston investigation, information from the investigation was not uploaded to PowerCase. If it was not for a retired officer seeing the "tweet" about Esen on *Twitter* and informing the officer on the Esen case of the other disappearances, connections would have been difficult to form (Epstein, 2021, p. 34).

Although there was more effort put forth by the Toronto Police when investigating the Esen case, the "Review" suggests that this effort only existed once the case became a part of Project Prism and not prior. In fact, like the previous four victims noted, prior to being included in Project Prism, Esen's case was not given 'major case status' even though he was missing for more than 30 days (Epstein, 2021, p. 34). His case status only changed when grouped with the Andrew Kinsman disappearance as "there was ample *circumstantial* evidence that indicated a strong possibility that these cases were connected …" (Epstein, 2021, p. 35).

Andrew Kinsman

In June of 2017, Andrew Kinsman, a white queer man, disappeared (Brockbank, 2019). His disappearance gathered a large amount of public and media attention due to, says the "Review", efforts made by his friends and family (Epstein, 2021, p. 35). After last being seen getting into a maroon Dodge Caravan, around twenty-five production orders were requested by Toronto Police, which gave them the power to look into Kinsman's email accounts, phone records, banking information, and Highway 407 records (Brockbank, 2019). By September of 2017, Toronto Police began to heavily monitor McArthur's mobile movements. Since only deeming McArthur a witness in Project Houston five years prior, this was the first time McArthur's name was used in a "request to seal a production order for Bell Canada" (Brockbank, 2019). Toronto Police followed said request by following McArthur's vehicles, one being the maroon Dodge Caravan that Kinsman was last seen getting into. This vehicle was found at and towed from Dom's Auto Parts after McArthur sold the vehicle to the business. It was thoroughly searched by police for evidence and both blood, which belonged to Kinsman, along with DNA, which belonged to Esen, were found in the van (Brockbank, 2019). In November of 2017, after the Mobile Surveillance Unit restarted watching McArthur, he was named a person of interest in the Kinsman case. Swiftly after being named a person of interest, the area behind his residence, located at 53 Mallory Crescent, was searched. It was in December of 2017 that Toronto Police obtained a warrant to search inside McArthur's residence. They duplicated some information from McArthur's "digital devices and storage media" that may have linked him to Kinsman but left soon after as someone else was returning home (Brockbank, 2019). A few days later on December 7th, 2017, the Toronto Police returned to McArthur's home and made copies of all of McArthur's computer hard drives, collected DNA swabs of his pillow "and a seven-to-nine-inch metal bar wrapped with tape" (Brockbank, 2019), and copied post-it notes that he had written his passwords and log-ins on (Brockbank, 2019). On McArthur's devices, Toronto Police found post-death photographs McArthur had attempted to delete, linking him to Kinsman, Esen, and some of the other victims. Following these findings on January 18th, 2018, McArthur was arrested by Toronto Police (Brockbank, 2019).

McArthur was "then charged with first-degree murder in the deaths of Esen and Kinsman, even though the men's bodies ... [had] yet been found" (Brockbank, 2019). Following McArthur's charges, pertaining to the homicides that he was accused of, Toronto Police announced a planned search of five other properties that McArthur had frequented. These included his apartment, and other properties, such as one in Scarborough, one in Madoc, and two in Toronto (Brockbank, 2019). During the searches, Toronto Police found evidence that connected three additional disap-pearances—those of Mahmudi, Kayhan, and Lisowick—to McArthur. He was then charged with their murders (Brockbank, 2019; Hardwick, 2019). It was at these differing locations that the remains of McArthur's other victims were also found. In sum, the Project Prism investigation led to McArthur being captured, the details of the eight queer men's disappearances being uncovered, and ultimately, charges laid for a total of eight counts of first-degree murder (Hardwick, 2019).

UNASSIGNED PROJECTS

> Kirushna Kumar Kanagaratnam. Dean Lisowick. And Many More...
> All loved. All deserving of thorough and prioritized investigations into their disappearances. All failed by Toronto Police.

Following the McArthur investigation, Detective Idsinga of the Toronto Police held a press con-ference in July of 2018. It was stated that after a four-month forensic investigation—one that col-lected 1,800 exhibits and 18,000 photos—there was no evidence that McArthur had additional victims (Hardwick, 2019). However, members of the Village community were not convinced, again, holding the suspicion that McArthur had killed more queer men from the Village commu-nity (Mayor et al., 2018).

Each year, approximately 4,300 "missing persons" are investigated by Toronto Police, overseen by the Missing Persons Unit since 2018 (Missing persons unit, n.d.). Of the total approximation of "missing persons" investigated, most return home or are returned home within one week of them initially being reported missing (Buckley, 2012, p. 1). However, the remaining cases can go cold or develop into 'major crime cases', such as homicide cases. Between 2010 and 2017, the period in which McArthur's confirmed eight victims had disappeared, an annual average of 60.875 intra-city homicides[7] were reported to Toronto Police (*Homicide—overview: Reporting period (2004-2020), n.d.*). Although the data on how many "missing persons" cases develop into homicide cases is inconclusive, available outlets indicate that the longer an individual (presumed to be in danger when reported missing) is missing, the likelihood that they are found alive decreases. In fact, if a "missing person" is not found within a couple weeks of their initial disappearance, investigations shift from attempting to find a person to finding a body (Jacobo, 2018). Although most of Toronto's yearly reported homicides between 2010 and 2017 likely did not originate as "missing persons" cases, the cases of six of McArthur's victims suggest that some did. In combination with this understanding is the realization that other "missing persons," such as Kanagaratnam and

---

[7]In 2010, a total of 65 intra-city homicides were reported to Toronto Police. Following, 51 cases were reported in 2011, 57 in 2012 and 2013, 58 in 2014, 59 in 2015, 75 in 2016, and in 2017, 65 homicide cases were reported to Toronto Police (*Homicide – overview: Reporting period (2004-2020), n.d.*).

Lisowick, are not reported at all (Brockbank, 2021). With many of these cases not being included in Toronto's official crime statistics, such as the *Public Safety Data Portal*, the dark figure of crime[8] is maintained (Quinet, 2007, p. 321). Knowing that some "missing persons" can go undetected if not reported or linked to other open cases come questions of why certain individuals can disappear unnoticed, making said individuals the serial killer's 'ideal' victims (Quinet, 2007, p. 321).

Strategically Targeting 'Ideal' Victims: Serial Killers and Marginalized Populations

The "Less-Dead"

Serial killers strategically target marginalized populations. These populations can include sex workers, queer folk, and the homeless (Hickey, 2003, p. 278; Quinet, 2007, p. 320). More specifically, serial killers target those whose marginal status situates them as vulnerable, making the likelihood of their deaths being overlooked high (Hickey, 2003, p. 278). These individuals, the serial killer's 'ideal victims', are known as the "less-dead" (see Egger, 2002) (Quinet, 2007, p. 320). To be "less-dead" is to be one that 'never was' (Hickey, 2003, p. 278). Meaning, the "less-dead" are those whose existences in any given community are essentially already "ignored and devalued" prior to their death. Their 'lesser than' status is formed through existing social understandings and arrangements that reinforce the notion that if said "less-dead" person disappeared, their disappearances would not be noticed, and they would "generally not [be] missed" (Hickey, 2003, p. 278).

Social Understandings and Arrangements

Social understandings and arrangements, attitudes shaped by existing stereotypes and stigma, are forms of pervasive injustice that become widespread and maintain unjust conditions that are "perceived as natural, normal, or simply "the way things are"" (Dean, 2015, p. 12). They shape the way certain populations, namely marginalized communities, are viewed and expose them to violent and non-ideal social conditions (Dean, 2015, p. 12–13, 116, 124, 133). For example, in their discussion of the disappeared women from Vancouver's Downtown Eastside (DTES), Dean (2015) examines failed police efforts when tasked with solving open "missing persons," later turned homicide, cases. Specifically, she notes that the disappearances of women from the DTES were rationalized and given low priority due to held views of the DTES area, which saw "outdoor sex work, addiction, and homelessness" (Dean, 2015, p. 77). Women from the DTES area were socially understood as criminal, deviant, and invaluable due to their proximity to such a "dangerous" community (Dean, 2015, p. 33, 77). Thus, when these women disappeared, their disappearances were normalized, with some officers stating that they were 'temporarily missing'; to re-appear when they wanted to return from the deviant activity that they were assumed to be partaking in (Dean, 2015, p. 26–28, 42). The social understandings and arrangements that formed a skewed view of the DTES area and in turn, the women that inhabited it, allowed for white Canadian serial killer Robert Pickton to long move undetected by police. By targeting victims that were part of a population whose disappearances were both not taken seriously or often discredited by police, Pickton killed dozens (Wahab, 2021, p. 13).

Like McArthur, Pickton was the target of police investigations, but evaded authorities for years until his ultimate conviction in 2007 (*Missing and Murdered Indigenous Women in British Columbia, Canada*, 2014, p. 34). Although arrested and charged with assault involving a weapon and the attempted murder of a women in 1997, the charges were stayed and he was released

---

[8]The dark figure of crime consists of committed acts that are not reported to the Criminal Justice System or are never discovered, which "puts into doubt the effectiveness and efficiency of the official crimes data" (*Section 2: Comparing police-reported crime statistics and victimization data (2015, November 27); The dark figure of crime and the reporting of crime (2021, August 26); A., 2013*).

(*Missing and Murdered Indigenous Women in British Columbia, Canada*, 2014, p. 33). After said release, he killed six other women from the DTES area before his second arrest in 2002 when he was recharged with twenty-seven counts of first-degree murder. Pickton was ultimately convicted of six counts of second-degree murder and sentenced to six terms of life in prison without the possibility of parole (CBC News, 2010; *Missing and Murdered Indigenous Women in British Columbia, Canada*, 2014, p. 34). The Pickton investigation, in which it was later determined that he killed 49 women, a fair number of which being Indigenous women, demonstrates how the McArthur investigation is not anomalous (Baynes, 2018; Miller, 2016; *Missing and Murdered Indigenous Women in British Columbia, Canada*, 2014, p. 34). In fact, the similarities between both the McArthur and Pickton investigations calls for further examination into why police (or state) responses to investigations involving marginalized populations, specifically populations concerning racialized identities, is slow.

Understanding State-Supported Violence Against Queer Folk of Color

A Brief History of the Queer as the 'Other'

Social understandings and arrangements in Western society have long upheld the homosexual-heterosexual binary, which has historically maintained queer folk as the 'other' when compared to their hetero- counterparts who are understood as the 'norm'. As early sociological research suggests, "homosexualities have been produced in a variety of ways in the Western world" (de Oliveira et al., 2013, p. 1476), making up a large part of the cause of public struggle throughout the 18th and 19th centuries (Seidman, 1997, p. 82–83). However, the culture that surrounded these 'sexual conflicts' was somewhat silent about them (Seidman, 1997, p. 83). Nearing the end of the 19th century, scholars, such as Foucault, published research on "the role of scientific and medical discourses" (de Oliveira et al., 2013, p. 1476). He argued that the role of these discourses impacted how sexuality was constructed and that it was this way of thinking that further characterized non-heterosexualities, associating them with 'abnormality' or as the 'other' (de Oliveira et al., 2013, p. 1476). Then, entering the first half of the 20th century, erotic autonomy and equality and 'sexual rebellion' or queerness became more visible and less silent in social movements (Seidman, 1997, p. 85-86). However, still, in the second half of the 20th century, emerging studies, such as constructionist studies, continued to pose gay or queer individuals as a social minority to their hetero- counterparts (Seidman, 1997, p. 90). For example, dating back to the 1970s, social understandings and arrangements labeled queer folk deviants that lacked morality and self-control (Guidotto, 2006, p. 84). In fact, newscasting, newspapers, and bulletins recorded the negative implications associated with being queer; synonymous with disease and criminality, and intentionally seeking to corrupt society (Guidotto, 2006, p. 37).

Intersecting Identities: Queer Folk of Color as 'Ungrievable' Bodies to the Nation-State

In the 21st century, Canada has reframed "normativity and citizenship" (Wahab, 2021, p. 2). Due to homonationalism (see Puar, 2007), white queer Canadians, meaning those that show "allegiance to the nation-state while indifferent to or participant in the targeted operations of state violence on marginal communities…" (Wahab, 2021, p. 2), are granted "queer citizenship" (Wahab, 2021, p. 3). However, such a reframing has resulted in a heightened exposure to violence for queer folk of color that cannot participate in homonationalist projects (Wahab, 2021, p. 3, 6, 11). What this means is that although 'other' sexualities can be "(homo)citizenize-able", meaning they can 'correctly' perform what would be hetero-domesticity, if one's identity is "outside of whiteness… [it] disqualifies their queerness" (Wahab, 2021, p. 2, 6). Wahab (2021) argues that for "the majority of McArthur's victims… their hyper-racialized nationalities, their non-quite-citizen status in Canada, [and] their Muslim and Muslim-looking identities…" (p. 6), made them "threats to the ... nation-state" (p. 2); "killable subjects" (p. 3). Thus, although queer folk in general carry a marginal, "less-dead" or 'other' status, making them 'ideal' victims for serial killers, queer folk of color are granted less protection from the nation-state due to their racialized identities (Hickey, 2003, p. 278; Quinet, 2007, p. 320; Wahab, 2021, p. 3). This lack of protection, leaving queer folk of color "marked for death", could explain why the open "missing persons" investigations prior to Kinsman's disappearance were not given the same amount of police effort (Haritaworn et al., 2014, p. 2; Wahab, 2021, p. 3, 7, 14). Kinsman, a white queer man, was a death that the state could mourn because his sexuality and whiteness placed him as "(homo)-citizenize-able" (Wahab, 2021, p. 2, 7). Whereas, McArthur's other reported victims, queer men of color, would not be viewed as losses to the nation-state; 'ungrievable' and deserving of their deaths (Haritaworn et al., 2014, p. 2, 8; Wahab, 2021, p. 2, 3, 6).

Butler's (2002) exploration of Antigone's relationships with her siblings and uncle in *Antigone's Claim* further supports how perceived "threats to the ... nation-state" (Wahab, 2021, p. 2) are deaths deemed 'ungrievable' (see Butler, 2004), and thus, not prioritized (Wahab, 2021, p. 14). After her brother, Polynices, is killed, Antigone demonstrates a desire to both mourn her loss and provide him with a proper burial. However, as Creon only wishes to properly bury her other brother, Eteocles, Antigone makes the choice to hold a proper burial for Polynices in secret (Oakes, 2006). From Antigone's actions is a clear and unquestioned prioritizing of grieving a specific life regardless of the punishment that she knows she will undoubtfully receive for going against Creon's wishes (Butler, 2002, p. 79; Oakes, 2006). However, it is Creon, who represents the state as he resumes power after Eteocles is killed, that demonstrates another clear and unquestioned prioritization; those who are threats "will be left for the dogs and vultures to eat" (Oakes, 2006). Evidently, Creon's views of Polynices navigate the proceedings following his death. Similarly, this paper argues that the investigations following the deaths of most of McArthur's victims, victims that were queer men of color, were not prioritized due to the men not being viewed as 'grievable' losses to the nation-state (Wahab, 2021, p. 2, 14).

To Be Missing or to Be Forcibly 'Disappeared'?

There is a distinction between when someone goes missing and when someone is forcibly 'disappeared' (Dean, 2015, p. 24). Missing as an adjective is defined as not being found in one's usual place or to be lost or absent (Dean, 2015, p. 22; *Missing*, n.d.). Whereas as a verb, 'disappeared' is defined as one ceasing to exist (Dean, 2015, p. 26; Disappear, n.d.). Drawing from Gordon (1997), Dean (2015) suggests that when 'disappeared', there is a state-supported system in place working to vanish specific groups (p. 26–28). This system, which allows for, accepts, and is often itself responsible for the mass disappearances of populations, is demonstrated through 1) the historical poor treatment of specific marginalized groups (paired with negative social understandings and arrangements), 2) slow police responses to violence against said groups, and 3) the state's neglect of certain geographic areas that are known to house said groups (Dean, 2015, p. 26–28).

Toronto's LGBTQ2S+ community, a population that carries a marginal or "less-dead" status, has a historically poor relationship with Toronto Police. For example, as demonstrated through the violence experienced during the Toronto bathhouse raids (Guidotto, 2006, p. 3, 39). Social developments constructing the queer as the 'other' have also remained somewhat constant over the last few decades, maintaining a binary that situates hetero as the 'norm' (de Oliveira et al., 2013, p. 1476). However, some queer folk, such as many of McArthur's victims, were also read as threats to white (settler) Canadian society, which additionally placed their bodies as readily killable with no protection from the nation-state (Wahab, 2021, p. 2, 3). These men experienced additional social understandings and arrangements outside of their sexualities, which were shaped by "the rise of state-sponsored Islamophobia, anti-brown racism and anti-immigration sentiment in post 9/11 Canada" (Wahab, 2021, p. 2) and naturalized their disappearances, rendering them 'ungrievable'. In addition, the "missing persons" cases of McArthur's first few reported victims, all queer men of color, were also met with a slow police response, only to be investigated when a white queer man disappeared and could be linked to said cases (Wahab, 2021, p. 7). Slow responses to violence against queer folk, however, is not surprising as the 1970s "missing persons" cases, presumed now as homicide cases, that involved queer men, remain open (Mayor et al., 2018). Lastly, during the McArthur investigation, Toronto Police failed individuals that frequented or inhabited the Village by refusing to acknowledge that a serial killer was targeting the community (Epstein, 2021, p. 40). Thus, in sum, the McArthur investigation clearly demonstrates "a wider neoliberal [state-supported] strategy of violently exploiting and casting out surplus populations" (Wahab, 2021, p. 6).

The "Review": Missing and Missed

"Missing and Missed: Report of The Independent Civilian Review into Missing Person Investigations" (the "Review") was released in April 2021 after a 31-month long investigation led by retired Ontario Court of Appeal Justice, Gloria Epstein (Woods, 2021). The "Review" was created with the purpose of improving the relationship between Toronto Police and the city's most marginalized and at-risk communities, such as the LGBTQ2S+ community. It found systemic issues at the base of investigations into "missing persons" cases and in its 151 recommendations, points to ways in which Toronto Police need to reform their procedures in order "to break down barriers to reporting and information-sharing … [and] to advance the investigations into disappearances within … [marginalized communities]" (Woods, 2021). Per Epstein, the "Review" can be transformative if translated from document into lived experience, even giving Toronto Police a timeline to develop a plan to implement all 151 recommendations into their practices and procedures. The plan must also detail how changes will be implemented and will be released to the public on or before April 2022 (Woods, 2021).

Highlights of the "Review": Emphasizing Communication and Trust

From the "Review" comes the clear desire to take on a holistic approach to "missing persons" (with potential to turn into homicide) investigations (Westoll, 2021). A holistic approach relies on the participation and actions of the community and its local services in order to achieve an overall goal. Using such an approach, says Epstein, will work to reallocate some of the components of "missing persons" investigations away from the police and instead, use the Village community and their connected social agencies as resources for solving open cases (Fox, 2021). It is believed that this shift in investigative procedure will act as a measure of accountability, resulting in more transparency from Toronto Police when handling investigations in the city (Woods, 2021). More specifically, of the 151 recommendations in the "Review," recommendations 36, 81, and 112 best represent the implementations needed for adoption so that the suggested holistic model can be achieved: enhancing communication and trust (Woods, 2021).

Recommendation 36. Recommendation 36[9] suggests that Toronto Police implement a new way of policing and handling "missing persons" cases. By using a model that uses a bottom-up approach, members of and resources from marginalized communities would be frequently consulted and used when an individual from the community is reported missing. Such a model, says Epstein, would "contemplate … [the] triaging of missing persons cases" (Woods, 2021), which

---

[9]"Recommendation 36: The Toronto Police Services Board and the Toronto Police Service should work with the City of Toronto, provincial and federal governments, and social service, public health, and community agencies and not-for-profit organizations to build capacity for non-policing agencies and organizations to assume responsibilities consistent with the proposed mid-term and long-term models" (Epstein, 2021, p. 101; Woods, 2021).

means "that the right people … [and] the right agencies are doing the work associated with these cases" (Woods, 2021). The hope with such a recommendation is that it will strengthen the existing investigative procedures, and in doing so, will avoid a repetition of history (Woods, 2021).

Recommendation 81. Recommendation 81[10] also addresses existing procedures in place, specifically in the form of public safety warnings. This recommendation works to mend the disconnect between Toronto Police and marginalized communities as it emphasizes the need for ongoing clear and open communication between the groups (Woods, 2021). Noting that "a key moment of the investigation into the McArthur murders came when police refused to acknowledge that the string of disappearances could be the work of a serial killer" (Woods, 2021), Epstein questions the Toronto Police's slow response during the McArthur investigation and argues that a public safety warning should have been released sooner than December of 2017. Thus, the "Review" recommends the need "for greater consultation between the … [Toronto Police] and the community … to ensure [that] these warnings are issued before it's too late" (Woods, 2021).

Recommendation 112. Lastly, recommendation 112[11] focuses on how the transferring of information between the Toronto Police and marginalized communities are conducted, emphasizing the need for repairing trust and confidence between the groups (Woods, 2021). Currently, there is an ongoing distrust between marginalized communities, such as the LGBTQ2S+ community, and Toronto Police regarding reporting processes. In fact, Hodge & Sexton (2020) state that the reporting relationship between the LGBTQ community and police "has long been a turbulent one" (p. 246) due to discriminatory treatment experienced by members of the LGBTQ community when they report a crime committed against them and must interact with officers on the force (p. 247). Although Hodge & Sexton's (2020) work focuses on the relationship between the police and the LGBTQ community in an American context, similar feelings of mistrust exist in a Canadian context as well. For example, in the "Review" is an outline of the interviews and consultations with Village community members, which point to fear of police interaction due to experiences with being targeted by members of the force (Epstein, 2021, p. 51-52). Thus, many view speaking with police as a "last option" and is why members of the LGBTQ2S+ community have grown to rely on each other rather than law enforcement (Epstein, 2021, p. 51; Hodge & Sexton, 2020, p. 247). The "Review" then suggests that Toronto Police need "to establish safe and secure reporting methods as a way to ensure that marginalized communities feel comfortable reporting missing persons to police without fear of personal repercussions" (Woods, 2021), such as additional targeting through secondary charges being laid (Epstein, 2021, p. 51-52).

In sum, the three highlights aim to reestablish a foundation between the Toronto Police and marginalized communities, such as the LGBTQ2S+ community, so that they can hopefully work with and rely on each other to create a new holistic system that is assumed as being more effective and efficient when solving "missing persons" (with the possibility to turn into homicide) investigations. However, while keeping these recommendations in mind, the following problematizes the "Review" and its conclusion of no overt bias or intentional discrimination (Epstein, 2021, p. 3, 61). Such a statement may make repairing the relationship between the Toronto Police and

---

[10]"Recommendation 81: The Toronto Police Service should re-evaluate its existing decision-making processes for issuing public safety warnings. At a minimum, in relation to major case investigations, the major case manager should make the ultimate decision, in consultation with the Service's Corporate Communications, as to whether a public safety warning is required. These types of decisions should be made, whenever possible, in partnership or in consultation with community leaders" (Epstein, 2021, p. 119; Woods, 2021).

[11]"Recommendation 112: The Toronto Police Service should consider incorporating into its Missing Persons Procedure, a third-party or "distance" reporting system (where trusted community leaders, organizations, or agencies are designated to transmit, anonymously if necessary, missing person reports or information to the police)" (Epstein, 2021, p. 129; Woods, 2021).

the LGBTQ2S+ community difficult as it excuses the experiences some queer folk may have had with officers and know to be true.

Questioning the "Review's" Conclusion: Blanket Statements as Tactics of Erasure

"In summary, … overt bias or intentional discrimination does not explain the deficiencies in the McArthur-related investigations. However, these deficiencies (prior to Project Prism) are partially explained by systemic practices that promoted differential treatment between how these men's disappearances were investigated and how empowered individuals' disappearances would be investigated" (Epstein, 2021, p. 61).

One investigation. Seven years. Eight confirmed victims. After the investigation into how Toronto Police handle the "missing persons" cases of marginalized communities, such as the LGBTQ2S+ community, Epstein did not conclude that overt bias or intentional discrimination are to be blamed for the flawed McArthur investigation (Epstein, 2021, p. 3, 61). Instead, in *Chapter Twelve* of the "Review," she points to systemic practices as the cause of the failures in the investigation, which resulted in some "missing persons" cases receiving more police involvement and attention than others (Epstein, 2021, p. 61). Although it is understood that the "Review" acted as a systemic review, meaning it was "designed to identify and address larger issues of systemic importance—issues involving an institution's systems, policies, or practices, rather than issues confined to an isolated or individual error or fault" (Epstein, 2021, p. 6), it is difficult to comprehend how Epstein can separately evaluate a system (and provide recommendations to address its failings) from the individuals that uphold and maintain it (Systemic reviews, 2020). In fact, she herself acknowledges that investigations of systems need to examine culture, environment, and practices to ensure that the structures in place do not put particular groups at a disadvantage (Epstein, 2021, p. 57). So then why are the practices and comments made by officers during the McArthur investigation excused when they make up the culture and environment of the Toronto Police?

The following questions how Epstein could have possibly concluded with the utmost amount of confidence that not one officer in an almost seven-year long investigation poorly performed their duty to protect due to intentional bias. To demonstrate reasonable doubt in Epstein's findings, the following addresses small fragments of the "Review" where she notes police discomfort when addressing the LGBTQ2S+ community and comments that she states were "closer on the spectrum to overt bias" (Epstein, 2021, p. 61). These examples demonstrate the potential for intentional discrimination when making procedural choices during the investigation and thus, rendering the blanket statement made by Epstein inappropriate.

Furthermore, in addition to emphasizing that the blanket statement made in the "Review" is likely inaccurate, the following is critical of the choice to use a blanket statement in the "Review" in general due to existing works demonstrating how state-supported efforts of erasure, as seen in other Canadian systemic reviews, have historically pardoned or silenced the victimization of marginalized, "less-dead," or 'othered' communities (Collard, 2015, p. 780; Epstein, 2021, p. 3, 61; Petticrew, 2015). Thus, the latter pages of this section will examine how written documents, such as the "Review" and systemic reviews in general, can also make the archives a site of violence themselves and allow for the ongoing victimization of marginalized communities, such as the LGBTQ2S+ community.

The Possibility of Police Discomfort and Comments of Overt Bias

Epstein's conclusion of no proof of overt bias or intentional discrimination draws reasonable doubt for a number of reasons (Epstein, 2021, p. 3, 61). First, there was little recorded during the McArthur investigation so it would be reasonable to believe that even after finding discrepancies with the handlings of the open cases, Epstein would still have had to heavily rely on interviews conducted with members of the Toronto Police to form her conclusions (Epstein, 2021, p. 22).

However, for an officer to willingly state on record that their discriminatory perceptions of the LGBTQ2S+ community led to them intentionally hindering members of said community's "missing persons" cases would be unlikely as it would be job-ending (Uyen, 2005). This thought process, however, is not further explored by Epstein in the "Review."

In addition to this thought, Epstein does provide minor details within the "Review" that can be used as proof to support concern of reasonable doubt toward her blanket statement. As demonstrated by the investigation into Navaratnam's disappearance, Toronto Police underutilized the Service's LGBTQ2S+ liaison officer and Village community resources, such as organizations and leaders tied to the force (Epstein, 2021, p. 15). The reasoning detailed in the "Review" was the unfamiliarity that many Toronto Police officers had with the Village community (Epstein, 2021, p. 60). In addition, Epstein points to the intersections of the men's sexualities and race as reasoning of why "these investigations were conducted differently... from investigations involving affected communities within the officers' expertise, or "comfort zone"" (Epstein, 2021, p. 60), pointing to a lack of training. However, Toronto Police have been given opportunity to partake in ongoing sensitivity training.

For example, in September of 2000, Toronto Police raided a lesbian bathhouse in the city (Uyen, 2005). The raid was led by five male officers and considered a *Canadian Charter of Rights and Freedoms* violation. The settlement that was decided later in December of 2005 consisted of a $350,000 payout to the seven women whose rights were violated, but also, mandatory gay and lesbian sensitivity training for all officers on the Toronto Police force; congruent with the positions of the Ontario Human Rights Commission and the queer community (Uyen, 2005). To suggest that the discomfort officers tasked with the McArthur investigation felt was due to their lack of training when a decision decided upon in 2005 indicates that these officers were trained, brings the question of whether it was a lack of training, or a lack of wanting to exhaust all available resources for members of a marginal, "less-dead," or 'other' community where historically, efforts have been made to 'disappear' them.

Such negative views are mentioned in *Chapter Twelve* of the "Review," noting that certain folks' intersecting identities could result in their disappearances being "dismissed or minimized" (Epstein, 2021, p. 61). In the chapter, Epstein makes the shocking omission that "several officers at the 51 Division expressed the view, about one of the missing men, that he had likely gone "on a sexual holiday"" (Epstein, 2021, p. 61). Making such an admission, says the "Review," demonstrates poor preconceptions of queer men. However, Epstein claims that although this comment was "closer on the spectrum to overt bias" (Epstein, 2021, p. 61), it does not prove that intentional bias or discrimination occurred during the McArthur investigation (Epstein, 2021, p. 61). Although Epstein is correct and the clear stereotypical understandings that these officers had of queer men may have not impacted their decision-making during the McArthur investigation, there is still the possibility that they could have, and that these officers, to protect their jobs, simply did not admit that (Uyen, 2005). Albert Bandura's (1997) *Social Learning Theory* further emphasizes how what one knows to be 'true' is often translated to their everyday practices and activity (Nabavi, 2012, p. 5). The translation—from observation to thought to practice—supports reservations about Epstein's claim that not one officer intentionally made the choice to not exhaust resources or to fully perform their duty to protect due to overt bias or intentional discrimination.

Nabavi (2012) argues that people "learn from ... [the] interactions [that they have] with others in a social context" (p. 5). Through their analysis of *Social Learning Theory*, Nabavi (2012) further notes that from watching the people around them, an individual will "assimilate and imitate" viewed behaviors, which translates into how they live their day-to-day lives (p. 5). This includes their mannerisms, beliefs, practices, motivation, and attention, which the individual will believe to be the 'correct' way of socializing (Nabavi, 2012, p. 5-6). With the work of Nabavi (2012) in mind, the following suggests that if the officers who made these statements had gathered this stereotypical and poor understanding of queer men from the culture around them, whether that be from the Toronto Police or the greater community, then it would be realistic to assume that over time, they adopted said understanding as 'correct', acceptable, or even accurate. Thus, it would not be unrealistic to suggest that even if all officers did participate in sensitivity training, at least one officer may still intentionally hold what they had come to know as a 'truth' about queer men, historical understandings that victimize them by labeling them as the 'other' or for some, even threats, and purposefully respond poorly (or not respond at all) to the "missing persons" cases (de Oliveira et al., 2013, p. 1476; Wahab, 2021, p. 2).

Systemic Reviews as the Archive: A Site of Violence and Continuing Victimization

The "Review" pardoning the possibility of intentional bias or discrimination can maintain the ongoing victimization of members of the LGBTQ2S+ community in an additional way, specifically within the archive (Epstein, 2021, p. 3, 6). Using the text *Silencing the Past: Power and the Production of History* by Michael-Rolph Trouillot, Hunt-Kennedy (2021) discuses "how social and political inequalities of the past shape the ways historical events are recorded in their moment and then archived, retrieved, and written about in the present" (p. 222). Similarly, Collard (2015) draws from the "Missing Women Commission of Inquiry" to demonstrate how the report acted as an exclusive and violent space, working to falsely rewrite in the present the historical wrongs conducted against Indigenous women (p. 780, 787). The final report, Collard (2015) notes, including its 63 recommendations on policing, are solutions that put little "fault ... [on] individual police actions, decisions, officials, and departments" (p. 790); a tactic used by British Columbia's provincial government to erase the province's historical mistreatment of Indigenous women at the hands of local and provincial police enforcement (Collard, 2015, p. 782, 790). Hunt-Kennedy (2021) also points to this process of silencing in the archive, although specifically discussing its application in "the archive of slavery" (p. 222). It is understood that the silences in the archive exist due to a lack of acknowledgement or representation, which in itself is a form of violence (Hunt-Kennedy, 2021, p. 222, 223). Combining the work of Hunt-Kennedy (2021) and Collard (2015), it becomes evident how the archive, in this instance, the creation of systemic reviews, "obscures and reveals" (Hunt-Kennedy, 2021, p. 223). Although there is an acknowledgement of those who were harmed in systemic reviews that provide 'next-step' recommendations, in actuality, the archive (what that review becomes) fails to point to the reality of the wrongdoings (usually at the hands of legal enforcement) or shed light on the experiences of those harmed, which in many instances, are members of marginalized communities, in order to maintain its "white colonial power" (Hunt-Kennedy, 2021, p. 223).

The "Review" does a good job of avoiding placing fault on intentional police actions and decisions, and the officers themselves involved in the McArthur investigation. This is due to Epstein's blanket statement, claiming that all officers assigned to the McArthur investigation did not carry overt bias or discrimination (Epstein, 2021, p. 3, 61). However, as stated, there are several reasons why one would believe that arriving at some concrete "impossible" is implausible. For example, as existing research suggests, members of the Toronto Police have admitted in the past to refraining from reporting that they witnessed intentional discrimination or harassment in order to avoid losing their job (Uyen, 2005). If officers fear losing their job as an outcome for reporting someone else intentionally discriminating against a member of a marginalized community during an investigation, then it is hard to imagine any coming forth during Epstein's investigation and admitting their own guilt. However, Epstein did not appear to consider the reasonable doubt that could be paired with her conclusion and in not shedding light on the possibility that purposeful police misconduct may have occurred due to understandings of the LGBTQ2S+ community, she unknowingly contributes to maintaining an archive that denies the possibility that such a victimization, one that has historically been ongoing, occurs. Such a denial allows for 'next-steps' (modelled after the recommendations in the "Review" and to be implemented into police procedure) to be based on inaccurate representations of victimization that fail to fully address the 'whole picture' of violence experienced by Toronto's LGBTQ2S+ community at the hands of the city's police (Collard, 2015, p. 781). In sum, the conclusion of the "Review" leaves opportunity for violence and victimization, both in police procedure and within the archive, to continue.

Moving Forward: Where to Go from Here?

Problematizing Community Policing-Like Initiatives

The stated purpose of the recommendations made in the "Review" is to improve the communication and trust between Toronto Police and marginalized communities, such as the LGBTQ2S+ community (Fox, 2021). However, blanket statements excusing any possibility of inherent police bias makes it difficult to improve the existing poor relationship between the two groups (Epstein, 2021, p. 3, 61). Epstein believes that a new holistic model or approach to investigations is the solution needed to mend the existing poor police-citizen relationship (Westoll, 2021). Although noble, what is suggested through the "Review's" recommendations still has some drawbacks as it appears to support a community policing-like initiative[12] (Kur, 2021).

Many local and grass-roots organizations have voiced concern over community policing-like initiatives, critiquing the police reform as not centering the needs of the community, and with forces only adopting community policing-like efforts into their procedure as a means of receiving more funding (Kur, 2021). In addition, existing opinion on community policing-like initiatives, based on experience, have not particularly noted much success in terms of the initiative repairing the police-citizen relationship. For example, the No Pride in Policing Coalition, Maggie's Toronto Sex Workers Action Project, and Butterfly: Asian and Migrant Sex Worker Support Network argue in a released statement that community policing-like initiates are "actually about the intensification of policing of Black, racialized, Indigenous, Two-Spirit, Queer and Trans communities and has nothing to do with safety" (Kur, 2021). Furthermore, the groups state that increased police presence does not lead to more transparency and accountability, but rather, results in higher reported levels of crime due to an increased number of arrests taking place (Kur, 2021). It is then no surprise that since the "Review" was released, members of the Village community have voiced their weariness of the recommendations suggested. In fact, for many queer folk, some recommendations are read as a way to "embed ... social workers and other 'civilians' in the police" (Kur, 2021), asking these individuals to surveille and regulate their own (Kur, 2021). In addition, other recommendations leave the level of collaboration to be done between Toronto Police and community, collaboration that is to be done under police observation and must meet police discretion, vague (Kur, 2021). Thus, arises the concern that the new implementations that will be released in a plan in or before April 2022 by Toronto Police, deriving from the "Review's" recommendations, will turn community members, leaders, and organizations working with Toronto Police into a part of the very institution that has been a source of their victimization. It is feared that the once reliable and safe outlets available for members of the Village community will be "shaped by and constrained" by Toronto Police who will still have the final say in all decisions, only faking an equal collaboration with the community (Kur, 2021).

---

[12]Community policing initiatives attempt to repair relationships between officers and communities by creating a partnership between the two. Instead of being the only enforcers of "law and order", officers are expected to work with community, allowing them to become 'allies' with the force and work along their side to "enhance ... safety in the[ir] community" (*Disadvantages of community policing*, n.d.).

Implementing a Hybrid Model of Crime Prevention: Centering Community Self-Policing and Community-Centred Initiatives

The fear that the "Review's" recommendations will result in a plan that does not repair the police-citizen relationship, and instead, works to turn community members, leaders, and individuals from local and grassroots organizations into "civilian officers" has resulted in members of the city's LGBTQ2S+ community reimagining community safety and what that could look like in the Village (Kur, 2021). Rooted in the belief that community safety approaches that involve police do not automatically equate to increased safety, especially for marginalized communities such as the LGBTQ2S+ community, is the desire to defund policing and instead, allocate said funds to community initiatives that can work independently from police (Kur, 2021).

Keeping the rising and voiced desire held by members of the Village community in favor of a community self-policing initiative in mind, the following will suggest a hybrid or modified model of crime prevention that Toronto Police should consider while they create a plan of implementation by or before April 2022. By considering two existing and successful community crime prevention initiatives based in the United States that have lowered crime rates and prevented violence with minimal to no police interference, the following encourages Toronto Police to 'take a step away' from community policing-like initiatives and instead to consider the efforts of Mothers/Men Against Senseless Killings (MASK), a community self-policing initiative, and the Dallas Domestic Violence Task Force (DDVTF), a community-centred or based model (*Rethinking community safety: A step forward for Toronto*, n.d., p. 19; Zerkel, 2021). Although not fully taking on the community self-policing initiative some queer folk have voiced a desire for, implementing a model to crime prevention that gives the responsibility of community safety to the people that know the community best (its members) while at the same time, uses physical presence to heighten feelings of comfort rather than distrust and intimidation, has the potential to successfully lower crime rates in the Village community and if victimization does occur, ensures that the 'right people' are tasked with investigating the matters (Woods, 2021).

Mothers/Men Against Senseless Killings (MASK)

MASK consists of a group of mothers and men in Chicago, Illinois, that have 'taken over' a block in their community and prevent crime without the presence or interference of police. The mothers and men "are present on the block every evening, barbecuing, feeding residents, and building relationships with the young people" (Zerkel, 2021). Their mission, which is to diffuse tensions that arise on their block, has proven to successfully reduce rates of violence (Zerkel, 2021). The key feature of importance to be taken from the MASK initiative is the physical presence of the mothers and men in the community. Acting as the opposite of civilian or police officers, the mothers and men are first and foremost neighbors to the members of their community (About us, n.d.). Unlike with the presence of police, which can be threatening, the women and men's presence, mainly their familiar and smiling faces, serve as a reminder to community members that they are not only welcomed and loved, but that as people, they (and their safety) matter (About us, n.d.).

The MASK initiative clearly demonstrates the process of adopting a collective responsibility regarding maintaining community safety, a stance to preventing violence that should be taken up by all prevention efforts. This is because collective responsibility rejects case-by-case approaches to prevention (Godderis & Root, 2017, p. 4). Instead, a collective stance would include the individuals of any given group prioritizing the overall wellbeing of all members of that community (Godderis & Root, 2017, p. 4). More specifically, in terms of violence prevention in the Village, a collective stance on community safety would involve all community members working together to educate themselves of the risks factors (in terms of victimization) in their community, to stay alert and 'look out" for each other's safety, to speak up and report to local organizations or leaders when they witness or suspect violence against members of their community, and to contribute to efforts that work toward ending violence and victimization in their community all together.

Dallas Domestic Violence Task Force (DDVTF)

The DDVTF, which is based in Dallas, Texas, addresses domestic violence by allocating most of the responsibility, in terms of addressing matters, to community members, service workers, and local agencies and organizations. The model "is made up of 40 plus members of various Dallas area agencies whose primary focus is the prevention and eradication of domestic violence and the support of victims" (*Dallas*, n.d.). Instead of acting as a community self-policing initiative like MASK, the DDVTF acts as a community-centered or based initiative that allows for law enforcement organizations to participate, but only as a "back-seat role". For example, within the initiative, law enforcement organizations only make up "13% of responding participants" (Rethinking community safety: A step forward for Toronto, n.d., p. 19). The remaining 87% of DDVTF is made up of survivor-oriented non-profits, survivor and victim services, counselling, emergency housing services, and additional education and labor support (*Rethinking community safety: A step forward for Toronto*, n.d., p. 19). Evidently, the overall goal of the initiative is the prioritization "of providing survivors with a comprehensive and enduring network of support" (*Rethinking community safety: A step forward for Toronto*, n.d., p. 19).

What the DDVTF initiative demonstrates is that violence prevention and safety measures can exist with limited police interaction and direction. For marginalized communities, such as the Village's LGBTQ2S+ community, the historically poor relationship with Toronto Police has resulted in them not feeling confident in officers' investigation processes (Mayor et al., 2018). Since this is the current status of the relationship between the two groups, safety measures need to be adjusted accordingly.

A Hybrid Model of Crime Prevention

As demonstrated by both the MASK initiative and the DDVTF, community-based prevention models that consist of community members acting as the main resource for intervention have promising outcomes and are best-suited to address marginalized groups. With the implementation of a model of crime prevention that centers the key components of both the MASK initiative and the DDVTF, comes several benefits. Some of these benefits include lower rates of violence and victimization, higher rates of reporting, more trusted support for survivors, and most surprisingly, a slight improvement in the police-citizen relationship that exists between the Toronto Police and the city's LGBTQ2S+ community.

By adopting the MASK initiative's use of community presence and collective responsibility as a method of crime prevention, all members of the Village will be best educated on pinpointing violence before it occurs as well as be trained in protocols in the case that they do witness violence in the community (*About us*, n.d.; *Dallas*, n.d.; *Rethinking community safety: A step forward for Toronto*, n.d., p. 20). For those that frequent or inhabit the Village, friendly faces that they know to be on their side with no police influence draws out a sense of comfort. The feeling of comfort replaces the paranoia or fear that exists in processes that involve police that would additionally charge individuals for separate matters when they report victimization (Epstein, 2021, p. 51). Not only would taking on a collective responsibility keep the community safer in terms of there always being a 'watchful eye', looking out for the best interests of the community's members, but by Toronto Police giving the responsibility of intaking reports of violence to local leaders or grassroots organizations, individuals may feel more compelled to come forth with reports of victimization (*About us*, n.d.).

In addition, as demonstrated by the DDVTF initiative, plans to be implemented by Toronto Police should consider the use of "non-police teams" to address and investigate existing matters of violence and to provide support to victims in the Village (Zerkel, 2021). Examples of "non-police teams" would include emergency care teams, trauma-informed crisis intervention teams, and climate de-escalation specialists, all of which would be made up of community members, leaders, and organizations (Zerkel, 2021). Instead of increasing funding for police services and "police-led, criminal-justice-oriented" approaches to crime prevention and investigation processes, funding should be reallocated, refocused, and funneled into these local "non-police teams" so that they can run successfully, able to access the materials and services that they need to both investigate the cases in and support the people of the Village community (Kur, 2021; *Rethinking community safety: A step forward for Toronto*, n.d., p. 17). For example, as demonstrated during the initial stages of the McArthur investigation, initiatives led by organizations, such as the Alliance for South Asian AIDS Prevention, which involved postering the Village community and holding information-sharing meetings, ultimately resulted in the community making connections between McArthur's victims sooner than Toronto Police (Kur, 2021). If community organizations were able to achieve such an outcome with no additional funding, the possibilities that they can achieve if transferred funding and the responsibility with investigating "missing persons" cases could exceed expectations (Kur, 2021).

By moving away from policing and instead, trusting the familiar individuals and organizations that are better equipped to support and serve members of their own community, Toronto Police can begin to mend the existing police-citizen relationship. By stepping aside, ridding any possibility of police bias in investigations, and implementing a model that would best protect members of the LGBTQ2S+ community from violence and victimization, Toronto Police would demonstrate a concern for the wellbeing of one of the city's most vulnerable communities. It is this demonstration, this act of care, that is a step in the right direction in terms of repairing the poor relationship between the Toronto Police and the city's LGBTQ2S+ community.

CONCLUSION

The "Missing and Missed: Report of The Independent Civilian Review into Missing Person Investigations" works to mend the relationship between Toronto Police and the city's most marginalized and at-risk communities, such as the LGBTQ2S+ community, by addressing police procedure and community safety (Fox, 2021). From the "Review" comes 'next-step' guidance in the form of recommendations for changes in investigative processes (Fox, 2021; Woods, 2021). However, Valerie Pruegger, a psychology professor at the University of Calgary, argues that police services do well with creating 'next steps', but "building them into a system of change" (Uyen, 2005) has proven to not have a "lasting impact" (Uyen, 2005). Thus, for members of the LGBTQ2S+ community, those that both frequent and inhabit the Village, their suspicion of the "Review" and weariness of Toronto Police's upcoming plan of implementation, which is to be released in or before April 2022, is justified (Kur, 2021; Woods, 2021). Implemented practices and procedures should provide members, leaders, organizations, and programs that are based out of or work alongside the Village community with the ability to approach investigations involving queer folk as they deem necessary since they are within the closest proximity to the area and know its people. In fact, the new practices and procedures put in place should not position Toronto Police at the forefront of investigations, directing members of the LGBTQ2S+ community on how to proceed with cases their way or dismissing them from fully contributing to and being involved with investigative processes (Kur, 2021). Such methods would maintain a system that allows for police to hold power over queer folk; power that has evidently resulted in years of victimization (Kur, 2021). Thus, by Toronto Police 'taking a back-seat' and adopting prevention models that provide LGBTQ2S+ community members with more and often sole responsibility when addressing crime that affect their own, officers would show an acknowledgement that they may not be the best suited for matters, demonstrating a taking of accountability for their historical failed policing efforts. Implementing a prevention model that meets, addresses, and minimizes many of the concerns and demands outlined by members of the Village community is a step in the right direction for both groups in terms of repairing their poor police-citizen relationship. At the same time, by implementing practices that demonstrate a care for what happens to members of Toronto's LGBTQ2S+ community, the existing archive that maintains a falsified history of the violence and victimization experienced by queer folk can begin to be rewritten. If considered when Toronto Police make their plan of implementation, this paper's suggestions can contribute to the start of the end of decades of violence against members of Toronto's LGBTQ2S+ community, making it so queer folk are no longer victimized for simply being "out on the street" (Out on the street Toronto, n.d.).

AUTHOR NOTE

In accordance with Taylor & Francis policy and the ethical obligation of a researcher, no potential competing interests are being reported.

REFERENCES

A. (2013, November). The dark figure of crime and the reporting of crimes. *LawTeacher*. https://www.lawteacher.net/free-law-essays/criminology/the-dark-figure-of-crime.php

Aamodt, M. G., Henriques, K., & Hodges, C. (2008). Profiling the age of serial killers. *Research Gate*.

About IACP. (n.d). IACP. https://www.theiacp.org/about-iacp

About us. (n.d). MASK. https://www.ontheblock.org/about

Bandura, A. (1997). *Social learning theory*. Prentice Hall.

Baynes, C. (2018, January 24). Serial killer Robert Pickton filmed admitting to 49 murders says he 'wanted to do one more.' *Independent*. https://www.independent.co.uk/news/world/americas/robert-pickton-video-serial-killer-women-murders-vancouver-canada-a8175716.html

Bradburn, J. (2013, February 03). *Toronto bathhouse raids (1981)*. The Canadian Encyclopedia. https://www.thecanadianencyclopedia.ca/en/article/toronto-feature-bathhouse-raids

Brockbank, N. (2019, February 08). From Project Houston to Bruce McArthur's life sentence: A timeline of what we know. *CBC News*. www.cbc.ca/news/canada/toronto/mcarthur-investigation-timeline-1.4697727

Buckley, M. (2012, March). Investigation of missing persons and suspected multiple homicides. *Missing Women Commission of Inquiry*. https://missingwomen.library.uvic.ca/wp-content/uploads/2010/10/POL-3-March-2012-MB-Policies-Practices-in-the-Investigation-of-Missing-Persons-Suspected-Multiple-Homicides.pdf

Butler, J. (2002). *Antigone's claim*. Columbia University Press.

Butler, J. (2004). *Precarious life: The powers of mourning and violence*. Verso.

CBC News. (2010, August 04). *Pickton escaped 1997 charge before murders*. https://www.cbc.ca/news/canada/british-columbia/pickton-escaped-1997-charge-before-murders-1.898052

Collard, J. (2015). Into the archive: Vancouver's Missing Women Commission of Inquiry. *Society and Space, 33*(5), 779–795. https://doi.org/10.1177/0263775815596170

Crime prevention 2019: You are crime prevention. (2019). OACP. https://www.oacp.ca/en/public-safety-and-awareness/resources/2019%20Crime%20Prevention%20Booklet.pdf

Dallas (n.d.). Domestic Violence Taskforce. https://dallascityhall.com/government/citycouncil/district13/dvtf/Pages/default.aspx

Daro, I. N. (2017, December 20). How Toronto's Gay Village is banding together after a string of deaths and disappearances. *BuzzFeed*, www.buzzfeed.com/ishmaeldaro/toronto-church-wellesley-community-response

de Oliveira, J. M., Costa, C. G., & Nogueira, C. (2013). The workings of homonormativity: Lesbian, gay, bisexual, and queer discourses on discrimination and public displays of affections in Portugal. *Journal of Homosexuality, 60*(10), 1475–1493. https://doi.org/10.1080/00918369.2013.819221

Dunn, T. (2017, June 14). With Pride approaching, concern in LGBT community about violent hate crimes. CBC News. https://www.cbc.ca/news/canada/toronto/hate-crimes-lgbtq-1.4159044

Dean, A. (2015). *Remembering Vancouver's disappeared women: Settler colonialism and the difficulty of inheritance*. University of Toronto Press.

Death investigations. (n.d.a). Justice. https://www.justice.gov.nt.ca/en/death-investigations/

Death investigations. (n.d.b). Ontario.ca. https://www.ontario.ca/page/death-investigations

Disadvantages of community policing. (n.d.). Cram. https://www.cram.com/essay/Disadvantages-Of-Community-Policing/PJCZK2VSHQU#google_vignette

Disappear. (n.d.). Macmillan Dictionary. https://www.macmillandictionary.com/dictionary/british/disappear

Egger, S. (2002). *The killers among us: An examination of serial murder and its investigation.* Prentice Hall.

Epstein, G. J. (2021). *Missing and Missed: Report of the independent civilian review,* into missing person investigations. 8e5a70b5-92aa-40ae-a0bd-e885453ee64c.filesusr.com/ugd/a94b60_eb1b274e75764885b9bf5a2347b5fad1.pdf?index=true

Fox, C. (2021, April 13). 'Misconceptions' about gay community may have 'impeded' search for Bruce McArthur's victims: Review. *CP24.* www.cp24.com/news/misconceptions-about-gay-community-may-have-impeded-search-for-bruce-mcarthur-s-victims-review-1.5385130

Godderis, R., & Root, J. L. (2017). Addressing sexual violence on post-secondary campuses is a collective responsibility. *Transformative Dialogues: Teaching & Learning Journal, 9*(3), 1–9.

Gordon, A. F. (1997). *Ghostly matters: Haunting and the sociological imagination.* University of Minnesota Press.

Guidotto, N. (2006). *Homo(sexual) sacer: Biopolitics and the bathhouse raids in Toronto, 1981.* Library and Archives Canada.

Hardwick, C. (2019, February 21). A comprehensive timeline of the Bruce McArthur case: From part of the community to convicted serial killer. *IN Magazine.* inmagazine.ca/2019/02/a-comprehensive-timeline-of-the-bruce-mcarthur-case-from-part-of-the-community-to-convicted-serial-killer/

Haritaworn, J., Kuntsman, A., & Posocco, S. (2014). *Queer necropolitics.* Routledge.

Hasham, A., Mathieu, E., Miller, J., Ngabo, G., Warren, M. (2019, January 29). After serial killer's guilty pleas, a Toronto community that hung 'in the balance' speaks about its relief, misery and anger. *The Star.* www.thestar.com/news/gta/2019/01/29/after-serial-killers-guilty-pleas-a-toronto-community-that-hung-in-the-balance-speaks-about-its-relief-misery-and-anger.html

Hickey, E. (2003). The less dead. *Encyclopedia of Murder and Violent Crime, 1,* 278. https://doi.org/10.4135/9781412950619.n255

Hodge, J., & Sexton, L. (2020). Examining the blue line in the rainbow: The interactions and perceptions of law enforcement among lesbian, gay, bisexual, transgender and queer communities. *Police Practice and Research, 21*(3), 246–263. https://doi.org/10.1080/15614263.2018.1526686

Home: The village. (n.d.). https://www.churchwellesleyvillage.ca/

Home. (n.d.). OACP. https://www.oacp.ca/en/index.aspx

Homicide – overview: Reporting period. (2004–2020) (n.d.). Toronto Police Services. https://app.powerbi.com/view?r=eyJrIjoiNmFiNjgyYzYtMjlhZi00ODA4LThkNjgtNDZmZWFjYjhhY2IyIiwidCI6Ijg1MjljMjI1LWFjNDMtNDc0Yy04ZmI0LTBmNDA5NWFlOGQ1ZCIsImMiOjN9

Howell, J. M. (1999). *Homicide investigation standard operating procedures.* DocPlayer. https://docplayer.net/10577046-Revised-3-01-homicide-investigation-standard-operating-procedures-john-m-howell.html

Hunt-Kennedy, S. (2021). Silence and violence in the archive of slavery. *English Language Notes, 59*(1), 222–224. https://doi.org/10.1215/00138282-8815104

Isai, V. (2018, February 02). Gay Village stalked by a serial killer … a second time? *The Star.* https://www.thestar.com/news/gta/2018/02/02/gay-village-stalked-by-a-serial-killera-second-time.html

Jacobo, J. (2018, October 08). Why the first 72 hours in a missing persons investigation are the most critical, according to criminology experts. ABC News. https://abcnews.go.com/US/72-hours-missing-persons-investigation-critical-criminology-experts/story?id=58292638

Kur, E. A. (2021). *Our response to the independent civilian review of missing persons reports.* Maggie's Toronto. https://www.maggiesto.org/post/missingpersonsreview

Leong, M. (2011, February 19). Queer and far: As many in the community move elsewhere, the Gay Village works to develop a new identity. *National Post.* nationalpost.com/posted-toronto/queer-and-far-as-many-in-the-community-move-elsewhere-the-gay-village-works-to-develop-a-new-identity

Levinson-King, R. (2019, January 29). Bruce McArthur: Toronto serial killer destroyed gay safe space. *BBC News.* www.bbc.com/news/world-us-canada-42980512

Mayor, L., White, J., Malik, S. (2018, April 04). Did a serial killer stalk Toronto's Gay Village in the '70s? *CBC News.* newsinteractives.cbc.ca/longform/toronto-gay-village-killings

Miller, M. E. (2016, February 23). 'Worst serial killer in history,' who fed prostitutes to pigs, sparks rage by publishing book. *The Washington Post.* https://www.washingtonpost.com/news/morning-mix/wp/2016/02/23/worst-serial-killer-in-history-who-fed-prostitutes-to-pigs-sparks-rage-by-publishing-book/

Missing. (n.d.). Macmillan Dictionary. https://www.macmillandictionary.com/dictionary/british/missing

Missing and Murdered Indigenous Women in British Columbia, Canada. (2014). Inter-American Commission on Human Rights. https://www.oas.org/en/iachr/reports/pdfs/indigenous-women-bc-canada-en.pdf

Missing persons unit. (n.d.). Toronto Police Service. https://www.torontopolice.on.ca/homicide/missing-persons-unit.php

Nabavi, R. T. (2012). Bandura's social learning theory & social cognitive learning theory. *Theories of Developmental Psychology, 2012*, 1–23.

Nangwaya, A. (2016, June 30). Toronto's bathhouse raids: Racialized, queer solidarity and police violence. *Pambazuka News.* https://www.pambazuka.org/gender-minorities/toronto's-bathhouse-raids-racialized-queer-solidarity-and-police-violence

Neighbourhood: The Gay Village. (n.d.). Destination Toronto. www.seetorontonow.com/explore-toronto/neighbourhoods/the-gay-village/

News Staff. (2019, February 08). Timeline of Bruce McArthur case in Toronto. *City News.* toronto.citynews.ca/2019/02/08/bruce-mcarthur-timeline/

Oakes, M. (2006, November 15). *Antigone plot summary.* https://www.uvm.edu/~jbailly/courses/tragedy/student%20second%20documents/oakes2.htm

Out on the street Toronto. (n.d.). Out on the Street. outonthestreet.ca

Petticrew, M. (2015). Time to rethink systematic review catechism? Moving from 'what works' to 'what happens'. *Systematic Reviews, 4*(36). https://doi.org/10.1186/s13643-015-0027-1

Puar, J. (2007). *Terrorist assemblages: Homonationalism in queer times.* Duke University Press.

Quinet, K. (2007). The Missing missing: Toward a quantification of serial murder victimization in the United States. *Homicide Studies, 11*(4), 319–339. https://doi.org/10.1177/1088767907307467

Rethinking community safety: A step forward for Toronto. (n.d.). Canadian Civil Liberties Association. https://neighbourhoodcentres.ca/sites/default/files/2021-01/Rethinking%20Community%20Safety%20-%20A%20Step%20Forward%20For%20Toronto%20-%20Full%20Report.pdf

Saini law. (2020, November 5). *How a Criminal Trial Works in Canada – An Overview.* Criminal Defence Law. https://www.saini-law.com/criminal-trial-process-in-canada/

Seidman, S. (1997). *Difference troubles: Queering social theory and sexual politics.* Cambridge University Press.

Section 2: Comparing police-reported crime statistics and victimization data. (2015, November 27). Statistics Canada. https://www150.statcan.gc.ca/n1/pub/85-004-x/2009001/part-partie2-eng.htm

Systemic reviews (2020, November 17). Office of the Independent Police Review Director. www.oiprd.on.ca/news/systemic-reviews/

Teitel, E. (2017, June 25). As the queer community spreads out, can the gay village remain vital? The Star. www.thestar.com/news/canada/2017/06/25/as-the-queer-community-spreads-out-can-the-gay-village-remain-vital.html

The dark figure of crime and the reporting of crime. (2021, August 26). Law Teacher. https://www.lawteacher.net/free-law-essays/criminology/the-dark-figure-of-crime.php

Understanding the Criminal Justice System. (n.d.). Windsor Police Service. https://www.police.windsor.on.ca/services/victim/Pages/Understanding-the-Criminal-Justice-System.aspx

Uyen, V. (2005). Toronto cops grudgingly accept sensitivity training. *Canadian HR Reporter, 18*(2), 1–3.

Wahab, A. (2021). When the closet is the grave: A critical review of the Bruce McArthur case. *Sexualities,* 1–18.

White, J. H., Lester, D., Gentile, M., & Jespersen, S. (2010). Serial murder: Definition and typology. *American Journal of Forensic Psychiatry, 31*(3), 17–36.

Welch, J. P. (2011). Profiling Serial Killers: A Stratified Look at Common Characteristics Spread Across Taxonomy, Race, and Gender. *Psychology of Criminal Behaviour.*

Westoll, N. (2019, February 09). Serial killer Bruce McArthur receives life sentence, no parole eligibility for 25 years. *Global News.* globalnews.ca/news/4937703/bruce-mcarthur-sentence-parole/

Woods, M. (2021, April 13). 'Profound systemic failure': 5 takeaways from the independent review of Toronto police. *Xtra**. https://xtramagazine.com/power/toronto-police-independent-review-198451

Zamon, R. (2017, June 27). Toronto comes in third in the world's most LGBT-friendly cities' ranking. Huffington Post. https://www.huffingtonpost.ca/2017/06/27/toronto-lgbt-friendly_a_23004014/

Zerkel, M. (2021, May 20). *Reimagining community safety.* American Friends Service Committee. https://www.afsc.org/blogs/news-and-commentary/reimagining-community-safety

Workplace Experiences of Lesbian and Bisexual Female Police Officers in the Royal Newfoundland Constabulary

Sulaimon Giwa (iD), Roddrick A. Colvin, Rosemary Ricciardelli, and Amanda P. Warren

ABSTRACT

Research into Canadian workplace experiences of lesbian, gay, bisexual, transgender, and queer (LGBTQ) public safety personnel is scant. This exploratory ethnographic study examined reasons for lesbian and bisexual female officers joining the police, their shared workplace experiences, perceived career barriers based on sexual orientation, and perceptions of police leadership in advancing the inclusion of LGBTQ officers in the profession. Informed by intersectionality theory and thematic analysis, indepth semistructured interviews were conducted with three active police officers in a medium-sized Canadian city. Four major themes emerged: (a) change in career paths in response to evolving life situations and desire for rewarding, nonmonotonous work; (b) latent stereotypes and biases within otherwise supportive organizational cultures; (c) sexual orientation not a barrier to career opportunities and advancement; and (d) strong support for LGBTQ diversity and inclusion at work but remaining challenges in police–LGBTQ community relations. Implications and recommendations for practice are discussed.

INTRODUCTION

Police organizations generally promote a mandate of diversity. They seek to reflect the kaleidoscope of the communities they serve, in terms of race, ethnicity, social class, gender, or sexual orientation (Bhugowandeen, 2013; Burke, 1993; Couto, 2014, 2018; Jones & Williams, 2015; Kirkup, 2013; Sklansky, 2006). Nevertheless, policing is still considered a male-dominated profession (Bevan & MacKenzie, 2012; Murray, 2021; Sklansky, 2006), underrepresenting equity-deserving groups such as women (Bikos, 2016; Franklin, 2005; Montgomery, 2012), members of visible minorities (Jain et al., 2000; Marcoux et al., 2016; Rigaux & Cunningham, 2021),[1] Indigenous people (Marcoux et al., 2016; Parent & Parent, 2019), and lesbian, gay, bisexual, transgender, and queer (LGBTQ) people (Colvin, 2012; Couto, 2014, 2018; van Ewijk, 2012). Attention has been paid to increasing the representation of women and visible minority groups in police ranks (Colvin, 2015; Gibbs, 2019; Statistics Canada, 2019). This effort has, recently, created a groundswell of need for police organizations to pursue parallel equity initiatives with LGBTQ people (Colvin, 2015; Kirkup, 2013; Pratka, 2008). Some improvement in LGBTQ representation in policing is evident due to these equity initiatives. For example, Sklansky (2006) observed that between 1992 and 2001 the number of LGBTQ officers in the San Diego Police Department increased from five to anywhere between 35 and 50. Likewise, in 2004, an estimated 20,000 LGBTQ people were reportedly employed as police officers in the UK (Blackbourn, 2006). In both contexts, the number is likely much higher today, given legal advancement in LGBTQ rights and changing attitudes toward LGBTQ people. Available Canadian data suggest that women now account for 22 percent of all police officers and that visible minorities and Indigenous people make up 8 percent and 4 percent of police officers respectively (Statistics Canada, 2019). Canadian data are not available for the number of currently active LGBTQ police members.

A growing body of international research has examined how LGBTQ officers perceive their workplace environment (Burke, 1993; Colvin, 2015; Jones & Williams, 2015; Mennicke et al., 2018; Miller et al., 2003). But, despite some improvement, LGBTQ officers still face subtle forms of discrimination such as attitudinal bias, differential treatment and stereotypes, bias allocation, workplace harassment, and challenges and barriers to promotion (Belkin & McNichol, 2002; Colvin, 2015; Mennicke et al., 2018; Miller et al., 2003). They may choose to not disclose their sexual orientation and gender identity at work, fearing isolation, harassment, bullying, and loss of participation in teams (Jones, 2015).

Most previous research on the workplace conditions of LGBTQ police officers has been conducted in the U.S. and the UK (Burke, 1993; Charles & Arndt, 2013; Colvin, 2015). Much less research has been done on the employment outcomes and experiences of Canadian LGBTQ people (Ng & Rumens, 2017; Waite et al., 2019) in general, and police officers in particular. In fact, only two such studies of LGBTQ police officers were found (Couto, 2014, 2018), both of which were gray literature—the first completed for an academic degree and the second produced for an academic institution.[2] Since workplace discrimination against LGBTQ people is a global phenomenon (Mendos, 2019), research from various social and cultural contexts is needed to improve the workplace experiences of LGBTQ police officers. Therefore, in our exploratory ethnographic study, we sought to gain insights into the workplace experiences of lesbian and bisexual female officers employed by the oldest police organization in North America (Government of Newfoundland and Labrador, n.d.).

LITERATURE REVIEW

LGBTQ Officers and Police Culture

Although there is no single police culture, police have historically regulated the construction of deviance in a society. Given the historical view of the LGBTQ identity as deviant (Burke, 1994), it too was thus policed. Couto (2014) attributed the discrimination of LGBTQ officers to police oppression of the LGBTQ community, such as the 1969 police raid on the Stonewall Inn. Applying Schein's model of organizational culture, Couto (2014) found that the police culture in Ontario, Canada, maintained and reinforced a hypermasculine and heterosexual character. Others, like Charles and Arndt (2013), noted the concept of "blue identity" to explain how inherently hypermasculine codes for behavior are reinforced through officer recruitment and training. These codes carry on throughout an officer's career.

LGBTQ-identifying police officers navigate their identities as a subculture within the larger police culture (Sklansky, 2006), which varies across services, time, and space (Chan, 1996). The level of organizational support from those in higher positions directly shapes the experiences of LGBTQ officers and impacts job satisfaction (Couto, 2014; Lloren & Parini, 2017). Although employee groups such as the Gay Officers Action League were created to address organizational concerns, ongoing exclusionary practices remain intact, causing issues for LGBTQ officers' engagement and satisfaction (Collins & Rocco, 2018; Githens & Aragon, 2007; Rennstam & Sullivan, 2018). Moreover, because the culture of policing privileges professionalism and duty over diversity (Couto, 2014), organizational support for LGBTQ officers might be perceived by some of these officers as forced (Jones & Williams, 2015).

Intersecting and Dual Identities

Charles and Arndt (2013) studied the dual identities—sexual and vocational—of lesbian and gay officers. Such officers have a unique experience compared to other socially marginalized groups, since they can choose to disclose or conceal their sexual identities (Hassell & Brandl, 2009). While their sexual identity can be marginalizing, their "blue identity" as a police officer is privileged—it is seen as the presenting identity. The decision to reveal one's sexual or gender identity at work takes into consideration physical safety and social isolation, alongside institutional considerations such as the potential impact on evaluations, opportunities for promotions, and assignments (Colvin, 2009, 2015). Miller et al. (2003) found that the decision to reveal one's sexual identity fell along a continuum; some officers were selective in who they told, whether they told anyone, or if they decided to keep their sexuality private. Disclosure often appeared at odds with police culture, which not only complicated decisions around managing a dual identity but also potentially affected LGBTQ officers' mental health, work performance, and personal relationships (Burke, 1994). A leading factor for LGBTQ officers' deciding whether to disclose was the perception and amount of discrimination experienced in the workplace; officers who were not open about their sexual orientation and gender identity faced reduced likelihood of discrimination (Jones & Williams, 2015).

The way that gender intersects with sexual orientation in police culture creates additional challenges that LGBTQ officers have to navigate. LGBTQ officers have differing experiences based on the different levels of intersecting identities. For example, Hassell and Brandl (2009) examined the impact of diversity on workplace stress, finding that individuals with the least amount of representation (e.g., lesbian, gay, and bisexual officers) had the least favorable experiences. Racialized LGBTQ officers, Miller et al. (2003) findings showed, were least likely to disclose their sexual orientation and gender identity, indicating that their intersecting identities impacted them negatively at work. They also found that gender stereotypes shape the experiences of lesbian and gay officers. Specifically, lesbian-identifying officers are viewed as more masculine than heterosexual female police officers, while gay male officers are viewed as more feminine than heterosexual male officers. Lesbian officers may experience greater acceptance within policing than their gay male counterparts, as they are seen to conform to masculine gender stereotypes (Charles & Arndt, 2013). In turn, lesbian officers are less likely to report workplace experiences of discrimination (Tucker et al., 2019). Couto (2018), however, challenged the perception that masculine stereotypes benefited lesbian-identifying officers, arguing their assumed masculinity and acceptance into the "boys' club" could be a threat to heterosexual female officers, resulting in discrimination and harassment.

Discrimination and Barriers

Charles and Arndt (2013) studied how sexual identity impacted work satisfaction for lesbian and gay officers. They found that police culture could be a hostile work environment for sexual minorities, lowering their job satisfaction. Discrimination was more common in contexts where greater supervisory discretion was perceptible, such as in the area of operational policing (Jones, 2015). Not all lesbian and gay officers in Charles and Arndt's study were open at work about their sexuality; they reported witnessing higher rates of homophobic attitudes in the workplace, influencing their decision to maintain their hidden sexuality at work.

Despite growing numbers of LGBTQ individuals joining police forces, attitudinal barriers, discrimination, and harassment still exist (Tucker et al., 2019), reflecting the experiences of the larger LGBTQ community (Mallory et al., 2015). Miller et al. (2003) lesbian, gay, and bisexual survey participants all reported experiencing antigay jokes, hearing derogatory slang, and seeing antigay graffiti or cartoons around the police station. Employment barriers—to promotion, assignments, or evaluation—were commonly experienced (Colvin, 2009). Derogatory insults, professional humiliation, physical violence, and refusal of heterosexual officers to work in close proximity with LGBTQ coworkers were also commonplace (Couto, 2014). The workplace experiences of transgender officers remains relatively unexplored, but some transgender officers have experienced harassment and discrimination (Tucker et al., 2019). Witnessed discrimination was higher than reported experienced discrimination; however, this could be attributed to the multiplier effect (Colvin, 2015). Galvin-White and O'Neal (2016) distinguished the unique barriers to advancement in employment for LGBTQ-identifying individuals as *the lavender ceiling*, which describes the struggle faced by LGBTQ officers to advance at the same rate as heterosexual coworkers.

THEORETICAL FRAMEWORK

This research study applies intersectionality as a framework for understanding the workplace experiences of lesbian and bisexual female officers. Intersectionality highlights the overlapping power relations of social identities—the ways that different aspects of identity interact and work simultaneously to shape multiple dimensions of people's experiences, especially those involving oppression and discrimination (Collins & Bilge, 2020; Crenshaw, 1989). Sexual orientation or gender identities, for example, are facets of a person's identity that influence how they experience the world (Collins & Bilge, 2020; Crenshaw, 1989; Giwa et al., 2021). In intersectionality, these identities—among others—are thought of as interlocking with the social categories of race, age, or class to create new patterns of experiences and perspectives (Razack, 2008). The characteristically White, male, hypermasculine police culture, laced with heteronormative ideals, reinforces dominant norms of sexual and gender identity (Sun & Payne, 2004). Researchers have underscored the differing experiences of lesbian versus gay officers (Bikos, 2016; Couto, 2018; Murray, 2021), noting how traditional gender stereotypes normalize the masculine characteristics of the ideal worker (Silvestri, 2017). Thus, intersectionality is ideal for understanding the ways that lesbian and bisexual female officers' multiple identities play out in the workplace, to either reproduce positions of privilege or disadvantage them.

METHODS

Study Setting and Design

In July 2014 the leading police organization for the province of Newfoundland and Labrador—the Royal Newfoundland Constabulary (RNC)—launched a video campaign aiming to remove barriers for LGBTQ people serving as police officers. The video's message of respect, tolerance, and diversity was consistent with the broader communication strategy of most police organizations in Canada, in its endorsement of a more diverse, respectful, and accepting workplace. Yet the actual quality of the climate at Canadian police organizations for nonheterosexual and gender-nonconforming officers remains understudied. In response, we employed a qualitative descriptive (Sandelowski, 2000) method of inquiry to explore how lesbian and bisexual female RNC officers experienced their work environment and the meanings they attributed to those experiences.

Recruitment and Procedures

To begin, the first author met with the RNC chief of police and one of his superintendents to discuss the goals of the research study. The chief then emailed a letter of support to the first author, signaling that the study could proceed, and delegating the aforementioned superintendent to provide ongoing support during the study period. Ethics approval for the research was obtained from the Interdisciplinary Committee on Ethics in Human Research (ICEHR Number 20181165-SW) at Memorial University of Newfoundland.

To recruit participants, a flyer was sent through the RNC's internal communication system, with the help of the superintendent. It specified that the study was not being conducted by the RNC and was not a job requirement. To protect the privacy of officers who did not wish to have their sexual orientation or gender identity known within the organization, interested participants were asked to contact the first author directly. Despite these measures, recruitment proved challenging. Over a period of three months (from February to April 2018), with recruitment extended month-by-month, only four officers indicated an interest in the study; in the end, three agreed to be interviewed.

Participants

In total, three female active-duty police officers were interviewed for the study. They self-reported as White, with a mean age of 33.6, and a combined police work experience of 22 years. They identified as either lesbian or bisexual. At the time of the study, they held at least a bachelor's degree. None of them had formally come out at work. However, they all said that their sexual orientation was known by others, suggesting that they had not kept their sexual orientation hidden. Given the small sample and the need for confidentiality and anonymity, information we can provide about the participants is limited.

Data Collection

The participants completed a consent form attesting to their understanding of the research study and their voluntary participation in it. The first author collected interview data in semistructured interviews, asking questions related to (a) reasons for choosing to become a police officer; (b) workplace treatment and experience as an LGBTQ officer; (c) impact of LGBTQ identity, if any, on career development opportunities and success; and (d) police leadership effectiveness in promoting workplace inclusion of LGBTQ officers. Interview questions were minimally to moderately structured and open-ended, to generate a detailed account of participants' experiences and to allow the research interviewer and participants to pursue additional topics of interest. The interviews took place at an agreed-upon location, and were audiorecorded and transcribed. Interviews lasted between one and two hours. Participants were offered CAD$15 compensation for their time and contribution to the study.

Data Analysis

To analyze the data, we followed Braun and Clarke's (2006) inductive thematic process. This data-driven approach to coding does not try to fit data into preexisting themes, coding frames, or researchers' analytic preconceptions, and is not bound to a theoretical framework. The first author and a graduate research assistant read the transcribed data for an overall understanding of the workplace treatment and experiences of research participants. Data saturation was reached when no new codes could be identified (Fusch & Ness, 2015). After coding all transcripts, the codes and their associated data were examined and organized in chronological order, with similarly related codes grouped into categories or themes. Selected quotations are used below, to support our research claims and to illuminate the experiences of research participants. Where necessary, quotations have been edited for grammar and readability. Pseudonyms are used to preserve the anonymity and confidentiality of research participants.

FINDINGS

Change in Career Paths in Response to Evolving Life Situations and Desire for Rewarding but Not Monotonous Work

Participants reported commonalities in the factors they described as motivating a career in policing. They described policing as paying well, and providing opportunities to engage in a range of duties and roles. Motivating factors included policing as a dependable and interesting career—particularly when other employment opportunities in the field of interest were grim. For example, one participant indicated that, despite her career interest in policy writing, she required a job that would help pay for her partner's education while supporting them both:

> My plan was to go into the not-for-profit sector, specifically policy writing or something of that nature. My wife was also going through university at the time and we were taking turns—she would go full-time and I would work full-time to pay for her university and then we would switch out. When she graduated it became very evident that I needed to perhaps find employment that was going to pay me. (Kendra)

In deciding to become a police officer, Kendra stated, she weighed her professional aspiration or interest against the practicalities of her home life and relationship, and found the latter more significant. For her, employment in the not-for-profit sector was not sustainable in the long term. She could maximize her earning potential as a police officer, to help meet her and her wife's evolving life situations; this might be harder to do in a lower-paying industry.

Participants noted a problematic lack of jobs matching their professional interests. This made policing—a good job with benefits—attractive. One participant said:

> I was working in the business field and I moved home due to something that happened in my personal life. One of my parents got sick so I moved back to Newfoundland and Labrador. I was living away and the job market here was not great for my field and I eventually applied to become a police officer. It's a good job. It's a government job, [with] good benefits. (Sandra)

Sandra had left Newfoundland and Labrador to pursue her interest in business elsewhere. She would have continued living and working outside of the province in the absence of exigent circumstances. However, on returning to care for her ill parent, she encountered the same problem that had driven her to leave in the first place—poor labor market conditions in her field of work. Believing that her business skills were transferable, she made the decision to become a police officer which, coupled with the prospect of job and financial security, enabled her to stay in Newfoundland and Labrador.

Participants were also motivated to work as police by their interpretation of the police role as nuanced and engaging rather than repetitive, thus providing them with a wealth of diverse learning experiences. As police, they would have the opportunity to interact regularly with the community and help citizens. Participating officers considered the RNC was an organization that served the community well; they wanted to be a part of it:

> I guess, in the simplest form, I joined so [that] I could help people. I wanted a career that I'd be active in doing something different every day. Something I guess where I'd be out in the community. I really like that I see different people every day—I mean, I see some of the same people every day as well, but I like that I'm out there dealing with people and every day is different. (Leslie)

According to Leslie, a career in policing offered the possibility of a dynamic, unpredictable work life, where repetitive and monotonous tasks were not the norm. She was drawn to the idea of working closely with community members and being challenged to find solutions to different and complex issues every day. The potential for direct impact, or making a change in people's lives, stood out for her as an advantage of being a police officer.

Sandra's narrative demonstrates that a person's primary reason for joining the police force might not always be altruistic. Although doing "good" and making the community "better" are ideas that resonated with Sandra, they were not the primary motivators. Sandra decided to become a police officer because it suited her lifestyle and views: "Yeah, it just suited my life at the time, so I applied and I got in. Of course, you want to do good and better the community and that stuff as well, but [those were] not my motivating factors" (Sandra). At the time, she prioritized a job matched to her current lifestyle; a perceived lack of fit might have caused her to look past the opportunity.

Supportive Organizational Culture and Confronting Latent Stereotypes and Biases

Participants described the workplace culture at the RNC as accepting and supportive. They did not feel targeted or excluded because of their sexual orientation. On the contrary, they portrayed a close-knit, family-like environment where coworkers supported them during major events in their personal and professional lives. For example, one participant who had been out at work noted:

> I can honestly say [that] my own workplace experiences have been overwhelmingly positive as an out member of the LGBTQ community. It really has been. I got engaged and married while I was working. My entire platoon came to my wedding. [B]eing a minority—as a woman—is far more damaging than being a minority as an LGBTQ at work. At work, I often have to remind the men that I work with … that I'm a lesbian and that … locker room talk and whatnot is fine, but I need [them] to reel it in because I am still a woman and I don't want to hear these things. (Kendra)

Echoing the description of other participants, Kendra shared that her workplace experience had been extremely positive. The camaraderie and sense of belonging and genuine connection she had with her coworkers were exemplified by their attendance at her wedding. This is not to say the she did not encounter challenges at work. However, her challenges were unrelated to her sexual orientation. Rather, being a woman and navigating thinly veiled treatment of women as incapable of performing police work was especially difficult:

> I just spoke to this on International Women's Day. We had a panel and I think they wanted us to say everything is great and everything is fine, but it's not. I still deal with leadership who will say, well, you can't do that by yourself; I'll send a guy with you. The same man at work would never get that treatment; he'd be able to go and do it himself. Simple small things, [such as] doing an alarm—that's a call we do 10 times a day. (Kendra)

Although Kendra did not think leadership had bad intentions in assigning a male officer to accompany her on the alarm call, for her this amounted to an underestimation of her and other women's ability to perform the duties of a police officer. This double standard was seen as unjustified; a male officer would not have been treated in the same way. During the panel on International Women's Day, leadership wanted to project the image of an organization embracing diversity and the inclusion of female officers. But their sexist practice contradicted this image, Kendra believed.

Participants described an unspoken expectation from their straight male colleagues that they would participate in the discussion of women's attractiveness in ways that objectified them. Participants believed their coworkers based this expectation on the women's emotional and sexual attraction to women. They observed that some of these male colleagues might have thought that indecorous speech about women would be okay—that it would be reciprocated, validated, and not found abhorrent. One participant had this to say:

> Like, sometimes, the guys kind of think that you have the same mindset as them. So you kind of have to put it out there that we're not the same… the way [they] see women is not how I see women and I don't really want to talk about [women] like that with them. (Leslie)

Leslie's and other participants' being sexually attracted to women became perceived, by their male colleagues, as a possible point of connection. Their male colleagues could see them as "one of the boys," unlike cisgender heterosexual women, and therefore say things to them that they might not say to heterosexual female colleagues. Having to continuously assert their gender as women, and women whose views about other women differed from their male colleagues, placed additional burdens on them.

Participants viewed their own agency and attributes as positively contributing to their experiences at work. The underlying narrative was that people "treat you the way you let them treat you." Having confidence and projecting it, participants suggested, helped them to maintain a lighthearted approach to situations that could be otherwise challenging or taboo. One participant noted:

> I'm a very confident person; I always have been. I just have never had any challenges, really… . There's a lot of black humor… . We're a bit more off color, I guess, in some of the comments that we make to each other. I'm pretty easy going: I don't take offense to very much either. (Sandra)

Sandra's self-confidence reportedly staved off any negative treatment from others and contributed to an overall positive workplace experience. Despite not encountering challenges, she thought that dark humor was pervasive in the workplace, but this was not taken seriously in a formal sense. Moreover, Sandra explained that "There's a lot of—I'm putting this in quotations—'harassment'"-type behaviors that were treated or downplayed as black humor, referring to the lighthearted way that officers talked among themselves about otherwise sensitive or taboo topics. Ultimately, though, she weathered the sometimes "off-color" culture at the RNC and maintained her easygoing demeanor by not taking things personally or as an offense.

All participants in our study believed that gay men had more challenging workplace experiences than lesbian and bisexual women. They expressed concerns that the police culture might not favor gay men coming out or self-identifying:

> I do feel like there is still work to do in terms of gay men in the policing culture. … The culture of how we talk about gay men … still [needs] a lot of work and the things that are said are still not right. So, I think the culture maybe isn't conducive to coming out if you were a gay man. (Leslie)

When asked to elaborate on this, Leslie continued:

> I think [that] as we diversify as a police force maybe that would minimize a bit, but right now, we still are predominantly White [and] cis male… . I think that … the culture especially on patrol is very much … hypermasculine… . Maybe that has something to do with it. (Leslie)

Although some progress had been made toward diversifying the workplace, the organization remained predominantly White and cis male. Leslie suggested that these factors combined with a hypermasculine police culture on patrol, where discussion about gay men might take a pejorative turn. For her, this culture reinforced the idea that being gay was incompatible with being a male police officer, an understanding that might discourage gay officers from coming out or being open about themselves. Thus, the interplay of intersectionality among gay officers was rendered invisible.

Sexual Orientation is Not a Barrier to Career Opportunities and Advancement

Participants unanimously said that their sexual orientation did not create barriers to accessing career advancement. Development opportunities and career advancement were based on seniority; there was no room there for decision-makers to discriminate against someone based on sexual orientation or gender identity. In the participants' eyes, the organization's seniority-based structure ensured that everyone was treated the same. Opportunities accrued to an individual officer based on their badge number; the person with the lowest badge number would be considered first for career development or promotion:

> Well, I feel like it's the same opportunities that anybody else with a similar badge number [would have access to], because a lot of our opportunities are based on seniority. I don't feel like my sexuality has come into any part of the equation. I'm not going to get a sergeant [position] until another few years because there are so many senior people above me who are going to get sergeant before I do. (Sandra)

While the current system of awarding career opportunities appeared equal and transparent, one participant seemed to raise doubt about the process's overall fairness, in ensuring a wider representation and advancement of LGBTQ people to leadership positions:

> [M]aybe there is something underlying there if there's only one out official that I can think of in the higher ranking but, again, that also speaks back [to the old] days. I don't think as many gay people were drawn to the profession of policing. (Leslie)

Because LGBTQ people only recently began joining the profession, and therefore had fewer years of service, in Leslie's view fewer of them were consequently in leadership positions. For Leslie, the current promotional structure might thus be contributing to the near invisibility of LGBTQ officers in leadership positions simply because it would take longer for those officers' badge numbers to reach the top of the queue.

Strong Support for LGBTQ Diversity and Inclusion at Work but Challenges Remain in Police-LGBTQ Community Relations

Participants agreed that police leadership was committed to a workplace culture inclusive of LGBTQ officers and to strong relationships with the LGBTQ community. Different initiatives evidenced this—trainings and workshops on LGBTQ language and rights, an LGBTQ recruitment video, gender-neutral washrooms, diversity bumper stickers, and rainbow flags. One commonly cited initiative was the LGBTQ diversity committee, created by police leadership to support LGBTQ officers:

> We meet and discuss ... you know, what needs to happen or bring any issues forward "..." That's something fairly new. So, we had someone in upper management who felt this [committee] was necessary ... to form, and it was put out force wide. [W]e welcome everyone's voices in this committee; it is primarily, you know, LGBTQ+-identified. But, there are also supervisors who have made the conscious decision to say, I want to sit on this committee, ... I want to have my finger on the pulse of what is happening and what needs to happen in this organization. (Kendra)

Kendra's words demonstrate that the existence of the LGBTQ diversity committee and its continued support by police leadership communicated the value that LGBTQ officers brought to the organization. Opening the committee for anyone to join empowered committee members, LGBTQ and non-LGBTQ alike, to work together to create a workplace culture that welcomed and included LGBTQ officers. However, one participant thought that external pressure for political correctness might have influenced police leadership actions regarding workplace diversity and inclusivity. When asked to clarify what she meant by "there's a lot of politics here and they [have] got to play the role," Sandra said:

> They [the RNC] want to appear to be proactive, which you know we're being by doing this. They try to keep everybody happy and, you know, the community is made [up] of LGBTQ [people] as well. We do want to recruit everybody because we want the best people to be police officers. We want LGBTQ people to want to apply. The same as any big organization, I'm sure. (Sandra)

For Sandra, the RNC was similar to any organization in which leadership aspired to work toward diversity and inclusivity. However, her use of "appear" seems to suggest a feigned commitment on the part of the leadership. For her, part of diversity and inclusion work involved keeping everyone—the LGBTQ community and the police—"happy." For the police, this could be helpful for recruiting eligible and qualified LGBTQ applicants. However, new recruits still needed to be "the best people to be police officers." In making decisions about who to hire, then, the overriding consideration should be who could do the job best and not whether one identified as LGBTQ.

Strain remains in existing police-LGBTQ community relations. One concern raised by participants was whether uniformed police should march in the local Pride parade. Discussion about a ban on uniformed police had, in their view, created a tense relationship between police and the LGBTQ community:

> I think people are frustrated about that. When part of the community doesn't want you involved in anything, I think that it kind of stings, and that's for straight police officers. I understand where they're coming from, but as a gay police officer, it stung a little bit because that's part of my identity; I identify as a police officer and I identify as a gay woman. So, when one part of my identity is saying … we don't want that part of you, it just kind of feels like I'm back there, where I could have been a police officer but I couldn't show my gay part. [I]t's a tricky thing because I understand where they're coming from and the fact that police officers can have triggering effects. I understand both sides, it's just too bad a compromise can't be made. I guess they're trying to strike a compromise. It's a hot topic for sure. (Leslie)

For Leslie the proposed ban was an organizational slight and a personal insult. It shunned police involvement in "anything" related to the LGBTQ community, which could undermine support from straight police officers. The proposed ban made her feel she had to choose between her LGBTQ identity and her police identity, rather than both identities intersecting and coexisting. Although she recognized that police could act as a trigger for some people, Leslie appealed for a compromise so police could participate in Pride in their uniforms.

Police leadership seemed to be moving in the right direction, but participants thought that more could still be done. In their view, system-wide changes were commendable but more was needed to inform officers about the LGBTQ community, which would serve to reduce intentional or unintentional offensive or derogatory treatment of certain members of the LGBTQ community:

> For sure, there is still a culture on patrol … [where a] … derogatory term or something like that [is used]. I think that maybe holding those people accountable for what they're saying and doing would suggest to the patrol that that's not going to work anymore… . [I]f we fix the culture on patrol, maybe that would spill out into our calls for services as well. So, like when we're dealing with trans members of the community, they wouldn't be snickering. I'm saying … snickering but there are comments being made, so maybe when everyone is on the same page and everyone has the same level of understanding of all the communities, the way we respond to calls will improve as well. (Leslie)

Leslie observed that holding officers accountable might help to shape their conduct on patrol, and send a clear message about unacceptable behaviors. Such accountability was required to inform existing practices when patrol responded to calls for services from LGBTQ community members. Otherwise, the potential existed for transgender individuals, for example, to be talked about in a negative or disparaging manner.

Biased or unfriendly attitudes toward LGBTQ people would be a definite barrier to LGBTQ people choosing a career in policing. However, participants felt confident that recruitment officers at RNC were neither biased nor unfriendly toward recruits who self-identified as LGBTQ. They felt that police leadership selected recruitment officers carefully for this role. Nonetheless, participants urged continued care with the selection process, to ensure the best possible outcome:

> I … think … they need to deal with the people who are like the face [of the organization], that are doing the recruiting or something like that, right. If they were biased or unfriendly toward LGBTQ [people] that would turn them off, but top management picks the recruiters, so they're not going to pick somebody who's either negative or not inclusive. (Sandra)

Sandra believed police leaders had mitigated the concern about biased or unfriendly treatment of the LGBTQ community by recruitment officers, yet continued vigilance needed to be maintained when appointing them, since they represented the face of the police organization to the public. Police recruiters who held negative opinions about LGBTQ people might inadvertently communicate the wrong impression about the workplace culture as unwelcoming to LGBTQ people, she thought, potentially driving away eligible and qualified applicants.

Participants expressed interest in having the role of an LGBTQ liaison officer included in the formal structures and operations of the organization, as part of a better practice approach to working with the LGBTQ community:

> I would like to see us have a formal LGBTQ liaison officer. We have one right now; it's not on paper, it's just sort of something that they are. But, there are other police forces [where] that's your job, you're the liaison officer, you know. (Kendra)

The role of LGBTQ liaison officer at RNC was not formally recognized. Doing so, Kendra believed, would legitimize the work being done by this person and bring the RNC in step with police organizations in other Canadian jurisdictions.

DISCUSSION

This research study sought to understand why participants chose a career in policing. We looked at their workplace experiences as self-identified lesbian and bisexual female officers, including whether their sexual orientation was a career barrier. Likewise, we investigated their perception of police leadership in advancing the inclusion of LGBTQ officers in policing. To our knowledge, this is the first study of its kind in eastern Canada, and among the first across Canada (for related studies, see Couto, 2014, 2018). Adopting an intersectionality framework was important in elucidating how the embodied identities of police officers who are LGBTQ are inseparable and mutually constitutive (Collins & Bilge, 2020; Crenshaw, 1989; Giwa et al., 2021). Some people might choose to keep their sexual orientation or gender identity hidden; nevertheless, intersectionality suggests that the experiences of LGBTQ officers might be qualitatively different from their heterosexual counterparts. Our findings provide a preliminary snapshot of the workplace experiences of lesbian and bisexual female officers in Newfoundland and Labrador, which future research could build upon.

In general, participants were motivated to join the RNC out of necessity, driven primarily by economic self-interest. They had either struggled to find work in their field or found employment opportunities and earnings in the not-for-profit sector inadequate to meet their personal, familial, and household needs. Although policing was not always participants' first career choice, it offered the potential for a higher salary and benefits. This finding corroborates that of previous studies, in which motivation among the general population for job security and benefits consistently ranked at the top of the list for why individuals joined the police (Lester, 1983; Moon & Hwang, 2004; Wu et al., 2009). Elntib and Milincic's (2021) study investigated motivations for becoming a police officer in 28 developing and developed countries. The authors found that the greater the financial pressures experienced by individuals, the more likely they were to apply to join the police. Thus, it is possible that the financial pressures experienced by participants in the current study—attributable to low-paying or poor employment opportunities in Newfoundland and Labrador—made policing a more appealing career option.

In previous research, an important reason for LGBTQ people joining the police was to help people or the community (Couto, 2014). This was the motive stated by some participants in the current study. Participants in Couto's (2014) study also indicated nonaltruistic goals, including being attracted to the paramilitary nature of policing; a desire for an exciting career; and an interest in fulfilling a childhood dream. Career opportunities, job security, and adventure were the three commonly identified nonaltruistic motives that participants in Colvin's (2015) study gave as reasons for joining the police. Colvin (2015) also reported that civic duty was ranked second as a motivation for lesbians to join the police force, and third for gay men. One participant in the current study mentioned not being motivated by altruism, though she recognized the importance of police officers doing good for others and the community. Most important for her was that the job fit her lifestyle.

Regarding their workplace experiences as lesbian and bisexual female officers, participants were unequivocally positive in their responses. None reported any negative experience relating to their sexual orientation or being out at work. They described a family-like work environment where they felt welcomed and accepted by colleagues. Being female was the more challenging issue (Couto, 2018). It was a common experience for them to be treated differently from their male colleagues who, the women sometimes felt, were perceived as more able to handle themselves on the job, such as when responding to an alarm call.

They did not report experiences relating directly to their identity as lesbian and bisexual female officers, yet their sexual orientation was leveraged by their male colleagues to hold conversations linked to the sexual objectification of women. Straight male colleagues would sometimes engage them in conversations about the sexual attractiveness of women, both inside and outside of the locker room, forcing them to assert that they did not share those views. In this way, the participants' sexual orientation became a convenient pretext for their male colleagues to reinscribe a culture of hegemonic masculinity (Connell & Messerschmidt, 2005), which served to uphold gender/sexual boundaries that still positioned women—regardless of sexual orientation—outside of the old boys' network and as objects of male sexual desire and pleasure. To some degree, these experiences mirrored those reported by Myers et al. (2004), who found that gender discrimination and homophobia in policing compounded the experiences of lesbian officers. Those officers described an overwhelming feeling of being seen by male colleagues as objects to "fuck," or having to prove themselves as female police officers. Male officers did not have to negotiate such gender-based experiences.

Burke (1994) argued that lesbian officers may experience fewer tensions at work because they are stereotyped as masculine, and therefore conforming to traditional macho police culture. Couto (2018) has suggested that LGBTQ female officers have to conform to the masculine norms of their police organizations by acting tough. However, this was not the overt sentiment found in the present study, for two possible reasons. First, participants were out at work, whereas in Couto's study this information was not evident. Because their sexual orientation was already known and accepted by colleagues, there was perhaps little or no pressure for them to act tough or masculine.

Second, participants found their confidence was a contributing factor to their generally positive experience at work. Exuding confidence sent the message that they were not to be crossed. In this way, participants constituted themselves as having agency, which allowed them to maintain a coherent sense of identity and also deal with workplace black humor. Lesbian and bisexual female officers perceived as less confident might be made to feel responsible for their negative treatment, instead of having attention focused on the employer's responsibility of addressing potentially toxic work behaviors.

Consistent with previous research, participants also viewed the workplace as much harder for gay men than for lesbian and bisexual female officers (Miller et al., 2003). Whether intentionally or unintentionally, police culture was thought to deter gay men from coming out. The perceived hypermasculine character of the workplace was understood to tacitly shape attitudes and behaviors that normalized cultural expectations of a nongay masculine identity. These expectations were reflected in how gay men were reportedly talked about at work, such as on patrol, for example. The effect of hegemonic masculinity, or what has been referred to in the literature as the "cult of masculinity" (Silvestri, 2017), may help to explain the lack of self-identified gay and bisexual male officers in the current study. Although participants referred to a well respected and out gay officer in a senior command rank, perhaps as evidence of progress, this officer's experience cannot be generalized to other gay or bisexual male officers in the organization who were not in a leadership position or had to work in contexts where their colleagues might make homophobic comments. According to the author of a post published in the *Harvard Business Review*, 71 percent of LGBT employees in senior management positions were out (Hewlett, 2011). It is possible that being in a senior leadership position provides a protective advantage that can shield one from the homophobic messages that junior-ranked gay officers, who choose to remain closeted, might be exposed to.

Colvin (2015) reported that LGBTQ officers might encounter work-related barriers due to their sexual orientation; while gay officers may be more likely to report barriers to equal employment, lesbian officers seem to experience or witness lower levels of employment-related barriers or discrimination. The current study does not support this previous finding. The participants' reported culture of acceptance and a seniority-based system for career-related opportunities and promotion might help to explain the difference in findings. Today there is an observed gap in LGBTQ officers among senior ranks, possibly because policing may not have been seen as an appealing career choice in the past, since LGBTQ people were traditionally not accepted in policing and were subjected to police violence (Mallory et al., 2015). Participants did raise the concern that since their limited years of service would underqualify them for many opportunities or promotions, the seniority-based system could be contributing to the near invisibility of LGBTQ officers in senior ranks. Diversity measures would support early opportunities for career development and promotion of LGBTQ officers into senior ranks.

Charles and Arndt's (2013) finding that institutional support can go a long way toward creating a police culture of acceptance was supported by the current study—all participants agreed that police leadership had been effective in promoting the workplace inclusion of LGBTQ people. The creation of the LGBTQ diversity committee, comprising senior command and rank-and-file officers, was evidence of the organization's commitment to being welcoming and inclusive of LGBTQ people. However, individuals still needed to be held responsible for any offensive or derogatory treatment of officers who identified with or were perceived to be LGBTQ people.

Despite participants' acknowledgment of the efforts being made to include LGBTQ officers in the workplace, they also agreed that there was room for improvement. Perhaps external rather than internal motivations could be driving current change efforts (see also Jones & Williams, 2015), one said, so that the police could be seen as progressive by the public. Such performative diversity, it was suggested, concealed the frustration among police members over the LGBTQ community's proposed ban on uniformed police in Pride.

As with all research, our study is not without limitations. First, the sample was small and consisted of only lesbian and bisexual female police officers who were White. It did not include accounts of gay, bisexual male, and transgender officers. Thus, findings cannot be said to reflect the realities of all LGBTQ police officers in the RNC, White or non-White. This is an issue for police leadership, with implications for their development of LGBTQ-inclusive workplace policies. Only participants with positive experiences chose to participate in the study, perhaps influenced by recent initiatives taken by the RNC to promote a LGBTQ supportive workplace culture. Moreover, because the study focused on LGBTQ officers, the perspectives of heterosexual cisgender officers were not considered. Future research could explore how heterosexual cisgender officers view their LGBTQ colleagues. This line of inquiry could further advance knowledge about LGBTQ officers' experiences in the workplace.

Implications and Recommendations

Knowledge of the reported motivations for why participants joined the police (financial reasons, dynamic and nonrepetitive work, and personal fit) could be used to connect with and recruit more LGBTQ people into policing (Elntib & Milincic, 2021), which could have the effect of increasing their representation in the frontline and leadership roles. We would recommend studying whether job satisfaction diminished (or not) over time with motive fulfillment (Elntib & Milincic, 2021), and possible implications for recruitment and retention of LGBTQ officers.

Even where workplace policies promote gender equity, stereotypes related to gender can operate at an implicit or unconscious level to uphold a hypermasculine culture (Connell & Messerschmidt, 2005), potentially deterring the advancement of women in policing. Although participants spoke positively about their workplace experiences as lesbian and bisexual female officers, they reported being perceived as less capable of police work than their male colleagues, due to their gender. Such possible gender-based bias and discrimination can undermine support for a gender-inclusive workplace and reinforce the view that women are not suited for policing (Veldman et al., 2017).

Stereotypical, traditional notions of masculinities in policing would be challenged if impacts on policewomen of the hypermasculinity in police culture were confronted. The macho image associated with policing operates as a barrier to women, who are seen as not measuring up in performing policing tasks due to sex- and gender-role typecasting (Bikos, 2016; Couto, 2018). Normalizing expectations of policewomen as capable professionals with valued skill sets, such as the ability to use communication to de-escalate and diffuse potentially volatile situations (Bolger, 2015) or to use weapons and excessive force less often than male officers (Schuck & Rabe-Hemp, 2005), could change police culture for the better. It could shift organizational culture away from assumptions about women's competency and ability, transgressing boundaries that limit men and women to their traditional traits. Such confrontation could also reduce the reluctance of gay or bisexual male officers to disclose their sexual orientation for fear of negative career impact or being perceived by peers as feminine or weak (Collins & Callahan, 2012; Colvin, 2015; Mennicke et al., 2018).

Participants acknowledged that police leadership had taken positive steps toward creating a diverse and more inclusive workplace culture, thus conveying the message to LGBTQ sworn police and civilian employees that they were valued. However, actions and inactions risk undermining progress, jeopardizing the gains made. Therefore, we recommend that police leadership:

Continue to support and promote the LGBTQ diversity committee as a communication channel for identifying and responding to LGBTQ issues, which may impact workplace environment and productivity. Such a committee could be effective in deliberately eliciting feedback from LGBTQ members on actions that could support gay and bisexual male officers in becoming comfortable with acknowledging their sexual orientation at work.

Offer ongoing professional development training to improve police members' understanding of implicit or unconscious gender bias and discrimination, to align policy and practice expectations on gender equality in the workplace, and communicate a zero-tolerance stance for violators.

Devise strategies to proactively combat homophobic and transphobic attitudes at all levels of the organization, especially on patrol. One way to do this would be to create an awareness campaign that educated and challenged non-LGBTQ officers to think about how their attitudes and actions (e.g., verbal comments) could be harmful to colleagues who might or might not identify as LGBTQ, and to LGBTQ community members. To keep the message of the awareness campaign fresh in officers' minds, it should be supplemented with ongoing LGBTQ training done in partnership with members of the LGBTQ community. This kind of collaborative training could help line officers and supervisors to understand the barriers faced by LGBTQ people in accessing public safety services; allay stereotypes; and support LGBTQ people, by using affirming language that is sensitive and respectful of trans- and gender-diverse people in the community.

Take steps to improve police and civilian personnel's understanding of how decisions are made regarding improving diversity and inclusion in the workplace. This could alleviate concern regarding the influence of external forces as motivating factors for organizational change.

Formalize the position of the LGBTQ liaison officer, to ensure continuous community policing support to members of the LGBTQ diversity committee and the broader LGBTQ community. This could help to address, among other things, current tension over the ban on uniformed police at Pride. When such formalization is made, senior command should communicate that throughout the organization.

Collect and analyze disaggregated workforce data to better understand how well (or not) the organization is doing in reflecting the communities they serve. Such data could then be used to improve the recruitment, hiring, and retention of police officers from historically underrepresented groups such as LGBTQ people.

CONCLUSION

Overall, we found that the culture of policing at the RNC promoted a workplace in which lesbian and bisexual female officers felt welcomed and valued. We could not ascertain the quality of the workplace environment for transgender, gay, and bisexual male officers, given their lack of participation in the research. Assumedly, such officers would benefit equally from the general actions taken by police leadership to promote LGBTQ inclusivity at work. However, the fact that none participated in the study invites the obvious question—why not?

Emerging from the research was a shared perception that the existing police culture perpetuated forms of hegemonic masculinity, reproducing traditional gender roles for women regardless of sexual orientation or gender identity, and regulating the cultural ideal of manhood for gay male officers. This culture ran counter to the goal of diversity and inclusion that the RNC sought to promote. Individuals needed to be held accountable for their role in creating a work environment that undermined women's agency or was discriminatory and paternalistic toward them. The same commitment must be made to foster attitudinal and behavioral change in the workplace, so that known or suspected gay officers would not be harmed by indignities or insensitive comments—intentional or not—made by others. Many police organizations such as the RNC are committed to embracing diversity and inclusion in all aspects of their operations; this commitment must be matched by concrete actions and strategies.

Notes

1. *Visible minority* is the term used by federal agencies in Canada, in connection with the *Employment Equity Act*, to describe people who are not Indigenous and White in race. Included in the category of visible minorities are South Asian, Chinese, Black, Filipino, Latin American, Arab, Southeast Asian, West Asian, Korean, Japanese, and others. The term is contested, and seen by many as outdated, in that it ignores the changing demographics of Canadian society. Visible minorities are, for example, the majority population in some provinces and cities across the country. Also, the term is criticized for disregarding the fact that race and ethnicity are social constructs; that barriers are rooted in historical and contemporary racial and cultural prejudices and are not a product of identities. We use the term in the current article only to be consistent with common parlance.
2. Gray literature is defined here as academic research, produced in print or electronic formats, that is not under the control of commercial publishers (Paez, 2017).

Funding

The present research was financially supported by School of Social Work Startup Funds, Memorial University of Newfoundland, SSHRC/VP Research Grant, Memorial University of Newfoundland.

ORCID

Sulaimon Giwa (ID) http://orcid.org/0000-0001-8076-0277

REFERENCES

Belkin, A., & McNichol, J. (2002). Pink and blue: Outcomes associated with the integration of open gay and lesbian personnel in the san diego police department. *Police Quarterly*, *5*(1), 63–95. https://doi.org/10.1177/109861102129198020

Bevan, M., & MacKenzie, M. H. (2012). 'Cowboy' policing versus 'the Softer Stuff'. *International Feminist Journal of Politics*, *14*(4), 508–528. https://doi.org/10.1080/14616742.2012.726095

Bhugowandeen, B. (2013). Diversity in the British Police: Adapting to a multicultural society. *Mémoire(s), identité(s), marginalité(s) dans le monde occidental contemporain*, *10*(10), 1340. https://doi.org/10.4000/mimmoc.1340

Bikos, L. J. (2016). I took the blue pill: The effect of the hegemonic masculine police culture on Canadian Policewomen's Identities [MA thesis]. Department of Sociology, Western University.

Blackbourn, D. (2006). Gay rights in the police service: Is the enemy still within? *Criminal Justice Matters*, *63*(1), 30–31. https://doi.org/10.1080/09627250608553116

Bolger, P. C. (2015). Just following orders: A meta-analysis of the correlates of american police officer use of force decisions. *American Journal of Criminal Justice*, *40*(3), 466–492. https://doi.org/10.1007/s12103-014-9278-y

Braun, V., & Clarke, V. (2006). Using thematic analysis in psychology. *Qualitative Research in Psychology*, *3*(2), 77–101. https://doi.org/10.1191/1478088706qp063oa

Burke, M. E. (1993). *Coming out of the blue: British police officers talk about their lives in "the Job" as Lesbians, Gays and Bisexuals*. Cassell.

Burke, M. E. (1994). Homosexuality as deviance: The case of the Gay Police Officer. *The British Journal of Criminology*, *34*(2), 192–203. https://doi.org/10.1093/oxfordjournals.bjc.a048402

Chan, J. (1996). Changing police culture. *British Journal of Criminology*, *36*(1), 109–134. https://doi.org/10.1093/oxfordjournals.bjc.a014061

Charles, M. W., & Arndt, L. M. R. (2013). Gay- and Lesbian-identified law enforcement officers: Intersection of career and sexual identity. *The Counseling Psychologist*, *41*(8), 1153–1185. https://doi.org/10.1177/0011000012472376

Collins, J. C., & Callahan, J. L. (2012). Risky business: Gay identity disclosure in a masculinized environment. *Human Resource Development International*, *15*(4), 455–470. https://doi.org/10.1080/13678868.2012.706427

Collins, J. C., & Rocco, T. S. (2018). Queering employee engagement to understand and improve the performance of gay male law enforcement officers: A phenomenological exploration. *Performance Improvement Quarterly*, *30*(4), 273–295. https://doi.org/10.1002/piq.21255

Collins, P. H., & Bilge, S. (2020). *Intersectionality* (2nd ed.). Polity Press.

Colvin, R. (2009). Shared perceptions among lesbian and gay police officers: Barriers and opportunities in the law Enforcement work environment. *Police Quarterly*, *12*(1), 86–101. https://doi.org/10.1177/1098611108327308

Colvin, R. (2012). *Gay and Lesbian Cops: Diversity and effective policing*. Lynne Rienner.

Colvin, R. (2015). Shared workplace experiences of Lesbian and Gay police officers in the United Kingdom. *Policing: An International Journal of Police Strategies & Management*, *38*(2), 333–349. https://doi.org/10.1108/PIJPSM-11-2014-0121

Connell, R. W., & Messerschmidt, J. W. (2005). Hegemonic masculinity: Rethinking the concept. *Gender & Society*, *19*(6), 829–859. https://doi.org/10.1177/0891243205278639

Couto, J. L. (2014). Covered in blue: Police culture and LGBT police officers in the province of Ontario. [MA thesis]. School of Communication and Culture, Royal Roads University.

Couto, J. L. (2018). Gay. Female. Cop.: The intersectionality of gender and sexual orientation in police culture. Retrieved August 12, 2020, from https://papers.ssrn.com/sol3/papers.cfm?abstract_id=3200082.

Crenshaw, K. W. (1989). Demarginalizing the intersection of race and sex: A black feminist critique of antidiscrimination doctrine. *University of Chicago Legal Forum*, *1989*(1), 139–168. https://chicagounbound.uchicago.edu/uclf/vol1989/iss1/8

Elntib, S., & Milincic, D. (2021). Motivations for becoming a police officer: A global snapshot. *Journal of Police and Criminal Psychology*, *36*(2), 211–219. https://doi.org/10.1007/s11896-020-09396-w

Franklin, C. A. (2005). Male peer support and the police culture: Understanding the resistance and opposition to women in policing. *Women & Criminal Justice*, *16*(3), 1–25. https://doi.org/10.1300/J012v16n03_01

Fusch, P. I., & Ness, L. R. (2015). Are we there yet? Data saturation in qualitative research. *The Qualitative Report*, *20*(9), 1408–1416.

Galvin-White, C. M., & O'Neal, E. N. (2016). Lesbian police officers' interpersonal working relationships and sexuality disclosure: A qualitative study. *Feminist Criminology*, *11*(3), 253–284. https://doi.org/10.1177/1557085115588359

Gibbs, J. C. (2019). Diversifying the police applicant pool: Motivations of women and minority candidates seeking police employment. *Criminal Justice Studies*, *32*(3), 207–221. https://doi.org/10.1080/1478601X.2019.1579717

Githens, R. P., Aragon, S. (2007). LGBTQ employee groups: Who are they good for? How are they organized?" Retrieved August 12, 2020, from https://scholarlycommons.pacific.edu/cgi/viewcontent.cgi?article=1309&context=ed-facpres.

Giwa, S., Colvin, R. A., Karki, K. K., Mullings, D. V., & Bagg, L. (2021). Analysis of "Yes" responses to uniformed police marching in pride: Perspectives from LGBTQ + Communities in St. John's, Newfoundland and Labrador, Canada. *SAGE Open*, *11*(2), 215824402110231. https://doi.org/10.1177/21582440211023140

Government of Newfoundland and Labrador. (n.d.). Police. Retrieved April 9, 2021, from https://www.gov.nl.ca/jps/childsupport/police/.

Hassell, K. D., & Brandl, S. G. (2009). An examination of the workplace experiences of police patrol officers: The role of race, sex, and sexual orientation. *Police Quarterly*, *12*(4), 408–430. https://doi.org/10.1177/1098611109348473

Hewlett, S. A. (2011). The cost of closeted employees. Retrieved March 16, 2021, from https://hbr.org/2011/07/the-cost-of-closeted-employees#.

Jain, H. C., Singh, P., & Agocs, C. (2000). Recruitment, selection and promotion of visible-minority and aboriginal police officers in selected Canadian Police Services. *Canadian Public Administration/Administration publique du Canada*, *43*(1), 46–74. https://doi.org/10.1111/j.1754-7121.2000.tb01560.x

Jones, M. (2015). Who forgot Lesbian, Gay, and bisexual police officers? Findings from a National Survey. *Policing*, *9*(1), 65–76. https://doi.org/10.1093/police/pau061

Jones, M., & Williams, M. L. (2015). Twenty years on: Lesbian, gay and bisexual police officers' experiences of workplace discrimination in england and wales. *Policing and Society*, *25*(2), 188–211. https://doi.org/10.1080/10439463.2013.817998

Kirkup, K. (2013). Best practices in policing and LGBTQ communities in Ontario. Retrieved August 13, 2020, from http://www.oacp.on.ca/Userfiles/Files/NewAndEvents/OACP%20LGBTQ%20final%20Nov2013.pdf.

Lester, D. (1983). Why do people become police officers: A study of reasons and their predictions of success. *Journal of Police Science and Administration*, *11*(2), 170–174.

Lloren, A., & Parini, L. (2017). How LGBT-supportive workplace policies shape the experience of Lesbian, Gay Men, and Bisexual Employees. *Sexuality Research and Social Policy*, *14*(3), 289–299. https://doi.org/10.1007/s13178-016-0253-x

Mallory, C., Hasenbush, A., Sears, B. (2015). Discrimination and harassment by Law Enforcement Officers in the LGBT Community. Retrieved August 12, 2020, from https://williamsinstitute.law.ucla.edu/wp-content/uploads/LGBT-Discrimination-by-Law-Enforcement-Mar-2015.pdf.

Marcoux, J., Nicholson, K., Kubinec, V.-L. (2016). Police diversity fails to keep pace with Canadian Populations. *CBC News*, July 14. Retrieved August 13, 2020, from https://www.cbc.ca/news/canada/police-diversity-canada-1.3677952.

Mendos, L. R. (2019). State-sponsored Homophobia. 13th ed. International Lesbian. Gay, Bisexual, Trans and Intersex Association. Retrieved August 13, 2020, from https://ilga.org/downloads/ILGA_State_Sponsored_Homophobia_2019.pdf.

Mennicke, A., Gromer, J., Oehme, K., & MacConnie, L. (2018). Workplace experiences of gay and Lesbian criminal justice officers in the United States: A qualitative investigation of officers attending a LGBT Law Enforcement Conference. *Policing and Society*, *28*(6), 712–729. https://doi.org/10.1080/10439463.2016.1238918

Miller, S. L., Forest, K. B., & Jurik, N. C. (2003). Diversity in blue: Lesbian and gay police officers in a masculine occupation. *Men and Masculinities*, *5*(4), 355–385. https://doi.org/10.1177/0095399702250841

Montgomery, R. (2012). "Gender audits in Policing Organizations." Retrieved August 13, 2020, from https://www.publicsafety.gc.ca/lbrr/archives/cnmcs-plcng/cn32523-eng.pdf.

Moon, B., & Hwang, E.-G. (2004). The reasons for choosing a career in policing among South Korean Police Cadets. *Journal of Criminal Justice*, *32*(3), 223–229. https://doi.org/10.1016/j.jcrimjus.2004.02.002

Murray, S. E. (2021). Seeing and doing gender at work: A qualitative analysis of Canadian male and female police officers. *Feminist Criminology*, *16*(1), 91–109. https://doi.org/10.1177/1557085120914351

Myers, K. A., Forest, K. B., & Miller, S. L. (2004). Officer friendly and the Tough cop: Gays and lesbians navigate homophobia and policing. *Journal of Homosexuality*, *47*(1), 17–37. https://doi.org/10.1300/J082v47n01_02

Ng, E. S., & Rumens, N. (2017). Diversity and inclusion for LGBT workers: cCurrent issues and new horizons for research. *Canadian Journal of Administrative Sciences/Revue Canadienne des Sciences de l'Administration*, *34*(2), 109–120. https://doi.org/10.1002/cjas.1443

Paez, A. (2017). Gray literature: An important resource in systematic reviews. *Journal of Evidence-Based Medicine*, *10*(3), 233–240. https://doi.org/10.1111/jebm.12266

Parent, R., & Parent, C. (2019). Diversity and policing in Canada. In J. F. Albrecht, G. den Heyer, & P. Stanislas (Eds), *Policing and minority communities: Contemporary issues and global perspectives* (pp. 145–161). Springer.

Pratka, R. (2008). Police forces are hiring more gay cops ... But can they keep us? *Xtra Magazine*, August 25. Retrieved August 13, 2020, from https://www.dailyxtra.com/police-forces-are-hiring-more-gay-cops-14937.

Razack, S. H. (2008). *Casting out: Race and the eviction of Muslims from Western Law and Politics*. University of Toronto Press.

Rennstam, J., & Sullivan, K. R. (2018). Peripheral inclusion through informal silencing and voice – A study of LGB officers in the Swedish Police. *Gender, Work & Organization, 25*(2), 177–194. https://doi.org/10.1111/gwao.12194

Rigaux, C., & Cunningham, J. B. (2021). Enhancing recruitment and retention of visible minority police officers in Canadian Policing Agencies. *Policing and Society, 31*(4), 454–482. https://doi.org/10.1080/10439463.2020.1750611

Sandelowski, M. (2000). Whatever happened to qualitative description? *Research in Nursing & Health, 23*(4), 334–340. https://doi.org/10.1002/1098-240X(200008)23:4<334::AID-NUR9>3.0.CO;2-G

Schuck, A. M., & Rabe-Hemp, C. (2005). Women police: The use of force by and against female officers. *Women & Criminal Justice, 16*(4), 91–117. https://doi.org/10.1300/J012v16n04_05

Silvestri, M. (2017). Police culture and gender: Revisiting the 'Cult of Masculinity.' *Policing: A Journal of Policy and Practice, 11*(3), 289–300. https://doi.org/10.1093/police/paw052

Sklansky, D. A. (2006). Not your Father's Police Department: Making sense of the new demographics of law enforcement. *Journal of Criminal Law & Criminology, 96*(3), 1209–1244. https://scholarlycommons.law.north-western.edu/jclc/vol96/iss3/9

Statistics Canada. (2019). Police Resources in Canada, 2018. Retrieved August 12, 2020, from https://www150.stat-can.gc.ca/n1/en/daily-quotidien/191003/dq191003a-eng.pdf?st=DON20XmH.

Sun, I. Y., & Payne, B. K. (2004). Racial differences in resolving conflicts: A comparison between Black and White Police Officers. *Crime & Delinquency, 50*(4), 516–541. https://doi.org/10.1177/0011128703259298

Tucker, J. M., Brewster, M. P., Grugan, S. T., Miller, L. M., & Mapp-Matthews, S. M. (2019). Criminal justice students' attitudes toward LGBTQ individuals and LGBTQ police officers. *Journal of Criminal Justice Education, 30*(2), 165–192. https://doi.org/10.1080/10511253.2018.1456555

van Ewijk, A. R. (2012). Diversity within Police Forces in Europe: A case for the comprehensive view. *Policing, 6*(1), 76–92. https://doi.org/10.1093/police/par048

Veldman, J., Meeussen, L., Van Laar, C., & Phalet, K. (2017). Women (Do Not) belong here: Gender-work identity conflict among female police officers. *Frontiers in Psychology, 8*(130), 130. https://doi.org/10.3389/fpsyg.2017.00130

Waite, S., Ecker, J., & Ross, L. E. (2019). A systematic review and thematic synthesis of Canada's LGBTQ2S+ employment, labour market and earnings literature. *PLoS One, 14*(10), e0223372. https://doi.org/10.1371/journal.pone.0223372

Wu, Y., Sun, I. Y., & Cretacci, M. A. (2009). A study of Cadets' motivation to become police officers in China. *International Journal of Police Science & Management, 11*(3), 377–392. https://doi.org/10.1350/ijps.2009.11.3.142

Surviving the Landings: An Autoethnographic Account of Being a Gay Female Prison Officer (in an Adult Male Prison in England)

Sarah Nixon

ABSTRACT
Female correctional staff face multiple challenges when working in a male prison environment. Perceptions of competence and gendered divisions of labor are prevalent in the negotiated order of a prison. Sexuality is a dynamic that is irrelevant to the demands of a correctional officer yet a significant identity to be managed and negotiated in interactions with both colleagues and prisoners. This study adopts an auto ethnographic approach to highlight discrimination in prison officer occupational culture. Drawing upon personal narratives whilst working in an adult male prison in England, lived experiences of homophobia and sexism are presented to identify the challenges faced as a gay female prison officer. Themes of sexual objectification, homophobia and workplace incivility identify failings within the English prison service in supporting workplace diversity and inclusivity.

INTRODUCTION

This paper explores the intersectionality between gender and sexuality in the role of prison officer and provides illustrative examples from the author's personal experience of working in a closed adult male prison in England. The aim is to contribute to the understanding of how gay[1] female prison officers experience gender, sexuality and sexual objectification during interactions with colleagues and prisoners. Themes of homophobia, heteronormativity, chivalry, benevolent sexism, sexual objectification, microaggressions, perceived levels of competence and workplace incivility are explored. This article considers the utility of autoethnography in offering an "Insider perspective" on discrimination in the workplace and through use of personal narratives, highlights distinct inadequacies that exist within the prison service around diversity and inclusion.

Whilst there has been research conducted on female prison officers (see Zimmer, 1986; Britton, 2003; Wood, 2015; Bruhn, 2013; Burdett et al., 2018) there is a gap in knowledge around the intersectionality of gender and sexuality in gay female prison officers. Female homosexuality has been researched in the police force (Burke, 1994; Couto, 2014), the military (Sinclair, 2009) and firefighters (Wright, 2008) but there is no research around LBGTQ+[2] prison officers. Therefore, this paper contributes to understanding the tensions encountered and the resilience

---

[1]The terms gay, lesbian and LGBTQ + are used interchangeably during this paper depending upon the focus given within research. LGB and LBGT precede LGBTQ + depending upon when research was conducted. The author of this paper identifies as a gay female.

[2]LGBTQ is an acronym for lesbian, gay, bisexual, transgender and queer or questioning. These terms are used to describe a person's sexual orientation or gender identity (www.gaycenter.org).

strategies adopted to working in a male prison environment. Sexuality and gender are both highly relevant to the lived experience of performing the role of prison officer, but also irrelevant to the completion of tasks that need to be done to meet prison service objectives.

The author worked at a category "B" male adult prison[3] between 2003 and 2009. The methodological approach taken in this paper is a retrospective autoethnography, by presenting an account of the lived experience of being a gay female prison officer and drawing upon insider positioning and emotional recall through reengagement with data (Gariglio, 2018). Whilst acknowledging existing research around prison officer culture and gender, autoethnography and its component of emotional recall serves as intellectual resources to help to do prison research differently (Jewkes, 2012). Personal experience methods are said to offer a new and unique vantage point from which to contribute to social science by considering macro and micro linkages between structure and agency and their intersection with each other (Laslett, 1999, p. 392 in Wall, 2016, p. 1). The distinctions and similarities between analytic and evocative autoethnography will be expanded up and this paper argues that there can be a synthesis between both branches of autoethnography. This is done through simultaneously "maintaining a strong focus upon the researcher's biographic and emotive self" (Wakeman, 2014, p. 705) and offering a more scholarly focus upon how the self is connected to a particular ethnographic context rather than merely the focus of it (Wall, 2016). This paper will engage with analytic issues rather than just telling stories (Gariglio, 2018). This synthesis allows for what Donovan (2011) identifies as the production of academically and artistically rigorous texts. This paper draws heavily upon the work of Zempi (2017), who adopted the Muslim veil to covertly explore the lived experience of discrimination from an autoethnographic perspective. The next section will present existing research around gender, sexuality and workplace culture.

SEXUALITY/IDENTITY IN THE WORKPLACE

Burke (1994, p. 189) found that heterosexuality was dominant in the police force and LBG police officers represented a "serious kind of contamination and a threat to the integrity of the British Police Service." People with an open non-heterosexual orientation at work reported discrimination and prejudice from across the police force, including derogatory discourse, professional humiliation, physical violence and a refusal from other officers to work in close proximity to LGB officers (Burke, 1994). Influential work by Scarman (1981) and Macpherson (1999) (cited in Jones & Williams, 2015) collectively highlighted the failings of the police as an institution, in accommodating and reflecting social differences as a result of their monolithic and antiquated practices.

Burke (1994) identified the double life strategies adopted by LGB officers, through an intentional disguising of sexual orientation and a strict, premeditated performance of heterosexuality throughout their careers. However, the emergence of organizations to support LGBTQ+ prison officers in England and Wales, for example, GALIPS[4] (Gays and Lesbians In the Prison Service, in England and Wales) and Pride in Prison and probation (PIPS)[5] highlight an orientation toward workplace inclusivity and diversity.

Rengers et al. (2019) explored the lived experiences of gay and lesbian humanitarian aid workers providing aid for Medicine Sans Frontier. They found that disclosure of sexual identity is

---

[3]Category 'B' prisons are either local or training prisons. Local prisons house prisoners that are taken directly from court in the local area (sentenced or on remand), and training prisons hold long-term and high-security prisoners. (from https://prisonjobs.blog.gov.uk/your-a-d-guide-on-prison-categories/).

[4]GALIPS (Gays and Lesbians in the Prison Service) (more information can be found here https://www.prisonofficers.org.uk/viewtopic.php?t=208).

[5]PIPS (Pride in Prison and Probation) More information can be found here: https://prisonjobs.blog.gov.uk/2019/07/08/openly-lgbti-in-the-prison-service-celebrating-pride/.

context dependent and has a front stage and back stage element to it. Their research participants were "out of the closet" in the office but when they entered the field of providing humanitarian aid, they hid their sexuality. Rengers et al. (2019) attribute this to different country contexts, which leads to different decisions concerning self-disclosure, which demonstrates the importance of careful sexual identity management. Crawley's (2004) research around the public and private lives of prison officers also illustrate front and back stage display of self, where identity is constantly managing and negotiated.

COMING OUT AT WORK

Denissen and Saguy (2014) state that lesbians in the building trade engage in complex risk assessments before coming out at work to their colleagues. Perceptions of organizational culture affect gay and lesbian workers' confidence around being open about their sexuality (Colgan et al., 2006 in Wright, 2013). Wood (2015) found that lesbian officers perceived that they were overlooked for promotion because of their sexuality. However, Frank (2001 in Wright, 2013) argues that many lesbian workers in male-dominated occupations find greater inclusivity than heterosexual women and may find greater levels of acceptance and comfort with male colleagues, once the possibility of a sexual relationship has been removed. Indeed, Wright (2008) argues that lesbians are often accepted into masculine cultures as "one of the lads." This aligns with Burke (1994) who argues that lesbian sexual orientations offer a waiver from social pressures to enact femininity.

Whilst this paper focuses upon female homosexuality and therefore a discussion of male sexuality is beyond the scope provided, it is important to identify how unprogressive the prison service can actually be in relation to respecting and celebrating diversity, despite the implementation of groups to support officers. In 2017, a male officer disclosed his bisexuality to colleagues at HMP Woodhill (In England) and endured 2 years of bullying around his disclosure, resulting in an employment tribunal. At the time of writing) the ex-officer was due to receive a landmark settlement from the Ministry of Justice, due to PTSD (post-traumatic stress disorder) from being bullied in the workplace (Taylor, 2019). Di Marco et al. (2018) identify that through coming out, employees can experience workplace incivility through ostracism, which is an omission of actions to involve members when it is considered appropriate according to social norm. This is evidenced through the incident at HMP Woodhill. This incident far exceeded workplace incivility and is an example of blatant homophobic bullying around sexual orientation.

GENDER, PERCEIVED COMPETENCE AND PRISON ORGANIZATIONAL CULTURE

This section highlights the role of chivalrous attitudes toward female prison officers from both male colleagues and male prisoners. Crawley (2004) suggested that male officers look to sexualize and protect female prison officers, suggesting that they are perceived to be less naturally capable than men of performing the prison officer role. However, female officers bring unique qualities to the role of prison officer and can diffuse tension between aggressive male officers and prisoners, which is supported in policing also (Lonsway, 2000). Female officers employ verbal de-escalation skills during heightened violent and aggressive incidents, which can have a calming effect on the prisoner being dealt with (Zimmer, 1986). Zimmer (1986) concludes that the macho-imperatives which characterize male-male relationships are absent with female officers and compliance is often achieved without resorting to physical force. Female officers however are afforded fewer opportunities than male colleagues to build skills or gain confidence when controlling violent prisoners in threatening situations (Zimmer, 1986). Indeed, Lawrence and Mahan (1998) identified male officers with the longest tenure of experience as being the most prone to hold negative views and opinions of the appropriateness of female officers working in male institutions. Burdett et al. (2018) found that sexism, hostility, paternalism and social alienation are maintained and reinforced in a prison environment. They state that female officers need to adopt coping strategies to build resilience in a highly gendered, masculine defined culture (Burdett et al., 2018).

Crewe (2006) identified that female prison officers are seen by male prisoners as sexual objects and deemed to be lesser attractive women who have chosen this role because they enjoy being desired. However, prisoners do demonstrate protective attitudes toward the "weaker sex" (Crewe, 2006). Crewe (2006) also found that older and married prisoners were most likely to regard female officers as worthy of respect in a way not extended to male officers. Sabo et al. (2001, p. 7) argue that prison culture "breathes masculine toughness and insensitivity and it impugns softness, caring and femininity." Prisoners are not averse to taking matters into their own hands if they feel a female officer has been treated harshly (Zimmer, 1986). Crewe (2006) states that for a large number of prisoners, assessments of female officers were not pre-determined by essentialist assumptions about femininity or sexuality. Interpersonal treatment and interest in them were deemed more important, and more often provided by female officers than male officers. Procedural legitimacy is identified as an important contributor to the social order of a prison and prisoners who feel they are treated with respect, neutrality and consistency are more likely to comply with the prison regime (Jackson et al., 2010). Zimmer (1986) argued that female officers have social worker orientations compared to male colleagues, placing value on listening to prisoner's personal problems, which Tait (2011) supports in her work around gendered approaches to caring for prisoners. This is a precarious position however because to care *too much* for prisoners is as detrimental as caring *too little*. In contrast, Murphy et al. (2007), who have all served time themselves as prisoners, found that during their custodial sentences, female officers adopted hyper masculine and aggressive personas, rather than nurturing and caring ones.

Female officers serve to soften the harsh prison environment and produce a normalizing experience for male prisoners in a hyper masculine-dominated environment (Newbold, 2005). Conversely, this can serve to remind male prisoners of "what they are missing," as they are deprived of heterosexual relationships (Sykes, 1958) and indeed many men are in prison for crimes against women, which might serve to antagonize them further. Often the presence of female authority figures had a provocative impact upon the sexual and emotional state of some prisoners (Zimmer, 1986; Richards et al., 2002). However, Crewe (2006) states that prisoners who are submissive to female officers on the basis of sexual desire or chivalry are perceived as weak or corrupted, having abandoned good judgment and are not following what it means to be a prisoner.

It is important to note that in the current penal climate, female prison officers are just as likely as male officers to be assaulted by male prisoners, as the inmate code of conduct (Sykes, 1958) around chivalry is changing. Former chief executive of HMPPS[6] Michael Spurr stated that gender equality is the reason why more female officers are assaulted by male prisoners, identifying the disappearance of long-standing traditions, norms and values amongst prisoners. The impact of austerity on staffing levels and staff competence have impacted the increasing number of assaults on female officers (see Ismail, 2019; Hymas, 2018).

INTERSECTIONALITY OF GENDER AND SEXUALITY

Couto (2014) argues that the intersectionality of gender and sexual orientation for LGBTQ female police officers exposes them to challenges regarding both their gender and sexual orientation, for example, workplace harassment and conformity to masculine norms. Couto's work highlights the

---

[6]Her Majesty's Prison and Probation Service is an executive agency of the Ministry of Justice responsible for the correctional services in England and Wales.

challenges which LGBTQ female officers face in finding inclusivity and support in the pursuit of finding their authentic self, legitimacy and respect as officers.

Intersectionality of gender and sexuality has been researched on females working in the construction industry (see Dennisen & Saguy, 2014; Wright, 2013). Findings suggest that male colleagues aim to establish women's sexual availability, with a readiness to label them as "dykes" if they appear to be unavailable (Paap, 2006). Paap's (2006) research explores the strategies that women adopt in presenting selves in relation to conceptions of masculinity and femininity and raises questions around the extent to which lesbians may avoid unwanted sexual attention once their sexuality is known. However, labeling women as lesbian (regardless of their actual sexual orientation) makes them less of a threat to ideologies of masculinity (Paap, 2006). Interestingly, Wright (2013) explores how women express gender and sexuality through appearances at work and how conceptions of masculinity and femininity are entwined with questions of sexuality. In the prison service appearance is homogenized through wearing a uniform, but other aspects of appearance, for example, hair style/length and jewelry can influence perceptions of sexuality and levels of femininity. Lesbians adopt a variety of gender presentations (Moore, 2006). Some are closely related to femininity, others are more closely related to masculinity and some combine elements of both. Appearance is key to treatment in the workplace and assumptions are made around body shape and appearance. Dennisen and Saguy (2014) identify the resilience strategies developed by tradeswomen, which are influenced by the intersection of sexual identity, gender presentation and body size. Androgyny and muscular appearance are synonymous with labeling of lesbians in the prison service, regardless of actual sexual orientation.

The next section will present an overview of and justification for the method used in this research, which is retrospective autoethnography. Combining analytic and evocative approaches, this paper supports synthesis between two often mutually hostile approaches (Donovan, 2011). The various theoretical and conceptual resources that have been used to make the data analytic are presented. Autoethnographic data is presented in the form of extracts from the journal kept by the author when serving as a prison officer. Extracts have been purposively selected to illustrate key themes around sexuality, gender and workplace discrimination.

METHODOLOGY

This section will outline autoethnography (AE) and discuss the utility of synthesizing evocative and analytic AE to explore the lived experience of gender and sexuality based discrimination within a prison setting. This section will detail the process of data collection and analysis, reflecting upon both the strengths and limitations of using AE as a method of critically analyzing personal experiences.

Autoethnography (AE)

According to Wall (2006), AE is a qualitative research method allowing the author to write in a highly personalized style, drawing upon their own particular experiences to extend understanding about a societal phenomenon. AE places the self as researcher and/or narrator within a social context exploring the relationship between the researcher's embodied experience, culture and cultural practices (Gariglio, 2018), with a view to offering a deeper understanding of it. AE is the critical analysis of lived experience (Ellis et al., 2011a), reflecting upon the self and the actions and reactions undergone during situated lives. Spry (2001, p. 710) defines AE as "a self-narrative that critiques the situatedness of self with others" and Ellis et al. (2011b, p. 274) state that AE "accommodates subjectivity, emotionality and the researcher's influence on research" rather than hiding from these matters or assuming that they do not exist.

AE is predominantly conceptualized as either evocative or analytic. However, these two strands of AE can be fused together to promote a greater understanding of a particular phenomenon. "Evocative" AE is a form of "writing lives and telling stories" (Bochner & Ellis, 2016) and I have drawn up on this aspect of AE to enhance understanding of my vulnerability through personal stories that demonstrate the oppressions that take place within a prison. This methodological approach allows for embodied experiences of homophobia and sexism from an informed subject position as a gay female prison officer. "Analytic" AE, grounded in Symbolic Interactionist epistemological assumptions (Gariglio, 2018), is where self and society are interconnected. This lens enhances the rigor and credibility of the account presented. Anderson's analytic AE (2006) allows for a convergence between personal experience and a commitment to theoretical analysis, allowing for analysis of data created by the self. Chang (2008, p. 51) supports Anderson's analytic AE by asserting that "mere self-exposure without profound cultural analysis and interpretation leaves … writing at the level of descriptive autobiography or memoir." Boylorn and Orbe (2014, p. 13) identify the connection between autoethnography and intersectionality, where cultural and social phenomena are used to write about personal experience from a racial, classed, gendered and sexed positionality, to identify the distinctions between the world viewed by the researcher and the world viewed by others. The value of this approach is therefore important for illuminating phenomena that is hard to reach through traditional qualitative research methods.

As Nowakowski (2016, p. 1617) argues, retrospective AE offers a "critical reflection on lived experience rather than planned research activity," which aligns with the approach taken here. The focus was upon multiple dimensions of personal biography, and use of a reflective journal kept as a prison officer allowed for critical reflection of other prison officer research, to either consolidate or challenge the personal experiences of the author. AE questions the dominant scientific paradigm and allows for other ways of knowing through sharing unique, subjective and evocative stories of experience that contribute to our understanding of the social world (Wall, 2006 in Zempi, 2017). Contreras (2013 in Wakeman, 2014) identifies what he calls a "standpoint crisis," which is the conflict between the desire to present a solid and rigorous academic contribution and the need to be honest in how biography influences research and theory. This tension is important to highlight when presenting retrospective accounts which are highly evocative and also claim to be analytic, which is the method used within this research (see also Zempi, 2017).

Using AE in Criminological Research: Insider Positioning

I am a gay female ex-prison officer with 6 years' experience in an adult male prison (in England), which positions me as having "insider" knowledge about the occupational culture of prisons. Hayfield and Huxley (2015 in Zempi, 2017) state that outsiders cannot understand or represent accurately the experiences of their participants, which is important if research is conducted around oppression, marginalization or "other" communities. However, it is important to note several things. There are several points to make here. Firstly, according to Wakeman (2014) "experience" does not directly equal "expertise." Whilst there is a lack of ex-prison officer research around occupational culture, gender and sexuality, the author does not claim ultimate authority; rather an opportunity to present an analytic account of data about self in relation to working within a prison. Much criminological research presents prison analysis in the form of inhuman data according to Bosworth et al. (2005), so the opportunity to present the lived experience of a gay female prison officer through a first-hand reflexive account of the self contributes to existing literature on gender and sexuality in a prison environment. Zempi (2017) uses AE to explore victimization through the wearing of a Muslim veil in public as part of her research. The author concludes that AE studies on victimization are extremely novel in criminological research and this paper aligns with her methodological approach in providing an insight into discrimination faced within a prison context. Wakeman (2014) suggests that prior involvement in the

various processes of criminal justice provides an enhanced heuristic perspective that criminologists should take heed of. Analytic autoethnography is not an exercise in narcissistic self-absorbed
reflection and the intention of this paper is to convey the dynamics at play surrounding gender
and sexuality in a masculine culture, through engaging with current prison sociological literature
to contextualize personal experiences.

Secondly, the researcher left the prison service in 2009 so "insider positioning" is partially relevant to today's prison climate. Accounts presented by the author are subjective and relevant to a
particular time, space and context and not representative of all gay female prison officer's experiences. Whilst the reflections in this account present valid analytic observations at the time of capture, working practices have changed in the prison service. I left the service in 2009 and the
Equality Act 2010[7] (for example) was introduced post departure, so the experiences presented in
this paper may not have unfolded in the way that they did, given recent legislation supporting
discrimination in the workplace.

Jewkes (2012) identifies how prison research can be done differently through drawing upon
autoethnography and emotion as intellectual resources. However, as Wakeman (2014) articulates,
both Sparks) and Jewkes (in Wakeman, 2014) experienced a gap of multiple years between the
autobiographical events unfolding and presentation as research, because of a trepidation around
accusations of self-absorption. There is also a gap of multiple years for me in experiencing these
events and then writing about them from an auto ethnographic perspective, but not for the reasons outlined above. Simply put, the opportunity did not arise until I was established within an
academic environment. Accomplishment of social sciences provided me with both the confidence
and critical insights to make sense of my experiences for an academic audience.

Researcher subjectivities and positionalities can enrich ethnographic accounts of the prison, as
demonstrated by Phillips and Earle (2010). The authors present a reflexive interrogation of their
prisoner identities, in which their own biographies, identities and memories framed their study
retrospectively (in Jewkes, 2012). However, Newbold et al. (2014) argue that subjective interpretation and an over-reliance on personal anecdote can endanger the credibility of research.
Newbold et al. (2014) further argue that convict criminologists (a movement of ex-prisoners who
have progressed into academia) have to put aside their prejudices, bitterness and resentments so
that it does not contaminate the credibility of their research. This paper however argues in opposition to this, as the methodological orientation adopted allows for a deep exploration of the
impact of negative emotions experienced as a result of discrimination. These emotions remain
with the author 10 years after leaving the service. The author is aware that these experiences are
located in a specific time, space and place (between 2003 and 2009 at a category "B" male adult
prison in England and Wales) and are therefore not representative of all gay female prison officer
experiences. They are not meant to be. The current academic literature to date on prison officers
has largely been written by "outsider" academics, not former officers, so this paper seeks to offer
an original contribution through autoethnography.

It is important to note the inclusion of obscene language (swearing) in the narratives, which is
an accurate representation of methods of communicating in a prison environment. According to
Baruch et al. (2017) swearing can lead to positive outcomes at the individual, interpersonal and
group levels, provide stress-relief, enrich communication and socialization, as well as being a con-
frontational method of communication. This paper demonstrates both aspects of this mode of
communication and swearing is an integral component of the narratives provided.

Wakefield (2014 in Zempi, 2017) states that AE can provide a sound epistemic platform upon
which meaningful challenges to prevailing theories of criminological subjects can be built, and a

---

[7]The **Equality Act 2010** legally protects people from discrimination in the workplace and in wider society. It replaced previous
anti-discrimination laws with a single **Act**, making the **law** easier to understand and strengthening protection in some
situations (https://www.gov.uk/guidance/equality-act-2010-guidance).

synthesis between evocative, analytic and retrospective AE seeks to contribute new knowledge around the complexities of the prison officer role.

DATA

During 6 years of employment a detailed journal was kept, documenting key events, observations and conversations that were pertinent around gender, sexuality, violence, humor and prison officer occupational culture more broadly. This gave a series of reflections to work from, although as stated already, I was unaware that at the time of recording my interactions they would be reproduced through academic writing. The original intention was to write an autobiographical account of being a female prison officer for a "lay audience," aligning with several publications to date written by prison officers. There are a range of popular nonacademic autobiographical accounts written by (mostly male) ex-prison officers (see Thompson, 2008; Samworth, 2018 for example), so a gay female perspective is a hidden narrative even within popular culture. Prison officer biographies are accessible to masses in the popular culture genre and expose the dramatic, exciting and largely violent aspects of the hidden prison world. It was upon reading one such book "Screwed" (Thompson, 2008) that I realized there was an opportunity to present my story, to compliment the array of highly masculinized views of the prison officer role. Making sense of discrimination and writing about these experiences was therapeutic and helped to cope with the stress of the job. This reflective journal serves as the data set for autoethnographic writing on prison officers. As stated already, I was not a researcher at the time of writing. However, transitioning into academia I realized that there are niche opportunities as a "pracademic" (ex-practitioner academic) to use these personal narratives in academic writing and criminology teaching. The original data was revisited using the methodological approach of retrospective autoethnography, drawing upon both evocative and analytic principles. Knowledge of penological and sociological literature on prisons and prison officer culture allowed for depth to be added to these experiences to make the data ready for analysis. Whilst the positive paradigm refutes methodologies such as AE, this account is valid, reliable and trustworthy through application of AE as a lens through which to make sense of the lived experiences around gender and sexuality. Ellis (2009 in Jewkes, 2012) asks why does social science have to be written in a way that makes detailed lived experience secondary to abstraction and statistical data. Zempi's (2017) work is of relevance here in defending criticism from more traditional methodologies on the basis that these do not allow for first-hand accounts of experiencing victimization and oppression.

DATA ANALYSIS

The data set was a collection of interactions and memories recorded in journal format from 6 years served as a prison officer (between 2003 and 2009). Often ethnographers write about epiphanies and place special emphasis on memories and emotions long after the given event has transpired (Ellis et al., 2011 in Worley, 2016). It was necessary to develop an analytical framework to code sections and generate themes that addressed the particular research focus whilst discarding other memories/stories that did not align with this focus. Whilst use of memory recall is not without criticism, each individual experience deemed relevant in the journal was relived, recalling the specifics of each interaction in terms of context, interpersonal dynamics and emotions. The reflective journal was updated to make these experiences more robust for analysis. I am a criminology lecturer and narratives/memories included in this AE piece are embedded into lecture content that I deliver to undergraduate and postgraduate students studying prison, punishment, rehabilitation and also wider criminological modules. In his memoirs of a guard research, Worley (2016) identifies the tensions around proximity, objectivity and immersion in the culture as both a prison officer and researcher. His autoethnography looks both inwardly at his own personal experiences as relevant, as well as focusing upon the wider prison culture (Worley, 2016), which has helped to synthesize the dimensions of this autoethnography.

According to Braun and Clarke (2006), a "theme" captures something important in the data in relation to the research focus, which in this paper relates to how sexuality and gender are experienced as a gay female prison officer. Braun and Clarke's (2006) model was used as a systematic approach to ensure academic rigor during analysis. Braun and Clarke (2006) identify familiarity with a data set as the initial step in thematic analysis (TA). However, an intimate familiarity with the data was already held and as I regularly draw upon these personal experiences in my academic teaching. Using the stages of the model, gender and sexuality were the initial overarching themes. Deductive TA (Braun & Clarke, 2006) was used to identify themes that I expected to find within the data to support the research focus. Symbolic interactionism largely guided the framing of key themes, as all personal experiences are grounded in interaction with prisoners, prison officers and senior management. Broader sociological constructions including Goffman's (1959) "presentation of self" and "impression management," heteronormative prison officer occupational culture, institutional homophobia, microaggression, workplace incivility and chivalry were used to code and organize narratives into meaningful sections. In addition, Syke's (1958) pains of imprisonment, particularly deprivation of heterosexual relationships is drawn upon to theorize sexual objectification from prisoners. The themes were shaped by extant literature on these topics and helped me to explore the relationships of the sub-themes in the context of gender and sexuality in the prison as a workplace. The findings, therefore, offer critical insight into discrimination and identity in a broader social context.

ETHICS

At the time of journal recordings, I did not identify as a researcher. I was a prison officer who sought to record and diarize my experiences. Reflections were recorded covertly, in the sense that they were for my own personal use. Nobody in the prison service knew about my journal. It was therefore not relevant at the time to establish boundaries around informed consent. As a result, I have been sensitive in maintaining the anonymity of all person's involvement in the writing of this paper. The interactions outlined in this paper would have happened organically anyway through my daily work interactions. Through placing myself 10 years later as the subject of inquiry, I do not feel that any ethical boundaries have been transversed. However, I am sensitive to the ethical boundaries relating to covert observations. Data collection and data analysis were conducted 10 years apart and whilst I keep in touch with many former colleagues, none of the people featured in this paper fit into this category. This makes the subject of relational ethics justifiable as ties were severed with these people when I left the service.

FINDINGS AND DISCUSSION

Sexual Objectification From Staff and Prisoners

It is evident from this following experience that prisoners like to force their masculinity upon female prison officers, asserting a level of masculinity that is intentionally threatening (Crewe, 2006). Prison deprives of heterosexual relationships (Sykes, 1958) and male prisoners use opportunities with female staff to express their virility and masculinity. In reality, unless they are engaging in sexual relations with other prisoners, prisoners are in a state of involuntary celibacy. The prisoner is "rejected, impoverished, and figuratively castrated" (Sykes & Messinger, 1960), which may pose profound threats to their personality or sense of personal worth (Sykes, 1958).

> The first time I worked on visits I experienced intense humiliation from the prisoners. We collect the prisoners from the wing and escort them to the visits hall. At the back of the hall, we have to rub down search them to make sure they are not carrying any contraband. It was a small space and there were 20 prisoners and me, and I had to take each prisoner in turn, search their upper body, then the waist band of their trousers and then their legs and arses. I learnt from day one that some prisoners enjoy being touched by a female officer and they like showing off to their mates, making inappropriate comments. On my first day, as I was crouched in front of one prisoner, searching him, he made the sexual reference of "while you're down there love". I had 20 pairs of eyes on me and I felt really intimidated. Straight out of training college, I didn't really know what to say. I could feel my face going red and knew that I was letting the cons know that I was intimidated. Same encounter, one of the cons said "miss, is it true that you like women?" Again, I didn't know how to reply. He said to his mates "I'll turn her straight lads". This was a massive reality check for me and over time I knew that I would harden up to comments like these, but it was going to be a steep learning curve and I felt really vulnerable.

In this instance, male (heterosexual) identity is threatened by the realization that a female officer may be in a same-sex relationship (and therefore engaging in sexual activity with a female, of which they are deprived). This prisoner attempted to compensate through hypermasculine behavior in front of peers, as proof of manhood. Men assert masculinity using the "coinage of women" (Cockburn, 1983) to impress others, and women become a "proving ground" for men to demonstrate their masculinity (Paap, 2006). This is certainly what my experience depicts. Crewe (2006, p. 403) found that female staff become "an outlet for fantasies of sexual contact and conquest." Close proximity to prisoners has been identified as a source of stress for prison officers (Bezerra et al., 2016) but this is something that gets routinized over time, pushed to the subconscious with a level of detachment. Officers may soon become desensitized to the impact of sexual innuendo, (I certainly did) but it is a daunting experience as a new officer, with little armory to protect self from humiliation.

The next experience identifies gender, power relations, prison officer humor and rank status in a male prison environment

> Today I was on visits and I was the only female officer working here. A prisoner had been sent some filthy (explicit) pictures of his partner and we needed to hand them back to her. I came back from lunch to find the officers having a 'very close look' at the pictures, making inappropriate sexual comments about this woman. I was drawn into this conversation when I didn't really want to be, and the officers held up the graphic images and asked me if I would "do her". This made me feel awkward and I didn't really know what to say. On the one hand they appeared to be comfortable with my sexuality, but one took it too far and said that he would love to watch. What the fuck! I could feel myself going red and getting really embarrassed. These weren't young good-looking guys, some of them would be of a similar age to my dad. I was told by the senior officer to return the photos to the woman on table X. As I walked over to her I could feel all eyes on me. They were clearly enjoying my discomfort. As a junior screw I had no choice but to follow orders. In my naivete, I actually had this conversation with her. I showed her the pictures and asked her "is this you", to which she looked embarrassed and said it was. Using humour to cope with awkwardness, I actually said "oh, I nearly didn't recognise you with your clothes on". "She saw the funny side, as did my colleagues, who were pissing themselves laughing at the front desk. But it made me feel awkward".

Sexual objectification is an integral part of masculine prison culture (Crewe, 2006). Regardless of the explicit nature of the photographs, they were only meant for the eyes of the prisoner. To have four male prison officers explicitly scrutinizing the level of sexualisation made for an uneasy encounter. Whilst somebody had to hand the photographs back, as the only female officer on duty in visits I felt there was an element of humiliation and power in making me take responsibility for this. Conversely, there was a collusive element as my colleagues treated me as "one of the lads" (see Burdett et al., 2018), which suggested a level of acceptance around sexuality. Inclusion as a lesbian prompts subjection to the rough and demeaning talk that characterizes many male interactions (Denissen, 2010), and inclusion in a misogynistic work culture (Denissen & Saguy, 2014) which is evident here. Humor is important in prisons and is an institutionalized part of prison life (Nielsen, 2011) However, it can foster both collaboration and inclusion, yet collusion and exclusion alongside friendliness and antagonism (Nielsen, 2011). Inclusive humor impacts less upon self-identity than humor that places self as the source of the joke. The context around this incident is confusing because to be the object of humor, yet to be included in a sexualized conversation, placed me in a very liminal position (Van Gennep, 1960).

The next extract illustrates hyper masculine aggressive behavior and sexual objectification. Prisoners have all day to think of ways to wind the staff up and make their lives difficult, through "playing mind games" (McDermott & King, 1988). One of the popular ways to do this is through intimidation, for example, invasion of personal space, looking female officers "up and down" and making inappropriate and sexualized remarks about their appearance. One of the most poignant experiences to illustrate this is as follows:

> I'd been in the job about 6 months and there was this con on my landing who made it a daily objective to get right in my personal space and try to intimidate me. He always said I looked sexy in my uniform. Male fantasy. He did this in a way that was actually more charismatic and less aggressive, but the subtle undertones were there. He saw me as bait. I used to call him 'Mr Curriculum Vitae' (which went right over his head) because every time I said 'hello' to him, he used to say "do you know how many banks I've robbed? Do you know how many guns I own?" to which I replied "I only asked you how you were, and to be honest, I'm not really that fucking interested!" This went on for a period of months and I refused to rise to it, although it was very stressful to have to keep my wits about me every day. One day, he was stood outside of his cell, sulking. I went up and asked him what was wrong. I actually did care about the welfare of the prisoners on my landing. He said "it's just not working, this me trying to wind you up Miss Nixon. Can you just let me in my cell please?" I even got manners! Result! He knew his place and I had stood my ground. A few weeks later, his cell mate put the bell on and I went to answer. Mr CV had taken his top off and was dominating the conversation, taking attention away from his cell mate who wanted to ask me something. Mr CV was heavily tattooed, strong body and he was flaunting it at me behind his cell door. I looked at his tattoos and said "thanks for reminding me, I need to get my nieces a new colouring book for their birthday!". His cell mate thought this was hilarious, as did I. To be fair, Mr CV saw the funny side and with no malice or aggression, he just said "fuck off you cunt". I didn't take it as malice. We were all laughing. In fact, keeping him at arm's length always, he became someone who looked out for me on the landings.

Denissen and Saguy (2013) argue that those who refuse to be sexually objectified may find themselves the target of open hostility. I agree with this to an extent during prisoner interactions. This prisoner constantly tried to undermine my authority through inappropriate behavior and used sexual language toward me, but we can see the change in his approach when he saw that it was having no impact. Worley (2016) highlights how staff prisoner interactions become normalized and can escalate toward boundary violations, which he refers to as "crossing over." Some offenders are extremely adept at breaking down the power differentials and establishing inappropriate relationships with staff (Worley, 2016). The above example demonstrates the vigilance required to keep relationships with prisoners professional and within acceptable boundaries, even if the above incident exhibits profanity toward me. Language and swearing is part of prison culture and generates shared meanings between prisoners and staff, providing that it does not cross a threshold of unacceptability. The language used by the prisoner (the "C" word) did not cross any lines for me as I had withheld a professional distance during his attempts at intimidation and accepted this was the way he communicated with others. Interestingly, once prison officers stand up to prisoners and assert their authority in a way that is perceived as appropriate (in my experience anyway), prisoners who were previously troublesome can be the best allies for officers (see Crewe et al., 2014 for an overview of staff prisoner relationships). However, when interacting with colleagues there was rarely any overt hostility but rather more subtler forms of banter and inappropriateness.

"Playing It Straight on the Landings"—Presentation of Self and Dual Identity

Sabharwal et al., (2018) research found that LBGT employees expressed a desire to hide their identity to avoid the stigma of being labeled LGBT. However, this was not an issue for me when working with colleagues, only the prisoners. Drawing upon the work of Rengers et al. (2019), having a dual sexual identity and having to constantly renegotiate sexual identity with different audiences proved to be stressful. Denial of self and adopting a false sexual identity consumed significant periods of time as I defended myself against aggressive homophobic remarks. "Presentation of self" and "impression management" (Goffman, 1959) on the landings became a survival strategy to cope in this environment and a heterosexual identity was preferred as a tool to cope with being in a hypersexualised environment.

> It occurred to me straight away that prisoners have a natural curiosity for the private lives of prison officers, and sexuality/sexual conduct is one of the popular topics of conversation aimed at new staff who are learning to be assertive and stand their ground. It's a way of intimidating and trying to break them down. I was labelled a 'lesbian' on day one, but rather than standing my ground and confirming this to the prisoners, I denied it. Why? Because I felt that in a masculine and hetersexist place like a prison, I would get an easier ride from the cons. I knew from day one though that I had a battle on my hands, for several reasons. I lived close to the jail, walked home with my girlfriend and was seen about town with her, holding hands. I even had one of them (ex-con) living on my road. Prisoners who are in and out of the nick all the time would bring with them a new level of knowledge about my sexual identity. It was a difficult time for me, as insults were banded around about my sexual identity, every time I used the word "no", which was quite a lot. Over time, when the cons got to know me and knew my work ethic, my sexuality became less relevant as they learnt to trust me. One prisoner even said that to me, which was nice, although slightly patronising. One day a con called me a "fucking dyke". I snapped and replied "Yeah, so what, does it change the way that I open and close a cell door, or hand out a toilet roll, which is what I spent most of my fucking day doing!" To my amazement, he started laughing, shrugged his shoulders and said "guess not!"

Denissen and Saguy (2014, p. 385) identify perceived risk toward coming out, falling on a continuum from "playing it straight," in which sexual orientation is hidden, to fully "coming out." It is interesting how different interactions yielded different points on the continuum in my role as prison officer. Crewe (2006) suggests that the insinuation around lesbian prison officers is that they dislike men. To keep the prisoners on side makes for an easier time as an officer on the landings and this influenced the decision to conceal my sexual identity at first; over time it became less important to most of the prisoners as they learnt to trust my integrity and my commitment to procedural legitimacy. However, I was placed in a "no-win situation" and either display of sexual identity resulted in sexual objectification from the prisoners. In a prison environment, institutional hetreosexism and heteronormative culture prevail. In agreement with Reimann (2001 in Denissen & Saguy, 2014) many lesbians adopted a hybrid strategy through selective revelation of sexual orientation in specific contexts.

WORKPLACE INCIVILITY AND STEREOTYPING

Zurbrügg and Miner (2016) identify workplace incivility as covert and subtle forms of workplace discrimination toward members of oppressed social groups. Incivility theory is defined as a low-intensity deviant workplace behavior with an ambiguous intent to harm (Anderson & Pearson, 1999). The following extract depicts how sexual identity as a gay female officer was used to categorize and stereotype, rather than the occupational identity I held as a prison officer

> I was going about my landing officer duties when I heard one of the female governors shout "Nicky, Nicky" (names changed) and I thought that was strange because I hadn't seen Nicky today. Nicky was also a gay female officer and we were mates from the gay scene. So, I carried on, ignoring the governor's shouts, but she got closer and continued to shout. She caught up with me and tapped me on the shoulder. "Nicky, I need to talk to you". I knew where this was going. I said "governor, I'm not Nicky, I'm Sarah", to which she replied, "oh, you are **the other one**!". I looked at her with amusement and said "the other one **what**, governor?" She instantly realised what she had said and went bright red. "Oh my God, I'm so sorry". To see a governor squirm though made the insult worth it.

Drawing upon incivility theory, Anderson and Pearson (1999) suggest that addressing a coworker inappropriately is an example of low-level workplace discrimination. To be addressed by the governor as *"the other one"* suggests a level of ignorance and a lack of consideration for individuality and preoccupation of identification through social group membership (Cortina, 2008) as a gay woman. Workplace incivility is not an objective phenomenon, but rather a reflection of people's interpretations of how their actions made them feel (Porath & Pearson, 2012). Multiple interpretations generate a sense of ambiguity as to the motivations behind the behavior; in this instance, it was not perceived to be threatening, just grossly inconsiderate, a poor choice of language (Di Marco et al., 2018) and arguably homophobic.

MICROAGGRESSIONS

According to Sue (2010), microaggressions are everyday slights, indignities, put downs and insults toward those who are marginalized. They are different from blatant homophobia, racism and sexism because they are outside the level of consciousness from the perpetrator and typically do not have any negative intent and hostility behind them (Sue, 2010). The following incident reflects a subtle microaggression, where intention toward harm was difficult to establish

> I had a forced absence at the weekend, to take my cat to the vets as she had been hit by a car. My job for this particular morning was to supervise the sex offenders cleaning the visits hall so I was just sat watching them, when the detail (job allocation) senior officer came in to discuss my absence. He demanded to know why I had been off at the weekend. I asked him if he thought that it was an appropriate time and place to have this conversation, in front of prisoners, which was ignored. I told him why I had been off and in ear shot of prisoners, he asked why couldn't **my girlfriend** have taken the cat to the vets, to which I replied that it was none of his business. It was obvious that the prisoners had heard this conversation and I felt humiliated that I had been 'outed', whether intentionally or not, through reference to my partner as female. I asked him if he would have had the same conversation with a male officer, to which he dismissed my question and walked off.

Assumptions were made around domestic arrangements and division of labor in a same sex relationship (Khor, 2007) and the incivility in the conduct of the senior officer indicates low level discrimination. Being "outed" in front of prisoners by a colleague is an example of a microaggression (rather than blatant homophobia), through a careless application of gender prefix to discuss my partner, which challenged the presentation of self and identity work that I did on the landings. A grievance was raised but intention could not be proved and the allegation was dropped. Mennicke et al. (2018) research identified instances where anti-harassment policies were in place but were not enforced for LGBT criminal justice workers in the US, and the example presented here suggests that policies to protect LGBTQ+ status in the prison service are ineffective.

In contrast to Charles and Rouse-Arndtl, who argue that, "the presence of homophobic microaggressions without institutional support to address the hostile environment significantly hampered job satisfaction and willingness to risk being out at work," this was a risk that I took. As part of a diversity training session in the first month of my employment, I told a large group of prison officers that I was gay, but this was not something I anticipated being shared with prisoners. Coult states that sexual orientation is a private matter and her research participants did not "wave a flag" to colleagues. I neither "waved a flag" to draw attention to my sexuality nor deceived colleagues of my sexuality, so the above situation was a violation of trust based around a very subtle and brave disclosure of sexuality at the start of my career.

Homophobia and Aggression

In contrast to low level incivility and microaggressions in the workplace, there are instances where there is a shift toward intentional and aggressive homophobia. The following extract evoked a range of emotions and highlighted a liminal status for me in the prison environment

I was on night shift and it was my turn to do the suicide checks. I went to a particular cell where a prisoner was on an ACCT document[8] and I opened the observation flap. I saw the 2 prisoners having sex, which caught me off guard. I didn't hang around too long, but I was confident that it was consensual and not rape. I went down to the wing office to tell my senior officer, mainly because I knew it would wind him up. He was everything "ophobic", but I wasn't prepared for the homophobic tirade he was about to give and his response made me really angry. He said "I hope that you are going to nick them for that[9], the dirty fucking bent bastards". He was very aggressive and clearly had an issue with homosexuality and/or male homosexual acts. I wasn't about to back down. "Who the fuck do you think you are talking to. I find that really disrespectful. I am gay, as you know". I waited for an apology, which never came. Instead, he grabbed my hand and marched me down to the segregation area to look at the prison rules. He was adamant that I should place them on report. It amused me however as I watched him struggle to fit my observations into infringements of prison rules. There is no direct rule about prisoners having sex. His lack of respect for my own sexuality really hurt though. I don't think it was intentional towards me, but this officer was "old school" and part of the homophobic culture in the prison service.

This illustrates blatant Institutional homophobia in the behavior and reaction toward male homosexual acts. Ironically, this same officer had met my partner and was openly warm to her. LaMar and Kite (1998) found attitudes toward gay men were more negative than attitudes toward lesbians, in terms of tolerance, morality and conduct, which is supported through the punitive and aggressive reaction from the senior officer. He expressed anger and a clear disgust at the idea of male homosexuality (see Tomsen, 2013). I experienced his conduct as indirect homophobia though, not intentionally directed at me but more at the physical act of two men having sex. The next example however involves an aggressive altercation with a prisoner who was explicitly contemptuous of the fact that I was perceived to be gay and also a female officer, which supports the double prejudice around gender and sexuality, as argued by Couto (2014)

I was working on the sex offenders landing (R45)[10] and there were 2 prisoners who were shouting offensive remarks aimed at me, calling me a "fucking dyke", a "chick with a dick" and "a fucking lesbo". I was getting really wound up, so I squared up to the prisoner nearest to me and asked him what his fucking problem was. He got right in my face, puffed his chest out and threated to knock me out if he ever saw me 'on road!' (outside of the prison). He said he didn't care that I was a woman, he would smash my face in. I called for assistance and another officer came over. I was shaking with anger at this point. He was escorted away to the office. I followed him into the office and told him I was going to nick him for threatening and abusive language and behaviour. He was angry, possibly on drugs. He changed tack and started saying that I didn't care about him and that he had had a shit life. I told him "you are damn right, I don't give a shit about you". Next time I worked on that landing he approached me. He had 2 black eyes and tried to offer me an apology. I refused his apology and told him to go away. One of the cleaners informed me that a few of the lads took exception to the way that he had spoken to me and they had battered him in the showers.

The prisoners had an audience on the landing and were showing off to it by behaving disrespectfully toward me. Prisoners look out for staff they trust and respect, which is supported by chivalry research between female staff and male prisoners (see Crewe, 2006). Whilst prison officers must never condone vigilante prisoner on prisoner violence, there are dynamics at play that make prisoners defend staff they trust and respect, and the boundaries become blurred in staff prisoner relationships (see Worley, 2016). Arguably, there were boundary violations from me in not reporting this violence, but I felt justified that all parties had learnt something from these interactions. Liebling (2011) identifies staff vulnerabilities working in dangerous conditions, through being isolated with violent and aggressive prisoners. I experienced a mix of complex emotions during the above incident, ranging from fear and anger to warmth toward the prisoners who believed in me as an officer.

---

[8]Using the Assessment, Care in Custody and Teamwork (ACCT) case management system prisoners are placed on a document to monitor their mood, behaviour and interactions with others.
[9]Place the prisoner on report and instigate an adjudication in front of a governor.
[10]R45 allows governors to isolate prisoners, either for their own protection or to ensure good order and discipline.

Gender and Perceived Levels of Competence

When females are judged negatively around their perceived ability to perform the role of prison officer, either by colleagues (see Zimmer, 1986; Wood, 2015) or prisoners (see Crewe, 2006), it impacts upon individual morale and creates tensions between the different groups. This is particularly noticeable when high levels of competence are needed to perform the more physical aspects of the prison officer role and female officers are questioned by (senior) members of staff

> One incident angered the fuck out of me and made me question my future in the prison service. Fortunately for me, a trusted colleague tipped me off for what was about to happen, which allowed me to manage my emotions. He told me that I was being redeployed to another part of the prison, because there was intelligence to suggest that there was going to be a fight on association[11]. Forewarned is forearmed. I attended the briefing and there were 14 officers on evening duty, a Principal officer and a female governor. This is what was said. "Officer Nixon, no disrespect to you because you are a woman, but we are expecting trouble on association and we need a male presence up there. So, I'm putting you on landing association [12]with officers x and x (both female). This was a poor decision all round because female officers can't patrol the shower/recess areas for reasons of decency. Because I knew this was coming I was able to manage my emotions more effectively than if I had heard it for the first time, but I was fucking fuming inside. I just wanted to throw my keys down and fuck off for the evening. As it happened, I had a right laugh with 2 of my female colleagues. It was the new number one female governors' first day and when she came up to ask us if everything was ok, she got it from me. I told her how this had made me feel. The Principal officer shouted up to ask us if we were ok, and I shouted back "no, you had better send a man up". This angered him, which pleased me because I wasn't done yet. I went to see him at the end of my shift, barged into his office and demanded to know what he was playing at. I asked "so, if there is a spontaneous incident on the landing, what am I supposed to do, wait for a male officer?" How dare he question my competence? I was always one of the first to jump in and react to prisoner violence. He said that he was trying to protect me. I called him a 'chauvinistic prick' and we met in the middle over a grievance procedure, which again was dismissed because of lack of proof around intent.

The implications here were around perceived competence and physical abilities of female officers and this served as a reminder of perceptions of female fragility (Burdett et al., 2018). This incident reinforces a chivalrous and overly protective attitude toward female officers, which links to benevolent sexism. Female officers spend long periods of time in places where assaults are likely, so this incident smacked of poor judgment. Gendered divisions of labor are common place in a masculine environment like a prison and female officers are often redeployed to "safe areas." Autoethnography allows for reflections around existential crises and/or transformational experiences and one of the major reasons that I left the prison service was because of the assault on my gender and perceived levels of competence.

The final extract illustrates a lack of tolerance from male prison officers toward female officers in the prison, with negative perceptions of our ability to complete physical tasks effectively. This serves to reinforce a highly gendered division of labor in a prison (Bruhn, 2013)

> We had a fight situation on evening duty and management were calling for staff to get 'kitted up' (Tornado team) [13]and go in and deal with this. I had never done this before, but was quite excited at the prospect of putting into practice what I had learnt at training college. I was laughed at, pushed out of the way by a muscular male officer and told to "go make the tea little girl". I felt dismissed and judged on the basis of my gender and perceived competence. Then I thought to myself "actually, we are all paid similar amounts of money. You go fight dickheads, I'll put the kettle on.

This particular incident highlights the hypermasculine culture of the prison environment and the perceived fragility of female officers (Burdett et al., 2018); nobody who witnessed this exchange challenged the officer who addressed me in a derogatory way. Working in a three

---

[11]A room where prisoners go to shower, make phone calls, play games and interact with other prisoners.
[12]This is where prisoners associate directly outside their cell doors on the same landing that they reside upon.
[13]'Kitted up' is prison jargon for when officers are required to change into protective uniform and go into a prison cell in a team of multiple officers, with shields to restrain and/or remove a prisoner.

officer team and using approved prison service control and restrain techniques (C and R),[14] prison officers outnumber the prisoner 3:1 in planned removals. The fact that I was not invited to participate as part of a team once again highlights the gendered assumption that a female officer should stay out of harm's way and let male officers control the situation. Crawley (2004) identifies that sexist language and a lack of perceived physical strength prevail in an environment that stresses male machismo (references of "split arses" was a very common insult toward female officers in the prison where I worked) Male prison officers thrive on the experience and performance of getting "kitted up" and using force and aggression toward prisoners. This aligns with Jester (2021), who identified a link between risk-taking masculinity and boys and toys masculinity, which are both congruent with hegemonic masculinity. This is not to say that female officers do not also behave in this way however. The gender dynamics may vary at different establishments, particularly female prisons, which reinforces the earlier point made that this paper is context specific, located in a particular time space and place. Having no direct experience working with female offenders, it is assumed that experiences of a gay female officer in the female estate might be very different to the ones outlined here in a male adult category "B" prison (see Wood, 2015 for an excellent overview of female prison officers in a female prison).

CONCLUSION

This paper draws upon autoethnography as a methodological approach to explore gender and sexuality in a male adult prison. There are several contributions that this approach has to offer the study of gay female experiences in the workplace. Combining evocative and analytic AE rather than seeing them as distinct polar opposites allows for personal stories to be merged with existing theoretical insights to make the data analytic. AE is useful in researching the lived experience of homophobia, sexism and workplace discrimination, adding depth, authenticity and credibility to recorded personal observations and experiences. Insider positioning offers a novel insight into prison officer culture and an embodied account of gender and sexuality. Moreover, the value of this approach enables sensitive and perhaps unresearchable topics to be illuminated. This paper will complement existing literature on prison officer culture, written largely from "outsider" or "partial insider" perspectives. Transitioning from prison officer to active researcher or "pracademic," personal narratives recorded a over a decade ago have been relived and reformulated, using an interactionist lens to interpret the significance of such experiences, in terms of what they can reveal about prison officer culture, from somebody who has first-hand experience of working in this environment.

Key findings from the paper include suggest that both prisoners and staff hold homophobic and sexist attitudes toward female prison officers. Gendered divisions of labor and perceived levels of competence based on gender are evident, and prisoners are not averse to behaving chivalrously around female officers, which can be both reassuring and patronizing. Presentation of self as a prison officer is integral to surviving in this environment and sexuality, whilst irrelevant to the task of prison officer, has to be managed during interactions with both staff and prisoners. However, during 6 years of service "procedural legitimacy" (Sparks & Bottoms, 1995) became more important to prisoners than sexuality and gender, as professional working relationships were established. Alarmingly, however, austerity has impacted upon and eroded the traditional "convict code" of chivalry toward female officers, meaning that female officers are just as likely to be assaulted by male prisoners in 2020 (Ismail, 2019). Shifting social and political practices are evident in my account of the prison as well as gender and sexuality. In extending this research I would recommend further focus on discrimination post austerity and the Equality Act 2010, to

---

[14]Control and restraint—where prison officers used approved prison service techniques to restrain and remove prisoners around the prison.

ascertain current experiences of homophobia and sexism within prison staff. An exploration around staff who hold discriminatory attitudes would prove insightful in further understanding the occupational culture within prisons.

This paper shines a light on the inadequacies of the prison service in tackling workplace discrimination, despite changes to legislation supporting protected characteristics of staff, for example, the Equality Act in the UK (2010). Professionalization aims to drive up standards of working practices and most public services have increased their involvement with the university sector, seeking higher standards of professional and intellectual excellence (see Green & Gates, 2014). As one of the few public services left to be professionalized, an overhaul of the prison service needs to be taken to bring the service in line with other public services around equality and diversity. The Woodhill incident (Taylor, 2019) demonstrates an urgent rethink of policy and practice to support and protect LGBTQ + staff working within the prison service. The culture of the prison service has changed immensely because of VEDS (Voluntary Early Departure scheme), however, deep-rooted discriminatory attitudes and practices still exist. Based on my analysis, the landscape of the prison demands a neater and more visible framework for addressing and eradicating discrimination. Whilst equality and diversity legislation is visible and forms part of new officer training, embodied accounts like the one presented here may help prison officers to thrive rather than merely "survive" the landings in prisons.

ACKNOWLEDGMENTS

I would like to thank Professor Rob Canton, Professor Vic Knight, Dr John Hockey and colleagues at the University of Gloucestershire for their time and effort to provide constructive feedback during the writing of this paper.

ORCID

Sarah Nixon (iD) http://orcid.org/0000-0003-4522-211X

REFERENCES

Anderson, L. (2006). Analytic autoethnography. *Journal of Contemporary Ethnography*, 35(4), 373–395. https://doi.org/10.1177/0891241605280449

Anderson, L. M., & Pearson, C. M. (1999). Tit for tat? The spiralling effect of incivility in the workplace. *Academy of Management Review*, 24(3), 452–472. https://doi.org/10.5465/amr.1999.2202131

Baruch, Y., Ollier-Malaterre, A., Prouska, R., & Bunk, J. (2017). Swearing at work: The mixed outcomes of profanity. *Journal of Managerial Psychology*, 32(2), 149–162. https://doi.org/10.1108/JMP-04-2016-0102

Bezerra, C. D. M., Assis, S. G. D., & Constantino, P. (2016). Psychological distress and work stress in correctional officers: A literature review. *Ciencia & Saude Coletiva*, 21(7), 2135–2146. https://doi.org/10.1590/1413-81232015217.00502016

Bosworth, M., Campbell, D., Demby, B., Ferranti, S. M., & Santos, M. (2005). Doing prison research: Views from inside. *Qualitative Inquiry*, 11(2), 249–264. https://doi.org/10.1177/1077800404273410

Braun, V., & Clarke, V. (2006). Using thematic analysis in psychology. *Qualitative Research in Psychology*, 3(2), 77–101. https://doi.org/10.1191/1478088706qp063oa

Britton, D. M. (2003). *At work in the iron cage: Prison as a gendered organization*. NYU Press.

Bochner, A. P., & Ellis, C. (2016). *Evocative autoethnography: Writing lives and telling stories*. Routledge.

Boylorn, R. M., & Orbe, M. P. (Eds.). (2014). *Critical autoethnography: Intersecting cultural identities in everyday life* (1st ed.). Routledge.

Bruhn, A. (2013). Gender relations and division of labour among prison officers in Swedish male prisons. *Journal of Scandinavian Studies in Criminology and Crime Prevention*, 14(2), 115–132. https://doi.org/10.1080/14043858.2013.845353

Burdett, F., Gouliquer, L., & Poulin, C. (2018). Culture of corrections: The experiences of women correctional officers. *Feminist Criminology*, 13(3), 329–349. https://doi.org/10.1177/1557085118767974

Burke, M. (1994). Homosexuality as deviance: The case of the gay police officer. *The British Journal of Criminology, 34*(2), 192–203. https://doi.org/10.1093/oxfordjournals.bjc.a048402

Chang, H. (2008). *Autoethnography as method*. Routledge.

Cockburn, C. (1983). *Brothers: Male dominance and technological change*. Pluto Press.

Cortina, L. (2008). Unseen injustice: Incivility as modern discrimination in organisations. *Academy of Management Review, 33*(1), 55–75.

Couto, J. (2014). *Covered in blue: Police culture and LGBT police officers in the province of Ontario* [MSc thesis]. Unpublished.

Crawley, E. M. (2004). *Doing prison work: The public and private lives of prison officers*. Willan Publishing.

Crawley, E. M. (2004). Emotion and performance: Prison officers and the presentation of self in prisons. *Punishment & Society, 6*(4), 411–427. https://doi.org/10.1177/1462474504046121

Crewe, B. (2006). Male prisoners' orientations towards female officers in an English prison. *Punishment & Society, 8*(4), 395–421. https://doi.org/10.1177/1462474506067565

Crewe, B., Liebling, A., & Rutherford, S. (2014). Staff-prisoner relationships, staff professionalism and the use of authority in public and private sector prisons. *Law & Social Inquiry, 2015*, 309–344.

Denissen, A. M. (2010). The right tools for the job: Constructing gender meanings and identities in the male-dominated building trades. *Human Relations, 63*(7), 1051–1069. https://doi.org/10.1177/0018726709349922

Denissen, A. M., & Saguy, A. C. (2014). Gendered homophobia and the contradictions of workplace discrimination for women in the building trades. *Gender & Society, 28*(3), 381–403. https://doi.org/10.1177/0891243213510781

Di Marco, D., Hoel, H., Arenas, A., & Munduate, L. (2018). Workplace incivility as modern sexual prejudice. *Journal of Interpersonal Violence, 33*(12), 1978–2004. https://doi.org/10.1177/0886260515621083

Donovan, N. (2011). Us and them: Seeking the autoethnographic 'we'. In D. Scott, J. Mc Carron, M. Mandere, R. Warwick, & S. Appiah (Eds.), *Creative connections: Exploring and discovering relationships* (pp. 40–45). Nottingham Trent University.

Ellis, C., Adams, T. E., & Bochner, A. P. (2011a). Autoethnography: An overview. *Historical Social Research, 36*(4), 273–290.

Ellis, C., Adams, T. E., & Bochner, A. P. (2011b). Autoethnography: An overview. *Forum: Qualitative Social Research. 12*(1), 10. https://www.qualitative-research.net/index.php/fqs/article/view/1589/3095

Gariglio, L. (2018). Doing (prison) research differently: Reflections on autoethnography and 'emotional recall'. *Oñati Socio-Legal Series, 8*(2), 205–224. https://doi.org/10.35295/osls.iisl/0000-0000-0000-0932

Goffman, E. (1959). *The presentation of self in everyday life*. Doubleday Anchor.

Green, T., & Gates, A. (2014). Understanding the process of professionalisation in the police organisation. *The Police Journal: Theory, Practice and Principles, 87*(2), 75–91. https://doi.org/10.1350/pojo.2014.87.2.662

Hymas, C. (2018). *Gender equality sees as many female prison officers assaulted as men, says head of service*. The Telegraph. https://www.telegraph.co.uk/news/2018/12/11/gender-equality-sees-many-female-prison-officers-assaulted-men/

Ismail, N. (2019). Rolling back the prison estate: The pervasive impact of macroeconomic austerity on prisoner health in England. *Journal of Public Health, 42*(3), 625–632.

Jackson, J., Tyler, T. R., Bradford, B., Taylor, D., & Shiner, M. (2010). Legitimacy and procedural justice in prisons. *Prison Service Journal, 191*, 4–10.

Jester, N. (2021). Army recruitment video advertisements in the US and UK since 2002: Challenging ideals of hegemonic military masculinity? *Media, War & Conflict, 14*(1), 57–74. https://doi.org/10.1177/1750635219859488

Jewkes, Y. (2012). Autoethnography and emotion as intellectual resources: Doing prison research differently. *Qualitative Inquiry, 18*(1), 63–75. https://doi.org/10.1177/1077800411428942

Jones, M., & Williams, M. L. (2015). Twenty years on: Lesbian, gay and bisexual police officers' experiences of workplace discrimination in England and Wales. *Policing and Society, 25*(2), 188–211. https://doi.org/10.1080/10439463.2013.817998

Khor, D. (2007). 'Doing gender': A critical review and an exploration of lesbigay domestic arrangements. *Journal of GLBT Family Studies, 3*(1), 35–73. https://doi.org/10.1300/J461v03n01_03

LaMar, L., & Kite, M. E. (1998). Sex differences in attitudes toward gay men and lesbians: A multidimensional perspective. *The Journal of Sex Research, 35*(2), 189–196.

Lawrence, R., & Mahan, S. (1998). Women corrections officers in men's prisons: Acceptance and perceived job performance. *Women and Criminal Justice, 9*(3), 63–86.

Liebling, A. (2011). Distinctions and distinctiveness in the work of prison officers: Legitimacy and authority revisited. *European Journal of Criminology, 8*(6), 484–499.

Lonsway, K. A. (2000). *Hiring & retaining more women: The advantages to law enforcement agencies*. National Center for Women & Policing.

McDermott, K., & King, R. D. (1988). Mind games: Where the action is in prison. *British Journal of Criminology, 28*(3), 357–375.

Mennicke, A., Gromer, J., Oehme, K., & MacConnie, L. (2018). Workplace experiences of gay and lesbian criminal justice officers in the United States: A qualitative investigation of officers attending a LGBT law enforcement conference. *Policing and Society*, 28(6), 712–718. https://doi.org/10.1080/10439463.2016.1238918

Moore, M. R. (2006). *Lipstick or timberlands? Meanings of gender presentation in black lesbian communities.* California Center for Population Research. https://escholarship.org/uc/item/3037s3mp

Murphy, D. S., Terry, C. M., Newbold, G., & Richards, S. C. (2007). Women guarding men. *Justice Policy Journal*, 4(2), 1–33.

Nielsen, M. M. (2011). On humour in prison. *European Journal of Criminology*, 8(6), 500–514. https://doi.org/10.1177/1477370811413818

Newbold, G. (2005). Women officers working in men's prisons. *Social Policy Journal of New Zealand*, 25, 105–117.

Newbold, G., Ian Ross, J., Jones, R. S., Richards, S. C., & Lenza, M. (2014). Prison research from the inside: The role of convict autoethnography. *Qualitative Inquiry*, 20(4), 439–448. https://doi.org/10.1177/1077800413516269

Nowakowski, A. C. (2016). You poor thing: A retrospective autoethnography of visible chronic illness as a symbolic vanishing act. *The Qualitative Report*, 21(9), 1615–1635.

Paap, K. (2006). *Working construction: Why white working-class men put themselves–and the labour movement–in harm's way.* Cornell University Press.

Phillips, C., & Earle, R. (2010). Reading difference differently? Identity, epistemology and prison ethnography. *British Journal of Criminology*, 50(2), 360–378. https://doi.org/10.1093/bjc/azp081

Porath, C. L., & Pearson, C. M. (2012). Emotional and behavioral responses to workplace incivility and the impact of hierarchical status. *Journal of Applied Social Psychology*, 42(S1), E326–E357. https://doi.org/10.1111/j.1559-1816.2012.01020.x

Rengers, J. M., Heyse, L., Otten, S., & Wittek, R. P. M. (2019). "It's not always possible to live your life openly or honestly in the same way" – Workplace inclusion of lesbian and gay humanitarian aid workers in doctors without borders. *Frontiers in Psychology*, 10, 320. https://doi.org/10.3389/fpsyg.2019.00320

Richards, S. C., Charles, M. T., & Murphy, D. S. (2002). Lady hacks and gentleman convicts. In L. F. Alarid & P. F. Cromwell (Eds.), *Correctional perspectives: Views from academics, practitioners and prisoners* (pp. 207–216). Roxbury Pub. Co.

Sabharwal, M., Levine, M. D'Agostino, H., & Nguyen, T. (2018). Inclusive work practices: Turnover intentions among LGBT employees of the U.S. Federal government. *American Review of Public Administration*, 49(4), 482–494.

Sabo, D., Kupers, T. A., & London, W. (2001). *Prison masculinities.* Temple University Press.

Samworth, N. (2018). *Strangeways: A prison officer's story.* Pan McMillan.

Sinclair, D. G. (2009). Homosexuality and the military: A review of the literature. *Journal of Homosexuality*, 56(6), 701–718. https://doi.org/10.1080/00918360903054137

Sparks, R., & Bottoms, A. E. (1995). Legitimacy and order in prisons. *The British Journal of Sociology*, 46(1), 45–62. p.60). https://doi.org/10.2307/591622

Spry, T. (2001). Performing autoethnography: An embodied methodological praxis. *Qualitative Inquiry*, 7(6), 706–732. https://doi.org/10.1177/107780040100700605

Sue, D. W. (2010). *Microaggressions in everyday life: Race, gender, and sexual orientation.* John Wiley & Sons Inc.

Sykes, G. (1958). *The society of captives: A study of a maximum-security prison.* Princetown University Press.

Sykes, G. M., & Messinger, S. (1960). *The inmate social system: Theoretical studies in social organisation of the prison* (pp. 5–19). Social Science Research Council.

Tait, S. (2011). A typology of prison officer approaches to care. *European Journal of Criminology*, 8(6), 440–454. https://doi.org/10.1177/1477370811413804

Taylor, D. (2019). *Bullied bisexual prison officer unlikely to work again, tribunal finds.* The Guardian. https://www.theguardian.com/society/2019/jun/19/bullied-bisexual-prison-officer-ben-plaistow-unlikely-work-again-tribunal

Thompson, R. (2008). *Screwed.* Headline Review.

Tomsen, S. A. (2013). Homophobic violence and masculinities in Australia. In S. Magaraggia & D. Cherubini (Eds.), *Men against women: The roots of male violence* (pp. 77–102).

Van Gennep, A. (1960). *The rites of passage* (M. B. Vizedom & G. L. Caffee, Trans.). The University of Chicago Press.

Wakeman, S. (2014). Fieldwork, biography and emotion: Doing criminological autoethnography. *British Journal of Criminology*, 54(5), 705–721. https://doi.org/10.1093/bjc/azu039

Wall, S. S. (2016). Toward a moderate autoethnography. *International Journal of Qualitative Methods*, 15(1), 1–9.

Wood, A. (2015). *Challenging occupational norms: An ethnographic study of female prison officers in a women's prison* [Unpublished PhD thesis]. University of Salford.

Worley, R. (2016). Memoirs of a guard researcher: Deconstructing the games that inmates play behind the prison walls. *Deviant Behaviour*, 37(11), 1215–1226.

Wright, T. (2008). Lesbian firefighters: Shifting the boundaries between masculinity and femininity. *Journal of Lesbian Studies*, 12(1), 103–114. https://doi.org/10.1300/10894160802174375

Wright, T. (2013). Uncovering sexuality and gender: An intersectional examination of women's experiences in UK construction. *Construction Management and Economics*, *31*(8), 832–844. https://doi.org/10.1080/01446193.2013.794297

Zempi, I. (2017). Researching victimisation using auto-ethnography: Wearing the Muslim veil in public. *Methodological Innovations*, *10*(1), 205979911772061. https://doi.org/10.1177/2059799117720617

Zimmer, L. (1986). *How women reshape the prison guard role*. University of Chicago Press.

Zurbrügg, L., & Miner, K. N. (2016). Gender, sexual orientation, and workplace incivility: Who is most targeted and who is most harmed? *Frontiers in Psychology*, *7*, 565. https://doi.org/10.3389/fpsyg.2016.00565

ᵭ OPEN ACCESS

From Victimization to Incarceration: Transgender Women in Costa Rica

Gloriana Rodriguez Alvarez ⓘ and Alejandro Fernandez Muñoz

ABSTRACT

In spite of a democratic governance model, due to cis-heteronormativity, the rights of incarcerated transgender women in Costa Rica are routinely undermined by pervasive direct, social and structural violence. In effect, their incarceration is often preceded by victimization in the public and private spheres. This paper will use in-depth interviews carried out with incarcerated transgender women to examine the social factors contributing to their vulnerability and the State's responsiveness to their needs. This will be complemented by a socio-legal analysis of the current criminal justice framework. Finally, will examine if there is compliance with international human rights conventions

INTRODUCTION

"It is said that no one truly knows a nation until one has been inside its jails. A nation should not be judged by how it treats its highest citizens, but its lowest ones" (Mandela, 1994, p. 23).

In spite of the advances made in LGBTQI rights worldwide, transgender individuals remain among the most vulnerable groups in Central America. First, it should be noted that the term transgender is "an umbrella term used to describe people with a wide range of gender identities that are different from the sex assigned at birth" (Thomas et al., 2017). In general, transgender women face high levels of violence and mass incarceration (Hereth et al., 2020). In addition, due to pervasive transphobia, transgender individuals are subjected to multiple forms of violence within their families and by the rest of society (Connell, 2021). Moreover, the lack of a trans-inclusive perspective in Costa Rica implies that the State perpetuates their marginalization and eventually criminalizes them.

This investigation will use a case study analysis based on interviews carried out in four different prisons across Costa Rica with incarcerated transgender women. The objective is to examine the social factors contributing to their vulnerability and the State's responsiveness to their needs. For this reason, the empirical research will be complemented by a socio-legal analysis of the current criminal justice framework. Finally, it will examine if there is compliance with international and regional human rights conventions during sentencing and the incarceration of transgender women.

This is an Open Access article distributed under the terms of the Creative Commons Attribution License (http://creativecommons.org/licenses/by/4.0/), which permits unrestricted use, distribution, and reproduction in any medium, provided the original work is properly cited.

It will investigate the case of Costa Rica, which is Latin America's oldest democracy, to illustrate how despite a democratic governance model, the persistence of transphobia continues to undermine their human rights. Notwithstanding the commitment to international human rights and democracy, Costa Rica remains a cis-heteronormative state. It refers to "a set of norms and values that privilege the straight line between designated sex at birth and the corresponding gender, gender roles, and gender presentation" (Rodgers et al., 2017). Applied to the State, it implies that laws, institutions, and policies operate under the assumption that citizens are heterosexual and cisgender. Far from being protected by a democratic State, their needs and vulnerabilities are not taken into account. Within the larger social context, they are treated as threats to the public order (Galindo et al., 2017). As a result, transgender women have had to carve out spaces of resistance and survival.

CURRENT STUDY

Thus far, the situation of transgender women remains under-researched. Most of the research is from the Global North. The result is that the "regimes of knowledge in Trans* Politics" are dominated by the experiences of transgender individuals in the United States and Europe (Nay, 2019). Furthermore, the legal protections, political rights and medical and psychological regulations are mainly based on those adopted by public and private institutions in the Global North. Even the "reports and surveys" about transgender individuals are mainly from the Global North (Nay, 2019).

Notwithstanding the gaps in knowledge, it should be noted that the transgender movement is gaining ground in the Global North. For instance, in the United States, since the 1980s, the term "transgender" has become an "informal umbrella term, and a 'collective political identity" (Taylor et al., 2018, p. 5). As a result of this political movement, there is growing awareness of transgender identities. There have also been notable advances regarding legal protections and policies (Taylor et al., 2018, p. 5). Likewise, in the European Union, LGBT rights have become an indicator by which "Europeanness" can be assessed. Given that the European Union is a supranational project, LGBT legislation and LGBT friendliness have become a means for creating a more regional identity (Slootmaeckers, 2020). To this end, the European Court of Human Rights and the Court of Justice of the European Union have established frameworks for transgender protection (Dunne, 2020).

In contrast, the research regarding the situation of transgender women in the Global South is limited. Gender is a social construct, which is often the result of specific social and political dynamics rather than biological truths (Freud, 1994). Hence, all the more reason to examine what this construct means in a specific social and cultural context. Transgender identities will be shaped by the social significance attached to gender. Because social context defines gender, this, in turn, affects how transgender women define themselves. In this regard, it is essential to "deconstruct the familiar perspective of gender as explained in binary opposition of Western understanding" (Ismoyo, 2020).

For this reason, it is vital to acknowledge local identity processes which inform social identities, the local institutional context which frames the pursuit of transgender rights, and the local socio-cultural context, which can either accept or reject a particular minority.

To begin with, the local identity processes in Costa Rica merit further research. It should be noted that regarding gender diversity, several terms refer to a person's identity, such as transgender, third gender, polygender, pangender, and gender-fluid (Beek et al., 2016, p. 2). Given that social identities vary depending on the temporal and spatial context, the terms employed to refer to gender-diverse individuals reflect the local identity processes. For example, in this paper, the term 'transgender' will be used since it is the most frequently used by members of the community. In the Costa Rican context, some individuals identify using the term '*trasvesti*'. Even though this term is considered offensive in some cultural contexts (Nissim, 2018; see also, BBC, 2015), in

Central America, it is sometimes "claimed by people assigned male at birth, who transit towards the female gender" (Human Rights Watch, 2020, p. 8). When used in this paper, it will appear italicized to indicate the current term selected by some individuals in Costa Rica.

In addition to exploring local identity processes, it is vital to examine the institutional context as well. The institutional context influences how transgender activism plays out. It will define the strategies used by transgender activists, and it will determine the degree of state responsiveness and State capacity when it comes to addressing those rights. For example, the rise in transgender activism in the United States is the result of grassroots organizations and alliances with gay rights groups, enabling the "incorporation into an existing social movement and its social movement organizations." (Taylor et al., 2018, p. 37). Additionally, laws and policies governing transgender rights can vary depending on the State (Taylor et al., 2018, p. 253). For this reason, "the appellate courts have played a role in how federal agencies have interpreted the definition of sex in statutes and regulations" (Taylor et al., 2018, p. 235). Hence, it is a legal strategy based on the unique legal federalism that defines the United States and which builds on previous social movements' victories. However, since Costa Rica has a different legal structure and social dynamics, this strategy is not applicable.

On a similar note, in Europe, the push for LGBT legislation reflects the supralegal structure which underpins the European Union. (Slootmaeckers, 2020). It is a legal strategy that relies on both appeals to a collective European identity and the influence of the European Union. It should be noted that Costa Rica is a member of the Organization of American States (OAS, 2021). Within the Interamerican system, the Inter-American Court of Human Rights, and the Inter-American Commission on Human Rights, are tasked with overseeing human rights. However, "its weakness lies in its lack of authority to enforce its recommendations" (Organization of American States, 2010). Subsequently, advancing human rights via regional integration is not as effective in Latin American.

Overall, in Costa Rica, much like the rest of Central America, the institutional context perpetuates discrimination against transgender individuals. However, it should be noted, an increasing number of countries have enacted laws recognizing transgender identities, such as Argentina, Colombia, Bolivia, Ecuador, and Uruguay, which have enacted laws recognizing transgender identity (REDLACTRANS, 2020). In contrast, in Central America, the protection offered to transgender rights is minimal (Campbell, 2019). To this end, Corrales (2020) analyzed LGBT legislation from 1999 to 2016 in Latin America and the Caribbean. The study examined whether each Latin-American country had legislation recognizing gender identity, same-sex marriage, same-sex civil unions, and hate crimes. Given that Costa Rica does not recognize gender identity, adoptions by LGBTQI individuals, or have anti-hate crime legislation, it is among the countries with "modest improvements" (Corrales, 2020).

Then, in 2017, the Interamerican Court of Human Rights issued *Advisory Opinion on Gender Identity, Equality, and Nondiscrimination of Same-Sex Couples (2017), OC-24/17*. This prompted a backlash within Costa Rica. According to national polls, the support for the presidential candidate from a small evangelical political party rose from 2% to 24,79% shortly after the advisory opinion was released. As a result, he came in first place during the first electoral round. He ultimately lost in the run-off election (Nájar, 2018). Nevertheless, his rapid rise on the national stage demonstrates how LGBTQ rights are still contested at the social and political levels.

Overall, the socio-cultural context can either accept or undermine transgender rights and identities. The socio-cultural context influences cognitive processes, which, in turn, determine a collective worldview, including a shared sense of right and wrong. Ultimately, "morality is in part grounded in culture" (Taylor et al., 2018, p. 5). Thus, for example, the Costa Rican socio-cultural context is influenced by dominant Christian and Catholic beliefs. As a result, the social construction of gender is often informed by these religious beliefs. It should be noted that both Catholics and Christians adhere to a strict interpretation of the gender binary (Darwin, 2020).

According to the Center for Research and Political Studies (CIEP) from the University of Costa Rica, only a third of the population supports same-sex marriage (Murillo, 2018). In effect, the legalization of same-sex marriage was not so much a reflection of popular sentiment as it reflects Costa Rica's commitment to international human rights. Although Costa Rica now recognizes same-sex marriage, it does not recognize transgender identity for men, women, or non-binary individuals. As a result, transgender and gender-expansive individuals are often rendered "invisible" (Caravaca-Morera & Padilha, 2018).

LITERATURE REVIEW

The term "transgender" is attributed to the psychiatrist John F. Oliven, who coined it in 1965. Similarly, the term was popularized by Virginia Prince (Currah et al., 2006). From an academic perspective, the field of transgender research flourishes in the nineties. Accordingly, in 1994, Susan Stryker described transgender individuals as "people who move away from the gender they were assigned at birth, people who cross over (trans-) the boundaries constructed by their culture to define and contain that gender" (Stryker, 2008). She then published the seminal text *Transgender History*, which examines the experience of transgender individuals within the United States from the 1850s to the 2000s (Stryker, 2008).

In the decades since, within the United States, transgender studies "gained the status of a recognized field". There are academic publications and university courses focused on transgender identities, experiences, and theories (Keegan, 2020). Currently, transgender research tends to examine identities within a social context, experiences within an institutional context and quantitative analyses of identities and experiences. (Schilt & Lagos, 2017).

Nevertheless, even in the United States, "little formal research on transgender prisoners exists" (Peek, 2004, p. 1218). In general, scholarship regarding incarcerated transgender women has focused on the role of patriarchy and heteronormativity within prison walls (Rosenberg & Oswin, 2015). Other studies have highlighted how incarcerated transgender individuals are subjected to "a shockingly inhumane daily existence" (Rosenblum, 1999). Moreover, research has proven that due to the prevalence of transphobia, transgender women are more likely to be incarcerated. Once incarcerated, their vulnerabilities are aggravated by prison conditions (Peek, 2004, p. 1218).

Regarding transgender women in Latin America, several studies have explored their identities, access to healthcare, motives for drug consumption, and experiences with violence in public and private settings. However, according to Loza et al. (2017), "they were generally not the target population, or, if so, the sample included a number of different Latina nationalities and cultures." Studying transgender individuals as if they were monolithic can be counterproductive because it erases the particularities of each cultural experience.

Furthermore, concerning incarcerated transgender women in Latin America, Johnson et al. (2020) carried out *An Exploratory Study of Transgender Inmate Populations in Latin America.* Their work is noteworthy because it investigates the experiences of five incarcerated women in Nicaragua and El Salvador. In other words, the neighboring Central American countries. The study concluded that incarcerated transgender women experience multiple inequities and violence because of their identities. Moreover, it affirmed the need for research to examine "how the state shapes the experiences and violence faced by transgender persons" (Johnson et al., 2020).

In Costa Rica, there is scant information regarding the situation of transgender women. For instance, there is no record of how many transgender women are in Costa Rica. This is because the national census adheres to a gender binary. Likewise, it is difficult to determine the nature and pervasiveness of violence that trans people have suffered. There are no statistics on the subject that are disaggregated by the gender identity of the victim. Victimization surveys in Costa Rica do not disaggregate data based on gender identity (INEC, 2020). Additionally, there is no category of hate crimes in the Costa Rican criminal code, making it impossible to assess its prevalence. Lastly, the police do not keep a record of complaints filed by transgender people.

With regards to *incarcerated* transgender women, there is even less information. There are previous investigations about incarcerated cisgender women carried out by NGOs (Fernández et al., 2015), universities (Palma Campos, 2011), and state institutions (ICD, 2014). However, the abovementioned investigations are limited to the ciswomen's prison system. As a result, the experience of transgender women is not included. Since there is no legal recognition of their gender identity, they are sent to men's prisons.

All in all, this investigation can contribute to the literature since it uses an intersectional lens to examine an extremely vulnerable group in a country that is often overlooked from an academic perspective. In this regard, it seeks to contribute to a gap in the literature. The paper will rely on a socio-legal analysis to appraise the current institutional and legal framework whose purpose is to guarantee the human rights of incarcerated transgender women. It will also examine if there is compliance with the human rights conventions on the topic. The legal perspective will be complemented by structured interviews with incarcerated transgender women in Costa Rica. Based on these interviews, the situation, vulnerabilities and needs of incarcerated transgender women will be explored.

METHODS

This paper seeks to explore the factors which have contributed to the incarceration of transwomen. Underlying an individual's incarceration are complex and interdependent social, political, economic, and legal factors. For this reason, the research explores the challenges (e.g., access to education, access to justice, access to work) faced by incarcerated transgender women in Costa Rica through empirical research.

Additionally, it also aims to provide a basic sociodemographic profile of incarcerated transgender women. Therefore, it was essential to explore their perspective regarding state responsiveness (or lack of) to their needs. To this end, they were asked about their experiences within the criminal justice system, the public education system, the security system, and the larger social context.

The research relied on mixed methods using structured interviews. An interviewer administered each questionnaire. All interviews were carried out in Spanish. Moreover, due to prison regulations, the interviews were not recorded. When requesting permission to enter the prison, we were only allowed to enter with printed versions of the questionnaires and pens. Hence, the interviewer would read aloud each question and then write down the answer provided by the respondent. After each question, the interviewee proceeded to the next. No follow-up questions were asked. There was a total of two interviewers: the authors of this paper. Each interviewer interviewed 8 participants each, for a total of 16 participants. Each interview lasted around an hour. The questionnaire consisted of 110 closed questions about nine main topics. For example, with regards to their education:

What is your education level?

	Complete	Incomplete (Include the last grade)
2.1.4 Primary school		
2.1.5 Highschool		
2.1.6 University		

Then, in the section regarding their work experience, the interviewees were asked the following:

What is the biggest obstacle to finding a job?

… … . Lack of education
… … . Lack of training
… … . Discrimination due to transgender/gender-expansive identity
… … . Other

These topics were selected using an intersectional lens. The intersectional perspective seeks to analyze the "multidimensionality' of marginalized subjects' lived experiences" (Crenshaw, 1989, p. 39). This approach allows for the exploration of the various intersecting forms of inequity faced by transgender women. Apart from gender identity, social characteristics like ethnicity, class and sexual orientation can also lead to discrimination. Indeed, "one's actions and opportunities are structured by one's placement along each of these dimensions" (Burgess-Proctor, 2006). The questions in the interview explored the past and present personal experience of respondents regarding the nine dimensions listed below:

1. **Social background.** Focused on childhood and family
2. **Education.** Examined their experiences with the educational system
3. **Work experience.** Focused on the level of insertion into the labor market
4. **Identity.** Analyzed self-identification, recognition of transgender identity by third parties and gender-reaffirming procedures
5. **Vulnerabilities.** Examined the prevalence of psychological violence, physical violence, sexual abuse, sexual violence, sexual exploitation, and economic violence
6. **Public security.** Analyzed how transgender women feel in public spaces, in the workplace and with regards to the national security apparatus (e.g., police officers)
7. **Health.** Examined mental health, drug consumption, VIH
8. **Crime.** Analyzed criminal antecedents and risk factors and causes of crime
9. **Access to Justice.** Focused on their experiences with the criminal justice system

These dimensions were selected based on a literature review of research that highlighted the many obstacles faced by transgender individuals. Given the lack of information regarding transgender women in Costa Rica, the aim was an explorative study. To this end, a comprehensive list of questions was developed. Moreover, this study is informed by the exploratory investigation by Loza et al. (2017) about transgender women living on the US-Mexican border. The study highlighted the need for researching the unique obstacles faced by transgender women in each national and cultural context. Since the type of vulnerabilities faced by transgender women can vary depending on the context, it is critical to understand the challenges resulting from a particular social, institutional and political framework. For this reason, we opted to give the study a national focus, Costa Rica.

Likewise, the research was also informed by the exploratory research carried out in Nicaragua and El Salvador (Johnson et al., 2020), highlighting the need for more research about how the State responds to the situation of incarcerated transgender women. For this reason, in addition to analyzing multiple dimensions of vulnerability, the study will also explore how State policy either addresses or neglects their needs.

SELECTION OF PARTICIPANTS

Currently, transgender women do not have their gender identity recognized legally in Costa Rica. As a result, they remain unrecognized and thus unprotected. Their presence is not noted according to their chosen gender identity in the official records when entering the prison system, but according to the gender they were assigned at birth. For this reason, the prison authorities are

Table 1. Prison visits.

Penitentiary	Province	Number of transwomen interviewed
CAI La Reforma	Alajuela	5
CAI Liberia	Limón	4
CAI Puntarenas	Puntarenas	5
CAI Centro de Atención para Personas con Enfermedades Mentales en Conflicto con la Ley (Capemcol).	San José	2

unaware of the exact number of incarcerated transgender women. According to an investigation carried out in 2017, 31 transgender women were in the Costa Rican prison system (Meléndez Segura, 2018).

For the purposes of this investigation, once permission was obtained to visit prisons, we had to rely on snowball methodology. Each day we arrived at the prison, we showed the necessary permits, explained the nature of the investigation, and passed through the security check. Since the prison authorities do not record the number, location, or names of incarcerated transgender women, we had to ask the prisoners and the correctional officers for information.

Usually, the first point of contact was the front-door correctional officer. We asked them if they were aware of any transgender women currently incarcerated. Although prison guards seldom use the term "transgender", they are aware of individuals who prefer to be referred to by a female name and have a feminine gender expression. Therefore, the guard would usually give us a name or two. Then, we would walk to the prison wing where this person was located. After interviewing them, we asked if they knew any other transgender women within the prison. In this regard, snowball sampling was used throughout. After the initial first point of contact via a prison guard, each informant was selected and interviewed through "contact information that is provided by other informants." (Chaim, 2008).

Four prisons in four provinces, Alajuela, San José, Puntarenas, and Liberia, were selected. The objective was to gauge if there was a rural-urban divide. Thus, Table 1 indicates each of the prisons visited, the province where it is located, and the number of transgender individuals interviewed.

During August 2019, structured interviews were carried out with sixteen incarcerated transgender women. The inclusion criteria were: (1) self-identified as a woman, a transgender woman, or any other gender-diverse term, (2) were assigned the 'male' sex at birth, (3) legal adults (i.e., 18 years or older), (4) currently incarcerated within the male prison system, (5) have been sentenced regardless of the crime. The exclusion criteria: (1) Individuals in pretrial detention were not included in the sample. Each participant was read out loud a consent form. This included information about the study's purposes, and it emphasized that their participation was confidential and voluntary. If they agreed to participate, they were asked to sign the consent form. It was then placed into a sealed manila envelope. It should be noted that all the participants were guaranteed confidentiality.

DATA ANALYSIS

Since this is an exploratory study based on 110 closed questions, data analysis involved evaluating a grid and then coding the answers. Once the sixteen interviews were completed, the results were first transferred from the paper questionnaires to a grid. To this end, an excel spreadsheet was used. Each dimension was given a separate spreadsheet. As a result, there were nine sheets overall. Then the answers to questions were inserted using a code. Since the questionnaire consisted of closed questions, the code was very simple (yes = 1, no = 0). To illustrate the analytical process, Table 2 provides an example of the data analysis involving physical violence. The transgender women were asked if they had experienced physical violence from the age interval

Table 2. Data analysis example.

Respondents	Physical violence 0–9 years
1	0
2	1
3	0
4	0
5	1
6	0
7	1
8	1
9	1
10	1
11	0
12	0
13	0
14	1
15	1
16	1
Totals	9

0–9 years old, i.e., during their childhood. If the respondent said yes, the code was 1, and if the answer was no, the code was 0. Once all the answers had been inserted for the age interval (0–9), the codes were added. The result was 9 out of 16, or 56%.

If the questions had multiple answers, the chart was divided into several categories. To this end, Table 3. provides an example of how the topic of public self-identification was analyzed. The question regarding public self-identification, the respondents answered transgender $(n = 6)$, women $(n = 6)$, gay $(n = 1)$, *travesti* $(n = 2)$ and *transsexual* $(n = 1)$. In this case, based on their answers, five categories were established. Each one was analyzed individually. For instance, the first category, "transgender", examined how many respondents publicly identified as transgender. The code was simple. If the respondents said yes, the code was yes = 1. If the respondents said no, the code was no = 0. The answers for that category were all added. Then, the same process was carried out for the next category, "women", and so forth.

RESULTS

The interviews provided a glimpse into the lives of incarcerated transwomen in Costa Rica. Their experiences and needs are at times rendered invisible. Although there is a growing awareness regarding the transgender experience in some countries, this is still lacking in Costa Rica.

In addition to the above, gender identity and sexual orientation do not have considerable weight when developing public policies and citizen security strategies. Indeed, "the sex binary has many negative effects on public policy" (Rosenblum, 2011). As it stands, the full impact of transphobic violence in Costa Rica is unknown. Subsequently, it is impossible to have a citizen security policy that is inclusive and nondiscriminatory. Since gender-based violence also affects transgender women, efforts to raise awareness and prevention measures should include them. At this time, the nature and extent of direct, structural, and cultural violence experienced by transgender people in Costa Rica are not fully known.

SOCIAL CONTEXT

The role of socialization agencies is crucial in the development of an individual. Based on social learning theory, individuals acquire certain attitudes, beliefs, and values from their peers and family. According to Akers (2006), "neighbors, churches, schoolteachers, doctors, legal figures and authorities and other people and groups in the community (….) have varying degrees of influence." In the case of Costa Rica, the abovementioned social actors adhere to a

Table 3. Data analysis example.

Respondent	How do you identify publicly	Transgender	Women	Gay	Travesti	Transsexual
1	Transgender	1	0	0	0	0
2	Gay	0	0	1	0	0
3	Woman	0	1	0	0	0
4	Transgender	1	0	0	0	0
5	Transgender	1	0	0	0	0
6	Transgender	1	0	0	0	0
7	Transsexual	0	0	0	0	1
8	Travesti	0	0	0	1	0
9	Woman	0	1	0	0	0
10	Transgender	1	0	0	0	0
11	Woman	0	1	0	0	0
12	Woman	0	1	0	0	0
13	Travesti	0	0	0	1	0
14	Woman	0	1	0	0	0
15	Transgender	1	0	0	0	0
16	Woman	0	1	0	0	0
	Totals	6	6	1	2	1

cis-heteronormative worldview. A clear example is the very vocal defense of "traditional" families by elected politicians, clergy, and activists in response to the increasing visibility of the LGBTQI community (Fattori & Quirós, 2019). In this context, "traditional family" implies a nuclear family composed of a cisgender and heterosexual man married to a cisgender and heterosexual woman and their children.

Regarding the social background of the incarcerated transgender women, it is worth noting that they were, on average, 31 years old. Only one of the people interviewed was a foreigner, and the remaining 15 respondents (94%), were born in Costa Rica. It is also worth mentioning that most of them were children of teen mothers, 11 respondents (68%). The average age of their mothers at the time of their first childbirth was 16 years old. In contrast, their father was 23 years old. On average, they had five siblings.

Many of the incarcerated transgender women have reported that their first experience of victimization happened within the family. On average, they left home at the age of 14. To examine this topic further, transgender women were asked the reasons for leaving home. Figure 1 illustrates their answers. When asked why they left their family home, 4 respondents, (25%), reported it was due to transphobic discrimination from their own family. For 3 respondents, (19%) it was due to domestic violence; for 3 respondents, (19%) it was because they wanted independence; for 1 respondent, (6%) it was due to drug consumption; for 1 respondent, (6%) it was due to poverty and for 1 respondent, (6%) it was to try to get a better education.

Access to Education

Education is frequently cited as one of the best pathways out of poverty (Awan et al., 2011). However, the education system is not a neutral actor in Costa Rica. Indeed, the public education system has become an ideological battlefield. Some activists have been campaigning to implement sexual education throughout the country, whilst others campaign to prevent it (Fattori & Quirós, 2019).

Given the importance of access to education, it was vital to explore the experiences of incarcerated transgender women. Accordingly, Figure 2 indicates access to education. In effect, 15 respondents (94%) of transgender women had access to formal education. However, only 11 respondents (73%) of the transgender women completed their primary school education. Although 9 respondents (60%) enrolled in high school, none completed it.

In the last fifteen years, Costa Rica has implemented education grants to assist students in completing their primary and secondary studies (Fondo Nacional de Becas, 2020). To this end,

REASONS FOR LEAVING HOME

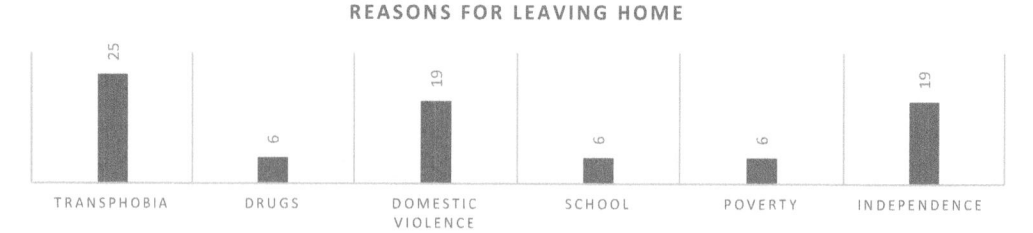

Figure 1. Reasons for leaving home.

EDUCATION

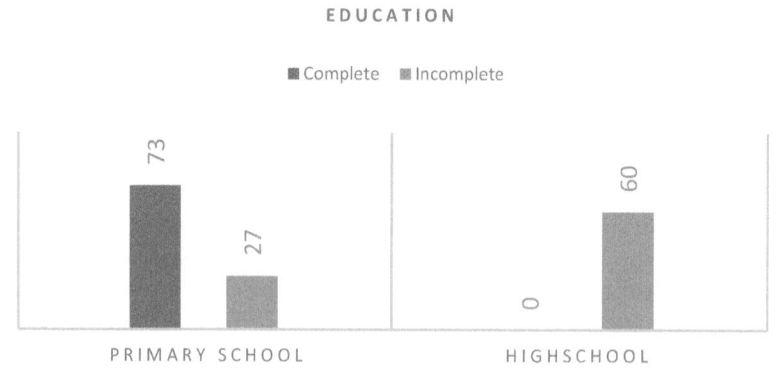

Figure 2. Education attainment.

DID YOU RECEIVE AN EDUCATION GRANT TO ATTEND SCHOOL

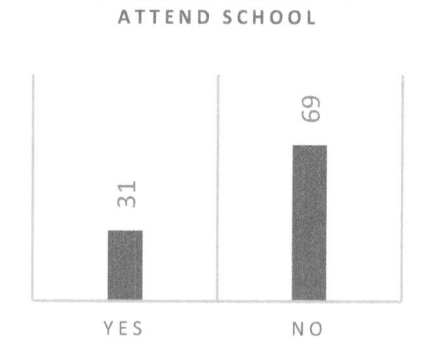

Figure 3. Education grant.

Figure 3 presents the data regarding education grants. Among the trans women interviewed, 5 respondents (31%) received an education grant to attend school. However, further research is required to explore why the grant is not reaching all the vulnerable groups.

The transwomen were also asked about their day-to-day experiences with the school system. In the United States, LGBTQI students have reported higher levels of bullying and harassment than their heterosexual counterparts (Earnshaw et al., 2017). Regarding transgender students, (90%) of students reported been victimized at school, and more than (25%) reported physical assault (Domínguez-Martínez & Robles, 2019). According to a previous study about gay and transgender individuals in Peru, the majority reported homophobic and transphobic bullying in schools (Juárez-Chávez et al., 2021). The extent of harassment in schools is illustrated in Figure 4. When asked about harassment during their time in school, 6 respondents (40%) of incarcerated transgender women reported being harassed by other students, 6 respondents (40%) reported being harassed by teaching staff, and 2

HARASSMENT IN SCHOOLS

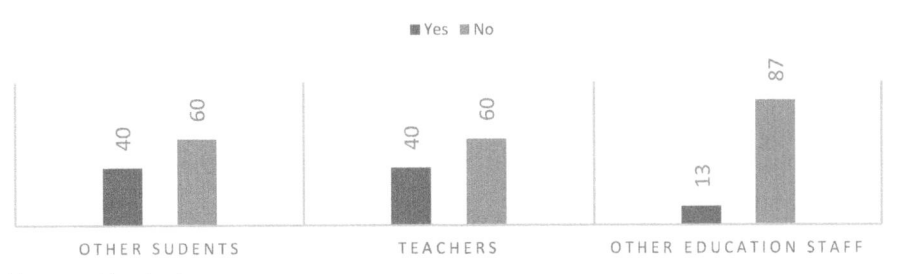

Figure 4. Harassment in schools.

respondents (13%) reported harassment by other members of the school staff. It should be noted that both fellow students and teaching staff victimized the transgender students.

In order to explore this topic further, transwomen were asked about verbal and physical violence. Figure 5 illustrates verbal violence. When asked about verbal violence, 8 respondents (56%) reported being victimized by other students, 6 respondents (40%) by teachers and 1 respondent (7%) by other education staff. Then, Figure 6 shows physical violence. Again, the transwomen were mainly targeted by other students, with 4 respondents (27%). Then, 2 respondents (13%) reported being physically victimized by teachers and 3 respondents (20%) by other education staff.

Only one person interviewed felt comfortable going through official channels to report the harassment or violence. It reveals that schools have failed to guarantee the psychological or physical safety of transgender students in at least four different provinces. Further research is required to determine the types of victimizations, such as harassment and bullying, transgender students are subjected to in school. In addition, it is vital to examine how the nature of the victimization varies depending on the perpetrator. For instance, it is important to determine if there is a difference in the type of violence inflicted by other students compared to teachers and other staff.

Given these circumstances, it is unsurprising that many transgender women are unable to complete their education. However, when asking them why they were unable to complete their education, the main reasons were transphobic discrimination at 3 respondents (27%) and the need to work at 3 respondents (27%). This was followed by poverty, 2 respondents (13%), domestic violence, 1 respondent (6%), drugs, 1 respondent (6%), sickness, 1 respondent (6%). To this end, Figure 7 exemplifies the reasons for leaving school.

Employment

Given that most transgender women interviewed leave home at a young age, they have to support themselves. Indeed, on average, they began working at the age of 15. Furthermore, transgender women face many difficulties obtaining work. According to a survey carried out in the United States, (44%) of transgender women were refused a job due to their identity. Moreover, even among those able to find employment, (50%) were harassed at work (DeSouza et al., 2017).

Article 33 of Costa Rica's *Political Constitution* enshrines the principle of equality. It prohibits any form of discrimination because it undermines human dignity. At the same time, Costa Rica's *Labor Code*, in its article 622, prohibits discrimination. Despite these legal protections, transgender women still face a great deal of difficulty finding work. For this reason, Figure 8 shows the percentage of transwomen who had difficulty obtaining work. It should be noted, 3 respondents (19%) reported they had never tried to find work in the formal sector. Then, 11 respondents (69%) reported they had had difficulty finding work.

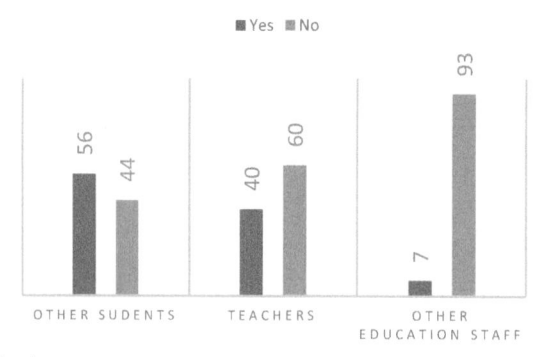

Figure 5. Verbal violence in schools.

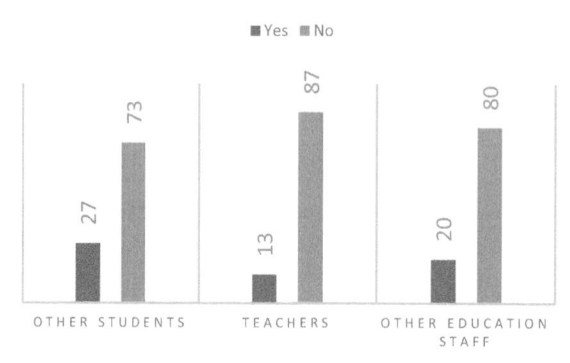

Figure 6. Physical violence in schools.

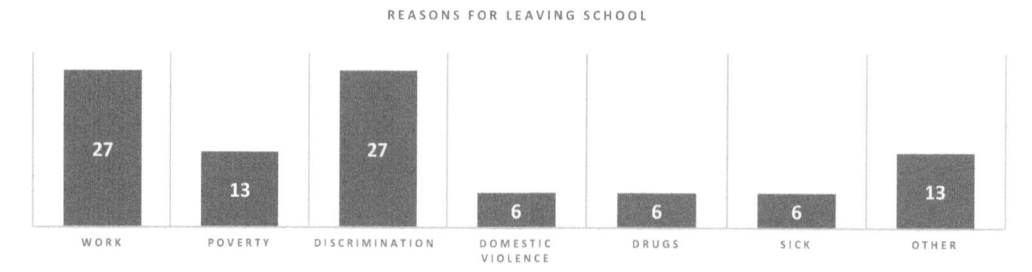

Figure 7. Reasons for leaving school.

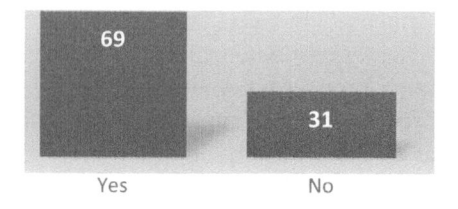

Figure 8. Difficulty finding work.

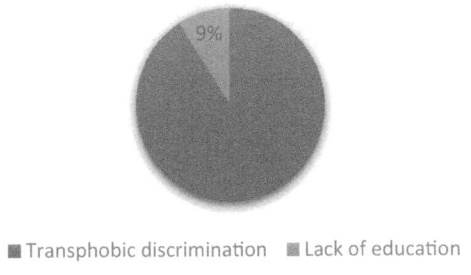

■ Transphobic discrimination   ■ Lack of education

Figure 9. The main obstacle for obtaining work.

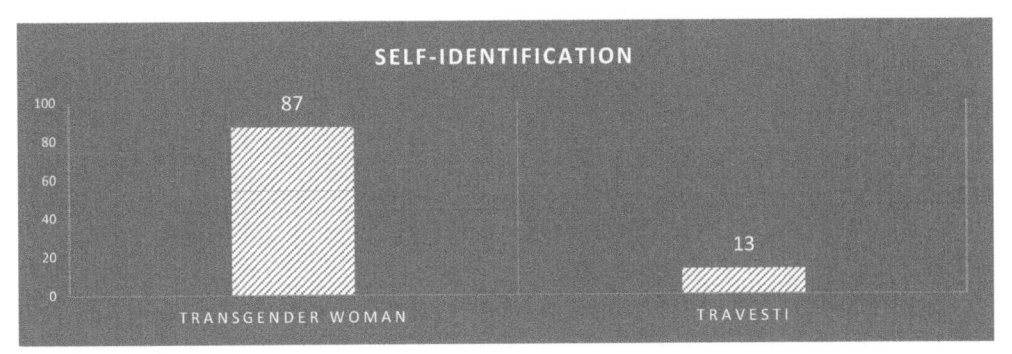

Figure 10. Self-identification.

In addition, transwomen were asked why they considered they had had difficulty finding work. Figure 9 demonstrates the results. Of the women who reported difficulties finding work, 1 respondent (9%) stated it was due to a lack of education, and 11 respondents (91%), said it was because of transgender discrimination. Lastly, 14 respondents (88%) of the transgender women interviewed reported having had to engage in sex work. Given that transgender women have reported difficulty finding work and stated transphobic discrimination is the main obstacle, further research is necessary.

Identity

The question of self-identification is fundamental. Figure 10 indicates how the interviewed individuals self-identify. To this end, 14 respondents (87%) said they identify as transgender women. Then, 2 respondents (13%) reported they identified as 'trasvesti' because they "had not had any reaffirming procedures." On average, they became aware of their gender identity at the age of nine.

Nonetheless, not all the respondents shared their identity with their social circles. To this end, Figure 11 reveals the first person they told. Usually, it was a parent: 8 respondents, (50%) first told a parent, 6 respondents, (38%) first told a friend, 1 respondent, (6%) a sibling and 1 respondent, (6%) an aunt. When gauging the reactions of the first person with whom they shared their trans-identity, 8 respondents (50%) reported the reaction was positive, in 4 respondents, (25%), the reaction was confusion, 2 respondents, (13%), it was negative, and 2 respondents, (13%), it was neutral or indifferent. More in-depth research regarding the experiences they had when sharing their identities with others is necessary. In addition, it is vital to explore how having a positive reaction instead of an adverse reaction impacted their sense of self.

It should be noted that not all of them feel safe publicly identifying as transwomen. In general, transgender individuals have reported "repressing" their gender identity and feminine behaviors

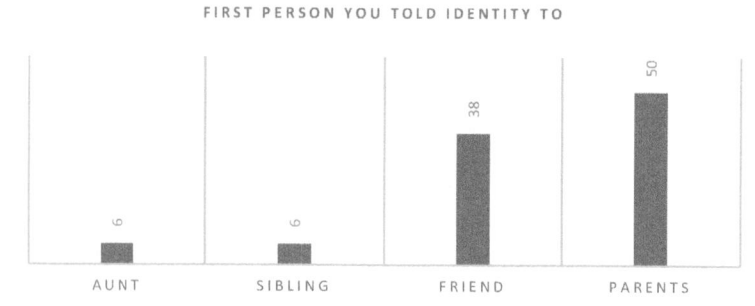

Figure 11. First-person you told identity to.

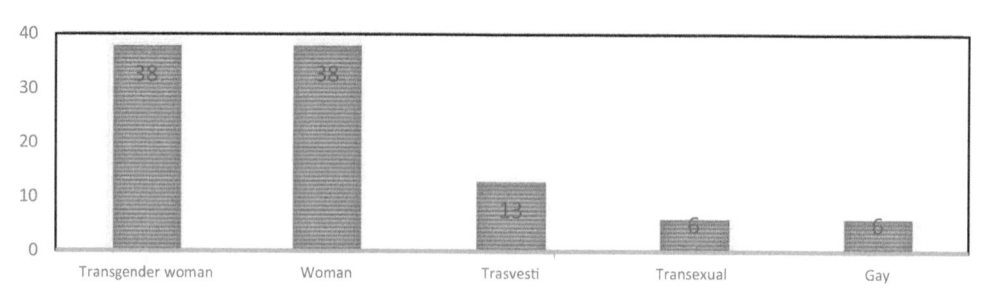

Figure 12. Public self-identification.

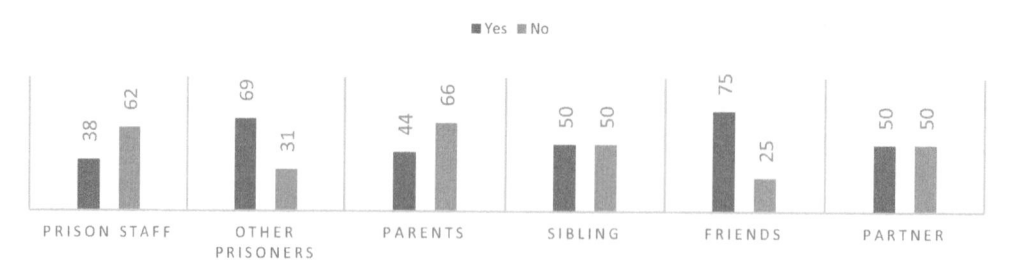

Figure 13. Referred to by chosen name.

to avoid discrimination and violence (Juárez-Chávez et al., 2021). Indeed, Figure 12 shows their public identification. Accordingly, 1 respondent (6%) stated that even though they are a trans-woman, they prefer to identify as a "gay man in the streets". Similarly, 6 respondents (38%) identify as women without disclosing that they are transgender. So then, 6 respondents (38%) identify as transgender, 2 respondents (13%) as *travesti* and 1 respondent (6%) as transexual. On average, the individuals who publicly identify as transgender, transexual or *travesti*, have done so since they were 15 years old.

Given that a significant number of transgender women publicly identify as such, it was important to assess if others respect their identity. Hence, the women were asked if they were referred to by their chosen name instead of the legal name they were assigned at birth. Figure 13 indicates the number of individuals who are referred to by their chosen name. Accordingly, 6 respondents (38%) of the prison staff used their chosen name and 11 respondents (69%) of other prisoners, 7 respondents (44%) of their parents, 8 respondents (50%) of their siblings, 12 respondents (75%) of their friends, and 8 respondents (50%) of their partners.

Health

In Costa Rica, the right to health is enshrined in article 50 of the Political Constitution. In addition, there is the public health system. The Caja Costarricense de Seguro Social (CCSS) was established in 1941 to provide healthcare to workers (Vargas & Muiser, 2013). Then 1994, the public healthcare system was reorganized. Clinics named *Equipo Básico de Atención Integral de Salud* (EBAIS, or basic integrated health care team) were added to provide primary healthcare. Within twelve years, health coverage increased to 93% (Pesec et al., 2017).

In spite of the advances in guaranteeing healthcare for the general population, transgender individuals are still excluded. In this regard, Costa Rica is not an exception. Throughout Latin America, transgender individuals are very vulnerable due to a lack of access to healthcare (PAHO, 2014). Healthcare is conceived from a cisnormative conceptualization. Consequently, the specific health needs of transgender people are unknown and unaddressed. There is even a lack of experts with regards to trans health. Due to the lack of trans-inclusive techniques and procedures, their right to health is undermined.

GENDER REAFFIRMING PROCEDURES

In 2007, an application for constitutional redress was interposed when the CCSS refused to provide a gender reaffirming surgery. The CCSS refused because the operation was not required for health reasons and based on the administrative principle of legality. Since the institution was not expressly authorized by law, they could not provide it (Constitutional Court of the Republic of Costa Rica, 2007). Moreover, the Acting Director-General of Mexico stated under oath that the purpose of the services provided by the public healthcare system was to "cure and prevent illness, for this reason, aesthetic and vanity are not within the institutional objectives" (Constitutional Court of the Republic of Costa Rica, 2007).

The transwomen were also asked with regards to gender reaffirming procedures. This can refer to "hormone therapy, genital reconstruction, breast reconstruction, facial plastic surgery, speech therapy, urologic and psychiatric services and primary care" (Johns Hopkins Medicine, 2020). In general, transgender individuals have reported "high levels of satisfaction" in response to the gender reaffirming procedures (Van de Grift et al., 2018).

Regarding gender reaffirming procedures, 11 respondents (69%) reported they had used hormone therapy. Of the 5 respondents, (31%) have not had hormone therapy. All of them want to. Then, 4 respondents (25%) have had a gender reaffirming surgery. Of the 12 respondents, (75%) have had no surgical procedures, all of them want to. In effect, all transgender women have either had or would like to have a gender reaffirming procedure.

However, transgender women face a myriad of "structural inequalities" when trying to obtain healthcare. These include a lack of access to housing, a lack of access to work, and a lack of access to health insurance (Clark et al., 2018). As a result of these numerous barriers, their transition is often dictated by their limited economic means rather than their actual needs. Even those who could obtain a gender reaffirming procedure still lacked access to proper medical care. Only 4 respondents (40%) of the cases obtained the treatment from a doctor. The remainder went to an unlicensed third party.

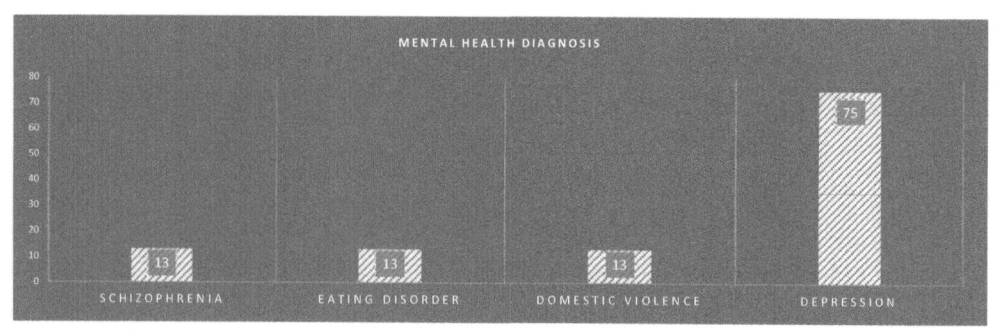

Figure 14. Mental health diagnosis.

DRUG CONSUMPTION

Previous studies have suggested there is a link between minority stress and drug consumption. Minority stress theory suggests that there are "stressors specific to sexual minorities", such as social rejection due to widespread discrimination and internalized feelings of self-devaluation (Gonzalez et al., 2017).

When the incarcerated transwomen were asked about drug consumption, many stated it was a coping mechanism given their lack of family and social support. Overall, 15 respondents (94%) have used illicit drugs at one point in their lives. Of these, 4 respondents (25%) have received treatment or gone to rehabilitation for their consumption. In some cases, the women sought treatment from a state institution, the Institute of Drug Abuse and Alcoholism (IAFA, 2020). Others from Hogares Crea, a nonprofit that offers a rehabilitation program for free. It should be noted, all of the transgender women who sought treatment reported a lack of gender sensitivity during treatment. Indeed, many transgender women cannot obtain proper treatment due to minority stress and prevalent transphobic attitudes among the staff (Lyons et al., 2015).

MENTAL HEALTH

The transgender women interviewed were also asked about their mental health. In general, transgender individuals report more mental health issues than their cisgender counterparts (Streed et al., 2018). According to an investigation carried among transgender women in Brazil, there was a "high prevalence of psychiatric diagnosis, including psychoactive drug use, suicide attempts, major depressive disorder, psychoses, social phobias, and obsessive-compulsive behavior" (Fontanari et al., 2018). In the United States, 57% of transgender individuals have reported experiencing depression, and 42.1% have reported anxiety. According to previous studies, "transphobia-based violence is related to increased depression and anxiety" (Klemmer et al., 2021).

It should be noted that 8 respondents (50%) of transwomen have been referred to a psychologist. Then, 3 respondents (19%) have been referred to a psychiatrist. Figure 14 illustrates the mental health diagnosis transwomen have received. Of the transwomen referred to a medical practitioner, 12 respondents (75%) were diagnosed with depression. Costa Rica is not an outlier. As mentioned above, the prevalence of depression has been confirmed in other studies. Then, 2 respondents (13%) were diagnosed with an eating disorder and 2 respondents (13%) with schizophrenia. An additional 2 respondents (13%) were referred to a psychologist, not because they had a particular mental health issue, but to cope with domestic violence.

It was also essential to examine the prevalence of self-injury because this mental health issue is the least researched among transgender individuals (Jackman et al., 2018). The previous meta-analysis has been "consistent" in concluding that LGBTQI individuals are more likely to be at

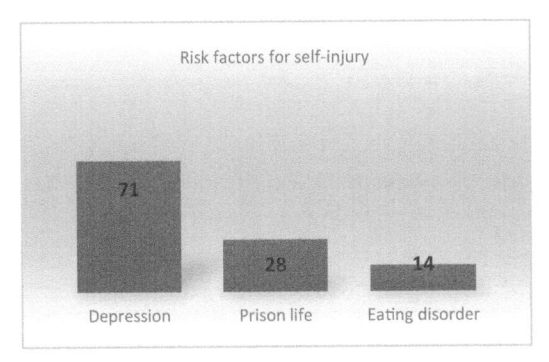

Figure 15. Risk factors for self-injury.

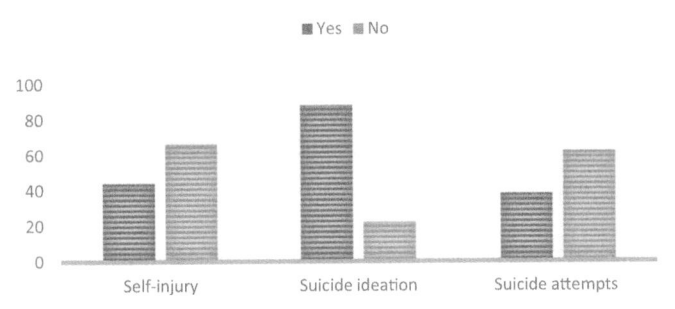

Figure 16. Self-injury, suicide ideation and suicide attempts.

risk for self-injury than their cis-heteronormative counterparts. However, there is still a gap in the literature regarding the extent and nature of the phenomenon (Liu et al., 2019).

It should be mentioned that 7 respondents (44%) of the transgender women interviewed reported self-injury. This is reflected in Figure 16. When asked why they hurt themselves, the transwomen identified three main reasons. Accordingly, as shown in Figure 15, 5 respondents (71%) stated it was a coping mechanism for their depression, 2 respondents (28%) stated it was to cope with the hardship of prison life, and 1 respondent (14%) used it to cope with an eating disorder.

In addition, the transgender women were asked about suicide ideation and suicide attempts. Previous studies have indicated that transgender women are at higher risk of suicide attempts (PAHO, 2014). For instance, in a study carried in the Dominican Republic, "between one fifth and one-quarter of respondents had attempted suicide (22.5%)" (Budhwani et al., 2018). Figure 16 describes the prevalence of suicide ideation and suicide attempts. In effect, 14 respondents (88%) of respondents, experienced suicide ideation, and 6 respondents (38%) have attempted suicide at least once.

Given the vulnerability of transgender women, there is a need for more significant social and psychological support. At the group level, this means community-building. At the individual level, it implies tailored support to address the toll of enduring transphobia and any mental health issues so that transgender women develop a "positive self-concept" (Kuper et al., 2018).

Lastly, there is the topic of HIV. According to previous studies, transgender women are considered a high-risk group for HIV. Moreover, many of them are undiagnosed and lack access to treatment (Ragonnet-Cronin et al., 2019). Nevertheless, a hundred percent of the respondents stated they are routinely tested for HIV. Currently, 3 respondents (19%) are HIV positive, and they are receiving anti-viral treatment.

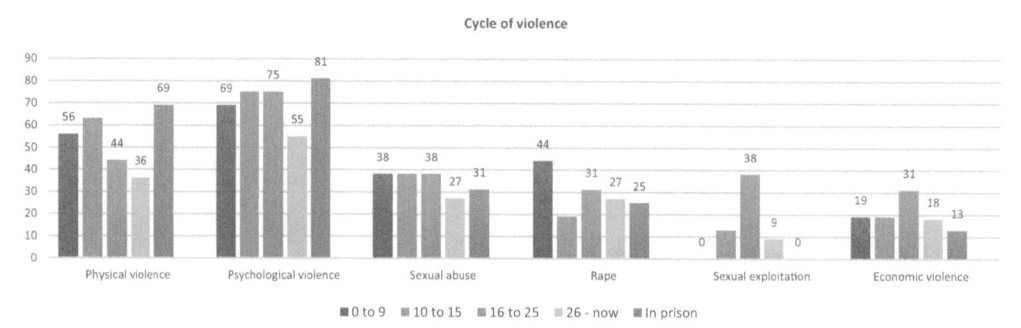

Figure 17. Cycle of violence.

Vulnerabilities

Transgender women are among the most vulnerable social groups (Wilson et al., 2017). In Costa Rica, they are marginalized from a cultural, political, and institutional perspective. Some of them are born in a situation of social marginality. At times, they are the victims of abuse and intrafamilial violence. Then, without exception, they are the victims of multiple forms of violence due to transphobia.

It is not a phenomenon limited to Costa Rica. Previous research in Barbados, El Salvador, Trinidad and Tobago, and Haiti has demonstrated that transgender women face very high levels of violence (Evens et al., 2019). In addition to gender-based violence, transgender women have also experienced high levels of sexual abuse and intimate partner violence compared to their cis-heterosexual peers (Garthe et al., 2018).

VICTIMIZATION

The participants were asked about their experiences with physical violence, psychological violence, sexual abuse, sexual exploitation, and economic violence to assess the different types of violence. The types of violence were defined using the legal terms in accordance with the Costa Rican *Law of criminalization of violence against women*, N° 8589. In addition, to evaluate the frequency of violence during their lifetime, the participants were asked if they had experienced it. Thus, Figure 17 represents the physical, psychological, sexual abuse, rape, sexual exploitation and economic violence experienced from the ages of 0–9, 10–15, 16–25, 26-now, and in prison.

PHYSICAL VIOLENCE

Physical violence is defined in article 22 of Law N° 8589. Physical violence refers to mistreating, hitting and any other physical harm. In a study among Latin American Transgender women in Washington DC, 92% were Central American migrants. Of the respondents, 76% reported experiencing physical violence during their lifetimes (Yamanis et al., 2018). As indicated in Figure 17, from the age of 0–9, 9 respondents (56%) reported physical violence, from the age of 10–15, 10 respondents (63%), from the age of 16–25, 7 respondents (44%), from the age of 26-now, 5 respondents (36%) and in-prison, 11 respondents (69%). Although high levels of physical violence were experienced during childhood, the highest frequency has been during their prison term. It reveals that prison is a site of violence for most transgender women.

PSYCHOLOGICAL VIOLENCE

Psychological violence is defined in article 26 of Law N° 8589. It includes the "threats of violence, intimidation, blackmail, or harassment." In a study among Latin American transgender women in Washington DC, 95% reported experiencing psychological violence during their lifetimes (Yamanis et al., 2018). As indicated in Figure 17, from the age of 0–9, 11 respondents (69%) reported psychological violence, from the age of 10–15, 12 respondents (75%), from the age of 16–25, 12 respondents (75%), from the age of 26-now, 9 respondents (56%) and in-prison, 13 respondents (81%). The highest frequency has been during their prison term. Thus, it reaffirms that prison is a site of violence for most transwomen.

SEXUAL ABUSE

Sexual abuse is defined in article 30 of Law N° 8589. It implies forcing another person to endure "sexual acts that cause pain or humiliation". According to the literature, LGBTQI individuals report experiencing high levels of sexual abuse (Grossman & D'Augelli, 2006). For example, in a study about incarcerated transgender women in California, 69.4% of respondents reported sexual victimization. For the study, it was defined as "including things they would "rather not do" (Jenness et al., 2019). As indicated in Figure 17, from the age of 0–9, 6 respondents (38%) reported sexual abuse, from the age of 10–15, 6 respondents (38%), from the age of 16–25, 6 respondents, (38%), from the age of 26-now, 4 respondents, (27%) and in-prison, 5 respondents, (31%).

RAPE

Rape is defined in article 29 of Law N° 8589. It specifies that it refers to oral, anal, or vaginal penetration without the person's consent. Given their social vulnerability, transgender women are at a higher risk of sexual assault (Seelman, 2015). According to the Bureau of Justice Statistics of the United States, one-third of incarcerated transgender women were sexually assaulted (Jenness et al., 2019). As indicated in Figure 17, from the age of 0–9, 7 respondents (44%) reported rape, from the age of 10–15, 3 respondents, (19%), from the age of 16–25, (31%), from the age of 26-now, 6 respondents (27%) and in-prison, 4 respondents (25%). It should be noted that transgender women were most likely to experience rape as young children.

SEXUAL EXPLOITATION

According to article 31 of Law N° 8589, sexual exploitation is when a person is forced to have sexual relations for another person's economic gain. More broadly, it can refer to "any actual or attempted abuse of a position of vulnerability, differential power, or trust for sexual purposes, including but not limited to profiting monetarily, socially, or politically from sexual exploitation" (Annan, 2003). Previous studies have demonstrated that transgender women report sexual abuse with more frequency than their cis-heterosexual peers (Rimes et al., 2019). As indicated in Figure 17, from the age of 0–9, no respondents reported sexual exploitation; from the age of 10–15, 2 respondents (13%), from the age of 16–25, 6 respondents (38%), from 26-now, 1 respondent (9%).

ECONOMIC VIOLENCE

Economic violence is defined in articles 38–40 of Law N° 8589. It refers to "when a third party deducts earnings from an economic activity for their benefit." It can also refer to when a person

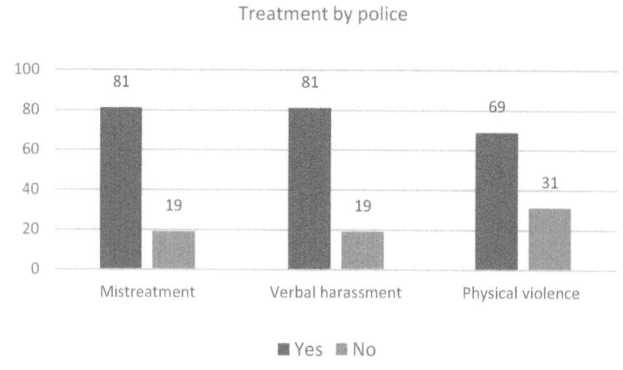

Figure 18. Treatment by police.

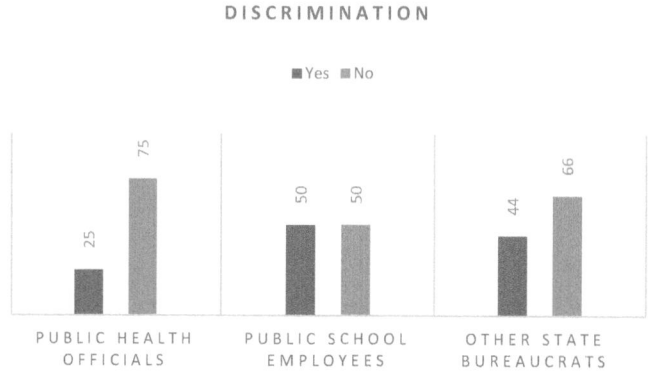

Figure 19. Discrimination.

coerces a woman to give away her earnings or refuses to pay a person after providing a service or good. It can also imply "limited access to funds and credit" (Fawole, 2008). As indicated in Figure 17, from the age of 0–9, 3 respondents (19%) reported economic violence, from the age of 10–15, 3 respondents (19%), from the age of 16–25, 5 respondents (31%), from the age of 26-now, 3 respondents (18%) and in-prison, 2 respondents (13%).

STRUCTURAL VIOLENCE

Structural violence is when "social structures or institutions that keep individuals from meeting basic needs—from a healthy existence" (Grauer & Buikstra, 2019). This can express itself as discriminatory laws, lack of access to education, lack of access to dignified work, and lack of access to housing (Ortiz & Jackey, 2019). For example, according to a study carried out in Peru, transgender women experience harassment and violence from police officers. Moreover, due to discriminatory laws and "social stigma," they are unable to report the extent of the violence (Rodríguez-Madera et al., 2017).

Regarding police violence, Figure 18 demonstrates that 13 respondents (81%) of the transgender women reported mistreatment, 13 respondents (81%) reported harassment, and 11 respondents (69%) reported physical violence. Thus, among incarcerated transgender women, the police are not equated with safety. Quite the contrary, for many, the security forces are a source of insecurity. Then, regarding discrimination, Figure 19 indicates that 4 respondents (25%) reported experiencing it from public health officials, 8 respondents (50%) from public school employees and, 7 respondents (44%) from other state bureaucrats.

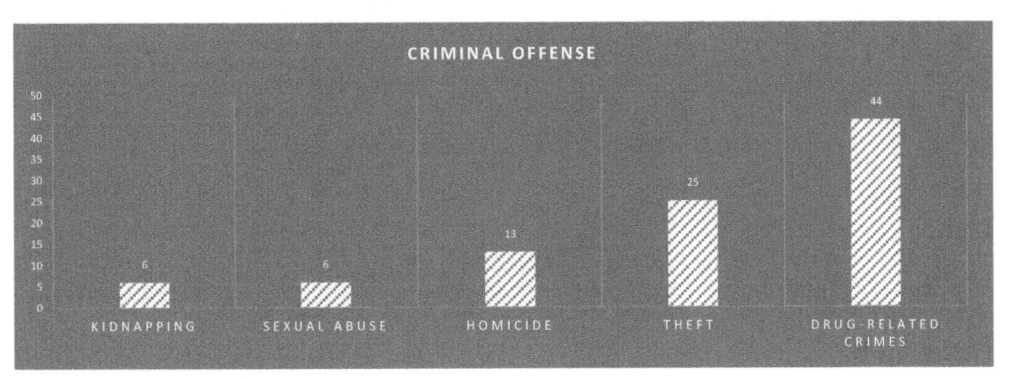

Figure 20. Criminal offense.

In general, transgender women are an at-risk social group. Once incarcerated, they face additional challenges to their safety (Wilson et al., 2017). The transgender women interviewed were asked the question, "do you feel safe?." Only 8 respondents (50%) reported feeling safe around the police, 7 respondents (44%) reported feeling safe around other prisoners, and 8 respondents (50%) reported feeling safe around the prison staff.

Given how widespread violence is, further research is merited. For example, to explore the types of violence inflicted on incarcerated transgender women by prison staff in comparison to other prisoners. Once incarcerated, transgender women are under custody of the State. For this reason, there is a state obligation to guarantee their safety. Additional research could highlight the institutional shortcomings in ensuring their physical and psychological well-being.

Criminal Justice System

Crime, much like gender, is a political and social construct. Kappeler and Potter (2017) argues that rather than respond to threats, criminal justice responds to dominant social myths (p. 444). In many cases, crime is "disproportionately attributed to the behaviors of those with marginalized racial, sexual, and gender identities" (Gaynor, 2018). As a result, in the public imaginary, crime is linked with anyone who is not cisgender, heterosexual (Gaynor, 2018) and middle-class (Francisco Simon, 2021, p. 245). The result is the criminalization of transgender women because of their gender identity (Lyons et al., 2017) and their poverty (Francisco Simon, 2021, p. 247).

Essentially, transgender women face multiple and persistent forms of violence. In many ways, incarceration adds another layer of violence. Criminalization is the result of 1) widespread transphobia (Lyons et al., 2017), 2) a lack of economic opportunities (Lyons et al., 2017), 3) punitive policies implemented against the criminal acts more likely to be committed by more impoverished individuals (in juxtaposition to the 'light' approach taken against white-collar crime) (Francisco Simon, 2021, p. 240), and 4) the influence of the War on Drugs. In the context of the War on Drugs, repressive criminal justice policies have been used to address insecurity. This has translated into harsher sentencing for drug-related crimes, resulting in a crisis of mass incarceration throughout Latin America (Chaparro Hernández & Pérez Correa, 2017).

Case in point, a significant proportion of the transgender women interviewed were incarcerated for drug-related crimes, as portrayed by Figure 20, 7 respondents, (44%). Given its geographic location between the countries where there is cocaine production and countries where there is cocaine consumption, Costa Rica has become a "bridge" for drug trafficking since the nineties. (Saborío, 2019). Moreover, as shown in Figure 20, the second criminal offense for which transgender women were most incarcerated was theft, 4 respondents (25%), homicide, 2 respondents (13%), kidnapping, 1 respondent (6%) and sexual abuse, 1 respondent (6%).

Figure 21. Reasons for crime.

Furthermore, it should be noted that the majority, 10 respondents (63%), were first-time-offenders. Since the '80s, the rise of mass incarceration has resulted in the rise of the alternative sentencing movement. It has led to more significant support for alternative sentencing and other measures besides incarceration (Mauer, 2018, p. 118). Yet, alternative sentencing, even for first-time offenders, is seldomly applied in Costa Rica. The Inter-American Commission on Human Rights has advocated for greater use of alternative sentencing, particularly with a "gender perspective and a differentiated approach with respect to at-risk groups" (Inter-American Commission on Human Rights, 2017, p. 16). Admittedly, transgender women should be candidates for alternative sentencing given their multiple vulnerabilities.

When asked about the reasons for the criminal offense, as indicated in Figure 21, transgender women identified economic necessity as the primary cause, 7 respondents (44%). Then, 2 respondents (13%) stated it was due to threats, 1 respondent (6%) attributed it to drug consumption, 1 respondent (6%) stated vengeance, and 5 respondents (31%) reported other.

The high number of transwomen driven by economic necessity proves that the punitive policies target primarily poor individuals. As demonstrated in Figure 21, it is also noteworthy that 2 respondents (13%) were incarcerated due to threats and 1 respondent (6%) due to drug consumption—two very vulnerable groups. In the first case, the individuals were under duress. In the second case, drug consumers need treatment. That requires collaboration between the penitentiary system and rehabilitation providers. These needs are often unmet (UNODC, 2003).

It was vital to examine if the criminal justice system is trans-inclusive. Gender is a deeply embedded social construct. It is reproduced through routine and discourse until it is deemed to be natural. As a result, many individuals adopt a rigid attitude toward gender identity and gender expression (Lorber, 2009, pp. 111–114). These attitudes permeate social, cultural, and legal norms (Buist & Stone, 2014). As a result, the criminal justice system, and by extension, the prison system, does not exist in a neutral space. Quite the contrary, "personal beliefs and cultural norms often play a part in legal decisions, particularly those regarding transgender criminal cases" (Buist & Stone, 2014).

As a means of assessing the degree of trans-inclusiveness during the criminal justice process, transgender women were asked if the other participants were aware of their identity. According to Figure 22, 7 respondents (44%) stated everyone was aware, 7 respondents (44%) states no one was aware, and 2 respondents (12%) stated only their defense attorney was aware of their identity. It should be noted that only 2 respondents (13%) had private representation. The rest had to rely on a public attorney. This implies that their experience provides an insight regarding the current state policies and norms governing the criminal justice system.

Prisons have historically been strictly segregated based on biological sex. This has resulted in a "somewhat hidden war on transgender women housed in men's facilities (as well as transgender men housed in women's facilities)" (Stohr, 2015). In effect, anyone who does not fall within the gender binary faces de facto marginalization.

During the process, were justice operators aware you are a transgender woman?

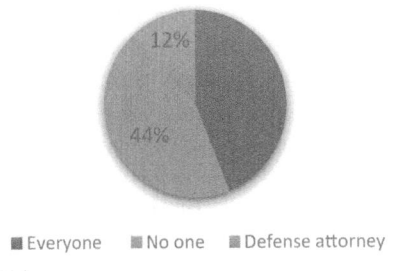

■ Everyone ■ No one ■ Defense attorney

Figure 22. Trans-awareness during the trial.

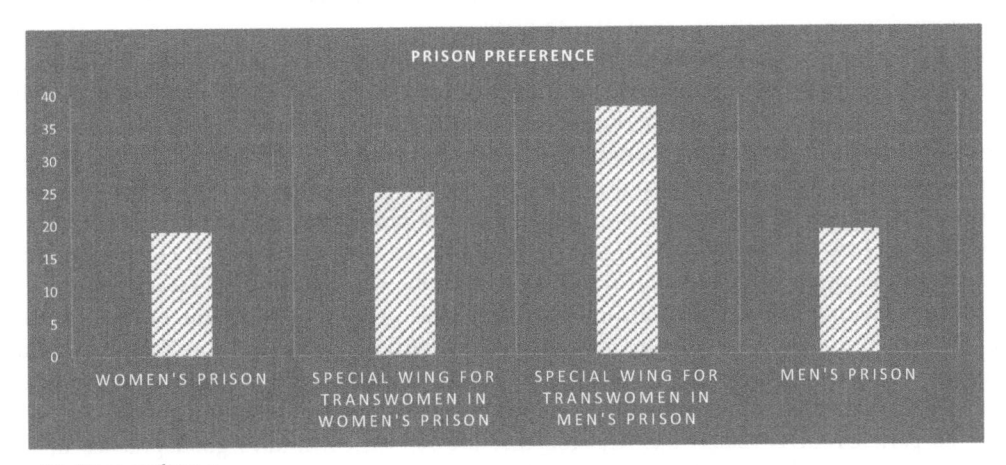

Figure 23. Prison preference.

Since being incarcerated within a men's prison often aggravates transgender women's vulnerabilities, it was essential to ask the transwomen about their prison preference- if they had a choice. Figure 23 shows the results regarding their prison preference, 3 respondents (19%) selected a women's prison, 4 respondents (25%) selected a special wing for transgender women in the women's prison, 6 respondents (38%) selected a special wing for transgender women in the men's prison, and 3 respondents (19%) selected staying in the men's prison system.

LEGAL FRAMEWORK

From a human rights perspective, the unique needs of vulnerable groups should be addressed when elaborating legal norms and public policies. For example, incarcerated transgender women are arguably among the most vulnerable social groups. To this effect, the United Nations Office on Drugs and Crime has declared that incarcerated women have a "particularly vulnerable status in prisons" (UNODC, 2009, p. 1). However, far from being directly addressed, their needs have thus far been brushed aside from a legal and an institutional standpoint.

In the case of Costa Rica, the country has expressed a profound commitment to human rights. Indeed, "its record of human rights promotion is enduring and multifaceted" (Brysk, 2005). To this end, there have been some noticeable advances with regards to ciswomen's rights. However, the legal system and institutional layout respond to a restrictive notion of gender.

Narcotics Law Reform 77bis

One of the positive advances in Costa Rica was the reform known as *"77 bis"* to the "Law on Narcotics, Psychotropic Substances, Unauthorized Drugs, Related Activities, Money Laundering and the Financing of Terrorism, Law No. 8204". However, this was a "modest" reform since its application was limited to the crime of smuggling drugs into the prison system (Mora Bolaños, 2019).

In 2013, this law was reformed to lessen the sanction for women incarcerated for "introducing drugs into the prison system" if they were first-time, nonviolent offenders and in a situation of extreme vulnerability. Based on pre-established criteria, judges are allowed to diminish the length of the prison sentence. Some of these requirements include that the woman must be living in poverty, be the sole head of the household, have dependents in her charge, or be elderly. Those who meet any of these requirements will have sentences of between three and eight years, which can be served through alternative measures to prison.

The legal reform was advocated because Costa Rica has not "fulfilled the commitments acquired due to ratifying international instruments for the protection of fundamental rights" (Orozco Álvarez, 2012). It should be noted that Costa Rica has ratified a significant number of international treaties, such as the *Convention on the Elimination of All Forms of Discrimination Against Women*, which was ratified by Law No. 6968 on October 2, 1984. Then the *Inter-American Convention on the Prevention, Punishment, and Eradication of Violence against Women*, was ratified by Law No. 7499 on 1995, May 2. Both treaties were invoked in the draft legislation. Thus, the gender perspective was added, in part, to comply with international commitments.

Besides upholding international norms, the draft legislation is also a critique of dominant cultural norms. It explicitly "condemns" discrimination against women "rooted in the cultural structures" (Orozco Álvarez, 2012). This part of the proposed bill is significant because it acknowledges that gender discrimination is embedded in state and cultural structures.

For its part, UNODC (2009) has declared that the reform constitutes good practice in drug regulations, "not only because it incorporates the gender perspective but also because it does not establish a minimum penalty for these crimes." However, *77bis* applies to the particular case of women at risk of introducing drugs to prisons. In practice, this has only been applied to *cisgender* women.

Despite reform *77 bis*, additional necessary measures have not been taken to deal with all groups at risk. The situation of transgender women is a case in point. The United Nations Committee Against Torture (2008, p. 4) and the Inter-American Commission on Human Rights (Comisión Interamericana de Derechos Humanos, 2015, p. 72) have expressed concern about the human rights violations of transgender people in Costa Rica. According to a study carried out in Latin America by REDLACTRANS (2020), 67% of the cases of abuse reported by transgender people "had as perpetrators State agents, mainly agents of the police forces" (p. 13).

Since 2014, the Costa Rican Public Defense Office has noticed a variation concerning the profile of the people sentenced for entering drugs into a penitentiary center under article 77. Of these, 30% of the offenders classified as "male" by the State are transgender women (Z. Molina, personal communication, December 14, 2016). They tend to have additional risk conditions, such as social exclusion, extreme poverty, HIV, and problematic drug consumption. By being incarcerated in the male penitentiary systems, they suffer abuse and mistreatment at the hands of both prison staff and fellow prisoners. Despite this, there are no clear administrative and legal policies to provide them with the proper technical attention. Nevertheless, the rights of transgender women are not on the political agenda.

Criminal Code Reform 71bis

Notwithstanding the neglect of transgender rights, since 2013, there have been even more advances regarding the protection of cisgender women. For example, on 2018, November 19, article 71 of the Criminal Code was reformed by Law N° 9628. The text was changed so that the judge could reduce the penalty for any crime based on several mitigating factors, including "the sentenced person is a woman in a vulnerable state, due to poverty, being the primary caregiver for dependent family members, disability or being the victim of gender violence."

According to the National Institute for Women (INAMU), the reform intends to guarantee "greater rationality and humanity" when sentencing first-time female offenders. The INAMU was part of an inter-institutional network whose aim was to reform the criminal justice system to address the myriad of structural injustices faced by women (INAMU, 2018). In this regard, this legal reform is a form of "affirmative action" favoring *cisgender* women (Mora Bolaños, 2019).

DISCUSSION

Although the Costa Rican legal framework enshrines universal human rights and multiple treaties which extend the realm of human rights, transgender women continue to be excluded from legal protections. Currently, the state practice is to restrict women's rights to *cisgender* women's rights. This restrictive legal interpretation stems from a transphobic perspective. Moreover, it is a symptom of more significant social phenomena. Transphobia begins at home and pervades the streets, the schools, the Courts, and the prison system.

Even the public institutions, national laws and international treaties that protect transgender women neglect them and contribute to their marginalization. In general, despite the substantial progress regarding women's rights in the last three decades in Costa Rica, these same protections are not applied to transgender women. From a legal perspective, there is growing consensus that the term "sex" should be interpreted in the broadest sense, thereby including "all kinds of sexes, including transgender, intersex and other differently-sexed and gendered people" (Holtmaat & Post, 2015).

It should be noted that neither CEDAW nor the *Inter-American Convention on the Prevention, Punishment, and Eradication of Violence against Women* explicitly defines the term "woman." Indeed, the "ordinary understanding" of the term "woman" often refers to sex and gender. For this reason, some authors have argued that the principles therein enshrined could be expanded to "protect lesbian, bisexual, and transgender ("LBT") women" (Gallagher, 2020). Moreover, given that these treaties aim to eliminate all forms of discrimination and violence against women, a "trans-inclusive interpretation" would align with the treaties core purpose. (Gallagher, 2020).

This viewpoint is supported by the Committee on the Elimination of Discrimination against Women. In effect, the Committee seems to be "cautiously" supporting a trans-inclusive interpretation of international law (Holtmaat & Post, 2015). Thus, for example, the General Recommendation No. 28 on the Core Obligations of States Parties (2010, October 19) stated the following:

> "*Intersectionality* is a basic concept for understanding the scope of the general obligations of States parties contained in article 2. The discrimination of women based on sex and gender is inextricably linked with other factors that affect women, such as race, ethnicity, religion or belief, health, status, age, class, caste, and sexual orientation and *gender identity.*"

The CEDAW Committee's attention to LBTQI issues remains scarce in all categories of documents except for the Concluding Observations. Our analysis of the Committee's Concluding Observations since 2010 shows that sexual orientation and some forms of gender identity (most notably transgender) are mentioned in over one-third of the documents concerning countries from all continents. (Holtmaat & Post, 2015)

On a similar note, the Inter-American Court of Human Rights has affirmed that the principle *pro homine* should guide conventional international law. Via its jurisprudence, the Court has established that a norm should be interpreted in the broadest sense and in a way that guarantees human dignity (Arrubia, 2018).

A trans-inclusive interpretation within international is more evident in *soft law*, such as in the "Principles on the application of international human rights legislation in relation to the sexual orientation and gender identity", commonly referred to as the Yogyakarta Principles (Arrubia, 2018). Although not legally binding, these principles signal the growing acceptance of transgender identity and rights.

From the perspective of Costa Rican national law and based on the constitutional *principle of nondiscrimination*, articles 77*bis* from Law No. 8204 and 71*bis* from the Criminal Code should be applied to transwomen. As it stands, the mitigating factors are not being applied due to a restrictive interpretation of gender.

There have been some positive advances with regards to protecting transgender rights. For instance, the Executive Decree No. 37071-S: Day Against Homophobia and Lesbophobia and Transphobia (2012), *Regulation of photographs for the identity card (Decree No. 08-2010)* from the Supreme Electoral Tribunal. The regulations allow transgender women to photograph according to their gender identity (Article 2), regardless of their legally assigned identity.

Despite these progressive regulations, the prevalence of violence is an indicator of the failure of current policies in ensuring trans-inclusive security. Additionally, cultural factors also guarantee impunity for perpetrators of crimes against transgender people. According to Fattah (2014), there is a cultural and structural propensity to victimization. A lack of power, economic deprivation and cultural stigmatization also makes certain social groups be deemed "easy prey' or as culturally legitimate victims" (p. 13).

There is a need for trans-inclusive interpretations of the laws and policies which underpin public institutions. For example, the Public Defender's Office has included sociodemographic measurement instruments to identify populations in vulnerable conditions and train public officials within its Strategic Plan (Z. Molina, personal communication, December 14, 2016). However, there are no trans-inclusive protocols to coordinate their treatment within the prison system. Likewise, it is essential to establish public policies to address the needs of transgender women throughout the criminal process. Yet, trans-inclusiveness needs to precede the prison system.

As this investigation demonstrated, transgender women are incarcerated in the aftermath of lives in which they have been subjected to multiple forms of violence. In this regard, their incarceration is often the result of extreme direct, social, and structural violence. In many cases, the victimization of incarcerated transgender women begins during their childhood. It continues when they enter the school system. Rather than being a place of learning, schools are, at times, a place of violence.

Moreover, the gender discrimination many transgender women experience when trying to obtain work demonstrates that they face many structural and social obstacles. In effect, transgender women are victimized by private and public actors. For instance, the public healthcare system also victimizes transgender women. There is scant information regarding the health needs of transgender individuals. By extension, there is also a gap in the treatment models being used for transgender individuals. Due to the lack of gender reaffirming procedures, the lack of trans-inclusive drug rehabilitation and the lack of mental health support, healthcare is a source of violence and not healing.

From a legal perspective, transgender identity remains unrecognized. Accordingly, transgender women are denied equal treatment under the law as cisgender women. With respect to the criminal justice system, they should be afforded the mitigating factors enshrined in articles 71*bis* and

77bis if they meet the same criteria as cisgender women. Similarly, following the guidelines established by the IAHRC and UNODC, there needs to be greater use of alternative sentencing.

Above all, further research is required. This research demonstrates that transgender women are often incarcerated due to economic, social, and structural marginalization. As it stands, they remain amongst the most marginalized citizens. Therefore, it is essential to fully understand the situation of incarcerated transgender women, taking into account their diverse identities, needs, and aspirations.

DISCLOSURE STATEMENT

The authors declare that there is no conflict of interest

ORCID

Gloriana Rodriguez Alvarez ⓘ http://orcid.org/0000-0002-6326-6813

REFERENCES

Akers, R. (2006). Aplicaciones de los principios del aprendizaje social. Algunos programas de tratamiento y prevención de la delincuencia. In Arús F.J. L.Dalbora & A.Maíllo (Eds.), Derecho penal y criminología como fundamento de la política criminal: estudios en homenaje al profesor Alfonso Serrano Gómez (pp. 1117–1138). *Editorial Dykinson.*

Annan, K. (2003). *Special measures for protection from sexual exploitation and sexual abuse.* United Nations Population Fund. https://www.tandfonline.com/doi/ref/10.1080/10911359.2014.991055?scroll=top

Arrubia, E. J. (2018). El derecho al nombre en relación con la identidad de género dentro del Sistema Interamericano de Derechos Humanos: el caso del Estado de Costa Rica. *Revista Direito GV, 14*(1), 148–168. https://doi.org/10.1590/2317-6172201808

Awan, M. S., Malik, N., Sarwar, H., & Waqas, M. (2011). *Impact of education on poverty reduction.* International Journal of Academic Research, Vol. 3, No. 1 (2011): pp. 659–664. Available at: https://mpra.ub.uni-muenchen.de/31826/1/MPRA_paper_31826.pdfpp.659-664.

BBC. (2015). *A guide to transgender terms.* https://www.bbc.co.uk/news/magazine-32979297

Beek, T., Cohen-Kettenis, P., & Kreukels, B. (2016). Gender incongruence/gender dysphoria and its classification history. *International Review of Psychiatry, 28*(1), 5–12. https://doi.org/10.3109/09540261.2015.1091293

Brysk, A. (2005). Global good Samaritans? Human Rights Foreign Policy in Costa Rica. *Global Governance: A Review of Multilateralism and International Organizations, 11*(4), 445–466. https://doi.org/10.1163/19426720-01104004

Budhwani, H., Hearld, K. R., Milner, A. N., Charow, R., McGlaughlin, E. M., Rodriguez-Lauzurique, M., Rosario, S., & Paulino-Ramirez, R. (2018). Transgender women's experiences with stigma, trauma, and attempted suicide in the Dominican Republic. *Suicide and Life-Threatening Behavior, 48*(6), 788–796. https://doi.org/10.1111/sltb.12400

Buist, C. L., & Stone, C. (2014). Transgender victims and offenders: Failures of the United States criminal justice system and the necessity of queer criminology. *Critical Criminology, 22*(1), 35–47. https://doi.org/10.1007/s10612-013-9224-1

Burgess-Proctor, A. (2006). Intersections of race, class, gender, and crime: Future directions for feminist criminology. *Feminist Criminology, 1*(1), 27–47. https://doi.org/10.1177/1557085105282899

Campbell, B. (2019). *Transgender-specific policy in Latin America.* Oxford Research Encyclopedia of Politics.

Caravaca-Morera, J. A., & Padilha, M. I. (2018). Trans necropolitics: Dialogues on devices of power, death and invisibility in the contemporary world. *Texto & Contexto – Enfermagem, 27*(2), 2-10. https://doi.org/10.1590/0104-07072018003770017

Chaim, N. (2008). Sampling knowledge: The hermeneutics of snowball sampling in qualitative research. *International Journal of Social Research Methodology, 11*(4), 327–344. https://doi.org/10.1080/13645570701401305

Chaparro Hernández, S. R., & Pérez Correa, C. (2017). *Sobredosis carcelaria y política de drogas en América Latina.* Centro de Estudios de Derecho, Justicia y Sociedad, Dejusticia. https://www.dejusticia.org/wp-content/uploads/2017/12/SobredosiscarcelariaypoliticadedrogasenAmericaLatina.pdf

Clark, K., Fletcher, J. B., Holloway, I. W., & Reback, C. J. (2018). Structural inequities and social networks impact hormone use and misuse among transgender women in Los Angeles county. *Archives of Sexual Behavior, 47*(4), 953–962. https://doi.org/10.1007/s10508-017-1143-x

Comisión Interamericana de Derechos Humanos. (2015). *Violencia contra Personas Lesbianas, Gays, Bisexuales, Trans e Intersex en América.* Comisión Interamericana de Derechos Humanos (p. 72).

Committee Against Torture. (2008). *Examen de los informes presentados por los Estados Parte en virtud del artículo 19 de la Convención/CAT/C/CRI/CO/2.* (4) http://www.acnur.org/t3/fileadmin/Documentos/BDL/2008/6319.pdf?view=1

Connell, R. (2021). Transgender health: On a world scale. *Health Sociology Review: The Journal of the Health Section of the Australian Sociological Association, 30*(1), 87–94. https://doi.org/10.1080/14461242.2020.1868899

Corrales, J. (2020). The expansion of LGBT rights in Latin America and the Backlash. *The Oxford handbook of global LGBT and sexual diversity politics* (pp. 185–200). Oxford Printing Press.

Crenshaw, K. (1989). *On intersectionality: Essential writings.* The New Press.

Currah, P., Juang, R., & Prince Minter, S. (2006). *Transgender rights.* University of Minnesota Press.

Darwin, H. (2020). Navigating the religious gender binary. *Sociology of Religion, 81*(2), 185–205. https://doi.org/10.1093/socrel/srz034

DeSouza, E. R., Wesselmann, E. D., & Ispas, D. (2017). Workplace discrimination against sexual minorities: Subtle and not-so-subtle. *Canadian Journal of Administrative Sciences, 34*(2), 121–132. https://doi.org/10.1002/cjas.1438

Domínguez-Martínez, T., & Robles, R. (2019). Preventing transphobic bullying and promoting inclusive educational environments: Literature review and implementing recommendations. *Archives of Medical Research, 50*(8), 543–555. https://doi.org/10.1016/j.arcmed.2019.10.009

Dunne, P. (2020). Transgender rights in Europe: EU and Council of Europe movements towards gender identity equality. In *Research handbook on gender, sexuality and the law* (pp. 134-147). Edward Elgar Publishing. https://doi.org/10.4337/9781788111157.00017

Earnshaw, V. A., Reisner, S. L., Juvonen, J., Hatzenbuehler, M. L., Perrotti, J., & Schuster, M. A. (2017). LGBTQ bullying: Translating research to action in pediatrics. *Pediatrics, 140*(4), e20170432. https://doi.org/10.1542/peds.2017-0432

Evens, E., Lanham, M., Santi, K., Cooke, J., Ridgeway, K., Morales, G., Parker, C., Brennan, C., de Bruin, M., Desrosiers, P. C., Diaz, X., Drago, M., McLean, R., Mendizabal, M., Davis, D., Hershow, R. B., & Dayton, R. (2019). Experiences of gender-based violence among female sex workers, men who have sex with men, and transgender women in Latin America and the Caribbean: A qualitative study to inform HIV programming. *BMC International Health and Human Rights, 19*(1), 1–14. https://doi.org/10.1186/s12914-019-0187-5

Fattah, E. (2014). Victimología: pasado, presente y futuro. *Revista Electrónica de Ciencia Penal y Criminología.* Bonachela, M, Trad. ISSN-e 1695-0194, N°. 16, 2014. https://dialnet.unirioja.es/servlet/articulo?codigo=4965987

Fattori, M., & Quirós, V. (2019). Tematizando la heteronormatividad. Una reflexión histórico-pedagógica sobre la educación sexual en Costa Rica. *UCR Reflexiones. Julio-Diciembre, 98*, 1–21. https://doi.org/10.15517/rr.v98i0.36795

Fawole, O. I. (2008). Economic violence to women and girls: Is it receiving the necessary attention? *Trauma, Violence & Abuse, 9*(3), 167–177. https://doi.org/10.1177/1524838008319255

Fernández, A., Rodríguez, G., Fallas, J., & Chinchilla, H. (2015). Privadas de libertad, vulnerabilidades extremas: Caso de Costa Rica. *Fundación Arias para la Paz y el Progreso Humano* (1ra. ed., pp. 41-53).

FONABE. (2020). *Tipos de Becas.* Fondo Nacional de Becas. https://www.fonabe.go.cr/centro-educativo/tipos-de-becas

Fontanari, A. M. V., Rovaris, D. L., Costa, A. B., Pasley, A., Cupertino, R. B., Soll, B. M. B., Schwarz, K., da Silva, D. C., Borba, A. O., Mueller, A., Bau, C. H. D., & Lobato, M. I. R. (2018). Childhood maltreatment linked with a deterioration of psychosocial outcomes in adult life for southern Brazilian transgender women. *Journal of Immigrant and Minority Health, 20*(1), 33–43. https://doi.org/10.1007/s10903-016-0528-6

Francisco Simon, S. (2021). Poéticas de la razón aporofóbica: testimonios de la prisión política y la criminalización de la pobreza en el Chile contemporáneo. *Revista de Humanidades,* (43), 237–264.

Freud, S. (1994). The social construction of gender. *Journal of Adult Development, 1*(1), 37–45. https://doi.org/10.1007/BF02252981

Galindo, D., Cazeiro, F., Serra, A. G., & Lemos de Souza, L. (2017). LGBTs and gender banned? Genealogical notes about law projects in Brazil. *Psicologia em Estudo, 22*(2), 253–265. https://doi.org/10.4025/psicolestud.v22i2.33506

Gallagher, R. (2020). Redefining "CEDAW" to include LGBT rights: incorporating prohibitions against the discrimination of sexual orientation and gender identity. *Southern California Interdisciplinary Law Journal, 29*(4), 637–658. https://gould.usc.edu/why/students/orgs/ilj/assets/docs/29-4-Gallagher.pdf

Garthe, R. C., Hidalgo, M. A., Hereth, J., Garofalo, R., Reisner, S. L., Mimiaga, M. J., & Kuhns, L. (2018). Prevalence and risk correlates of intimate partner violence among a multisite cohort of young transgender women. *LGBT Health, 5*(6), 333–340. https://doi.org/10.1089/lgbt.2018.0034

Gaynor, T. S. (2018). Social construction and the criminalization of identity: State-sanctioned oppression and an unethical administration. *Public Integrity*, 20(4), 358–369.

Gonzalez, C. A., Gallego, J. D., & Bockting, W. O. (2017). Demographic characteristics, components of sexuality and gender, and minority stress and their associations to excessive alcohol, cannabis, and illicit (noncannabis) drug use among a large sample of transgender people in the United States. *The Journal of Primary Prevention*, 38(4), 419–445. https://doi.org/10.1007/s10935-017-0469-4

Grauer, L. A., & Buikstra, E. J. (2019). *Ortner's Identification of Pathological Conditions in Human Skeletal Remains* (3rd ed.). Arizona State University.

Grossman, A. H., & D'Augelli, A. R. (2006). Transgender youth: Invisible and vulnerable. *Journal of Homosexuality*, 51(1), 111–128. https://doi.org/10.1300/j082v51n01_06

Hereth, J., Garthe, R. C., Garofalo, R., Reisner, S. L., Mimiaga, M. J., & Kuhns, L. M. (2020). Examining patterns of interpersonal violence, structural and social exclusion, resilience, and arrest among young transgender women. *Criminal Justice and Behavior*, 48(1), 54–75.

Holtmaat, R., & Post, P. (2015). Enhancing LGBTI rights by changing the interpretation of the convention on the elimination of all forms of discrimination against women? *Nordic Journal of Human Rights*, 33(4), 319–336. https://doi.org/10.1080/18918131.2016.1123502

Human Rights Watch. (2020). "Every Day I Live in Fear" *Violence and Discrimination Against LGBT People in El Salvador, Guatemala, and Honduras, and Obstacles to Asylum in the United States.* https://www.hrw.org/sites/default/files/media_2020/10/centralamerica_lgbt1020_web_0.pdf

IAFA. (2020). *Información Especial.* Instituto sobre Alcoholismo y Farmacodependencia. https://www.iafa.go.cr/

ICD. (2014). *Relación entre el delito y el consumo de drogas en mujeres sentenciadas en el Centro Penal Buen Pastor.* Instituto Costarricense sobre Drogas. https://www.icd.go.cr/portalicd/images/docs/uid/investigaciones/Relacin_delito_drogas_mujeressentenciadas_PenalBuenPastor.pdf

INAMU. (2018). *Proyecto de Ley mejorará la condición de las mujeres en situaciones de vulnerabilidad en procesos penales.* https://www.inamu.go.cr/proyecto-de-ley-mejorara-las-condicion-de-las-mujeres-en-situaciones-de-vulerabilidad-en-procesos-penales

INEC. (2020). *Costa Rica en cifras 2020.* Instituto Nacional de Estadística y Censos de Costa Rica https://www.inec.cr/sites/default/files/documetos-biblioteca-virtual/recostaricaencifras2020_0.pdf

Inter-American Commission on Human Rights. (2017). *Informe sobre medidas dirigidas a reducir el uso de la prisión preventiva en las Américas.* Relatoría sobre los Derechos de las Personas Privadas de Libertad de la Comisión Interamericana de Derechos Humanos.

Ismoyo, P. J. (2020). Decolonizing gender identities in Indonesia: a study of Bissu 'The Trans-religious leader' in. *Paradigma: Jurnal Kajian Budaya*, 10(3), 277–288. https://doi.org/10.17510/paradigma.v10i3.404

Jackman, K. B., Dolezal, C., Levin, B., Honig, J. C., & Bockting, W. O. (2018). Stigma, gender dysphoria, and non-suicidal self-injury in a community sample of transgender individuals. *Psychiatry Research*, 269, 602–609. https://doi.org/10.1016/j.psychres.2018.08.092

Jenness, V., Sexton, L., & Sumner, J. (2019). Sexual victimization against transgender women in prison: Consent and coercion in context. *Criminology*, 57(4), 603–631. https://doi.org/10.1111/1745-9125.12221

Hopkins Medicine, J. (2020). *Gender Affirmation Nonsurgical Services.* https://www.hopkinsmedicine.org/health/wellness-and-prevention/gender-affirmation-nonsurgical-services

Johnson, R. G., McCandless, S., & Renderos, H. (2020). An exploratory study of transgender inmate populations in Latin America. *Public Integrity*, 22(4), 1–14. https://doi.org/10.1080/10999922.2018.1557027

Juárez-Chávez, E., Cooney, E. E., Hidalgo, A., Sánchez, J., & Poteat, T. (2021). Violence experiences in childhood and adolescence among gay men and transgender women living in Perú: A qualitative exploration. *Journal of Interpersonal Violence*, 36(9–10), 4235–4255. https://doi.org/10.1177/0886260518787811

Kappeler, V. E., & Potter, G. W. (2017). *The mythology of crime and criminal justice.* Waveland Press.

Keegan, C. M. (2020). Getting disciplined: What's trans about queer studies now? *Journal of Homosexuality*, 67(3), 384–314. https://doi.org/10.1080/00918369.2018.1530885

Klemmer, C. L., Arayasirikul, S., & Raymond, H. F. (2021). Transphobia-based violence, depression, and anxiety in transgender women: The role of body satisfaction. *Journal of Interpersonal Violence*, 36(5–6), 2633–2655. https://doi.org/10.1177/0886260518760015

Kuper, L. E., Adams, N., & Mustanski, B. S. (2018). Exploring cross-sectional predictors of suicide ideation, attempt, and risk in a large online sample of transgender and gender nonconforming youth and young adults . *LGBT Health*, 5(7), 391–400. https://doi.org/10.1089/lgbt.2017.0259

Liu, R. T., Sheehan, A. E., Walsh, R. F., Sanzari, C. M., Cheek, S. M., & Hernandez, E. M. (2019). Prevalence and correlates of non-suicidal self-injury among lesbian, gay, bisexual, and transgender individuals: A systematic review and meta-analysis . *Clinical Psychology Review*, 74, 101783. https://doi.org/10.1016/j.cpr.2019.101783

Lorber, J. (2009). The social construction of gender. In E. Disch (Ed.), *Reconstructing gender: A multicultural anthology* (pp. 111–119). McGraw-Hill Higher Education.

Loza, O., Beltran, O., & Mangadu, T. (2017). A qualitative exploratory study on gender identity and the health risks and barriers to care for transgender women living in a US–Mexico border city. *International Journal of Transgenderism*, *18*(1), 104–118. https://doi.org/10.1080/15532739.2016.1255868

Lyons, T., Krüsi, A., Pierre, L., Kerr, T., Small, W., & Shannon, K. (2017). Negotiating violence in the context of transphobia and criminalization: The experiences of trans sex workers in Vancouver, Canada. *Qualitative Health Research*, *27*(2), 182–190. https://doi.org/10.1177/1049732315613311

Lyons, T., Shannon, K., Pierre, L., Small, W., Krüsi, A., & Kerr, T. (2015). A qualitative study of transgender individuals' experiences in residential addiction treatment settings: Stigma and inclusivity. *Substance Abuse Treatment PreventionPolicy*, *10*, 17. https://doi.org/10.1186/s13011-015-0015-4

Mandela, N. (1994). *A long walk to freedom*. Little, Brown and Company.

Mauer, M. (2018). Long-term sentences: Time to reconsider the scale of punishment. *UMKC Law Review*, *87*(1), 118.

Meléndez Segura, J. (2018). *Discriminación por identidad género en la ubicación de la población trans privada de libertad en materia Penal Juvenil: internamiento en centros especializados*. Licentiate thesis, University of Costa Rica, San José. http://repositorio.sibdi.ucr.ac.cr:8080/jspui/handle/123456789/5670

Molina, Z., personal communication, (December 14, 2016)

Mora Bolaños, J. (2019). Perspectiva de género y privación de libertad: Algunas reflexiones sobre una (reciente y necesaria) reforma al Código Penal Costarricense. *Revista Nuevo Humanismo*, *7*(2). 51-60. https://doi.org/10.15359/rnh.7-2.3

Murillo, Á. (2018). *Una batalla sin fin: Costa Rica abraza al matrimonio igualitario*. Seminario Universidad. https://semanariouniversidad.com/pais/una-batalla-sin-fin-costa-rica-abraza-al-matrimonio-igualitario/

Nájar, A. (2018). El "shock religioso" que puso a Fabricio Alvarado, predicador de una iglesia evangélica, como favorito para las elecciones presidenciales de Costa Rica. BBC Mundo. https://www.bbc.com/mundo/noticias-america-latina-42884219

Nay, Y. E. (2019). The atmosphere of trans politics in the global north and west. *TSQ: Transgender Studies Quarterly*, *6*(1), 64–79. https://doi.org/10.1215/23289252-7253496

Nissim, M. (2018). *Transvestite, Transsexual, Transgender: Here's what you should actually call trans people*. PinkNews. https://www.pinknews.co.uk/2018/03/19/transsexual-transgender-transvestite-what-should-you-call-trans-people/

OAS. (2021). *Inter-American Treaties*. Organization of American States. http://www.oas.org/en/sla/dil/inter_american_treaties_signatories_member_states.asp

Organization of American States. (2010, May 4). *The European Union and the Americas: The challenges of multilateralism*. XXIII OAS Policy Roundtable Summary.

Orozco Álvarez, J. (2012). *Reforma del artículo 77, de la Ley de Estupefacientes, Sustancias Psicotrópicas, Drogas de uso no autorizado, actividades conexas, legitimación de capitales y financiamiento al terrorismo y su reglamento*. Proyecto de Ley. https://cgrfiles.cgr.go.cr/publico/jaguar/USI/normativa/2011/PROYECTO/PROYECTO-17980.pdf

Ortiz, J. M., & Jackey, H. (2019). The system is not broken, it is intentional: The prisoner reentry industry as deliberate structural violence. *The Prison Journal*, *99*(4), 484–503. https://doi.org/10.1177/0032885519852090

PAHO. (2014). *Blueprint for the provision of comprehensive care for trans persons and their communities in the Caribbean and other Anglophone countries*. Pan-American Health Organization. https://www.paho.org/hq/dmdocuments/2014/2014-cha-blueprint-comprehensive-anglo-countries.pdf

Palma Campos, C. (2011). Delito y sobrevivencia: las mujeres que ingresan a la cárcel El Buen Pastor en Costa Rica por tráfico de drogas. *Anuario de Estudios Centroamericanos*, *37*, 245–270.

Peek, C. (2004). Breaking out of the prison hierarchy: Transgender prisoners, rape, and the eighth amendment. *Santa Clara Law Review*, *44*(4), 1211–1248.

Pesec, M., Ratcliffe, H. L., Karlage, A., Hirschhorn, L. R., Gawande, A., & Bitton, A. (2017). Primary health care that works: The Costa Rican experience. *Health Affairs*, *36*(3), 531–538. https://doi.org/10.1377/hlthaff.2016.1319

Ragonnet-Cronin, M., Hu, Y. W., Morris, S. R., Sheng, Z., Poortinga, K., & Wertheim, J. O. (2019). HIV transmission networks among transgender women in Los Angeles County, CA, USA: A phylogenetic analysis of surveillance data. *The Lancet HIV*, *6*(3), e164–e172. https://doi.org/10.1016/S2352-3018(18)30359-X

REDLACTRANS. (2020). *Aproximación a un mapeo de las barreras legales para la plena vigencia de los derechos humanos de las mujeres trans en América Latina y el Caribe*. https://issuu.com/redlactrans/docs/aproximaci_n_a_una_mapeo_de_las_barreras_legales_p

Rimes, K. A., Goodship, N., Ussher, G., Baker, D., & West, E. (2019). Non-binary and binary transgender youth: Comparison of mental health, self-harm, suicidality, substance use and victimization experiences. *International Journal of Transgenderism*, *20*(2-3), 230–240. https://doi.org/10.1080/15532739.2017.1370627

Rodgers, J., Asquith, N. L., & Dwyer, A. (2017). Cisnormativity, criminalization, vulnerability: Transgender people in prisons. *Tasmanian Institute of Law Enforcement Studies Briefing Paper*, *12*, 1–13.

Rodríguez-Madera, S. L., Padilla, M., Varas-Díaz, N., Neilands, T., Vasques Guzzi, A. C., Florenciani, E. J., & Ramos-Pibernus, A. (2017). Experiences of violence among transgender women in Puerto Rico: An underestimated problem. *Journal of Homosexuality, 64*(2), 209–217. https://doi.org/10.1080/00918369.2016.1174026

Rosenblum, D. (1999). Trapped' in sing sing: Transgendered prisoners caught in the genderbinarism. *Michigan Journal of Gender and Law, 6*, 499–571.

Rosenblum, D. (2011). Unisex CEDAW, or what's wrong with women's rights. *Columbia Journal of Gender and Law, 20*, 98.

Rosenberg, R., & Oswin, N. (2015). Trans embodiment in carceral space: Hypermasculinity and the US prison industrial complex. *Gender, Place & Culture, 22*(9), 1269–1286. https://doi.org/10.1080/0966369X.2014.969685

Saborío, S. (2019). Estado del arte sobre narcoviolencia en Costa Rica. *Revista Reflexiones, 98*(2), 23–38. https://doi.org/10.15517/rr.v98i2.34956

Schilt, K., & Lagos, D. (2017). The development of transgender studies in sociology. *Annual Review of Sociology, 43*(1), 425–443. https://doi.org/10.1146/annurev-soc-060116-053348

Seelman, K. L. (2015). Unequal treatment of transgender individuals in domestic violence and rape crisis programs. *Journal of Social Service Research, 41*(3), 307–325. https://doi.org/10.1080/01488376.2014.987943

Slootmaeckers, K. (2020). Constructing European union identity through LGBT equality promotion: Crises and shifting othering processes in the European union enlargement. *Political Studies Review, 18*(3), 346–361. https://doi.org/10.1177/1478929919877624

Stohr, M. (2015). The hundred years' war: The etiology and status of assaults on transgender women in men's prisons. *Women & Criminal Justice, 25*(1–2), 120–129. https://doi.org/10.1080/08974454.2015.1026154

Streed, C. G., Jr, McCarthy, E. P., & Haas, J. S. (2018). Self-reported physical and mental health of gender nonconforming transgender adults in the United States . *LGBT Health, 5*(7), 443–448. https://doi.org/10.1089/lgbt.2017.0275

Stryker, S. (2008). *Transgender history*. Seal Press.

Taylor, J. K., Haider-Markel, D. P., & Lewis, D. C. (2018). *The remarkable rise of transgender rights*. University of Michigan Press.

Thomas, R., Pega, F., Khosla, R., Verster, A., Hana, T., & Say, L. (2017). Ensuring an inclusive global health agenda for transgender people. *Bulletin of the World Health Organization, 95*(2), 154–156. https://doi.org/10.2471/BLT.16.183913

UNODC. (2003). *Drug abuse treatment and rehabilitation: A practical planning and implementation guide*. UN Office on Drugs and Crime. https://www.unodc.org/docs/treatment/Guide_E.pdf

UNODC. (2009). *Handbook on prisoners with special needs*. UN Office on Drugs and Crime. https://www.refworld.org/docid/4a0969d42.html

Van de Grift, T., Elaut, E., Cerwenka, S., Cohen-Kettenis, P., & Kreukels, B. (2018). Surgical satisfaction, quality of life, and their association after gender-affirming surgery: A follow-up study. *Journal of Sex & Marital Therapy, 44*(2), 138–148. https://doi.org/10.1080/0092623X.2017.1326190

Vargas, J. R., & Muiser, J. (2013). Promoting universal financial protection: a policy analysis of universal health coverage in Costa Rica (1940–2000). *Health Research Policy and Systems, 11*(1), 28–29. https://doi.org/10.1186/1478-4505-11-28

Wilson, M., Simpson, P. L., Butler, T. G., Richters, J., Yap, L., & Donovan, B. (2017). You're a woman, a convenience, a cat, a poof, a thing, an idiot': Transgender women negotiating sexual experiences in men's prisons in Australia. *Sexualities, 20*(3), 380–402. https://doi.org/10.1177/1363460716652828

Yamanis, T., Malik, M., del Río-González, A., Wirtz, A., Cooney, E., Lujan, M., Corado, R., & Poteat, T. (2018). Legal immigration status is associated with depressive symptoms among Latina transgender women in Washington, DC. *International Journal of Environmental Research and Public Health, 15*(6), 1246. https://doi.org/10.3390/ijerph15061246

ORCID

Gloriana Rodriguez Alvarez (iD) http://orcid.org/0000-0002-6326-6813

LAWS

Advisory Opinion on Gender Identity, Equality, and Non-Discrimination of Same-Sex Couples, (2017), OC-24 / 17

Costa Rica. Constitución Política. (1949) *Political Constitution of Costa Rica*. San Jose. Article 33

Constitutional Court of Costa Rica, Resolution No. 2007-07128, Dossier No. 06-001874-0007-CO. May 23, 2007

Criminal code, article 71bis, (Costa Rica, 2018)

Executive Decree No. 37071-S: Day Against Homophobia, Lesbophobia and Transphobia (2012)

Regulation of photographs for the identity card (Decree No. 08-2010)

Labour Code, article 622, (Costa Rica, 1943)

Law on Narcotics, Psychotropic Substances, Unauthorized Drugs, Related Activities, Money Laundering and the Financing of Terrorism. Article 77bis, (Costa Rica, 2013).

Organization of American States (OAS), *Inter-American Convention on the Prevention, Punishment and Eradication of Violence against Women ("Convention of Belem do Para")*, 9 June 1994

UN General Assembly, *Convention on the Elimination of All Forms of Discrimination Against Women*, 18 December 1979, United Nations, Treaty Series, Vol. 1249

Litigation on Gender Confirmation Surgery and Hormonal Therapy among Trans Women Prisoners: Views from the U.S. Circuit Courts of Appeals

Claire Nolasco Braaten and Michael S. Vaughn

ABSTRACT

This article analyzes U.S. Circuit Courts of Appeals' cases involving Title 42 U.S.C. §1983 actions filed by trans women inmates against corrections and/or medical officers for failure to provide hormone therapy and/or gender confirmation surgery ("GCS") ($N = 24$). The courts varied in their decisions. The Ninth Circuit has been more progressive toward trans rights, holding that GCS can be medically necessary depending on the individualized needs of the transgender inmate because there is a medical consensus on the appropriateness of these treatments. The First and Fifth Circuits rejected requests for GCS because of the lack of medical consensus on the necessity of GCS. Both the Seventh and Eleventh Circuits held that failure to provide medically recommended care for a non-medical reason and unexplained delays in treatment can constitute deliberate indifference, violating the Eighth Amendment. Under Tenth Circuit precedent, prison officials are not deliberately indifferent for failing to provide hormone treatments.

INTRODUCTION

Trans gender women face a plethora of difficulties living in male prisons. *First,* corrections officers perceive them as security risks, disrupting prison disorder because they do not conform to the inherently masculinist prison environment (Jenness, 2010; Jenness & Fenstermaker, 2014). *Second,* they face higher risks of victimization and are 13 times more likely than nontrans female inmates to be sexually assaulted (Jenness, 2011; Jenness et al., 2010). Paradoxically, trans women inmates in all-male prisons report higher levels of self-perceptions of femininity while incarcerated, especially for those who report sexual victimization by other inmates (Jenness & Gerlinger, 2020). *Third,* classification decisions by prison officials also pose problems for trans women inmates in several ways: (1) general population placement according to their biological sex coerces them into a subordinate position in the prison hierarchy (Brown & Jenness, 2020; Brown & McDuffie, 2009; Dolovich, 2011; Donaldson, 2001; Sumner & Jenness, 2014); (2) segregation can be demoralizing and lead to dangerous labeling (Hwang, 2016), and limit access to programming and other opportunities available to general population inmates (Jenness, 2021); and (3) restrictive isolation may lead to deterioration in their mental health (Wildeman & Andersen, 2020). Housing classification for trans women inmates is a "sine qua non policy and practice concern" due to the well-documented and pressing threats to their safety and deprivation of their rights (Jenness, 2021, p. 8). *Fourth,* medical care for trans women inmates also pose significant legal and policy issues for courts and correctional facilities (Van Hout et al., 2020). Failure of prisons to provide necessary medical care, including hormonal therapy and gender confirmation surgery (GCS), have resulted in significant psychological and mental stress among transgender female inmates (Jenness, 2011) and substantial court litigation (Garcia, 2014).

Meeting the medical needs of trans women inmates presents a compelling set of issues for correctional medical and custodial personnel (Redcay et al., 2020; Routh et al., 2017). The complexities of issues related to the treatment of gender dysphoria (GD) is further evident within court settings, as medical experts have varied in their approaches to the symptoms and their resolution. Levine (2016, p. 237) notes that in court settings, medical experts on both sides of the litigation base their testimonies on three different paradigms: *First,* the medical illness paradigm assumes that diagnosis of the illness automatically necessitates treatment. As applied to male-to-female trans prisoners with GD, these experts opine that ameliorative measures, such as facial hair removal, hormone therapy, rhinoplasty, and/or augmentation mammoplasty are medically necessary to lessen subjective suffering. Under this paradigm, GD is presented in courtrooms as a "serious medical condition" and experts view GCS to be a "cure for gender dysphoria" (Levine, 2016, p. 237). *Second,* the developmental paradigm focuses on the developmental processes from childhood to adulthood, including those experiences while incarcerated. Levine (2016) approves of this paradigm, which assumes that a diagnosis of GD does not automatically require hormone treatment and/or GCS. The developmental paradigm recognizes that GD is a psychiatric disorder in the DSM-5, not a health problem to be treated as a medical necessity. To ameliorate suffering, treatment of GD requires a holistic approach, considering the patient's history, comorbidities, and motivations. Clinicians using the developmental model must "acknowledge the pain of gender dysphoria" and work with patients to make life more palatable—to ease anxiety and reduce depression (Levine, 2016, p. 238). Treatment options for incarcerated inmates include addressing the inmate by her preferred name, staff education, providing female accessories, and hormone treatment. *Finally,* the minority rights paradigm assumes that the treatment of GD is primarily determined by the patient's wishes. Gender confirmation surgery requires diagnosis of GD by a qualified mental health professional (MHP) expert who endorses the World Professional Association for Transgender Health (WPATH) standards and the lapse of one year of hormone treatments for the patient. Levine (2016, p. 239) criticizes this paradigm because it assumes that GCS "is a cure that, if withheld, constitutes a gross violation of the Eighth Amendment."

The varying approaches of medical experts described above have led to divergent outcomes within U.S. Circuit Courts of Appeals in litigation involving requests of transgender inmates for gender confirmation surgery and hormone therapy. It is important to look at the U.S. Circuit Courts of Appeals because the U.S. Supreme Court has not decided a case on transgender prisoners. Other than the Supreme Court, the federal circuit courts are the most influential courts in the United States, as they are situated directly below the Court of last resort. Since the Supreme Court only hears around 70 cases a year out of the thousands decided by the lower courts across the country (Grant, 2012), it is important to know how the U.S. Circuit Courts of Appeals are ruling on the medical rights of trans gender female inmates. Thus, this article addresses this gap in the literature by analyzing how the 12 federal circuits have ruled on requests for gender confirmation surgery and requests for hormone treatment therapy among trans women prisoners. The article also analyzes similarities and differences of outcomes among the federal circuits that have litigated issues involving the Constitutional rights of trans women inmates. The discussion is based on U.S. Circuit Courts' descriptions of the testimony of medical experts and the Circuits' own assessments of their veracity. Since the article is a legal analysis, it summarizes experts' opinions as described in the decisions of U.S. Circuit Courts of Appeals without commenting on the accuracy of these medical assessments; however, the article explains the disagreements and variation in the medical community on how to approach GD and its treatment for individual trans women prisoners.

Legal and Scientific Context of Transgender Inmates' Rights

Gender Dysphoria and its Treatment

Transgender individuals have a gender identity that does not align with their biological sex (American Psychological Association, 2015). An estimated 1.4 million U.S. adults or 0.6 percent of the adult population identify as transgender (Flores, 2016). The *Diagnostic and Statistical Manual of Mental Disorders* (American Psychiatric Association, 2013, pp. 453, 458) ("DSM-5") lists two conditions for a diagnosis of gender dysphoria: (1) "marked incongruence between one's experienced/expressed gender and assigned gender" for at least 6 months; and (2) the person's condition must be associated with "clinically significant distress" that severely impairs or limits the ability to meaningfully function (*Gibson v. Collier*, 2019, p. 217; WPATH, 2012, p. 5). Gender dysphoria is associated with "clinically significant distress or impairment in social, occupational, or other important areas of functioning" (DSM-5). It constitutes a "form of psychological pain" and in court proceedings is represented as "a steady state of distress, often described as suffering" (Levine, 2016, p. 242). According to the Ninth Circuit, without treatment, it can lead to "debilitating distress, depression, impairment of function, substance use, self-surgery to alter one's genitals or secondary sex characteristics, self-injurious behaviors, and even suicide" (*Edmo v. Corizon, Inc.*, 2019, p. 769).

The WPATH standards (2012, p. 60) for GCS in male-to-female patients include: (1) "persistent, well documented gender dysphoria"; (2) "capacity to make a fully informed decision" and "consent for treatment"; (3) "age of majority"; (4) "if significant medical or mental health concerns are present, they must be well controlled"; (5) "12 continuous months of hormone therapy" appropriate to the patient's "gender goals"; and (6) "12 continuous months of living in a gender role that is congruent with their gender identity." The WPATH standards (2012, p. 54) state that many individuals "find comfort with their gender identity, role, and expression without surgery"; however, GCS may be essential for others and "medically necessary to alleviate their gender dysphoria." The latter group cannot obtain relief from gender dysphoria "without modification of their primary and/or secondary sex characteristics to establish greater congruence with their gender identity" (WPATH, 2012, p. 555; Sevelius & Jenness, 2017, p. 36). The consensus view, although not universally, in the medical and mental health communities is that GCS is safe, effective, and medically necessary in appropriate circumstances for gender dysphoric individuals, including those who are incarcerated (Ettner, 2016; Frey et al., 2017; Osborne & Lawrence, 2016; Stroumsa, 2014).

Osborne and Lawrence (2016, p. 1650) point out that the WPATH standards are "not without controversy." The WPATH recommendations formulated by experienced clinicians and scholars were based on low-quality evidence, including case series and expert opinion (Byne et al., 2012; De Cuypere & Vercruysse, 2009). Importantly, the WPATH standards also do not reflect the practices and experiences of all GD experts (Levine, 2018; Levine & Solomon, 2008; Zucker et al., 2016). Osborne and Lawrence (2016, p. 1651), however, concurred that despite the complexities involved, prisons must "make reasonable efforts to provide medically necessary treatments," including GCS to inmates. They also acknowledged that, the "medical necessity" of gender GCS is a "fundamental issue" because U.S. courts have consistently ruled that failure to provide inmates with appropriate medical treatment to serious medical needs is deliberate indifference, violating the Eighth Amendment's prohibition against cruel and unusual punishment (Osborne & Lawrence, 2016, p. 1651).

Other scholars vary in their approach to treatment. Berlin (2016, p. 247) considers GD as "similar to a depressive disorder" that may require psychiatric intervention to facilitate improvement. In correctional institutions, treatment must be provided within a safe and secure setting that is "responsive to the legitimate concerns of administrators, staff, and other inmates" (Berlin, 2016, p. 251). According to McHugh (2015), however, individuals diagnosed with GD should not be treated with surgery or hormone therapy but with psychotherapy that focuses on dissuading patients of the idea that they are in the wrong body, and of the idea that they can only be happy (less dysphoric) through GCS. McHugh (2015) argues that surgical removal of a completely healthy and fully functioning organ (e.g., the penis) represents a radical departure from acceptable medical practice.

Research indicates a low regret rate of 1%–2% for individuals who undergo GCS (Byne et al., 2012; Osborne & Lawrence, 2016, p. 1660). Reasons for regret include "inadequate social adaptation, comorbidity with certain psychiatric disorders, poor psychological and psychiatric evaluation, and dissatisfaction with aesthetic or functional outcome of GCS" (Bizic et al., 2018, p. 5). Scientific literature provide mixed results when analyzing morbidity rates and well-being of patients who underwent GCS (Simonsen et al., 2016). Asscheman et al. (2011) conducted a long-term follow-up study of 1,331 individuals in the Netherlands who received hormone treatment (966 biological men received estrogen and 365 biological women received testosterone). They found that biological males receiving feminizing hormones experienced only minimal bodily effects, significant decrease in libido, and had a 51 percent higher mortality rate than the general population, most from suicides, AIDS, and drug abuse. Current estradiol use was also associated with three times the increased risk of cardiovascular death and increased risk of lung and hematological disease. Dhejne et al. (2011) followed 324 persons in Sweden (191 male-to-female and 133 female-to-male) who underwent GCS over a 30-year period from 1973 to 2003. They found that although GCS diminished the distress of individuals with GD, transgenders who underwent GCS had approximately a three times higher risk of all-causes of mortality than controls. Their rates of attempted suicide was 4.9 times higher, completed suicide rates was 19.1 times higher, and psychiatric inpatient care was 2.8 times higher than comparable rates in the general population.

Contrary studies indicate positive outcomes of gender-affirming surgery on transgender and gender diverse individuals, including relief from gender dysphoria and improvement of psychosocial distress (Marano et al., 2021). These studies, however, used observational methods that lack either control groups or adequate sample size (Bränström & Pachankis, 2020; Murad et al., 2010; Stroumsa, 2014). Moreover, Almazan and Keuroghlian (2021) performed a secondary analysis of the 2015 U.S. Transgender Survey, which contained data from 27,715 transgender adults in 50 states, Washington, D.C., U.S. territories, and U.S. military bases abroad. They found that "respondents who had undergone all desired surgeries had significant reductions in adverse mental health outcomes, and these reductions were more profound than those among respondents who had received only some desired surgeries" (Almazan & Keuroghlian, 2021, p. E4).

Gender-affirming surgeries such as GCS were also not associated with measures of lifetime mental health including lifetime suicidal ideation, lifetime suicide attempts, lifetime alcohol use, or lifetime smoking (Almazan & Keuroghlian, 2021). Prunas et al. (2017) found similar results among 76 transgender patients (45 male-to-female and 31 female-to-male) in a hospital in Milan, Italy between 2011 and December 2014. Those who already received GCS showed higher scores of self-acceptance on the Psychological Well-being Scale. The male-to-female sample also had higher scores on environmental mastery, and all transsexuals showed higher levels of eudaimonic well-being after GCS.

Legal Requirements Under The Eighth Amendment Deliberate Indifference Claims

The Eighth Amendment of the U.S. Constitution prohibits cruel and unusual punishments, embodying "broad and idealistic concepts of dignity, civilized standards, humanity, and decency"

(*Brown v. Plata*, 2011, p. 510; *Estelle v. Gamble*, 1976, p. 105). Courts have interpreted the Eighth Amendment's prohibition against cruel and unusual punishment when considering permissible conditions of confinement and medical treatment for inmates (*Farmer v. Brennan*, 1994). The Eighth Amendment prohibits undue suffering unrelated to any legitimate penological purposes, including "unnecessary and wanton infliction of pain" that is "repugnant to the conscience of mankind" (*Estelle v. Gamble*, 1976, pp. 105–106). The government is obliged to provide for the medical care of incarcerated inmates because society deprives them of the means to provide for their own needs (*Brown v. Plata*, 2011, p. 510).

The Eighth Amendment prohibition on cruel and unusual punishments includes "deliberate indifference to serious medical needs of prisoners" (*Estelle v. Gamble*, 1976, p. 104). To prove an Eighth Amendment violation, a prisoner must satisfy two prongs: (1) an objective prong requiring proof of a serious medical need and (2) a subjective prong requiring proof of prison administrators' or medical officials' culpability that rises to the level of deliberate indifference to the prisoner's serious medical need (*Estelle v. Gamble*, 1976; *Farmer v. Brennan*, 1994, *Wilson v. Seiter*, 1991). Deliberate indifference requires that a prison or medical official: (1) had subjective knowledge that an inmate was at risk of serious harm, and (2) recklessly disregarded that risk (*Farmer v. Brennan*, 1994). This level of blameworthiness requires more than mere negligence, which is actionable in medical malpractice lawsuits filed by free-world plaintiffs (Vaughn & Carroll, 1998), but medical malpractice or negligence is not actionable for prisoners suing correctional or medical personnel under Section 1983.

The objective prong requires that a physician diagnosed the serious medical need as mandating treatment (Nolasco & Vaughn, 2020) or that failure to treat the medical condition could result in "unnecessary and wanton infliction of pain" (*Jett v. Penner*, 2006, p. 1096). The need must be so obvious that even a layperson would recognize the necessity of treatment (*Gaudreault v. Municipality of Salem Mass*, 1990; *Keohane v. Florida DOC Secretary*, 2020a). Serious medical needs can refer to physical, dental, and/or mental health needs (*Hoptowit v. Ray*, 1982, p. 1253). Under this prong, however, prison administrators or medical officials are not required to provide the best available care (*Harris v. Thigpen*, 1991) or the inmate's preferred treatment (*United States v. Derbes*, 2004). Prison administrators or health care personnel are only required to provide adequate treatment (*Estelle v. Gamble*, 1976; Vaughn & Carroll, 1998) that is reasonably plausible within modern medical science and can be tied to the doctor's professional medical judgment (*Hamby v. Hammond*, 2016; Vaughn & Carroll, 1998). Medical treatment violates the Eighth Amendment when it is "so grossly incompetent, inadequate, or excessive as to shock the conscience or to be intolerable to fundamental fairness" (*Harris v. Thigpen*, 1991, p. 1505).

The subjective prong requires deliberate indifference of prison administrators or health care personnel to the prisoner's serious medical needs (*Farmer v. Brennan*, 1994; *Wilson v. Seiter*, 1991). Deliberate indifference requires evidence that the failure in treatment was not negligent or inadvertent but was reckless as defined in the criminal law (*Farmer v. Brennan*, 1994). Wanton disregard to a prisoner's needs may also constitute deliberate indifference if the disregard rose to the level of criminal recklessness where the prison or health care official was aware of "impending harm" to the inmate that was "easily preventable" (*Battista v. Clarke*, 2011, p. 453; *Kosilek v. Spencer*, 2014b, p. 83). Wide-ranging deference, however, must be granted to prison administrators in the adoption and execution of policies and practices necessary to maintain institutional safety and security (*Turner v. Safley*, 1987; *Whitley v. Albers*, 1986). A temporary, not a permanent, denial of care based on legitimate prisoner safety and institutional security does not violate the Eighth Amendment (*Cameron v. Tomes*, 1993).

The Fifth Circuit held that a plaintiff alleging defendants' deliberate indifference must show that defendants "acted with malicious intent," knowing that they were withholding medically necessary care (*Gibson v. Collier*, 2019, p. 220). The Ninth Circuit, however, countered that neither it nor the Supreme Court has ever required proof that a prison official acted with "sinister" or "improper motives" (*Edmo v. Corizon, Inc.,* 2019, p. 793). An inmate does not need to prove complete denial and/or delay of medical care to bring an Eighth Amendment claim (*Lopez v. Smith,* 2000, p. 1132). Instead, inmates' denial of treatment claims must allege that the denial and/or delay was medically unacceptable and made in conscious disregard of excessive risks to their health (*Jackson v. McIntosh,* 1996). An incarcerated transgender inmate's release from prison pending litigation moots claims for injunctive relief from the prison's policies unless the suit was classified as a class action (*Dilley v. Gunn,* 1995; *Norsworthy v. Beard,* 2015). The Seventh and Eleventh Circuits require more than "[m]ere negligence"—the plaintiff must provide evidence that an official "actually knew of and disregarded a substantial risk of harm" (*Campbell v. Kallas,* 2019, p. 544; *Keohane v. Florida DOC Secretary,* 2020a, p. 1266; *Petties v. Carter,* 2016, p. 728).

METHOD

The NEXIS-UNI computerized database contains electronic copies of published and unpublished court decisions. A keyword search was used to gather all cases decided by the U.S. Circuit Courts of Appeals as of March 22, 2021 where transgender inmates filed a §1983 action against corrections officers or medical personnel. The advanced search parameters required that all the terms "transgender," "inmate," and "prison" appeared at least once in the "main body" of the case, producing 53 cases decided in the federal appellate courts. This article focuses exclusively on GCS and hormonal therapy requested by trans women prisoners housed in male prisons; thus, cases that pertained to other issues, such as failure to protect and housing classification decisions, were removed, leading to a total of 24 circuit court decisions presented in this article. The authors conducted an inductive doctrinal analysis (Nolasco et al., 2010) to synthesize U.S. Circuit Courts of Appeals decisions on transgender female inmates seeking hormonal therapy and GCS, creating a framework from which to organize the analysis (Nolasco et al., 2015; Nolasco & Vaughn, 2011).

U.S. Circuit Courts of Appeals Rulings on Trans Women Prisoners' Requests for Gender Confirmation Surgery and Hormonal Therapy

Request for Gender Confirmation Surgery

First circuit. Kosilek, a transgender inmate with gender dysphoria, sued defendants, alleging that the prison's chosen treatment plan of supportive therapy instead of GCS violated the Eighth Amendment (*Kosilek v. Spencer,* 2014b). The First Circuit affirmed the district court's ruling in *Kosilek v. Spencer* (2014a) ("*Kosilek I*") that Department of Correction's ("DOC") failure to provide GCS because of security concerns was not deliberate indifference and did not violate the Eighth Amendment. After *Kosilek I,* the DOC revised its policy for gender dysphoria treatment. Contrary to the old policy that only allowed continuation of whatever treatment an inmate received prior to incarceration, the revised policy allowed new treatment if recommended by the DOC's health-services contractor. The DOC then provided Kosilek with hormone treatment, mental health treatment, gender-appropriate clothing and personal effects, and hair removal electrolysis. The DOC did not allow GCS for Kosilek based on: (1) peer reviews indicating disagreement on the medical necessity of GCS as treatment for gender dysphoria; and (2) security concerns if Kosilek would be given GCS.

In *Kosilek v. Spencer* (2014b) ("*Kosilek II*"), the First Circuit en banc reversed the district court's injunction that required the DOC to provide GCS. The district court considered detailed expert witness testimony on both sides who all disagreed on the medical necessity of GCS as treatment for Kosilek's dysphoria. The court-appointed expert concluded that treatment of gender dysphoria was an evolving field and that practitioners reasonably differed in their preferred treatment methods. The DOC also submitted a security report detailing possible security concerns if Kosilek was provided GCS. The district court in *Kosilek II* concluded that: (1) GCS was medically necessary to treat Kosilek's serious medical need; (2) DOC's security concerns were merely pretextual due to public and political pressure; and (3) DOC was deliberately indifferent under the Eighth Amendment. A panel of the First Circuit affirmed the decision of the district court (*Kosilek v. Spencer,* 2014a). On rehearing *en banc,* the First Circuit Court of Appeals reversed, holding that the DOC's decision not to provide GCS to treat the inmate's gender dysphoria did not constitute deliberate indifference and did not violate the Eighth Amendment (*Kosilek v. Spencer,* 2014b).

The First Circuit relied on accredited medical professionals, holding that the DOC's alternative treatment sufficiently alleviated Kosilek's gender dysphoria and exceeded the level of care that would be "inadequate as to shock the conscience" (*Kosilek v. Spencer,* 2014b, p. 86). The en banc First Circuit held that they should not "second guess medical judgments" or require the prison administrators to adopt "the more compassionate" of two alternative courses of medical treatment (*Kosilek v. Spencer,* 2014b, p. 90). The court also granted the prison administrators wide deference in the adoption of security measures deemed necessary to preserve internal order and discipline. The DOC officials reported security concerns post-surgery, including the high risk of placing Kosilek in either an all-male prison or in an all-female prison with inmates who were domestic violence survivors. The First Circuit concluded that it did not create a "de facto ban" against GCS as a medical treatment for any inmate because: (1) DOC specifically disclaimed a blanket policy regarding GCS; and (2) such policy would conflict with the necessity of individualized medical care based on the particular prisoner's serious medical needs. The court also doubted that their decision would foreclose all litigants from successfully seeking GCS because the court based its decision on the specific facts of the case.

Third circuit. In *Pinson v. United States* (2020), the Third Circuit vacated the dismissal of the district court of a federal transgender inmate's Bivens action (*Bivens v. Six Unknown Named of Federal Bureau of Narcotics,* 1971), holding that there was a factual dispute on whether defendants denied her request for GCS for political or retaliatory reasons. Upon intake, Pinson was diagnosed with gender dysphoria and received psychological treatment and hormone therapy throughout her incarceration. She was recommended for the general prison population but was placed in the Special Housing Unit ("SHU") pending final determination. After a brief transfer to the general prison population, she was returned to SHU pending investigation under the Prison Rape Elimination Act ("PREA") of physical and sexual threats from another inmate. Upon return from hospitalization for multiple self-injuries, she was placed on suicide watch. After three months in the current facility, her requests for GCS were denied by a prison administrator because of her failure to meet the requirements specified by WPATH standards. She was transferred to another facility after four months of incarceration.

The Third Circuit held that a prison official is deliberately indifferent in the following instances: (1) he knew of but "intentionally refused" to provide medical treatment for an inmate's serious medical needs; (2) he delayed necessary medical treatment based on a "non-medical reason"; or (3) he prevented a prisoner from receiving needed or recommended medical treatment (*Pinson v. United States,* 2020, p. 241). Here, the district court erred in granting summary judgment for defendants because Pinson presented evidence that defendants denied her request for GCS for non-medical reasons (retaliatory or political). They informed her that "for political reasons" the prison would "never actually follow through" with GCS "because 'FOX News and Republicans would go crazy" (*Pinson v. United States,* 2020, p. 242). Pinson's allegations "were sufficient to withstand the defendants' summary judgment motion" (*Pinson v. United States,* 2020, p. 242).

Fourth circuit. De'lonta, a transgender inmate suffering from gender dysphoria, on several occasions attempted to self- castrate herself (*De'lonta v. Johnson,* 2013). In *De'lonta v. Angelone*

("*De'lonta I*") (2003), she filed a §1983 lawsuit, alleging that defendants had a policy that wrongfully prevented her from receiving treatment. The district court dismissed De'lonta's first complaint for failure to state a claim. The Fourth Circuit reversed and remanded, holding that De'lonta's need for protection against continued self-castration was a serious medical need under the Eighth Amendment and that she had sufficiently alleged defendant's deliberate indifference. In a settlement agreement, defendants agreed to provide continuing hormone treatment and allow De'lonta to dress and live as a woman. Despite these accommodations, De'lonta's symptoms persisted and she was hospitalized after an attempt of self-castration. Although she requested GCS, she was not evaluated by a specialist concerning her need for GCS.

In *De'lonta v. Johnson (2013)* (*De'lonta II*), she filed another suit under §1983 against defendants, alleging that their continued denial of GCS constituted deliberate indifference to her serious medical needs in violation of the Eighth Amendment. The district court dismissed the complaint without prejudice for failure to state a claim. The Fourth Circuit reversed and remanded, holding that De'lonta's complaint on its face stated a plausible Eighth Amendment claim. The Fourth Circuit held that De'lonta alleged an objectively serious medical need for protection against continued self-mutilation and that defendants were deliberately indifferent to her serious medical needs. Although defendants provided De'lonta with some treatment consistent with WPATH standards to alleviate her symptoms, this may not have been constitutionally adequate (*De'lonta v. Johnson*, 2013). Total deprivation of care is not necessary for a constitutional violation to exist; grossly incompetent or inadequate care can also constitute deliberate indifference (*Langford v. Norris*, 2010). Although a prisoner does not enjoy a constitutional right to a preferred treatment, the treatment chosen by a prison facility must be adequate to address the prisoner's serious medical needs (*De'lonta v. Johnson*, 2013).

Fifth circuit. Fifth Circuit precedent establishes that prison officials are not deliberately indifferent to trans women prisoners' serious medical needs by declining to provide GCS (*Gibson v. Collier*, 2019; *Williams v. Kelly*, 2020) if they provide the trans female prisoners' hormonal therapy. In *Gibson v. Collier* (2019), transgender inmate Gibson was diagnosed with gender dysphoria and was provided mental health counseling and hormone therapy while in the custody of the Texas Department of Criminal Justice ("TDCJ"). TDCJ Policy ("Policy") provides that transgender inmates must be evaluated for treatment on a case-by-case basis by appropriate health professionals based on "current, accepted standards of care" (*Gibson v. Collier*, 2019, p. 218). The doctors, however, denied Gibson's requests because the Policy did not designate GCS as a treatment for gender dysphoria. Gibson sued *pro se* the TDCJ Director, arguing that TDCJ's Policy of preventing evaluation of the medical necessity for her GCS violated her Eighth Amendment rights. The district court granted summary judgment on the merits of the Eighth Amendment claim. On appeal, the Fifth Circuit affirmed the district court and granted summary judgment, holding that Gibson did not establish deliberate indifference because she did not prove universal acceptance in the medical community of the necessity and efficacy of GCS as treatment for gender dysphoria.

The Fifth Circuit agreed with the First Circuit's *en banc* ruling in *Kosilek v. Spencer* (2014b) regarding the absence of consensus in the medical community on the necessity of GCS as treatment for gender dysphoria. The Fifth Circuit affirmed that the "on-going medical debate doom[ed] Gibson's claim" (*Gibson v. Collier*, 2019, p. 221). The court also noted the "sparse record" in *Gibson v. Collier* (2019) that included only WPATH standards, which declared GCS as an effective and necessary treatment for gender dysphoria. The Fifth Circuit, however, characterized the WPATH standards as "merely one side in a sharply contested medical debate" and not a medical consensus over GCS (*Gibson v. Collier*, 2019, p. 221). Remanding the case to allow evidence of Gibson's individual need for GCS would not change the court's decision because GCS was "fiercely debated within the medical community" (*Gibson v. Collier*, 2019, p. 224). She would not be able to establish on remand that GCS was universally accepted as an effective or necessary treatment for gender dysphoria. TDCJ was not deliberately indifferent to her serious medical needs because TDCJ provided her with other treatment plans. The Fifth Circuit also held that TDCJ was not required to make an individualized assessment of the inmate's particular medical needs and that *Kosilek v. Spencer* (2014b) allowed a blanket ban of GCS.

Seventh circuit. Campbell, a gender dysphoric inmate in state prison undergoing hormone therapy, repeatedly requested for GCS (*Campbell v. Kallas,* 2019). Defendants consulted an outside expert in gender dysphoria, who determined that Campbell was a potential surgical candidate subject to a safe, workable solution to the real-life-experience requirement. Citing security concerns, the officials denied Campbell's request. Campbell sued the DOC officials under §1983. The district court denied the defendant's motions for summary judgment and rejected their qualified immunity defense, concluding that case law clearly established a constitutional right to effective medical treatment. On appeal, the Seventh Circuit reversed, holding that it was not clearly established that the Eighth Amendment required defendants to provide inmates with gender dysphoria treatment beyond hormone therapy.

The Seventh Circuit held that qualified immunity shielded a public official from suit for damages unless caselaw clearly puts him on notice that his action is unconstitutional. Contrary to the mandate that clearly established law cannot be framed at a high level of generality (*Ashcroft v. al-Kidd,* 2011), the district judge's discussion of qualified immunity was brief and highly general (*Campbell v. Kallas,* 2019). The proper inquiry was whether existing precedent clearly established a constitutional right to gender-dysphoria treatment beyond hormone therapy. According to the Seventh Circuit, the two Circuit precedents of *Roe v. Elyea* (2011) and *Fields v. Smith* (2011) relied on by Campbell did not provide the required level of specificity. In both cases, prison officials refused to provide any treatment at all for serious diseases based solely on categorical rules. Here, defendants consulted a medical expert before denying Campbell's request for GCS. Prisons are not obliged to provide every requested treatment once medical care begins. In a deliberate indifference case challenging the medical decisions of prison doctors who diagnosed and treated an inmate's medical condition, the court defers to these medical decisions "unless no minimally competent professional would have" made such a treatment decision (*Campbell v. Kallas,* 2019, p. 548).

Campbell's reliance on the court's decision in *Mitchell v. Kallas* (2018) was similarly erroneous because in that case, prison officials refused a gender dysphoric inmate's request for hormone therapy despite a medical doctor's endorsement of the treatment. The refusal was based on a DOC policy requiring a 13-month evaluation prior to eligibility for hormone treatment. The court rejected the qualified immunity defense, interpreting the refusal to begin hormone therapy as a complete denial of care. The Seventh Circuit held that prison officials were on notice that total absence of treatment for serious medical conditions, including gender dysphoria, can amount to deliberate indifference and is unconstitutional (*Campbell v. Kallas,* 2019; *Mitchell v. Kallas,* 2018). *Mitchell v. Kallas* (2018) had not been decided when the defendants made decisions about Campbell's care—it did not provide sufficient notice for purposes of the qualified immunity analysis. *Mitchell v. Kallas* (2018) illustrated the difference between a complete denial of care and context-specific medical judgments. Deciding whether to provide the inmate's preferred course of treatment that posed challenges to prison administration was not equivalent to complete absence of treatment. When the defendants denied Campbell's request for GCS, there was no precedent clearly establishing a right to gender dysphoria treatment beyond hormone therapy.

Ninth circuit. The Ninth Circuit in *Rosati v. Igbinoso* (2015) and *Edmo v. Corizon, Inc.* (2019) ruled in favor of plaintiffs. In *Rosati v. Igbinoso* (2015), the district court dismissed a transgender inmate's *pro se* §1983 claim, alleging that defendants were deliberately indifferent to her gender dysphoria because they refused to provide GCS. The Ninth Circuit reversed and remanded for further proceedings, cautioning that it expressed no opinion on whether GCS was medically necessary for Rosati or whether prison officials had other legitimate reasons for denying her that treatment. The Ninth Circuit explained that Rosati's complaint credibly alleged that: (1) she has severe gender dysphoria, describing repeated episodes of attempted self-castration despite continued hormone treatment; (2) the medically accepted treatment for her dysphoria is GCS, citing provisions of WPATH; and (3) prison officials were aware of her medical history but denied GCS because of a blanket policy against it. During oral argument, the state also acknowledged that no California inmate has ever received GCS. Even without a blanket policy, Rosati plausibly alleged her symptoms were so severe that prison officials recklessly disregarded an excessive risk to her health by denying GCS based on the opinion of a medical assistant without any experience in transgender medicine.

In *Edmo v. Corizon, Inc.* (2019), transgender inmate Edmo was diagnosed with gender dysphoria while incarcerated. Despite hormone treatments provided by the prison to alleviate her gender dysphoria, she continued to experience significant distress due to her male genitalia that made her feel "depressed, embarrassed, [and] disgusted" (*Edmo v. Corizon, Inc.*, 2019, p. 772). After her first unsuccessful attempt at self-castration, a prison doctor evaluated her for GCS. The DOC's policy on the treatment of inmates with gender dysphoria required an individual medical determination on the necessity of GCS for that specific inmate (*Edmo v. Corizon, Inc.*, 2019). Contrary to WPATH, the consultant opined that GCS would be medically necessary only in three situations: (1) "congenital malformations or ambiguous genitalia," (2) "severe and devastating dysphoria" primarily due to genitals, or (3) "some type of medical problem" where "endogenous sexual hormones were causing severe physiological damage" (*Edmo v. Corizon, Inc.*, 2019, p. 773). The doctor concluded that hormone therapy and supportive counseling were adequate treatments and that GCS was not medically necessary because Edmo did not meet any of the criteria.

Edmo filed a *pro se* complaint against the defendants, alleging that their failure to provide her with GCS violated her Eighth Amendment rights. The Ninth Circuit affirmed the district court's decision but cautioned that its analysis was particularized to Edmo based on the idiosyncratic facts of the case. It did not endeavor to answer whether individuals in other cases would meet the threshold to establish an Eighth Amendment violation. It further denied a petition for rehearing *en banc* (*Edmo v. Corizon, Inc.*, 2020). The Ninth Circuit held that Edmo's gender dysphoria was a serious medical need that triggered the state's obligations under the Eighth Amendment (*Allard v. Gomez*, 2001; *Battista v. Clarke*, 2011; *De'lonta v. Johnson*, 2013; *Kosilek v. Spencer*, 2014b; *Meriwether v. Faulkner*, 1987; *Norsworthy v. Beard*, 2015; *Rosati v. Igbinoso*, 2015; *White v. Farrier*, 1988). Moreover, defendants acted with deliberate indifference—the prison doctor knew of Edmo's gender dysphoria and her multiple attempts at self-castration and self-injury but did not recommend GCS. Defendants are liable for deliberate indifference even if they did not act with "malice, intent to inflict pain, or knowledge" that the chosen treatment was medically inappropriate (*Edmo v. Corizon, Inc.*, 2019, p. 793). While differences in medically acceptable treatments between an inmate and physician or between medical professionals and inmates is not deliberate indifference (*Toguchi v. Chung*, 2004), the defendants' chosen treatment was medically unacceptable because GCS was medically necessary in Edmo's case. The prison's physician substituted his own criteria that was contrary to WPATH standards, which are widely accepted, evidence-based criteria.

Tenth circuit. Transgender inmate Lamb was diagnosed with gender dysphoria and received hormone treatment and weekly counseling sessions while incarcerated (*Lamb v. Norwood*, 2018). The Tenth Circuit affirmed the dismissal of her §1983 action, holding that prison officials are not deliberately indifferent when they provide subpar medical treatment that is different from what the inmate wants (*Lamb v. Norwood*, 2018) or if they made an informed judgment about treatment options in the face of disagreement within the medical community (*Supre v. Ricketts*, 1986).

Lamb was provided psychological counseling and hormone treatments, including estrogen and testosterone-blocking medication. Although prison officials did not authorize GCS or increased the hormone dosages preferred by the inmate, the existing treatments and sparseness of the summary judgment record precluded a finding of deliberate indifference.

Summary of issues and distinctions among circuits involving requests for gender confirmation surgery

Medical consensus on gender confirmation surgery. The First Circuit rejected the WPATH standards as indication of a medical consensus, noting that the detailed conflicting expert testimony reflected a division in the medical community about the necessity and efficacy of GCS (*Kosilek v. Spencer*, 2014b). The Ninth Circuit and Fifth Circuit have taken opposite positions on the medical necessity of GCS to treat gender dysphoria. The Fifth Circuit in *Gibson v. Collier* (2019, p. 220) disputed the necessity of GCS for gender dysphoria because there was no "universal acceptance" in the medical community. Prison officials are not deliberately indifferent if a "genuine debate" exists within the medical community about the "necessity or efficacy" of GCS (*Gibson v. Collier*, 2019, p. 220) or if the inmate disagrees with the doctor's prescribed medical treatment (*Mayweather v. Foti*, 1992; *Norton v. Dimazana*, 1997). Universal acceptance does not require unanimity—a single dissenting expert does not defeat a medical consensus about the necessity of a particular treatment; however, the presence of a "robust and substantial good faith disagreement" among experts in the medical community negates an Eighth Amendment claim (*Gibson v. Collier*, 2019, p. 220).

The Ninth Circuit refuted the Fifth Circuit's approach, countering that there is a medical consensus that GCS is effective and medically necessary under certain circumstances (*Edmo v. Corizon, Inc.*, 2019). According to the Ninth Circuit, WPATH standards have been endorsed by various medical, psychiatric, psychological, and health professional associations, including members of the medical community (Frey et al., 2017; Tran et al., 2018). The Ninth Circuit concluded that most courts and the medical community agree that WPATH standards: (1) are the internationally recognized guidelines for the treatment of individuals with gender dysphoria; (2) represent the medical consensus regarding appropriate treatment for transgender and gender dysphoric individuals; (3) apply equally to all transgender individuals regardless of their housing situation; and (4) require that health care for incarcerated transgender inmates should approximate those available in a non-institutional setting and must be individualized according to their particular medical needs (*Edmo v. Corizon, Inc.*, 2019; *De'lonta v. Johnson*, 2013). Failure to provide adequate treatment for gender dysphoria can expose transgender individuals to serious risks of psychological and physical harm and GCS should be provided when found to be a serious medical need (*Edmo v. Corizon, Inc.*, 2019).

The Ninth Circuit also opined that the Fifth Circuit's decision in *Gibson v. Collier* (2019) was an "outlier" based on a "dismaying disregard for procedure" (*Edmo v. Corizon, Inc.*, 2019, p. 795). The Ninth Circuit further dismissed *Gibson v. Collier* (2019) as unpersuasive for the following additional reasons: (1) it "directly conflicted" with the Ninth Circuit, Fourth Circuit, and Seventh Circuit precedents which held that denying GCS for gender dysphoria can pose a cognizable Eighth Amendment claim (*De'lonta v. Johnson*, 2013; *Fields v. Smith*, 2011; *Rosati v. Igbinoso*, 2015); (2) it contradicted Eighth Amendment precedent requiring a case-by-case determination of the medical necessity of a particular treatment (*Colwell v. Bannister*, 2014); (3) it contradicted and misconstrued *Kosilek v. Spencer* (2014b, p. 91) as allowing a blanket ban on GCS although the First Circuit expressly cautioned that it did not "create a de facto ban" against GCS as a medical treatment for any incarcerated individual because a blanket prohibition would conflict with the requirement that medical care "be individualized based on a particular prisoner's serious medical needs" (*Edmo v. Corizon, Inc.*, 2019, p. 796).

The Seventh Circuit noted in *Campbell v. Kallas* (2019, p. 539) that the WPATH standards (2012, p. 67) required transgender individuals considering GCS to undergo one-year of hormone therapy and "12 continuous months of living in a gender role that is congruent with their gender identity." The court construed WPATH standards as requiring real-life experience outside prison in the desired gender role. According to the Seventh Circuit, the real-life experience outside of prison provides ample opportunities for patients to socially adjust in their desired gender role before undergoing irreversible surgery (*Campbell v. Kallas*, 2019). The Ninth Circuit, however, disagreed that this requirement necessitates real-life experiences of a trans female outside of prison because the WPATH standards apply "to all transsexual, transgender, and gender noncon-forming people, irrespective of their housing situation" and that "medically necessary treatments should not be denied on the basis of institutionalization or housing arrangements" (*Edmo v. Corizon, Inc.*, 2019, p. 789; WPATH, 2012, p. 67).

Medical necessity and the exercise of professional judgment. Medical necessity is determined by physicians or health care professionals who may either be retained or consulted by the correc-tional facility. During transgender inmate litigation, courts allow the parties to present testimony from medical experts qualified in treating gender dysphoria and with experience in gender con-firmation surgery. In certain situations, though, the physician's exercise of professional judgment is not granted deference by courts. A recommended treatment is "medically necessary" if a quali-fied professional exercising "prudent clinical judgment" determines that it is necessary (Osborne & Lawrence, 2016, p. 1651); however, professionals sometimes disagree about the medical neces-sity of certain treatments, including GCS as a treatment for GD (Osborne & Lawrence, 2016, pp. 1652). When discussing deliberate indifference, federal circuit courts explained the implications of defendants' exercise of professional medical judgment. Liability may be imposed only when the professional's decision was a "substantial departure from accepted professional judgment" (*Doe 4 by and through Lopez v. Shenandoah Valley Juvenile Center Commission*, 2021, p. 342; *Youngberg v. Romeo*, 1982, pp. 320–323). Under this standard, courts do not determine the "correct" or "most appropriate" medical decision (*Patten v. Nichols*, 2001, p. 845). The proper inquiry is whether the decision was "so completely out of professional bounds as to make it explicable only as an arbitrary, nonprofessional one" (*Doe 4 by and through Lopez v. Shenandoah*, 2021, p. 343; *Patten v. Nichols*, 2001, p. 845). Courts defer and accord the presumption of validity to the "subjective aspects of the decisional process of institutional medical professionals" (*Patten v. Nichols*, 2001, p. 845). Courts defer to prison decisions when they reflect an "actual exercise of medical judgment" (*Inmates of Allegheny County Jail v. Pierce*, 1979, p. 762).

The First Circuit held that prison officials were not deliberately indifferent when they chose one of two alternatives that are both "reasonably commensurate with the medical standards of prudent professionals" and provide inmates with "significant … relief" (*Kosilek v. Spencer*, 2014b, p. 90). According to the Seventh Circuit, medical treatment decisions are entitled to deference by courts unless "no minimally competent professional would have so responded under those cir-cumstances" (*Campbell v. Kallas*, 2019. p. 544; *Sain v. Wood*, 2008, pp. 894–895). A prison doctor faces liability only if his or her course of treatment substantially departs from accepted profes-sional judgment (*Campbell v. Kallas*, 2019).

The Fourth Circuit explained that the standard of "professional judgment" differs from the "deliberate indifference" standard. The standard of professional judgment is a "lower standard of culpability" compared to the Eighth Amendment standard for deliberate indifference because the U.S. Supreme Court in *Youngberg v. Romeo* (1982) did not require proof of subjective intent (*Doe 4 by and through Lopez v. Shenandoah*, 2021, p. 343). To apply *Youngberg v. Romeo* (1982) to a claim of inadequate medical care, prison officials must establish that their treatment was adequate to address a person's needs under a relevant standard of professional judgment. The

Fourth Circuit noted that its decisions in *De'lonta v. Angelone* (2003) (*"De'lonta I"*) and *De'lonta v. Johnson* (2013) (*"De'lonta II"*) offer further guidance on whether defendants adequately exercised professional judgment. In *De'lonta I*, the Fourth Circuit reversed the district court's dismissal of the prisoner's suit, holding that defendants' refusal to provided hormone treatments to De'lonta was based solely on prison policy rather than the exercise of professional medical judgment. The higher standard of deliberate indifference required defendants to base their decisions on a medical judgment concerning the individual's specific needs, not based on policy or the availability of services at the facility (*Doe 4 by and through Lopez v. Shenandoah, 2021*, p. 343). In *De'lonta II*, the Fourth Circuit reversed the district court's dismissal of De'lonta's suit based on deliberate indifference, holding that although defendants provided her with "some treatment" consistent with WPATH standards, they may not have necessarily provided her with "constitutionally adequate treatment" (*De'lonta v. Johnson*, 2013. p. 526). Although an inmate does not enjoy a constitutional right to their preferred treatment, the prison facility must provide adequate treatment to address the inmate's serious medical needs (*De'lonta v. Johnson*, 2013).

Distinctions among cases. The cases of *Edmo v. Corizon, Inc.* (2019), *Gibson v. Collier* (2019), and *Kosilek v. Spencer* (2014b) arrived at different results on the issue of the medical necessity of GCS to treat gender dysphoria in trans women prisoners. Both *Edmo v. Corizon, Inc.* (2019) and *Kosilek v. Spencer* (2014b) were based on extensive medical testimony offered during trial and individualized to the inmates' specific health needs, while *Gibson v. Collier* (2019) was based on a sparse record containing only a copy of the WPATH standards.

The Ninth Circuit's decision in *Edmo v. Corizon, Inc.* (2019) was based on detailed and exhaustive expert medical testimony during the trial that showed WPATH standards reflected the medical consensus regarding appropriate treatment for transgender and gender dysphoric prisoners. Its decision was also based on its own conclusions that the defendants' medical experts were not sufficiently qualified and did not have the appropriate experience in treating gender dysphoric inmates. In contrast, the trans prisoners' medical experts who had extensive experience in treating gender dysphoric inmates testified on the necessity of GCS for Edmo. The Ninth Circuit conducted a fact-specific analysis of the record to determine deliberate indifference (*Roe v. Elyea*, 2011). The Ninth Circuit distinguished *Kosilek v. Spencer* (2014b) because of the absence of security concerns present in that case and the agreement of plaintiff's qualified medical experts on the medical necessity of GCS for Edmo's severe gender dysphoria.

The First Circuit's ruling in *Kosilek v. Spencer* (2014b) also used a fact-based approach to evaluate a gender dysphoric inmate's Eighth Amendment claim seeking GCS. Defendants solicited multiple medical experts and were provided with two alternative treatment plans. The qualified experts also disagreed on whether GCS was medically necessary because the inmate's treatment plan significantly stabilized her mental state. There were significant security concerns if the inmate underwent GCS. The First Circuit concluded that GCS was not medically necessary for the inmate's gender dysphoria. The extensive record in *Kosilek v. Spencer* (2014b) was not decided by summary judgment and contained testimony from numerous medical experts (including gender-dysphoria specialists who evaluated Kosilek regarding the medical necessity of GCS). The First Circuit in *Kosilek v. Spencer* (2014b, p. 90) also cautioned that it was inappropriate for it to "second guess medical judgments" or require prison officials to adopt "the more compassionate of two adequate options." It also warned that its opinion did not "create a de facto ban" or "blanket policy" against GCS as a medical treatment for any inmate because the Eighth Amendment required individualized assessment of an inmate's medical needs (*Kosilek v. Spencer*, 2014b, pp. 90–91; *Roe v. Elyea*, 2011, pp. 862–863). Rather, the court's holding was based on Kosilek's specific circumstances, where prison officials solicited the opinions of multiple medical experts and chose a course of treatment from two alternative treatment plans recommended by different medical experts.

The Fifth Circuit in a split decision in *Gibson v. Collier* (2019) held that failure to provide GCS to an inmate did not violate the Eighth Amendment's cruel and unusual punishment clause. The sparse record in that case only included the WPATH standards without medical experts' testimony. The 2–1 majority in *Gibson v. Collier* (2019, p. 221) concluded that "there is no consensus in the medical community" about the necessity and efficacy of GCS for gender dysphoria." The dissent pointed out that the Fifth Circuit could not determine subsequent developments in the medical community regarding the necessity of GCS for treating gender dysphoria because there was no expert testimony or any evidence as to the medical necessity aside from the WPATH standards. The majority stated that to constitute deliberate indifference, the medical procedure must be universally accepted. The majority, however, provided no citation to any caselaw regarding the requirement for a "universal-acceptance standard" (*Gibson v. Collier*, 2019, p. 235). In Gibson's case, a TDCJ doctor ordered evaluation for GCS, but TDCJ refused to offer the surgery because of a blanket policy and not due to conflicting medical opinion.

The dissent in *Gibson v. Collier* (2019) also argued that TDCJ's blanket ban on an evaluation for GCS was contrary to *Kosilek v. Spencer's* (2014b) holding. Other circuits have held that prison officials were deliberately indifferent for refusing to evaluate for treatment based on a blanket policy instead of individualized medical judgment (*Colwell v. Bannister*, 2014; *Fields v. Smith*, 2011; *Rosati v. Igbinoso*, 2015). The majority cited two cases where trans women prisoners did not prevail (*Praylor v. Texas Department of Criminal Justice*, 2005; *Supre v. Ricketts*, 1986), but the dissent criticized the *Gibson* majority, saying they "missed the mark" because the issue was not whether there was broad medical controversy but whether there was disagreement about the efficacy of GCS for Gibson based on her individual serious medical needs (*Gibson v. Collier*, 2019, p. 240).

Requests for Hormone Treatment Therapy

Seventh circuit. The Seventh Circuit in the cases of *Fields v. Smith* (2011) and *Mitchell v. Kallas* (2018) considered whether the failure or delay of defendant prison officials to provide hormonal treatment constituted deliberate indifference. Prior to the passage of the Inmate Sex Change Prevention Act ("Act 105"), Wisconsin DOC ("WDOC") inmates with gender dysphoria were provided hormone treatments. Act 105 prohibited the WDOC from providing transgender inmates with certain medical treatments, including hormone therapy and GCS (*Fields v. Smith*, 2011). In response, inmates filed a §1983 lawsuit, alleging that defendants violated their constitutional rights by enforcing a statutory provision that prevented WDOC medical personnel from providing hormone therapy or GCS to trans women prisoners. The Seventh Circuit affirmed the district court, holding that the statute's enforcement constituted deliberate indifference to inmates' serious medical needs and facially violated the Eighth Amendment.

Defendants relied on dicta in two Seventh Circuit decisions where the court stated that: (1) an inmate did not have a right to any particular type of hormone treatment (*Meriwether v. Faulkner*, 1987); and (2) the Eighth Amendment does not require prison officials to provide "esoteric" treatments like hormone therapy and GCS that are "protracted and expensive" and not generally available to non-affluent individuals (*Maggert v. Hanks*, 1997, pp. 671–672). The Seventh Circuit explained that its discussion of hormone therapy and GCS in those two cases assumed that their costs were high and that adequate alternatives existed (*Fields v. Smith*, 2011). More than a decade after, the district court in *Fields v. Smith* (2011) ascertained that the annual costs of hormone therapy was significantly less than that of an antipsychotic drug and other major surgeries (e.g., heart bypass surgery and kidney surgery) used to treat many DOC inmates.

Moreover, the Seventh Circuit stated that defendants did not prove that another treatment could be an adequate replacement for hormone therapy (*Fields v. Smith*, 2011). The Eighth

Amendment's cruel and unusual punishment clause does not allow a state to deny effective treatment for prisoners' serious medical needs. Since defendants did not establish any security benefits associated with a ban on hormone therapy, refusing to provide effective treatment for a serious medical condition does not serve any valid penological purpose and "amounts to torture" (*Fields v. Smith,* 2011, p. 556). The deference granted to prison administrators in the adoption of security policies and practices did not extend to "actions taken in bad faith and for no legitimate purpose" (*Fields v. Smith,* 2011, p. 558).

In another case, the Seventh Circuit considered the claims of Mitchell, a trans women inmate at the WDOC diagnosed with gender dysphoria who requested, but was denied, hormone treatment upon her incarceration (*Mitchell v. Kallas,* 2018). Based on DOC policy, her clinician conducted a preliminary assessment that was submitted to the prison's Gender Dysphoria Committee. The committee referred her request for hormone therapy to its outside consultant who recommended hormone therapy after a 13-month delay. The WDOC mental health director denied Mitchell's request, explaining that she was not eligible for treatment because she was scheduled for release that same month. The director alluded to DOC policy that allowed hormone therapy only for inmates who had at least six months left on their sentences to allow for medical stabilization. Upon Mitchell's release, her parole officers forbade her from seeking hormone therapy because her parole conditions required her to dress and present as a man. In response, Mitchell filed a *pro se* Section 1983 lawsuit in federal court. On appeal, the Seventh Circuit held that the district court erred in dismissing her claim because she sufficiently stated an Eighth Amendment deliberate indifference claim against the director of corrections and her parole officers.

Failure to provide medically recommended care for a non-medical reason (*Perez v. Fenoglio,* 2015) and inexplicable delays in treatment that serve no penological purpose (*Petties v. Carter,* 2016) can constitute deliberate indifference (*Mitchell v. Kallas,* 2018; Nolasco & Vaughn, 2020). Because Seventh Circuit precedent clearly establishes that an absence of treatment for serious medical needs related to gender dysphoria is unconstitutional, the director may not claim qualified immunity for the denial of Mitchell's request for care (*Fields v. Smith,* 2011; *Meriwether v. Faulkner,* 1987; *Mitchell v. Kallas,* 2018). The Seventh Circuit noted that Mitchell's complaint alleged total denial of care because she did not receive the hormone therapy recommended by the prison's medical consultant. There were also material disputes of fact on whether defendants exercised professional medical judgment. The director alluded to an unwritten WDOC rule, requiring that an inmate have at least six months remaining on her sentence prior to the commencement of hormone therapy. This requirement, however, was not contained in DOC's written policy on gender dysphoria. The denial of hormone therapy based on a "blanket rule" instead of an "individualized medical determination" constitutes deliberate indifference in violation of the Eighth Amendment (*Allard v. Gomez,* 2001; *De'lonta v. Angelone,* 2003; *Kosilek v. Spencer,* 2014b).

Mitchell sufficiently stated a claim against the parole officers who forbade her from dressing as a woman and seeking hormone treatment on her own. The parole officers had notice that a bar to hormone treatment would cause her harm because they received copies of her medical records. Although there is no Seventh Circuit precedent finding that parole officers are liable for deliberate indifference to a parolee's serious medical needs, their actions implicate the Eighth Amendment in some situations (*Hankins v. Lowe,* 2015). One district court held that parole officers can be liable for deliberate indifference by placing conditions on a parolee that prevented her from obtaining medical treatment (*Stewart v. Raemisch,* 2009). Parole officers may be constitutionally obligated not to impose parole conditions that prevent a parolee from seeking medical treatment on their own (*Mitchell v. Kallas,* 2018).

Tenth circuit. The Tenth Circuit in *Druley v. Patton* (2015) held that a transgender inmate who received hormone treatments was unlikely to succeed on the merits of her Eighth Amendment claim. Prior to her incarceration, Druley was diagnosed with gender dysphoria and had two partial GCS (*Druley v. Patton,* 2015). She filed a §1983 complaint against employees of the Oklahoma DOC ("ODOC"). Relying on Tenth Circuit precedent, the district court concluded that Druley failed to show a likelihood of success on the merits. In *Supre v. Ricketts* (1986), the Tenth Circuit declined to recognize a constitutional right under the Eighth Amendment to hormone therapy for inmates with gender dysphoria because hormone treatment was medically controversial and the prison officials "made an informed judgment" as to the "appropriate form of treatment" (*Supre v. Ricketts,* 1986, p. 963). The Tenth Circuit noted that the WPATH standards provide "flexible directions" for gender dysphoria treatment—"individual professionals and organized programs may modify" the requirements in response to a patient's "unique situation" or "an experienced professional's evolving treatment methodology" (*Druley v. Patton,* 2015, p. 635; *Kosilek v. Spencer,* 2014b, p. 70). Druley did not establish that the ODOC defendants failed to consider the WPATH's flexible guidelines, make an informed judgment as to the appropriate hormone treatment level, or deliberately ignored her serious medical needs.

Eleventh circuit. Eleventh Circuit precedent since 1986 has established that intentional refusal to provide medically necessary treatment constitutes deliberate indifference and violates the Eighth Amendment (*Ancata v. Prison Health Servs.,* 1985; *H.C. by Hewett v. Jarrard,* 1986). In *Keohane v. Florida DOC Secretary* (2020a), the Eleventh Circuit considered the §1983 claims of Keohane, a Florida DOC ("FDOC") trans female inmate who was formally diagnosed with gender dysphoria at age 16 and was receiving hormone therapy prior to her arrest. After her transfer to prison, her continual requests over a two-year period were repeatedly ignored due to a policy that specified that treatment for inmates with gender dysphoria will be maintained "only at the level of change that existed at the time they were received by the Department" (*Keohane v. Florida DOC Secretary,* 2020a, p. 1263). Under this freeze-frame policy, the treatment of inmates with gender dysphoria was determined by the treatment that they were receiving at the time of incarceration. Keohane's grievances in 2014 began to include requests for social transitioning or the ability to live consistently with one's gender identity. In response, the FDOC refused her social-transitioning requests, and Keohane alleged that the prison policy (requiring male inmates to wear male undergarments and have short to medium cut hair) was not a security risk. During this period, Keohane made multiple attempts at self-harm, including hanging and self-castration. Keohane brought a §1983 action for declaratory and injunctive relief, alleging that the FDOC's denial of her hormone-therapy and social-transitioning requests violated the Eighth Amendment.

After the complaint was filed, the Florida DOC: (1) referred Keohane to an outside endocrinologist who immediately prescribed her hormone therapy and (2) formally repealed its freeze-frame policy, replacing it with a policy requiring individualized assessment and treatment of inmates with gender dysphoria. The FDOC, however, continued to refuse Keohane's social-transitioning requests. On appeal, the Eleventh Circuit reversed the district court and denied a petition for rehearing *en banc* (*Keohane v. Florida DOC Secretary,* 2020a).

The Eleventh Circuit acknowledged that policies creating blanket bans on gender-dysphoria treatments amount to deliberate indifference to inmates' serious medical needs (*Fields v. Smith,* 2011; *Keohane v. Florida DOC Secretary,* 2020a). However, the challenge to the Florida DOC freeze-frame policy was moot because the FDOC already repealed and replaced it with a new policy that considers the individualized medical needs of inmates. The court also held the denial of her social-transitioning requests was mere negligence; thus, not enough culpability to invoke a Section 1983 lawsuit. The Eleventh Circuit gave two reasons for this finding. *First,* medical experts disagreed as to the medical necessity of her social transitioning. Differences in medical opinion between the prison's medical staff and the inmate as to diagnosis or treatment do not violate the Constitution (*Keohane v. Florida DOC Secretary*, 2020a; *Kosilek v. Spencer*, 2014b; *Lamb v. Norwood*, 2018). *Second*, the FDOC denied Keohane's social-transitioning requests because of security concerns, including the likelihood of attacks from other inmates in an all-male prison. The court concluded that prison administrators have wide deference in adopting and executing policies and practices needed to preserve internal order and discipline and maintain institutional security (Keohane v. *Florida DOC* Secretary, 2020a; Kosilek v. Spencer, 2014b).

Summary of issues and distinctions among circuits involving requests for hormone therapy
Failure to provide hormone treatment. The Seventh, Tenth, and Eleventh Circuits have taken different approaches to requests for hormone therapy by trans female inmates. Seventh Circuit precedent clearly establishes that failure to provide medically recommended care for a non-medical reason (*Perez v. Fenoglio*, 2015) and inexplicable delays in treatment that serve no penological purpose (*Petties v. Carter*, 2016) constitute deliberate indifference (*Fields v. Smith*, 2011; *Mitchell v. Kallas*, 2018). Denying hormone therapy based on a "blanket rule" instead of "individualized medical determination" constitutes deliberate indifference in violation of the Eighth Amendment (*Allard v. Gomez*, 2001; *De'lonta v. Angelone*, 2003; *Kosilek v. Spencer*, 2014b). Under Tenth Circuit precedent, prison officials are not deliberately indifferent for failing to provide hormone treatments to trans female inmates with gender dysphoria because hormone treatment was medically controversial and the prison officials "made an informed judgment" as to the "appropriate form of treatment" (*Druley v. Patton*, 2015; *Supre v. Ricketts*, 1986, p. 963). Eleventh Circuit precedent since 1986 establishes that intentional refusal to provide medically necessary treatment constitutes deliberate indifference and violates the Eighth Amendment (*Ancata v. Prison Health Servs. & Inc*, 1985; *H.C. by Hewett v. Jarrard*, 1986; *Kothmann v. Rosario*, 2014).

CONCLUSION

Transitioning is difficult in the most supportive environment, but it is uniquely problematic while incarcerated (Glezer, 2013; Whitman, 2017), where there is limited family support, mental health professionals, and other support systems such as social workers, physicians, and gender identity organizations (Bochicchio, 2019; Norman, 2017; Routh et al., 2017). Research shows that "transphobia-based violence [is] significantly associated with anxiety, depression, and body satisfaction" (Klemmer et al., 2021, p. 2634). Trans "women's satisfaction with the way their body looks is an important internal psychological evaluation that is a component of one's gender identity affirmation and an important factor in the overall health of transgender women" (p. 2634). When satisfied with their bodies, trans gender women have less "self-injurious behavior and improved mental health" (p. 2634). In contrast, their mental health suffers when correctional policies "deny transgender individuals' affirmation of their identity," such as limiting hormonal therapy and banning GCS, which forces trans women prisoners to "present their sex assigned at birth rather than as their authentic gender" (Klemmer et al., 2021, p. 2635).

Correctional facilities require a diagnosis of GD by medical personnel for transgender inmates to receive appropriate treatment (Alexander & Meshelemiah, 2010; von Dresner et al., 2013). Even with a diagnosis of GD, however, a majority of states do not allow transgender inmates to obtain medical treatment once incarcerated, 13 states allow for the initiation of hormone treatment (Arkansas, California, Colorado, Delaware, Idaho, Massachusetts, Michigan, Minnesota, New Hampshire, New York, North Carolina, Texas, and Washington), 20 states do not allow for the continuation of hormone therapy, and 8 states allow for GCS (Arizona, Arkansas, California, Colorado, Georgia, Idaho, Michigan, and New Hampshire) (Routh et al., 2017).

Federal circuit courts also varied in their decisions concerning requests for GCS by transgender inmates. The Ninth Circuit has traditionally been more progressive toward trans rights, holding that GCS can be medically necessary depending on the individualized needs of the transgender inmate because of the presence of a medical consensus on the appropriateness of these treatments for gender dysphoria pursuant to expert witnesses and WPATH standards. Conversely, the First and Fifth Circuits rejected requests for GCS because of the lack of medical consensus on the necessity and efficacy of GCS for transgender inmates with gender dysphoria. The courts also differ in their interpretation of the 12-month requirement of living in a role corresponding with their gender identity prior to consideration for GCS. The Seventh Circuit construed WPATH standards as requiring real-life experience outside of prison in the desired gender role. The Ninth Circuit, however, disagreed that real-life experiences must occur while living in the free world and considered time spent within correctional institutions as meeting this requirement.

The Seventh, Tenth, and Eleventh Circuits have also taken divergent approaches to requests for hormone therapy by trans female inmates. Both the Seventh and Eleventh Circuits clearly established that failure to provide medically recommended care for a non-medical reason and unexplained delays in treatment can constitute deliberate indifference, violating the Eighth Amendment. Under Tenth Circuit precedent, prison officials are not deliberately indifferent for failing to provide hormone treatments to inmates with gender dysphoria because hormone treatment was medically controversial.

Besides the legal issues regarding hormonal therapy and GCS, there remains a need for research on the types of medical procedures available for transgender prisoners. Future research, for example, needs to focus on the types of hormonal therapy approved for transgender prisoners, and the health impacts of these treatments, with special emphasis directed to bone health (Marano et al., 2021; Wiepjes et al., 2020). While research shows that finding a surgeon to conduct GCS in the free world is difficult (Esmonde et al., 2019), additional research is needed to uncover just how problematic it is within prisons to find a surgeon to perform GCS (Cohen et al., 2020). Moreover, future research should explore the requests for and specific types of GCS actually performed on trans women prisoners, such as labiaplasty, clitoroplasty, penectomy (penis removal), orchiectomy (testicular removal), vulvoplasty, vaginoplasty, breast enhancement, and/or facial feminization surgery (Ferrando, 2020; Jiang et al., 2018; Nolan et al., 2019). In conclusion, much more needs to be known about the legal issues transgendered prisoners face when seeking medical intervention and the health repercussions that transgender prisoners experience when receiving such treatment.

REFERENCES

Alexander, R., & Meshelemiah, J. C. A. (2010). Gender identity disorder in prisons: What are the legal implications for prison mental health professionals and administrators? *The Prison Journal, 90*(3), 269–287. https://doi.org/10.1177/0032885510373498

Almazan, A. N., & Keuroghlian, A. S. (2021). Association between gender-affirming surgeries and mental health outcomes. *JAMA Surgery, 156*(7), 611–618. https://doi.org/10.1001/jamasurg.2021.0952

American Psychiatric Association. (2013). *Diagnostic and statistical manual of mental disorders* (5th ed.). American Psychiatric Association Publishing.

American Psychological Association. (2015). Guidelines for psychological practice with transgender and gender nonconforming people. *American Psychologist, 70*, 832–864.

Asscheman, H., Giltay, E. J., Megens, J. A. J., de Ronde, W. P., van Trotsenburg, M. A. A., & Gooren, L. J. G. (2011). A long-term follow-up study of mortality in transsexuals receiving treatment with cross-sex hormones. *European Journal of Endocrinology, 164*(4), 635–642. https://doi.org/10.1530/EJE-10-1038

Berlin, F. S. (2016). A conceptual overview and commentary on gender dysphoria. *Journal of the American Academy of Psychiatry and the Law, 44*(2), 246–252.

Bizic, M. R., Jeftovic, M., Pusica, S., Stojanovic, B., Duisin, D., Vujovic, S., Rakic, V., & Djordjevic, M. L. (2018). Gender dysphoria: Bioethical aspects of medical treatment. *BioMed Research International*, *2018*, 9652305–9652306. https://doi.org/10.1155/2018/9652305

Bochicchio, L. (2019). [Book Review: K. Norman. 2017. *Socialising transgender: Support in transition*. Dunedin Academic Press.]. *Journal of Social Work*, *19*(6), 835–837. https://doi.org/10.1177/1468017319837422

Bränström, R., & Pachankis, J. (2020). Reduction in mental health treatment utilization among transgender individuals after gender-affirming surgeries: A total population study. *American Journal of Psychiatry*, *177*(8), 727–734. https://doi.org/10.1176/appi.ajp.2019.19010080

Brown, G. R., & McDuffie, E. (2009). Health care policies addressing transgender inmates in prison systems in the United States. *Journal of Correctional Health Care*, *15*(4), 280–291. https://doi.org/10.1177/1078345809340423

Brown, J., & Jenness, V. (2020). LGBT people in prison: Management strategies, human rights violations, and political mobilization. In E. Erez & P. Ibarra (Eds.), *Oxford encyclopedia of international criminology* (1–25). Oxford University Press.

Byne, W., Bradley, S. J., Coleman, E., Eyler, A. E., Green, R., Menvielle, E. J., Meyer-Bahlburg, H. F. L., Pleak, R. R., & Tompkins, D. A. (2012). Report of the American Psychiatric Association task force on treatment of gender identity disorder. *Archives of Sexual Behavior*, *41*(4), 759–796. https://doi.org/10.1007/s10508-012-9975-x

Cohen, W., Maisner, R. S., Mansukhani, P. A., & Keith, J. (2020). Barriers to finding a gender affirming surgeon. *Aesthetic Plastic Surgery*, *44*(6), 2300–2307. https://doi.org/10.1007/s00266-020-01883-z

De Cuypere, G., & Vercruysse, H. Jr.(2009). Eligibility and readiness criteria for sex reassignment surgery: Recommendations for revision of the WPATH standards of care. *International Journal of Transgenderism*, *11*(3), 194–209. https://doi.org/10.1080/15532730903383781

Dhejne, C., Lichtenstein, P., Boman, M., Johansson, A. L. V., Långström, N., & Landén, M. (2011). Long-term follow-up of transsexual persons undergoing sex reassignment surgery: Cohort study in Sweden. *PLoS One*, *6*(2), e16885. https://doi.org/10.1371/journal.pone.0016885

Dolovich, S. (2011). Strategic segregation in the modern prison. *American Criminal Law Review*, *48*(1), 1–110.

Donaldson, S. (2001). A million jockers, punks, and queens. In D. Sabo, T. A. Kupers, & W. London (Eds.), *Prison masculinities* (pp. 118–126). Temple University Press.

Esmonde, N. O., Heston, A. L., Morrison, T., Rogers, E., Liem, T., Amling, C., Dugi, D. D., Hansen, J., & Berli, J. U. (2019). Providing gender confirmation surgery at an academic medical center: Analysis of use, insurance payer, and fiscal impact. *Journal of the American College of Surgeons*, *229*(5), 479–486. https://doi.org/10.1016/j.jamcollsurg.2019.07.002

Ettner, R. (Eds.). (2016). *Principles of transgender medicine and surgery* (2nd ed.). Routledge.

Ferrando, C. (2020). Adverse events associated with gender affirming vaginoplasty surgery. *American Journal of Obstetrics and Gynecology*, *223*(2), 267.e1–267.e6. https://doi.org/10.1016/j.ajog.2020.05.033

Flores, A. R. (2016). *How many adults identify as transgender in the United States?* The Williams Institute. https://williamsinstitute.law.ucla.edu/wp-content/uploads/Trans-Adults-US-Aug-2016.pdf

Frey, J. D., Poudrier, G., Thomson, J. E., & Hazen, A. (2017). A historical review of gender-affirming medicine: Focus on genital reconstruction surgery. Journal of Sexual Medicine, *14*(8), 991–1002. https://doi.org/10.1016/j.jsxm.2017.06.007

Garcia, N. (2014). Starting with the man in the mirror: Transsexual prisoners and transitional surgeries following Kosilek v. Spencer. *American Journal of Law & Medicine*, *40*(4), 442–463.

Glezer, A. (2013). Transgendered and incarcerated: A review of the literature, current policies and laws, and ethics. *Journal of the American Academy of Psychiatry and the Law*, *41*(4), 551–559.

Grant, E. (2012). The ideological divide: Conflict and the supreme court's certiorari decision. *Cleveland State Law Review*, *60*(3), 559–583.

Hwang, R. Y. (2016). Accounting for carceral reformations: Gay and transgender jailing in Los Angeles as justice impossible. *Critical Ethnic Studies*, *2*(2), 82–103.

Jenness, V. (2010). From policy to prisoners to people. *Journal of Contemporary Ethnography*, *39*(5), 517–553. https://doi.org/10.1177/0891241610375823

Jenness, V. (2021). The social ecology of sexual victimization against transgender women who are incarcerated: A call for (more) research on modalities of housing and prison violence. *Criminology & Public Policy*, *20*(1), 3–18. https://doi.org/10.1111/1745-9133.12540

Jenness, V., Maxson, C. L., Sumner, J. M., & Matsuda, K. N. (2010). Accomplishing the difficult, but not impossible. *Criminal Justice Policy Review*, *21*(1), 3–30. https://doi.org/10.1177/0887403409341451

Jenness, V. (2011). *Transgender inmates in California prisons. Report to the California department of corrections and rehabilitation*. University of California.

Jenness, V., & Fenstermaker, S. (2014). Agnes goes to prison: Gender authenticity, transgender inmates in prisons for men, and pursuit of "the real deal. *Gender & Society*, *28*(1), 5–31. https://doi.org/10.1177/0891243213499446

Jenness, V., & Gerlinger, J. (2020). The feminization of transgender women in prisons for men: How prison as a total institution shapes gender. *Journal of Contemporary Criminal Justice, 36*(2), 182–205. https://doi.org/10. 1177/1043986219894422

Jiang, D., Witten, J., Berli, J., & Dugi, D. (2018). Does depth matter? Factors affecting choice of vulvoplasty over vaginoplasty as gender-affirming genital surgery for transgender women. *The Journal of Sexual Medicine, 15*(6), 902–906. https://doi.org/10.1016/j.jsxm.2018.03.085

Klemmer, C. L., Arayasirikul, S., & Raymond, H. F. (2021). Transphobia-based violence, depression, and anxiety in transgender women: The role of body satisfaction. *Journal of Interpersonal Violence, 36*(5–6), 2633–2655. https:// doi.org/10.1177/0886260518760015

Levine, S. B. (2016). Reflections on the legal battles over prisoners with gender dysphoria. *Journal of the American Academy of Psychiatry and the Law, 44*(2), 236–245.

Levine, S. B. (2018). Ethical concerns about emerging treatment paradigms for gender dysphoria. *Journal of Sex & Marital Therapy, 44*(1), 29–44. https://doi.org/10.1080/0092623X.2017.1309482

Levine, S. B., & Solomon, A. (2008). Meanings and political implications of "psychopathology" in a gender identity clinic: A report of 10 cases. *Journal of Sex & Marital Therapy, 35*(1), 40–57. https://doi.org/10.1080/ 00926230802525646

Marano, A. A., Louis, M. R., & Coon, D. (2021). Gender-affirming surgeries and improved psychosocial health out-comes. *JAMA Surgery, 156*(7), 685–687. https://doi.org/10.1001/jamasurg.2021.0953

McHugh, P. (2015, June 10). *Transgenderism: A pathogenic meme.* The Witherspoon Institute. https://www.thepu-blicdiscourse.com/2015/06/15145/

Murad, M. H., Elamin, M. B., Garcia, M. Z., Mullan, R. J., Murad, A., Erwin, P. J., & Montori, V. M. (2010). Hormonal therapy and sex reassignment: A systematic review and meta-analysis of quality of life and psycho-social outcomes. *Clinical Endocrinology, 72*(2), 214–231. https://doi.org/10.1111/j.1365-2265.2009.03625.x

Nolan, I. T., Kuhner, C. J., & Dy, G. W. (2019). Demographic and temporal trends in transgender identities and gender confirming surgery. *Translational Andrology and Urology, 8*(3), 184–190. https://doi.org/10.21037/tau. 2019.04.09

Nolasco, C. A. R. I., Vaughn, M. S., & del Carmen, R. V. (2010). Toward a new methodology for legal research in criminal justice. *Journal of Criminal Justice Education, 21*(1), 1–23. https://doi.org/10.1080/10511250903518944

Nolasco, C. A. R. I., del Carmen, R. V., Steinmetz, K. F., Vaughn, M. S., & Spaic, A. (2015). Building legal compe-tency: Foundations for a more effective criminology and criminal justice discipline. *Journal of Criminal Justice Education, 26*(3), 233–252. https://doi.org/10.1080/10511253.2015.1006648

Nolasco, C., & Vaughn, M. S. (2011). Judicial scrutiny of gender-based employment practices in criminal justice agencies. *Journal of Criminal Justice, 39*(2), 106–119. https://doi.org/10.1016/j.jcrimjus.2010.11.002

Nolasco, C. A., & Vaughn, M. S. (2020). Section 1983 civil liability against prison officials and dentists for delaying dental care. *Criminal Justice Policy Review, 31*(5), 721–745. https://doi.org/10.1177/0887403419860899

Norman, K. (2017). *Socialising transgender: Support in transition.* Dunedin Academic Press.

Osborne, C. S., & Lawrence, A. A. (2016). Male prison inmates with gender dysphoria: When is sex reassignment surgery appropriate? *Archives of Sexual Behavior, 45*(7), 1649–1663. https://doi.org/10.1007/s10508-016-0700-z

Prunas, A., Fisher, A. D., Bandini, E., Maggi, M., Pace, V., Todarello, O., De Bella, C., & Bini, M. (2017). Eudaimonic well-being in transsexual people, before and after gender confirming surgery. *Journal of Happiness Studies, 18*(5), 1305–1317. https://doi.org/10.1007/s10902-016-9780-7

Redcay, A., Luquet, W., Phillips, L., & Huggin, M. (2020). Legal battles: Transgender inmates' rights. *The Prison Journal, 100*(5), 662–682. https://doi.org/10.1177/0032885520956628

Routh, D., Abess, G., Makin, D., Stohr, M. K., Hemmens, C., & Yoo, J. (2017). Transgender inmates in prisons: A review of applicable statutes and policies. *International Journal of Offender Therapy and Comparative Criminology, 61*(6), 645–666. https://doi.org/10.1177/0306624X15603745

Sevelius, J., & Jenness, V. (2017). Challenges and opportunities for gender-affirming healthcare for transgender women in prison. *International Journal of Prisoner Health, 13*(1), 32–40. https://doi.org/10.1108/IJPH-08-2016-0046

Simonsen, R. K., Giraldi, A., Kristensen, E., & Hald, G. M. (2016). Long-term follow-up of individuals undergoing sex reassignment surgery: Psychiatric morbidity and mortality. *Nordic Journal of Psychiatry, 70*(4), 241–247. https://doi.org/10.3109/08039488.2015.1081405

Stroumsa, D. (2014). The state of transgender health care: Policy, law, and medical frameworks. *American Journal of Public Health, 104*(3), e31–e38. https://doi.org/10.2105/AJPH.2013.301789

Sumner, J., & Jenness, V. (2014). Gender integration in sex-segregated prisons. In D. Peterson & V. R. Panfil (Eds.), *The handbook of LGBT communities, crime, and justice* (pp. 229–259). Springer.

Tran, B. N. N., Epstein, S., Singhal, D., Lee, B. T., Tobias, A. M., & Ganor, O. (2018). Gender affirmation surgery: A synopsis using American college of surgeons national surgery quality improvement program and national inpatient sample databases. *Annals of Plastic Surgery, 80*(4 Suppl 4), S229–S235. https://doi.org/10.1097/SAP. 0000000000001350

Van Hout, M. C., Kewley, S., & Hillis, A. (2020). Contemporary transgender health experience and health situation in prisons: A scoping review of extant published literature (2000–2019). *International Journal of Transgender Health, 21*(3), 258–306. https://doi.org/10.1080/26895269.2020.1772937

Vaughn, M. S., & Carroll, L. (1998). Separate and unequal: Prison versus free-world medical care. *Justice Quarterly, 15*(1), 3–40. https://doi.org/10.1080/07418829800093621

von Dresner, K. S., Underwood, L. A., Suarez, E., & Franklin, T. (2013). Providing counseling for transgendered inmates: A survey of correctional services. *International Journal of Behavioral Consultation and Therapy, 7*(4), 38–42. https://doi.org/10.1037/h0100965

Whitman, C. (2017). Transgender criminal justice: Ethical and constitutional perspectives. *Ethics & Behavior, 27*(6), 445–457. https://doi.org/10.1080/10508422.2016.1183490

Wiepjes, C. M., Blok, C. J., Staphorsius, A. S., Nota, N. M., Vlot, M. C., Jongh, R. T., & Heijer, M. (2020). Fracture risk in transgender women and transgender men using long-term gender-affirming hormonal treatment: A nationwide cohort study. *Journal of Bone and Mineral Research, 35*(1), 64–70. https://doi.org/10.1002/jbmr.3862

Wildeman, C., & Andersen, L. H. (2020). Long-term consequences of being placed in disciplinary segregation. *Criminology, 58*(3), 423–453. https://doi.org/10.1111/1745-9125.12241

World Professional Association for Transgender Health. [WPATH] (2012). *Standards of care for the health of transsexual, transgender, and gender-nonconforming people.* https://www.wpath.org/media/cms/Documents/SOC%20v7/SOC%20V7_English2012.pdf?_t=1613669341

Zucker, K. J., Lawrence, A. A., & Kreukels, B. P. C. (2016). Gender dysphoria in adults. *Annual Review of Clinical Psychology, 12*, 217–247. https://doi.org/10.1146/annurev-clinpsy-021815-093034

Cases Cited

Allard v. Gomez, 9 Fed.Appx. 793 (9th Cir. 2001).

Ancata v. Prison Health Servs., Inc., 769 F.2d 700 (11th Cir. 1985).

Ashcroft v. al-Kidd, 563 U.S. 731 (2011).

Battista v. Clarke, 645 F.3d 449 (1st Cir. 2011).

Bivens v. Six Unknown Named of Federal Bureau of Narcotics, 403 U.S. 368(1971).

Brown v. Plata, 563 U.S. 493 (2011).

Cameron v. Tomes, 990 F.2d 14 (1st Cir. 1993).

Campbell v. Kallas, 936 F.3d 536 (7th Cir. 2019).

Colwell v. Bannister, 763 F.3d 1060 (9th Cir. 2014).

De'lonta v. Angelone, 330 F.3d 630 (4th Cir. 2003).

De'lonta v. Johnson, WL 5157262 (W. Va. 2011), *rev'd and remanded*, 708 F.3d 520 (4th Cir. 2013). *on remand, De'lonta v. Clarke*, WL 4584684 (W. Va. 2013).

Dilley v. Gunn, 64 F.3d 1365 (9th Cir. 1995).

Doe 4 by and through Lopez v. Shenandoah Valley Juvenile Center Commission, 985 F.3d 327 (4th Cir. 2021).

Druley v. Patton, 601 Fed.Appx. 632 (10th Cir. 2015).

Edmo v. Idaho Department of Correction, 358 F.Supp.3d 1103 (D. Idaho 2018), *aff'd in part vacated in part and remanded, Edmo v. Corizon, Inc.*, 935 F.3d 757 (9th Cir. 2019), *reh'g en banc denied*, 949 F.3d 489 (9th Cir. 2020), *stay denied, Idaho Department of Correction v. Edmo*, 140 S.Ct. 2800 (2020), *cert. denied*, 141 S.Ct. 610 (2020).

Estelle v. Gamble, 429 U.S. 97. (1976).

Farmer v. Brennan, 511 U.S. 825. (1994).

Fields v. Smith, 653 F.3d 550 (7th Cir. 2011).

Gaudreault v. Municipality of Salem, Mass., 923 F.2d 203 (1st Cir. 1990).

Gibson v. Collier, 920 F.3d 212 (5th Cir. 2019). *cert. denied*, 140 S.Ct. 653 (2019).

Hamby v. Hammond, 821 F.3d 1085 (9th Cir. 2016).

Hankins v. Lowe, 786 F.3d 603 (7th Cir. 2015).

Harris v. Thigpen, 941 F.2d 1495 (11th Cir. 1991).

H.C. by Hewett v. Jarrard, 786 F.2d 1080 (11th Cir. 1986).

Hoptowit v. Ray, 682 F.2d 1237 (9th Cir. 1982).

Inmates of Allegheny County Jail v. Pierce, 612 F.2d 754 (3rd Cir. 1979).

Jackson v. McIntosh, 90 F.3d 330 (9th Cir. 1996).

Jett v. Penner, 439 F.3d 1091 (9th Cir. 2006).

Keohane v. Jones, 328 F.Supp.3d 1288 (N.D. Fla. 2018), *order vacated, Keohane v. Florida DOC Secretary*, 952 F.3d 1257 (11th Cir. 2020a), *reh'g en banc denied*, 981 F.3d 994 (11th Cir. 2020b).

Kosilek v. Maloney, 221 F.Supp.2d 156 (D. Mass. 2002), *aff'd, Kosilek v. Spencer,* 740 F.3d 733 (1st Cir. 2014a). *reh'g en banc granted, opinion withdrawn Feb. 12, 2012, on reh'g en banc,* 774 F.3d 63 (1st Cir. 2014b), *cert. denied, Kosilek v. O'Brien,* 575 U.S. 989 (2015).
Kothmann v. Rosario, 558 Fed.Appx. 907 (11th Cir. 2014).
Lamb v. Norwood, 899 F.3d 1159 (10th Cir. 2018).
Langford v. Norris, 614 F.3d 445 (8th Cir. 2010).
Lopez v. Smith, 203 F.3d 1122 (9th Cir. 2000) (en banc).
Maggert v. Hanks, 131 F.3d 670 (7th Cir. 1997).
Mayweather v. Foti, 958 F.2d 91 (5th Cir. 1992).
Meriwether v. Faulkner, 821 F.2d 408 (7th Cir. 1987).
Mitchell v. Kallas, 895 F.3d 492 (7th Cir. 2018).
Norsworthy v. Beard, 802 F.3d 1090 (9th Cir. 2015).
Norton v. Dimazana, 122 F.3d 286 (5th Cir. 1997).
Patten v. Nichols, 274 F.3d 829 (4th Cir. 2001).
Perez v. Fenoglio, 792 F.3d 768 (7th Cir. 2015).
Petties v. Carter, 836 F.3d 722 (7th Cir. 2016) (en banc).
Pinson v. United States, 826 Fed.Appx. 237 (3rd Cir. 2020).
Praylor v. Texas Department of Criminal Justice, 430 F.3d 1208 (5th Cir. 2005).
Roe v. Elyea, 631 F.3d 843 (7th Cir. 2011).
Rosati v. Igbinoso, 791 F.3d 1037 (9th Cir. 2015).
Sain v. Wood, 512 F.3d 886 (7th Cir. 2008).
Stewart v. Raemisch, WL 3754173 (E.D. Wis. 2009).
Supre v. Ricketts, 792 F.2d 958 (10th Cir. 1986).
Toguchi v. Chung, 391 F.3d 1051 (9th Cir. 2004).
Turner v. Safley, 482 U.S. 78. (1987).
United States v. Derbes, 369 F.3d 579 (1st Cir. 2004).
Whitley v. Albers, 475 U.S. 312. (1986).
White v. Farrier, 849 F.2d 322 (8th Cir. 1988).
Williams v. Kelly, 818 Fed.Appx. 353 (5th Cir. 2020).
Wilson v. Seiter, 501 U.S. 294. (1991).
Youngberg v. Romeo, 457 U.S. 307 (1982).

Laws Cited

Inmate Sex Change Prevention Act ("Act 105") (Wis.).
Prison Rape Elimination Act ("PREA"), 28 C.F.R. § 115 et seq.
Title 42 U.S.C. § 1983, 1871 Civil Rights Act.

No Such Thing as Acceptable Sexual Orientation Change Efforts: An International Human Rights Analysis

Sonia Boulos and César González-Cantón

ABSTRACT
Sexual orientation change efforts (SOCE) have received well-founded criticism from multiple fronts for their discriminatory effects and variegated harmful consequences on LGBTQ + people. International human rights institutions had voiced their concern over extreme forms and coercive SOCE, labeling them as torture. However, the legal status of "soft" non-coercive practices (i.e., psychological interventions willingly sought by consumers) is less clear. This article argues that a proper understanding of the prohibition on torture and other forms of ill-treatment, and of the positive obligations attached to the right to equality requires banning SOCE in all its forms, even when pursued by consenting consumers.

INTRODUCTION

Sexual orientation change efforts (hereinafter, SOCE) have received well-founded criticism from multiple fronts for their discriminatory effects and variegated harmful consequences on LGBTQ + individuals (Beckstead 2002; Beckstead & Morrow 2004; Davison 1991; Glassgold et al. 2009; Haldeman 2002b; Schroeder & Shidlo 2001). SOCE are based on the assumption that minority sexual orientations are sinful and/or abnormal, changeable, and require healing or fixing. A wide variety of practices are deployed across the globe to pressure or even force people to renounce their non-heterosexual orientations. Those range from highly invasive techniques that cause severe physical and psychological damage—such as electroshock therapy, induced vomiting, surgery, corrective rape, etc.—through psychoanalysis and other talking therapies (Bothe 2020). The latter, even though "softer" in appearance, may also result in numerous negative impacts on their consumers, such as anxiety, suicidal ideation, depression, impotence, relationship dysfunction, and exacerbating the victims' feelings of inadequacy, self-worthlessness, and shame (Glassgold et al. 2009).

While international human rights institutions have raised various concerns over the compatibility of SOCE with international human rights standards, they have focused primarily on extreme forms of SOCE that meet the definition of torture. Even then, coercion and lack of consent served as a condition for classifying SOCE as torture. This erroneously suggests that extreme forms of SOCE could be justified if they involve a consenting consumer. Furthermore, the focus on extreme forms of SOCE fails to prevent and remedy the damage of "soft" practices, such as "psychoanalytical" methods, or informal SOCE exercised by religious ministries and "ex-gays." Such "soft" practices violate the right of members of sexual minorities to live a dignified life free of humiliation.

The aim of this paper is to criticize the failure of international human rights institutions to capitalize on the full potential of international human rights law to assert that SOCE, in all their forms, contravene basic human rights, guaranteed by international human rights conventions, even when they involve consenting adults.

To the best of our knowledge, human rights literature dealing with the application of the terms torture, and cruel, inhuman or degrading treatment (CIDT) to SOCE, has overlooked the fact that international human rights institutions used the label "torture" and other forms of ill-treatment only in relation to coercive and non-consensual treatments. Therefore, this article fills this gap by addressing the implications of consent in the application of the prohibition on torture and other forms of prohibited ill-treatment to SOCE.

An additional contribution of this article is that it carries out a fine-grained analysis of the positive human rights obligations attached to the right to non-discrimination on the ground of sexual orientation, and later suggests that such positive obligations entail a clear duty to ban all forms of SOCE, even when offered by private entities, or offered to consenting adults.

Besides framing SOCE as a torture or CIDT, this article has practical implications for policy-makers regarding the banning of SOCE by providing a multidimensional analysis of the legal obligations of States in relation to such harmful and discriminatory practices.

The organization of this article is as follows. Section 2 presents an overview of SOCE by providing definitions of key terms and a brief history of SOCE. It also explores the main harms that SOCE inflict on participants, including practices that are considered "soft".

Section 3 demonstrates that SOCE meet the definitions of torture and of CIDT under international law. We begin this section by clarifying the question whether the definition of torture or CIDT could be applied to SOCE, especially when offered by private entities, since the commission of torture and CIDT under the Convention Against Torture and Other Cruel, Inhuman or Degrading Treatment or Punishment (the Torture Convention) (UN, 1984) requires some level of state involvement (UN, 1984). In this section we focus, *inter alia*, on the positive obligations of States in relation to torturous acts and other forms of ill-treatment inflicted by private entities, and the duty of States to take positive measures to prevent such acts. Then, the article argues that the application of the term torture should not be limited to nonconsensual forms of SOCE. It further highlights that consent cannot justify an act that amounts to a violation of a peremptory norm of international law, such as the prohibition on torture. The article proceeds further by arguing that, even when SOCE do not amount to torture for the lack of *severe* physical or mental pain, they still amount to ill-treatment prohibited under international law. We further argue that positive obligations of States in relation to the right to non-discrimination on the ground of sexual orientation require States to ban all forms of SOCE, including "soft" ones, even when pursued by consenting consumers.

SOCE: AN OVERVIEW

Definitions

In this article, we utilize the definition of "sexual orientation" and of "sexual orientation identity" as presented in the 2009 report of the American Psychological Association Taskforce (Glassgold et al., 2009). Both are elements of the more general construct of "sexual identity" (Dillon et al., 2011; Shively & De Cecco, 1977). The term sexual orientation "refers to an individual's patterns of sexual, romantic, and affectional arousal and desire for other persons based on those persons' gender and sex characteristics" (Glassgold et al., 2009, p. 30). As it is connected to physiological and biological dynamics, sexual orientation is "beyond conscious choice" (Glassgold et al., 2009, p. 30). Sexual orientation identity, "refers to acknowledgment and internalization of sexual orientation and reflects self-exploration, self-awareness, self-recognition, group membership and affiliation,culture, and self-stigma" (Glassgold et al., 2009, p. 30). While a person's sexual orientation is hardly susceptible to modification, self-identification and self-labeling as heterosexual, or bisexual or gay and so on can change over time. Therefore, sexual orientation identity "involves private and public ways of self-identifying and [...] creates a foundation for the formation of community, social support, role models, friendship, and partnering" (Glassgold et al., 2009, p. 30).

Attempts to modify sexual orientation received different names, which are often used interchangeably: "sexual conversion therapy," "reparative theory," "sexual reorientation therapy," and, more recently, "sexual orientation change efforts" or SOCE. The term "conversion" points to the heavy religious load of the practice (George, 2016, p. 795, n. 792). George (2016, p. 815), citing ethnographer Tanya Erzen (2006), suggests that the emphasis of conversion therapists on change and malleability is "completely entwined with religious conversion." Whereas religiously motivated conversion therapy feeds on interpretations of same-sex attraction as "sin," "temptation," "diabolic possession," etc., reparative theory seeks "scientific" grounds and provides etiological explanations in the context of psychoanalytic theory. Thus, homosexuality is deemed a pathology whose origin may lie, for instance, in a pathological attachment to parents in early life or in defective learning of sexual patterns (Haldeman, 1994). As a "pathology," the homosexual person requires "fixing" or "reparative" action (Bothe, 2020; Glassgold et al., 2009).

This article uses SOCE, following the *Report of the American Psychological Association Task Force on Appropriate Therapeutic Responses to Sexual Orientation* (2009), as this term is broader in scope and describes more accurately than the previous ones the nature of these harmful interventions. SOCE refer to varied psychological and "therapeutic" practices that aim at altering non-heterosexual sexual orientations toward heterosexuality in professional and non-professional settings alike, including, but not limited to, those performed by unlicensed ministers and "ex-gay" volunteers inside churches, religious support groups, etc. Along these lines, too, we choose the term "consumers" (Drescher, 2001a) over "patients" to refer to people who undergo SOCE.

Description of SOCE Practices

The ethicality of SOCE has been discussed by both their advocates and opponents (Schroeder & Shidlo, 2001). Ethical concerns about extreme practices are widespread. Some of those practices are labeled as torture. Even so, they are still used on sexual minority people across the globe. Those include (Bothe 2020, pp. 7–12):

Aversive treatment: This practice consists in pairing discomfort with presentation of non-heterosexual stimuli. This "discomfort" can range from nausea induced by apomorphine as the aversive stimulus, to electroshocks to the hands, head, genitals, etc. that can be very painful (Smith et al., 2004). It is practiced in countries such as China, Ecuador, Australia, or United States of America.

Electroconvulsive therapy: The passing of an electric current between two electrodes attached to the head. If administered without anesthesia, it produces violent convulsions that can result in bones fractures. It is an extreme form of SOCE that leads to heavy cognitive deficits. Since it can sometimes be mixed up with aversive electroshocking, it is unclear in how many countries it is practiced; however, it is certainly practiced in Iran and India.

Medication: The use of anti-psychotics and anti-depressants, as well as hormone treatments, such as testosterone, sedatives in conjunction with hypnosis, and Viagra. In Russia and Vietnam, they have been administered forcibly; in other countries, such as France or the United Arab Emirates, consent has been obtained in coercive settings or through misleading information.

Forced confinement: Confinement in psychiatric facilities (for instance, in Mauritius), clinics (Ecuador) or even at home (Nigeria). In Ecuador, there are reports of subjects being exposed to long-term isolated confinement, humiliation (such as being handcuffed to a toilet for more than three months), forced sexual relations with other residents, verbal and physical abuse, and food and water deprivation.

Psychotherapy: In addition to talking therapy, which will be discussed in the next section, practitioners have tried Eye Movement Desensitization and Reprocessing (EMDR). This technique includes deep brain stimulation and is meant to ease the stress associated with traumatic memories; in this case, it targets the subject's "negative" attitude toward hetero-sexual attraction. Hypnotherapy is also a therapy of choice. Psychotherapy is widely used at least in 25 countries, including Egypt, Germany, Panama, Tunisia, or United Kingdom.

Corrective violence: This includes rape or "curative sex" and can also include beatings, flogging or carving. It is used in several countries, including South Africa, Sri Lanka, and Uganda. It is frequently perpetrated by family members and neighbors, who are asked for "help" to provide victims with an opposite sexual experience in the hope that they change her/his "choice."

Exorcisms and ritual cleansing: These typically involve prayer and Scripture reading. It may also include the usage of oil and water on the subject's body, beating, isolation, burns, or extreme fasting. Such practices are used in New Zealand, South Korea, Spain, Germany, France, or Ethiopia.

Gender reassignment surgery: It may be practiced when other SOCE "fail" to yield the expected results. For example, in Iran when victims "fail" therapy, they are pressured to undergo gender reassignment surgery to "facilitate" their involvement in "opposite sex" relations. Earp (2014) also mentions brain surgery but without providing further details.

SOCE and Psychoanalysis

Today, the most common forms of SOCE are "soft," i.e., those consisting of talking therapies, such as psychoanalysis. This section argues that "talk therapies" are not backed by sound psycho-analytical theories, instead, they were influenced by and perpetuate conservative socio-cultural beliefs about human sexuality. In that sense, SOCE are the battlefield of broader "culture wars" (Drescher, 2001a), revealing that "[t]he status of homosexuality is a political question, representing a historically rooted, socially determined choice regarding the ends of human sexuality" (Bayer, 1981, p. 5).

Homosexuality was discussed in a psychoanalytical context from the very beginning of the discipline. Freud (1960/1905, 1960/1935), for instance, regarded it as an imperfect developmental stage, although not a pathology. As time progressed, Forstein (2002, p. 168) claims that "[t]he cultural acceptance of homosexuality as an illness pushed clinicians, therapists, doctors, and religious counselors to accept homosexuality as pathological without applying the same rigorous scientific principles as was expected in other fields of medicine." The psychoanalytic view became, then, slowly coopted by religious conservatism (Bieber et al., 1962; Moberly, 1983; Nicolosi, 1991).

Among the most influential works pathologizing same-sex attraction was Socarides' (1968) treatment of homosexuality as manifestation of intrapsychic conflict, caused by the combination of overbearing mothers and "absent, weak, detached or sadistic" (Socarides, 1968, p. 38) fathers. The idea that homosexuality is related to unhealthy family dynamics was further developed by Moberly (1983), who is credited with introducing the concept of "reparative therapy." Moberly popularized the idea that homosexuality is the result of a "gender deficit" (Moberly, 1983, p. 36), i.e., deficit in the ability to relate to same-sex parent. This would lead to the pathological sexualization of child's unmet needs for her/his same-sex parent's love. According to this view, homosexuality is a "reparative drive" (Moberly, 1983, p. 37) to compensate this deficit through same-sex relationships.

This perspective dominated the conversation until 1973, when the American Psychiatric Association ceased to consider homosexuality an illness (Drescher, 2001b). This change was prompted, to a great extent, by a different understanding of homosexuality coming from fields such as biology, biochemistry, endocrinology, ethology, evolutionary studies, experimental psychology, genetics, sex studies, history, literary theory, neuroanatomy, the social sciences, and philosophy (Drescher, 2001a; Tozer & McClanahan, 1999).

In this line, various studies show that family dynamics cannot be associated with any particular sexual orientation (Bell et al., 1981; Bradley & Zucker, 1998; Freund et al., 1974; Freund & Blanchard, 1983; Siegelman, 1974; Storms, 1980; Zucker, 2008). Other studies highlight the conceptual shortcomings of the pathological approach to minority sexual orientation (Drescher 2001a, 1998; O'Connor & Ryan, 1993), whereas others take an empirical route. Among the latter, two pioneering researchers stand out: Alfred Kinsey and Evelyn Hooker. In his studies on sexual behavior in men (1948) and women (1953), Kinsey (and collaborators) found that many of the subjects under study were actually showing bisexual inclinations; thus, he first introduced, against the rigid polarity of heterosexuality and homosexuality, the idea of a *continuum* of sexual orientations. Further studies have later expanded the Kinsey's model across cultures and lifespans (McWhirter et al., 1990). On her part, psychologist Evelyn Hooker (1957) administered different psychological tests, such as the Rorschach Inkblot Test, to a sample of homosexual and heterosexual men and found no difference in terms of healthy mental functioning. Same results were obtained by Thompson and collaborators (1971) regarding differences in wellbeing and adjustment between male and female homosexuals and their heterosexual counterparts. Along these lines, some studies have focused on the question of personality differences between heterosexual and homosexual women (Armon, 1960; Ohlson & Wilson, 1974), or between heterosexual and homosexual men, and between homosexual men who seek treatment and those who do not (Turner et al., 1974), without finding any relevant differences that might justify therapeutical intervention.[1]

The therapeutic view is also lacking on the methodological side. Glassgold and collaborators (2009) offer the most comprehensive review to date of the methodological problems of SOCE-supporting studies. Beyond identifying internal and construct validity concerns, they highlight significant ambiguity surrounding SOCE "success stories." Some early studies reported rates of sexual reorientation as high as 67% (Nicolosi, 1991) and, at large, they expressed reasonable confidence in the effectiveness of therapeutic efforts (Bieber et al., 1962; Byrd & Nicolosi, 2002; Hadden, 1966; Masters & Johnson, 1979; Mayerson & Lief, 1965; Mintz, 1966; Nicolosi et al., 2000; Spitzer, 2003). However, according to Glassgold et al., in the last 50 years only a handful of studies have met scientific standards for assessing efficacy of outcomes,[2]—among which some recognize that SOCE fail in changing sexual orientation (Birk, 1980; Conrad & Wincze, 1976; Curran & Parr, 1957; Rangaswami, 1982). Also, there are few follow-up studies, and the existing ones show that, at best, changes work for a short term or work mostly for participants self-identified as bisexual or having had previous heterosexual experiences.

The main shortfall of SOCE-supporting studies is their significant ambiguity regarding the definition of "successful change." A variety of outcome measures has been proposed: reduction in sexual arousal and imagery in the presence of LGBTQ + erotic stimuli—through the usage of aversive conditioning therapy (Cautela, 1967; Cautela et al., 1987; McConaghy et al., 1981);

---

[1]Other empirical studies are Ford and Beach (1951), Marmor (1965, 1980), Bell et al. (1981), and Gonsiorek (1991). Pierce (1973) researched the difference between active and situational homosexuality in a study among inmates whose homosexual behavior was present before incarceration or, occasionally, after it. On their part, DeCecco and Parker (1995) curated a collection of essays examining state of the art research at the time about whether homosexuality is determined by heredity, hormones or by the structure of the brain.

[2]Other researchers have carried out reviews of particular studies, with similar conclusions (Cramer et al., 2008; Gonsiorek, 1981; Haldeman, 1991, 1994; Morrow & Beckstead, 2004; Sandfort, 2003; Tozer & McClanahan, 1999); a telling example is Spitzer (2012), who debunks his own 2003 study.

reduction in LGBTQ + erotic behavior (acting on those urges); and, in the last years, increased well-being for being able to "live with it", namely, to integrate the undesired sexual orientation in one's own life (Beckstead & Morrow, 2004; Shidlo & Schroeder, 2002).

Reframing goals of SOCE in terms of wellbeing, as opposed to changing the actual attraction, is very telling. It is an admission of defeat, i.e., that promises of sexual orientation change cannot be kept. SOCE become about coming to terms with one's own undesired feelings and, in the context of a religious life, with the ability to commit to God. The goal is to become a (Christian) with a homosexual problem, not a homosexual who believes in (Jesus) (George, 2016). This is possibly the reason why a significant number of consumers report successful outcomes and increased levels of well-being: it is no longer about developing a heterosexual orientation but being able to have a life within institutional religion, which usually means celibacy. It is about having reoriented toward asexuality rather than toward majority sexuality (Storms, 1980, cited by Beckstead, 2002).

Once SOCE have become discredited among care professionals, SOCE's supporters have increasingly moved away from scientific discussion and shifted to political action. A most representative instance of this trend is the establishment of the National Association for Research and Treatment of Homosexuality (NARTH) in 1999 by Socarides (Drescher, 2001b). At the same time, this move has also taken place in the opposite direction. The growing body of research coupled with political activism led the American Psychiatric Association (APA) to remove homosexuality from its diagnostic list in 1973. Successive declarations, resolutions, position statements, policies and practice guidelines by professional bodies came in, first slowly, then across-the-board during the following years (Byne, 2016; Drescher, 2001a; Haldeman, 2002a; Schroeder & Shidlo, 2001), also in other countries (Forstein 2002) and at the global level, such as the World Health Organization (WHO, 2017). Just recently, over 400 religious leaders, including Desmond Tutu and the Bishop of Liverpool, called for ending conversion therapy (Greenhalgh, 2020). Along with this growing trend, there has been an increasing banning of conversion therapies in some US States (Byne, 2016; Drescher et al., 2016; George, 2016)—although Trump presidency may have implied a setback in this regard. Other countries, such as Canada, Australia or Spain have also regional bans, and only four countries (Germany, Brazil, Ecuador and Malta) ban the practice in their whole territory (Wareham, 2020).

SOCE is Harmful

While coercive and physically invasive techniques, such as forced confinement, electrotherapy, and rape, have received wide condemnation (Bothe, 2020), a broad array of harms caused by psychological and psychoanalytical therapies remain insufficiently addressed by international human rights institutions.

Many behavior therapists have been concerned with the potential harms of aversive therapies (Bancroft, 2003; Davison, 1976, 1978; Davison & Wilson, 1973; King et al., 2004; Silverstein, 1991, 2007). Also, the field of psychoanalysis has increasingly recognized that, even though consumers may feel supported in the short term, negative effects are likely to be more prevalent in the long term (Beckstead, 2002). Several studies (Beckstead, 2002; Beckstead & Morrow, 2004; Davison, 1991; Glassgold et al., 2009; Haldeman, 2002b; Schroeder & Shidlo, 2001) take stock of these negative impacts that could be summarized in the following:

First, SOCE proponents disseminate misleading information regarding the efficacy of the treatment and the characterization of LGBTQ + sexuality as a psychological disorder that needs to be treated.

Second, SOCE have been found to have physical consequences, such as inability to get sexually intimate. These physical effects can be also related to severe psychological damage.

Third, in regard to that psychological impact, the report of the American Psychological Association Taskforce (Glassgold et al., 2009), which surveyed available studies on the efficiency and effects of SOCE, suggests that stigmatizing minority sexual orientations can have a variety of negative consequences throughout the victims' life span. This includes anxiety, confusion, depression, grief, guilt owing to internalizing treatment failure, hopelessness, loss of faith (which can also be tied back to depression), poor self-image, intimacy difficulties, suicidal ideation, and self-hatred.

Fourth, social relationships are also harmed, as the consumers may blame their parents for causing their sexual orientation; they may lose friends and potential romantic partners, as well as social support in general; or, more broadly, they could develop increased alienation, loneliness, and social isolation.

Fifth, prejudices toward members of sexual minorities get reinforced by considering their lives as less worth living. As Haldeman (1994) and Davison (1991) put it, the professional speaks from a position of power—there is not such a thing as therapist's neutrality. Therefore, by saying that there is a cure for non-heterosexual orientations, the professional is sanctioning homophobic values and beliefs.

What makes SOCE most troubling is the assumption that a person can give up such an important part of oneself, such as one's sexual and emotional identity, for objectionable reasons, and still be better off. For somebody to consensually undergo SOCE, they must feel a strong need to conform to social group expectations, which requires them to decouple their sexual and emotional identity from their social and religious identity, and reduce the former to a superficial aspect of one's life (Beckstead & Morrow, 2004).

According to Begelman (1975) and Whitman et al. (2006), the very existence of the therapy conveys the idea that non-heterosexual orientations are inferior to hetero-sexual orientation. Therefore, it "violates the principles of integrity and respect for the rights and dignity of minority individuals" (Cramer et al., 2008; Halpert, 2000). SOCE also perpetuate prejudicial social and religious values and beliefs (Cramer et al., 2008; Halpert, 2000), preventing and delaying social reform. Therefore, even interventions that would be painless and voluntary, such as "reorientation pills" (if they came into existence some day), remain unacceptable (Earp et al., 2014). Social prejudices can be very strong and coerce individual behaviors and beliefs in a manner that is as effective as physical and emotional violence, or even more. Silverstein (1977, p. 4) paints the nature of this coercion very eloquently:

> To grow up in a family where the word "homosexual" was whispered, to play in a playground and hear the words "faggot" and "queer," to go to church and hear of "sin" and then to college and hear of "illness," and finally to the counseling center that promises to "cure," is hardly to create an environment of freedom and voluntary choice.

The source of distress for consumers is not their sexual orientation *per se* but "internalized homophobia and societal pressures" (Cramer et al., 2008). In the absence of such pressure, the person feels no need to change their orientation. This explains the absence of change efforts in the opposite direction, i.e., from hetero-sexuality to minority orientation (Forstein, 2002).

SOCE AS TORTURE, CRUEL, INHUMAN OR DEGRADING TREATMENT

The prohibition on Torture and CIDT is a central tenet of international human rights law. Article 5 of the Universal Declaration of Human Rights states "[n]o one shall be subjected to torture or to cruel, inhuman or degrading treatment or punishment" (UN, 1948, p. 217 (III) A). Article 7 of the International Covenant on Civil and Political Rights (ICCPR) reiterates the same language (UN, 1966). Article 2.1 of the Torture Convention states: "Each State Party shall take effective legislative, administrative, judicial or other measures to prevent acts of torture in any territory under its jurisdiction" (UN, 1984). Likewise, Article 16.1 of the Torture Convention requires States to "undertake to prevent in any territory under its jurisdiction other acts of cruel, inhuman or degrading treatment or punishment." The prohibition on torture and CIDT is also central to regional human rights treaties.[3] The prohibition on torture is a rule of customary international law regarded peremptory norm of international law (*jus cogens*), from which no derogation is permitted (ICTY, 1998).

While the prohibition on torture and CIDT emerged in the realm of the criminal justice system (Burgers & Danelius, 1988), international human rights institutions have expanded the reach of these prohibitions beyond this traditional context.[4] According to the UN Committee against Torture (CAT), States must prohibit, prevent and redress torture and ill-treatment not only in prisons and detention facilities, but also in hospitals, schools, the military, and in institutions that engage in the care of children, the aged, the mentally ill or disabled. More broadly, the duty to prevent torture and ill-treatment applies to all institutions where the failure of the State to intervene "encourages and enhances the danger of privately inflicted harm" (CAT 2008, para 15).

The Prohibition on Torture and CIDT and the Question of Private Actors

According to the Torture Convention, both torture and CIDT require the State's involvement for ill-treatment to amount to torture or CIDT. This is embedded in the requirement that the prohibited act must be inflicted by, or at the instigation of, or with the consent or acquiescence of a State agent (UN, 1984, arts. 1 and 16). This raises the question whether the terms torture and CIDT are applicable to ill-treatment inflicted by private entities. International human rights institutions have long interpreted human rights norms as encompassing both negative and positive obligations. Negative obligations require states to refrain from violating human rights. Positive obligations require states to take active measures to prevent violations of rights, even when committed by private actors (Lavrysen, 2014). For example, Article 2 of the ICCPR states that each State party must undertake "to respect and to ensure" to all individuals within its territory and subject to its jurisdiction the rights recognized in the ICCPR without distinction of any kind. According to the UN Human Rights Committee (HRC), the duty to "ensure" requires States to protect the individual from the violation of her rights by private persons or private entities (CCPR, 2004). States could be held accountable for human rights violations, committed by a private actor, for "permitting or failing to take appropriate measures or to exercise due diligence to prevent, punish, investigate or redress the harm caused by such acts" (CCPR, 2004, para 8). The obligation to prevent human rights violations was applied to torturous acts committed by private actors, especially in cases involving gender violence. According to the UN Committee on the Eliminations of all forms of Discrimination against Women (CEDAW Committee), gender violence violates, inter-alia, the right of women to be free from torture and CIDT. Therefore, States could be held responsible for private acts violence if they fail to act with due diligence to prevent such acts or to investigate and punish them, and provide compensation for the victim (CEDAW, 1992).

In the *Velásquez Rodríguez v. Honduras* (The Velasquez Rodriguez case), the Inter American Court of Human Rights (IACtHR) emphasized that (IACtHR, 1988, para17)

> an illegal act which violates human rights and which is initially not directly imputable to a State (for example, because it is the act of a private person or because the person responsible has not been identified)

---

[3]These prohibitions are found, *inter-alia*, in Article 3 of the European Convention on Human Rights, Convention for the Protection of Human Rights and Fundamental Freedoms (COU, 1956); Article 5.2 of the American Convention on Human Rights (UN, 1969); and Article 5 of the African (Banjul) Charter on Human and Peoples' Rights (OAU, 1981).

[4]For example, the prohibition on CIDT was applied to racial discrimination (see, e.g. ECtHR, 2001a) and house demolitions (see CAT, 2002).

can lead to international responsibility of the State, not because of the act itself, but because of the lack of due diligence to prevent the violation or to respond to it.

Both the European Court of Human Rights (ECtHR) and the IACtHR have found States responsible for the violation of the prohibition on torture and CIDT for failing to exercise due diligence to prevent or to respond to gender violence committed by private persons.[5] In *López Soto v. Venezuela* the IACtHR (2019) ruled that when acts of violence against women are perpetrated by private actors with the State's tolerance, this amounts to acquiescence to torture, i.e., a violation by the State of its duty not to torture, and not simply a violation of its positive obligations to prevent or respond to private acts of violence.

A similar position was expressed by the Rapporteur against Torture and Other Cruel, Inhuman or Degrading Treatment or Punishment (UN Rapporteur on Torture), Juan E. Méndez, who argued that the failure of the State to prevent, investigate and punish domestic violence suggests its consent, acquiescence and or even justification for such acts (HRC, 2016, para 11). Adding that "States are internationally responsible for torture when they fail—by indifference, inaction or prosecutorial or judicial passivity—to exercise due diligence to protect against such violence or when they legitimize domestic violence by, for instance, allowing husbands to 'chastize' their wives or failing to criminalize marital rape, acts that could constitute torture" (HRC, 2016, para 55).

State's obligation to protect all persons from torture and ill-treatment applies equally to members of sexual minorities. This entails a duty to prohibit, prevent, investigate, and redress torture and ill-treatment of members of sexual minorities, including when committed by private actors (HRC, 2015). As highlighted by the Office of the High Commissioner of Human Rights, States become complicit in violence against members of sexual minorities "whenever they create and implement discriminatory laws and practices that trap them in abusive circumstances or foster a climate in which such violence by both State and non-State actors is condoned and met with impunity" (OHCHR, 2019a, p. 28). Applied to SOCE, States' tolerance of such practices, which are advocated openly in the public sphere, amounts to acquiescence to torture.

SOCE as Torture

The term torture is defined in Article 1 of the Torture Convention (UN, 1984):

> Torture means any act by which severe pain or suffering, whether physical or mental, is intentionally inflicted on a person for such purposes as obtaining from him or a third person information or a confession, punishing him for an act he or a third person has committed or is suspected of having committed, or intimidating or coercing him or a third person, or for any reason based on discrimination of any kind, when such pain or suffering is inflicted by or at the instigation of or with the consent or acquiescence of a public official or other person acting in an official capacity. It does not include pain or suffering arising only from, inherent in or incidental to lawful sanctions.

This definition involves four elements: the infliction of *severe* pain, either physical or mental; the infliction of the pain is intentional; it aims to achieve a certain purpose; and there is a state involvement, at least through acquiescence. Article 4 of the Torture Convention requires States to criminalize acts of torture, the attempt to commit torture, and complicity or participation in torture.

The above-mentioned definition is easily applicable to SOCE practices ordered by the State if they involve severe physical or mental pain, such as the use of sexual violence, force-feeding, food deprivation, isolation, confinement, or any other practices that induce severe physical or mental pain. It is not surprising, then, that international human rights institutions have started to

---

[5]See e.g. Opuz v. Turkey (ECtHR, 2009), Talpis v. Italy (ECtHR, 2017), E.M. v. Romania (ECtHR, 2012, §§ 41 and 43), Valiulienė v. Lithuania (ECtHR, 2013).

use terminology related to torture almost two decades ago in addressing SOCE. In his capacity as the UN Special Rapporteur on Torture, Nigel Rodley highlighted that members of sexual minorities are disproportionately subjected to torture and other forms of ill-treatment, for failing to conform to socially constructed gender expectations (OHCHR, 2001, p. 19). His report described, *inter-alia*, the ill-treatment inflicted on sexual minorities for the purpose of changing their sexual orientation using terminology that resonates with the definitional elements of torture (OHCHR, 2001, p. 24):

> In a number of countries, members of sexual minorities are said to have been involuntarily confined to state medical institutions, where they were allegedly subjected to forced treatment on grounds of their sexual orientation or gender identity, including electric shock therapy and other "aversion therapy", reportedly causing psychological and physical harm.

However, international human rights institutions have been willing to attach the label of torture to SOCE practices that are *coercive*. For example, in 2013, the former UN Rapporteur on Torture, Juan E. Mendez, called upon States to repeal all laws allowing intrusive and irreversible treatments, including "conversion therapies" when enforced or administered without the free and informed consent of the person concerned (HRC, 2015, para 88). In 2019, the current UN Rapporteur on Torture, Nils Melzer, argued that when "conversion therapy" involves inflicting severe pain or suffering, *in the absence of a free and informed consent*, rooted in discrimination based on sexual orientation or gender identity, it could amount to torture or CIDT (OHCHR, 2019b, para 50).

CAT followed the same approach. For example, in its Concluding Observations on Ecuador, CAT expressed its concern over the "*involuntary* placement and ill-treatment of lesbian, gay, bisexual and transgender persons in private centers in which "sexual reorientation or dehomosexualization therapies" are practiced" (emphasis added) (CAT, 2017, para 49). In its Concluding observation on China, CAT expressed its concern over "gay conversion therapy" offered by private and public clinics, which included, inter-alia, the administration of electroshocks and the involuntary confinement in psychiatric and other facilities. CAT recommended that China adopts the necessary legislative, administrative and other measures to guarantee respect for the autonomy of members of sexual minorities and to prohibit "conversion therapy" and other forced, involuntary or otherwise coercive or abusive treatments (CAT, 2016, para 55–56).

Also, the former High Commissioner for Human Rights, Zeid Ra'ad Al Hussein, limited the use of the word torture to coercive practices. In one of his reports, he emphasized that certain medical procedures, including "conversion therapy," "when forced or otherwise involuntary, breach the prohibition on torture and ill-treatment" (Al Hussein 2015, para 38). Most recently, in 2020, the Independent Expert on protection against violence and discrimination based on sexual orientation and gender identity issued a special report on "conversion therapy." While he recommended to ban SOCE, he stated that "conversion therapy" *may* engage the international responsibility of the State due to inconsistency with the prohibition on torture on CIDT (HRC, 2020).

It seems that the reference to consent could shield minors who are coerced into therapy by their parents but it fails to guarantee the same protection to adults.

This continuous emphasis on the coercive and involuntary nature of certain SOCE as a precondition for labeling them as torture, could open the door for legitimizing "freely" chosen practices, even when they involve acts that could otherwise amount to torture. While International law allows States to rely on consent as a justification for a conduct that, without a consent, would constitute a breach of an international obligation (ILC, 2001, ch. IV.E.1), consent can never justify a violation of a peremptory norm of international law, such as the prohibition on torture (ILC, 2001, ch. IV.E.1). Therefore, international human rights institutions must declare unequivocally that SOCE practices involving severe physical and mental pain constitute torture, even if the victim had consented to it. International human rights institutions have endorsed the criminalization of serious physical injuries even when the injured party consented to the injury and found pleasure in it. Therefore, the insistence on linking SOCE to torture only in the existence of coercion and lack of consent is unmerited and baffling. In *Laskey, Jaggard and Brown v. The United Kingdom* (the Laskey case), the applicants, all adults, claimed that their conviction of assault and wounding as a result of engaging in consensual sado-masochistic activities violated their right to privacy under Art. 8 of the European Convention (ECtHR, 1997). The ECtHR ruled that States are entitled to regulate, through the operation of criminal law, activities which involve the infliction of physical harm regardless of the consent of the parties involved. The Court noted that applicants' sado-masochistic activities involved a significant degree of injury, which could not be characterized as trifling or transient. Therefore, the prosecution and conviction of the applicants could be considered as necessary in a democratic society for the sake of protecting public health.

The decision of the ECtHR was criticized by some scholars for being paternalistic (Nowlin, 2002); after all, the *Laskey case* dealt with acts that took place in the private sphere pursued by adults as gratifying and enjoyable. In comparison, SOCE are institutionalized practices that perpetuate the pathologization of non-heterosexual orientations and have broader societal implication for members of sexual minorities. Even when "freely" chosen, they are chosen not for pleasure, but as a response to public pressure to conform to socially constructed gender stereotypes.

Additionally, in most legal systems, consent is valid only when the individual's choice is autonomous and free of external pressure (Dubber & Hörnle, 2014). But as explained above, social prejudices can be extremely coercive and impact individual behaviors and beliefs in a manner that is as effective as physical and emotional violence, or even more Silverstein (1977, p. 4). As mentioned before, Holtmaat argues that gender stereotypes impair the autonomy of people of all genders "to live their lives according to their own interests and convictions about their personal and unique contribution to sustaining and developing humanity" (2013, p. 113). Therefore, consent is irrelevant for the purpose of labeling certain SOCE practices as torture.

SOCE as CIDT

Even when SOCE practices do not amount to torture due to the lack of *severe* physical or mental pain, they still amount to ill-treatment prohibited under international law. While human rights institutions have not delved much on the definition of cruel, inhuman and degrading treatment, they have used the severity of the pain as one of the main criteria to distinguish torture from CIDT (Boulos, 2019). In *T v. UK* the ECtHR (1999, para 69) defined inhuman treatment as a treatment that causes either actual bodily injury or intense physical and mental suffering. In *Bouyid v. Belgium* the Grand Chamber of the ECtHR ruled that minor bodily injuries that do not involve serious physical or mental suffering cannot be described as inhuman or, *a fortiori*, torture. Waldron criticizes the lack of clear definitions of these prohibitions and suggests to understand inhuman treatment as a treatment "which cannot be endured in a way that enables the person suffering it to continue the basic elements of human functioning" (2010, p. 308). He maintains that the prohibition on inhuman treatment protects what we value about elementary human functioning, such as self-control, care of self, and the ability to interact with others and so on (Waldron, 2010). Applied to SOCE, certain practices can easily qualify as inhuman because they result in a serious disruption of the victim's ability to love and to have an emotional attachment to others, to maintain social relations, and to enjoy satisfying sexual relations.

SOCE also violate the prohibition on degrading treatment. International human rights institutions have emphasized the intimate link between degrading treatment and human dignity. While they fall short of explaining with sufficient clarity how degradation constitutes a particular form of harm to human dignity, an emphasis has been put on key concepts such as humiliation and debasement. In *Ireland v. UK*, Judge Fitzmaurice argued that degrading treatment denotes "something seriously humiliating, lowering as to human dignity, or disparaging, like having one's head shaved, being tarred and feathered, smeared with filth, pelted with muck, paraded naked in front of strangers, forced to eat excreta [...] or dress up in a way calculated to provoke ridicule or contempt" (ECtHR, 1977). In *T. v. UK* the ECtHR defined degrading treatment as a treatment that arouses in its victims "feelings of fear, anguish and inferiority capable of humiliating and debasing them" (ECtHR, 1999, 69). The ECtHR further emphasized that, even if the purpose of the treatment was not to humiliate or to debase the victim, this does not immediately rule out finding a violation of the prohibition on degrading treatment.

In *Peers v. Greece* the Court further added that in considering whether a treatment is degrading, as far as the consequences are concerned, it must adversely affect the victim's personality (ECtHR, 2001b, para 68).

In *Tyrer v. the UK,* the ECtHR (1978, para 104) ruled that the humiliating act does not need to be executed in public to amount to degrading treatment, it suffices that the victim was humiliated in his own eyes, even if not in the eyes of others. It seems that in addition to the subjective element of humiliation, in evaluating the compatibility of an objectionable treatment, the court evaluates whether the applicant was in fact placed in a state of humiliation or degradation (Kaufmann et al., 2010). The ECtHR (2006) considered a treatment degrading also when it could get the victim to act against her will or conscience.

The prohibition on degrading treatment was also applied to cases involving discriminatory treatment based on group-affiliation, when discrimination was found to reach the severity threshold required for breaching Article 3 of the European Convention, which prohibits ill-treatment. In *Cyprus v. Turkey* the ECtHR (2001a) concluded that compelling Karpas Greek Cypriots to live isolated, restricted in their movements, controlled and with no prospect of renewing or developing their community is debasing.

Linking degrading treatment to humiliation is found also in the jurisprudence of the IACtHR. For example, in *Loayza-Tamayo v. Peru* the Court held that "[t]he degrading aspect is characterized by the fear, anxiety and inferiority induced for the purpose of humiliating and degrading the victim and breaking his physical and moral resistance" (IACtHR, 1997, para 57). The HRC also linked degrading treatment to humiliation (HRC, 1989, para 9.2).

Margalit defines humiliation as "any sort of behavior or condition that constitutes a sound reason for a person to consider his or her self-respect injured" (Margalit, 1996, p. 9). He further maintains that self-respect is "the honor persons bestow upon themselves by virtue of their own humanity" (Margalit, 1996, p. 24). Since the freedom to shape one's life is a unique feature of humans that animals and things lack, a "severe diminution of human freedom and control" constitutes humiliation (Margalit, 1996, p. 119). Holtmaat (2013, p. 113) argues that gender stereotypes deny people of all genders "the autonomy to live their lives according to their own interests and convictions about their unique contribution to sustaining and developing humanity." Adding that people of all genders "have a fundamental right not to be confined to constructed (essentialist) understandings of femininity or masculinity [...] that are entrenched in their culture, tradition or religion, as well as in the main social and legal institutions or organizations of their society" (2013, p. 113).

SOCE practices are not only prejudicial to the individual's ability to control her life, they are also built on the idea that the person should fully renounce her right to self-determination. More so, as Margalit (1996) and Waldron (2010) point out, treating individuals or groups of people as the embodiment of evil debases them and treats them as unhuman.

Therefore, even "soft" SOCE practices are inherently debasing for the mere fact that they pathologize and stigmatize minority sexual orientations, provoking guilt and self-loathing sentiments. As expressed by the Independent Expert on protection against violence and discrimination based on sexual orientation and gender identity, attempts to pathologize and erase the identity of individuals of diverse sexual orientations and genders, negate their existence and provoke self-loathing, and hence have profound consequences on their physical and psychological integrity and well-being (HRC, 2020, para 19). A similar view was expressed by an Independent Forensic Expert Group, who concluded the following (Alempijevic et al., 2020):

> All practices attempting conversion are inherently humiliating, demeaning and discriminatory. The combined effects of feeling powerless and extreme humiliation generate profound feelings of shame, guilt, self-disgust, and worthlessness, which can result in a damaged self-concept and enduring personality changes. The injury caused by practices of "conversion therapy" begins with the notion that an individual is sick, diseased, and abnormal due to their sexual orientation or gender identity and must therefore be treated. This starts a process of victimization.

They further emphasized that SOCE are based on the belief that sexual minority persons are somehow inferior morally, spiritually and even physically to their heterosexual and cisgender counterparts and must modify their orientation or identity to remedy that inferiority (Alempijevic et al., 2020).

Here too one might pose the question whether States are allowed to interfere in freely chosen SOCE when the harm inflicted on the individual does not amount to torture, nor it involves physical injury. Answering this question requires understanding the nature of the positive obligations that international law imposes on States in relation to respecting and ensuring human rights.

International human rights institutions have expanded the right to non-discrimination to include people of diverse sexual orientations and gender identities. Both the HRC and UN Committee on Economic, Social and Cultural Rights (CESCR) have clarified that the principle of non-discrimination prohibits discrimination based on sexual orientation or gender identity (CESCR, 2016, paras 9 & 23; CESCR, 2009, para 32; HRC, 1994). Also, the Committee on the Rights of the Child (CRC) interpreted the right to non-discrimination, guaranteed in Article 2 of the Convention on the Rights of the Child, to include sexual orientation (CRC, 2003b, para 6, 2003a, para 8), gender identity (CRC, 2011, paras 60 & 72(g), 2013, para 8), and intersex status (CRC, 2016, para 34). The CEDAW Committee has recognized that the discrimination of women based on sex and gender is inextricably linked with other factors that affect women, such as sexual orientation and gender identity (CEDAW, 2010, para 18, 2015, para 8). Likewise, the Committee on the Rights of Persons with Disabilities (2016b, para 15, 2017, para 19, 2016a, paras 8-9) and the Committee on the Elimination of Racial Discrimination (CERD, 2017, para 27, 2015, para 16) have referred to sexual orientation or gender identity in addressing intersectional discrimination.

Recognizing sexual-orientation as a prohibited ground for discrimination carries positive obligations with it. Article 2 of the ICCPR requires States "to respect and to ensure to all individuals within its territory and subject to its jurisdiction the rights recognized in the present Covenant, without distinction of any kind" (UN, 1966). According to the HRC, the duty to ensure rights requires States to "adopt legislative, judicial, administrative, educative and other appropriate measures in order to fulfill their legal obligations" (CCPR, 2004, para 7). The HRC further clarified that the duty to ensure rights requires States to protect the individual "not just against violations of Covenant rights by its agents, but also against acts committed by private persons or entities that would impair the enjoyment of Covenant rights" (CCPR, 2004, para 8). These obligations equally apply to members of sexual minorities, who are entitled to enjoy their human rights without any discrimination. States are under the obligation to protect the human rights of members of sexual minorities by "preventing abuses by third parties and proactively tackling barriers to the enjoyment of human rights, including […] discriminatory attitudes and practices" (HRC, 2015, para 10).

In the *Velasquez Rodriguez case,* the IACtHR emphasized that the duty to "ensure" rights entails the duty to adopt "all those means of a legal, political, administrative and cultural nature that promote the protection of human rights" (IACtHR, 1988, para 175). In *Castillo Petruzzi et al. v. Peru* the IACtHR further clarified that the duty to protect rights requires the elimination of norms and practices that violate human rights, and the promulgation of norms and the development of practices conducive to the enjoyment of rights (IACtHR, 1999, para 207).

The HRC and the CESCR have also recognized the duty of States to adopt of legislative, judicial, administrative, educational, and other measures to ensure the full enjoyment of all human rights to all. In addressing gender equality, the HRC has clarified that States must "ensure that traditional, historical, religious or cultural attitudes are not used to justify violations of women's right to equality before the law and to equal enjoyment of all Covenant rights" (HRC, 2000, para 5). The CESCR specifically requires States to adopt measures to eliminate "prejudices, customary and all other practices that perpetuate the notion of inferiority or superiority of either of the sexes, and stereotyped roles for men and women" (CESCR, 2005, para 19).

The same principles apply to discrimination based on sexual orientation. An exemplification of this is found in *Atala Riffo and Daughters v. Chile*, which dealt with the discriminatory treatment and arbitrary interference in the private life of a lesbian mother, who was stripped of the custody of her daughters for being a lesbian. There, the IACtHR ordered transformative reparations to the victim with the aim of achieving "structural changes, dismantling certain stereotypes and practices that perpetuate discrimination against LGBT groups" (IACtHR, 2012, para 267).

The Convention and the Elimination of all Forms of Discrimination against Women (CEDAW) (UN, 1979) takes a transformative approach to equality with the objective of transforming structures that perpetuate discrimination. Transformative equality aims at "changing society in such a way that those features of existing cultures, religions or traditions and of legal, social and economic structures that obstruct the equality and human dignity of women are subjected to fundamental change" (Holtmaat, 2013, p. 111; see also Fredman, 2011, pp. 25–29, 2019a, p. 283).

Cusack and Pusey (2013) argue that the principle of transformative equality, as advanced by CEDAW Committee, embodies two categories of obligations. The first category focuses on the transformation of "institutions, systems and structures that cause or perpetuate discrimination and inequality" (Cusack & Pusey, 2013, p. 64). The second category focuses on "the transformation of harmful norms, prejudices and stereotypes" (Cusack & Pusey, 2013, p. 64). The notion of transformative equality is reflected, inter alia, in Article 5(a) of CEDAW, which requires States to "modify the social and cultural patterns of conduct of men and women, with a view to achieving the elimination of prejudices and customary and all other practices which are based on the idea of the inferiority or the superiority of either of the sexes or on stereotyped roles for men and women" (UN, 1979). The pathologization of diverse sexual orientations is intimately tied to harmful gender stereotypes. Enforcing heterosexuality as *the normative* form of sexuality forms part of the construction and conservation of patriarchal gender relations (Butler, 1990; Holtmaat & Post, 2015).

While the CEDAW Committee had referred to sexual orientation and gender identity in the context of intersectional discrimination and not as a stand-alone violation of CEDAW, Dianne Otto (2015) argues that it is possible to interpret CEDAW as prohibiting all forms of sex discrimination, including forms of discrimination against gay men and intersex and transgender people. Holtmaat and Post (2015, p. 325) argue that "[g]ender stereotypes and fixed parental gender roles directly affect the lives of all persons who renounce traditional heterosexual and patriarchal feminine and masculine gender identities and gender roles. Through an expansive interpretation of article 5a, all of these situations may be brought under the scope of the Convention."

Even without settling the debate on whether CEDAW's asymmetrical application to women only must be reevaluated, the duty to eradicate SOCE still falls within the scope of the positive obligations of States under CEDAW. The CEDAW Committee explicitly recognized that one of the three main objectives of CEDAW is to address prevailing gender relations and the persistence of gender-based stereotypes. The penalization and the stigmatization of sexual attractions, behaviors, and identities that do not conform to hetero-patriarchal norms constitute one of the main pillars sustaining the patriarchal order of society. Gender stereotypes harmful to women are not going to disappear in societies where non-heterosexual attractions, behaviors, and identities are treated as an evil and an illness that requires treatment. Therefore, eradicating practices that perpetuate the stigmatization of individuals of diverse sexual orientations and gender identities is at the core of the positive obligations embodied in Article 5 of CEDAW, and States must proactively combat them, even if certain consumers consent to them. Just like the consent of women to the institution of polygamy does not absolve the State from its duty to eradicate this discriminatory institution, the same should apply to SOCE.

CONCLUSIONS

In this article, we surveyed the harms of SOCE, especially those resulting from "soft" practices, such as "talk therapy." We have demonstrated that the definition of torture and CIDT can be applied to SOCE not only in relation to extreme practices such as rape, electroshock therapy, forced confinement, induced vomiting and so forth, but also in relation to "softer" practices, such as talking therapies and psychoanalysis, since they inflict myriad and serious emotional harms on victims and reinforce the view that non-heterosexual orientations are sinful, abnormal, sick, and require fixing. We have also argued that consent cannot serve as a justification for SOCE, even in relation to "soft" forms. This conclusion is not only based on the peremptory character of the prohibition on torture, but also on the positive obligations attached to the right to nondiscrimination that require States to eradicate laws, practices and customs that perpetuate discrimination against members of sexual minorities. States that tolerate discriminatory and debasing practices, such as SOCE, violate their international obligations to ensure the right to equality for all and are legally responsible for such acts of torture and CIDT, whether performed by State institutions or by private entities.

DISCLOSURE STATEMENT

No potential competing interest was reported by the author(s).

REFERENCES

Al Hussein, Z. R. A. (2015). *Discrimination and violence against individuals based on their sexual orientation and gender identity*. Human Rights Council.

Alempijevic, D., Beriashvili, R., Beynon, J., Birmanns, B., Brasholt, M., Cohen, J., Duque, M., Duterte, P., van Es, A., Fernando, R., Fincanci, S. K., Hamzeh, S., Hansen, S. H., Hardi, L., Heisler, M., Iacopino, V., Leth, P. M., Lin, J., Louahlia, S., … Viera, D. N. (2020). Statement on conversion therapy. *Journal of Forensic and Legal Medicine*, 72, 101930. https://doi.org/10.1016/j.jflm.2020.101930

Armon, V. (1960). Some personality variables in overt female homosexuality. *Journal of Projective Techniques*, 24(3), 292–309. https://doi.org/10.1080/08853126.1960.10380972

Bancroft, J. (2003). Can sexual orientation change? A long-running saga. *Archives of Sexual Behavior*, 32(5), 419–421.

Bayer, R. (1981). *Homosexuality and American psychiatry: The politics of diagnosis*. Basic Books.

Beckstead, A. L. (2002). Cures versus choices: Agendas in sexual reorientation therapy. *Journal of Gay & Lesbian Psychotherapy*, 5(3–4), 87–115. https://doi.org/10.1300/J236v05n03_07

Beckstead, A. L., & Morrow, S. L. (2004). Mormon clients' experiences of conversion therapy: The need for a new treatment approach. *The Counseling Psychologist*, 32(5), 651–690. https://doi.org/10.1177/0011000004267555

Begelman, D. A. (1975). Ethical and legal issues of behavior modification. In M. Hersen, R. Eisler, & P. M. Miller (Eds.), *Progress in behavior modification* (pp. 159–189). Academic Press.

Bell, A. P., Weinberg, M. S., & Hammersmith, S. K. (1981). *Sexual preference: Its development in men and women*. Indiana University Press.

Bieber, I., Dain, H. J., Dince, P. R., Drellich, M. G., Grand, H. G., & Gundlach, R. H. (1962). *Homosexuality: A psychoanalytic study*. Basic Books.

Birk, L. (1980). The myth of classical homosexuality: Views of a behavioral psychotherapist. In J. Marmor (Ed.), *Homosexual behavior: A modern reappraisal* (pp. 376–390). Basic Books.

Bothe, J. (2020). *It's torture, not therapy. A global overview of conversion therapy: Practices, perpretrators, and the role of states* (pp. 1–24). International Rehabilitation Council for Torture Victims (IRCT).

Boulos, S. (2019). Towards reconstructing the meaning of inhuman treatment or punishment: A human capability approach. *The Age of Human Rights Journal, 12*(12), 35–61. https://doi.org/10.17561/tahrj.n12.3

Bradley, S., & Zucker, K. (1998). Drs. Bradley and Zucker reply. *Journal of the American Academy of Child & Adolescent Psychiatry, 37*(3), 244–245. https://doi.org/10.1097/00004583-199803000-00002

Burgers, J. H., & Danelius, H. (1988). *The United Nations convention against torture: A handbook on the convention against torture and other cruel, inhuman, or degrading treatment or punishment.* Martinus Nijhoff Publishers.

Butler, J. (1990). Gender trouble, feminist theory, and psychoanalytic discourse. In *Feminism/postmodernism* (p. 327, x). Routledge.

Byne, W. (2016). Regulations restrict practice of conversion therapy. *LGBT Health, 3*(2), 97–99. https://doi.org/10.1089/lgbt.2016.0015

Byrd, A. D., & Nicolosi, J. (2002). A meta-analytic review of treatment of homosexuality. *Psychological Reports, 90*(3 Pt 2), 1139–1152.

CAT. (2002). *Hajrizi Dzemajl et. al. v. Yugoslavia.* In U. C. a. Torture (Ed.). Geneva.

CAT. (2008). *General Comment No. 2: Implementation of Article 2 by States Parties.* In U. C. a. Torture (Ed.), (Vol. Un Doc. CAT/C/GC/2). Geneva.

CAT. (2016). *Concluding observations on the fifth periodic report of China.* In U. C. a. Torture (Ed.), (Vol. UN Doc. CAT/C/CHN/CO/5). Geneva.

CAT. (2017). *Concluding observations on the seventh periodic report of Ecuador.* In U. C. a. Torture (Ed.), (Vol. Un Doc. CAT/C/ECU/CO/7). Geneva.

Cautela, J. R. (1967). Covert sensitization. *Psychological Reports, 20*(2), 459–468. https://doi.org/10.2466/pr0.1967.20.2.459

Cautela, J., Kearney, A., & Dryden, W. (1987). The covert conditioning handbook. *Journal of Cognitive Psychotherapy, 1*(4), 264.1–264. https://doi.org/10.1891/0889-8391.1.4.264

CCPR. (2004). *General comment no 31: The nature of the general legal obligation imposed on States Parties to the Covenant.* UN Human Rights Committee.

CEDAW. (1992). *CEDAW general recommendation no. 19: Violence against women.* UN Committee on the Elimination of Discrimination Against Women (CEDAW).

CEDAW. (2010). *General recommendations no. 28.* Committee on the Elimination of Discrimination against Women.

CEDAW. (2015). *General Recommendations No. 33.* Committee on the Elimination of Discrimination against Women.

CERD. (2015). *Concluding Observations on Germany.* CERD.

CERD. (2017). *Concluding Observations on Uruguay.* CERD.

CESCR (2005). *General comment no. 16: The equal right of men and women to the enjoyment of all economic, social and cultural rights (Art. 3 of the Covenant).* UN Committee on Economic, Social and Cultural Rights (CESCR).

CESCR. (2009). *General comment no. 20. Non-discrimination in economic, social and cultural rights (art. 2, para. 2, of the International Covenant on Economic, Social and Cultural Rights).* UN Committee on Economic, Social and Cultural Rights (CESR).

CESCR. (2016). *General comment no. 22 on the right to sexual and reproductive health (article 12 of the International Covenant on Economic, Social and Cultural Rights).* UN Committee on Economic, Social and Cultural Rights (CESR).

Conrad, S. R., & Wincze, J. P. (1976). Orgasmic reconditioning: A controlled study of its effects upon the sexual arousal and behavior of adult male homosexuals. *Behavior Therapy, 7*(2), 155–166. https://doi.org/10.1016/S0005-7894(76)80271-7

COU. (1956). *European convention on human rights, convention for the protection of human rights and fundamental freedoms* (Vol. 5). Council of Europe.

Cramer, R. J., Golom, F. D., LoPresto, C. T., & Kirkley, S. M. (2008). Weighing the evidence: Empirical assessment and ethical implications of conversion therapy. *Ethics & Behavior, 18*(1), 93–114. https://doi.org/10.1080/10508420701713014

CRC. (2003a). *General Comments No. 3.* Committee on the Rights of the Child.

CRC. (2003b). *General Comments No. 4.* Committee on the Rights of the Child.

CRC. (2011). *General Comments No. 13.* Committee on the Rights of the Child.

CRC. (2013). *General Comments No. 15.* Committee on the Rights of the Child.

CRC. (2016). *General Comments No. 20.* Committee on the Rights of the Child.

CRPD. (2016a). *Concluding Observations on Chile.* Committee on the Rights of Persons with Disabilitie.

CRPD. (2016b). *Concluding Observations on Lithuania.* Committee on the Rights of Persons with Disabilitie.

CRPD. (2017). *Concluding Observations on Canada*. Committee on the Rights of Persons with Disabilitie.

Curran, D., & Parr, D. (1957). Homosexuality: An analysis of 100 male cases seen in private practice. *British Medical Journal, 1*(5022), 797–801. https://doi.org/10.1136/bmj.1.5022.797

Cusack, S., & Pusey, L. (2013). CEDAW and the rights to non-discrimination and equality. *Melbourne Journal of International Law, 14*, 54–92.

Davison, G. C. (1976). Homosexuality: The ethical challenge. *Journal of Consulting and Clinical Psychology, 44*(2), 157–162. https://doi.org/10.1037/0022-006X.44.2.157

Davison, G. C. (1978). Not can but ought: The treatment of homosexuality. *Journal of Consulting and Clinical Psychology, 46*(1), 170–172. https://doi.org/10.1037/0022-006X.46.1.170

Davison, G. C. (1991). Constructionism and morality in therapy for homosexuality. In J. C. Gonsiorek, & J. Weinrich (Eds.), *Homosexuality: Research implications for public policy* (pp. 137–148). Sage.

Davison, G. C., & Wilson, T. G. (1973). Attitudes of behavior therapists toward homosexuality. *Behavior Therapy, 4*(5), 686–696. https://doi.org/10.1016/S0005-7894(73)80160-1

DeCecco, J., & Parker, D. A. (Eds.). (1995). *Sex, cells, and same-sex desire: The biology of sexual preference.* Harrington Park Press.

Dillon, F. R., Worthington, R. L., & Moradi, B. (2011). Sexual identity as a universal process. In *Handbook of identity theory and research* (pp. 649–670). Springer.

Drescher, J. (1998). *Psychoanalytic therapy and the gay man.* Analytic Press.

Drescher, J. (2001a). Ethical concerns raised when patients seek to change same-sex attractions. In J. Drescher, A. Shidlo, & M. Schroeder (Eds.), *Sexual conversion therapy: Ethical, clinical and research perspectives* (Vol. 5, pp. 181–210). CRC Press.

Drescher, J. (2001b). I'm your handyman: A history of reparative therapies. In J. Drescher, A. Shidlo, & M. Schroeder (Eds.), *Sexual conversion therapy: Ethical, clinical and research perspectives* (Vol. 5, pp. 5–24). CRC Press.

Drescher, J., Schwartz, A., Casoy, F., McIntosh, C. A., Hurley, B., Ashley, K., Barber, M., Goldenberg, D., Herbert, S. E., Lothwell, L. E., Mattson, M. R., McAfee, S. G., Pula, J., Rosario, V., & Tompkins, D. A. (2016). The growing regulation of conversion therapy. *Journal of Medical Regulation, 102*(2), 7–12. https://doi.org/10.30770/2572-1852-102.2.7

Dubber, M., & Hörnle, T. (2014). *Criminal law: A comparative approach.* Oxford University Press.

Earp, B. D., Sandberg, A., & Savulescu, J. (2014). Brave new love: The threat of high-tech "conversion" therapy and the bio-oppression of sexual minorities. *AJOB Neuroscience, 5*(1), 4–12.

ECtHR. (1977). *Ireland v. The United Kingdom.* European Court of Human Rights (ECtHR).

ECtHR. (1978). *Tyrer v. UK.* European Court of Human Rights (ECtHR).

ECtHR. (1997). *Laskey, Jaggard and Brown v. the United Kingdom.* European Court of Human Rights (ECtHR).

ECtHR. (1999). *T. v. United Kingdom.* European Court of Human Rights (ECtHR).

ECtHR. (2001a). *Cyprus v. Turkey.* European Court of Human Rights (ECtHR). Grand Chamber.

ECtHR (2001b). *Peers v. Greece.* European Court of Human Rights (ECtHR).

ECtHR (2006). *Jalloh v. Germany.* European Court of Human Rights (ECtHR). Judgment of the Grand Chamber.

ECtHR (2009). *Opuz v. Turkey.* European Court of Human Rights (ECtHR).

ECtHR (2012). *E.M. v. Romania.* European Court of Human Rights (ECtHR).

ECtHR. (2013). *Valiuliene v. Lithuania.* European Court of Human Rights (ECtHR).

ECtHR. (2017). *Talpis v. Italy.* European Court of Human Rights (ECtHR).

Erzen, T. (2006). *Straight to Jesus: Sexual and Christian conversions in the ex-gay movement.* Univ of California Press.

Ford, C. S., & Beach, F. A. (1951). *Patterns of sexual behavior.* Harper.

Forstein, M. (2002). Overview of ethical and research issues in sexual orientation therapy. *Journal of Gay & Lesbian Psychotherapy, 5*(3–4), 167–179. https://doi.org/10.1300/J236v05n03_10

Fredman, S. (2011). *Discrimination law.* Oxford University Press.

Freud, S. (1960/1905). Three essays on the theory of sexuality. In J. Strachey (Ed.), *The standard edition of the complete psychological works of Sigmund Freud* (Vol. 7, pp. 123–143). Hogarth.

Freud, S. (1960/1935). Anonymous (Letter to an American mother). In *The letters of Sigmund Freud* (pp. 423–424). Basic Books.

Freund, K., & Blanchard, R. (1983). Is the distant relationship of fathers and homosexual sons related to the sons' erotic preference for male partners, or to the sons' atypical gender identity, or to both? *Journal of Homosexuality, 9*(1), 7–25. https://doi.org/10.1300/J082v09n01_02

Freund, K., Langevin, R., Chamberlayne, R., Deosoran, A., & Zajac, Y. (1974). The phobic theory of male homosexuality. *Archives of General Psychiatry, 31*(4), 495–499.

George, M.-A. (2016). Expressive ends: Understanding conversion therapy bans. *Ala. L. Rev, 68*, 793.

Glassgold, J. M., Beckstead, L., Drescher, J., Greene, B., Miller, R. L., Worthington, R. L., et al. (2009). *Report of the American Psychological Association task force on appropriate therapeutic responses to sexual orientation* (p. 130). American Psychological Association.

Gonsiorek, J. C. (1981). Review of Homosexuality in perspective, by Masters and Johnson. *Journal of Homosexuality*, 6(3), 81–88.

Gonsiorek, J. C. (1991). The empirical basis for the demise of the illness model of homosexuality. In J. C. Gonsiorek & J. Weinrich (Eds.), *Homosexuality: Research implications for public policy* (pp. 115–136). Sage.

Greenhalgh, H. (2020). Hundreds of Religious Leaders Call for LGBTQ 'Conversion Therapy' Ban. (2020, Dec 17). *HuffPost*.

Hadden, S. B. (1966). Treatment of male homosexuals in groups. *International Journal of Group Psychotherapy*, 16(1), 13–22. https://doi.org/10.1080/00207284.1966.11642896

Haldeman, D. C. (1991). Sexual orientation conversion therapy: A scientific examination. In J. C. Gonsiorek, & J. Weinrich (Eds.), *Homosexuality: Research implications for public policy* (pp. 149–160). Sage.

Haldeman, D. C. (1994). The practice and ethics of sexual orientation conversion therapy. *Journal of Consulting and Clinical Psychology*, 62(2), 221–227. https://doi.org/10.1037/0022-006X.62.2.221

Haldeman, D. C. (2002a). Gay rights, patient rights: The implications of sexual orientation conversion therapy. *Professional Psychology: Research and Practice*, 33(3), 260–264. https://doi.org/10.1037/0735-7028.33.3.260

Haldeman, D. C. (2002b). Therapeutic antidotes: Helping gay and bisexual men recover from conversion therapies. *Journal of Gay & Lesbian Psychotherapy*, 5(3–4), 117–130. https://doi.org/10.1300/J236v05n03_08

Halpert, S. C. (2000). "If it ain't broke, don't fix it": Ethical considerations regarding conversion therapies. *International Journal of Sexuality and Gender Studies*, 5(1), 19–35. https://doi.org/10.1023/A:1010133501054

Holtmaat, R. (2013). CEDAW: A holistic approach to women's equality and freedom. In *Women's human rights: CEDAW in international, regional and national law* (pp. 95–124). Cambridge University Press.

Holtmaat, R., & Post, P. (2015). Enhancing LGBTI rights by changing the interpretation of the convention on the elimination of all forms of discrimination against women? *Nordic Journal of Human Rights*, 33(4), 319–336. https://doi.org/10.1080/18918131.2016.1123502

Hooker, E. (1957). The adjustment of the male overt homosexual. *Journal of Projective Techniques*, 21(1), 18–31. https://doi.org/10.1080/08853126.1957.10380742

HRC. (1989). *Antti Vuolanne v. Finland*. HRC.

HRC. (1994). *Toonen v. Australia*. CCPR.

HRC. (2000). *General Comment No. 28, Equality of rights between men and women (article 3)*. HRC.

HRC. (2015). *Report of the special rapporteur on torture and other cruel, inhuman or degrading treatment or punishment, Juan E. Méndez: addendum*. UN Human Rights Council.

HRC. (2016). *Report of the Special Rapporteur on torture and other cruel, inhuman or degrading treatment or punishment. Note by the Secretariat*. UN Human Rights Council.

HRC. (2020). *Practices of so-called "conversion therapy". Report of the Independent Expert on protection against violence and discrimination based on sexual orientation and gender identity*. UN Human Rights Council.

IACtHR. (1988). *Velásquez Rodríguez v. Honduras*. Inter-American Court of Human Rights (IACrtHR).

IACtHR. (1997). *Loayza Tamayo v. Perú*. Inter-American Court of Human Rights (IACrtHR).

IACtHR. (1999). *Castillo Petruzzi et al. v. Peru*. Inter-American Court of Human Rights (IACrtHR).

IACtHR. (2012). Atala Riffo and Daughters v. Chile. Inter-American Court of Human Rights (IACrtHR).

IACtHR. (2019). *López Soto y otros vs. Venezuela*. Inter-American Court of Human Rights (IACrtHR).

ICTY. (1998). Prosecutor v. Anto Furundzija (Trial Judgement). *IT-95-17/1-T* (10 December 1998 ed.). Bosnia and Herzegovina | Serbia: International Criminal Tribunal for the former Yugoslavia (ICTY).

ILC. (2001). *Draft articles on responsibility of states for internationally wrongful acts*. International Law Commission.

Kaufmann, P., Kuch, H., Neuhaeuser, C., & Webster, E. (Eds.). (2010). *Humiliation, degradation, dehumanization: human dignity violated* (Vol. 24). Springer Science & Business Media.

King, M., Smith, G., & Bartlett, A. (2004). Treatments of homosexuality in Britain since the 1950s—an oral history: The experience of professionals. *BMJ (Clinical Research ed.)*, 328(7437), 429–432.

Kinsey, A. C., Pomeroy, W. B., & Martin, C. E. (1948). *Sexual behavior in the human male*. W. B. Saunders.

Kinsey, A. C., Pomeroy, W. B., Martin, C. E., & Gebhard, P. H. (1953). *Sexual behavior in the human female*. W. B. Saunders.

Lavrysen, L. (2014). Positive obligations in the jurisprudence of the Inter-American Court of Human Rights. *Inter-Am. & Eur. Hum. Rts. J*, 7, 94.

Margalit, A. (1996). *The decent society*. Harvard University Press.

Marmor, J. (Ed.). (1965). *Sexual inversion: The multiple roots of homosexuality*. Basic Books.

Marmor, J. (Ed.). (1980). *Homosexual behavior: A modern reappraisal*. Basic Books.

Masters, W. H., & Johnson, V. E. (1979). *Homosexuality in perspective*. Little, Brown & Co.

Mayerson, P., & Lief, H. (1965). Psychotherapy of homosexuals: A follow-up study of nineteen cases. In J. Marmor (Ed.), *Sexual inversion: The multiple roots of homosexuality* (pp. 302–344). Basic Books.

McConaghy, N., Armstrong, M. S., & Blaszczynski, A. (1981). Controlled comparison of aversive therapy and covert sensitization in compulsive homosexuality. *Behaviour Research and Therapy, 19*(5), 425–434. https://doi.org/10.1016/0005-7967(81)90132-7

McWhirter, D. P., Sanders, S. A., & Reinisch, J. M. (Eds.). (1990). *Homosexuality/heterosexuality: Concepts of sexual orientation.* Oxford University Press.

Mintz, E. E. (1966). Overt male homosexuals in combined group and individual treatment. *Journal of Consulting Psychology, 30*(3), 193–198. https://doi.org/10.1037/h0023381

Moberly, E. R. (1983). *Homosexuality: A new Christian ethic.* James Clarke & Co.

Morrow, S. L., & Beckstead, A. L. (2004). Conversion therapies for same-sex attracted clients in religious conflict: Context, predisposing factors, experiences, and implications for therapy. *The Counseling Psychologist, 32*(5), 641–650. https://doi.org/10.1177/0011000004268877

Nicolosi, J. (1991). *Reparative therapy of male homosexuality: A new clinical approach.* Jason Aronson.

Nicolosi, J., Byrd, A. D., & Potts, R. W. (2000). Retrospective self-reports of changes in homosexual orientation: A consumer survey of conversion therapy clients. *Psychological Reports, 86*(3 Pt 2), 1071–1088.

Nowlin, C. (2002). The protection of morals under the European Convention for the Protection of Human Rights and Fundamental Freedoms. *Human Rights Quarterly, 24*(1), 264–286. https://doi.org/10.1353/hrq.2002.0014

OAU. (1981). *African (Banjul) charter on human and peoples' rights* (Vol. 21, p. 58). Organization of African Unity.

O'Connor, N., & Ryan, J. (1993). *Wild desires and mistaken identities: Lesbianism and psychoanlaysis.* Columbia University Press.

OHCHR. (2001). *Report of the Special Rapporteur on the question of torture and other cruel, inhuman or degrading treatment or punishment.* Office of the High Commissioner for Human Rights (OHCHR).

OHCHR. (2019a). *Born free and equal: Sexual orientation and gender identity in international human rights law.* Office of the High Commissioner for Human Rights (OHCHR).

OHCHR. (2019b). *Interim report of the Special Rapporteur on torture and other cruel, inhuman or degrading treatment or punishment. Relevance of the prohibition of torture and other cruel, inhuman or degrading treatment or punishment to the context of domestic violence.* Office of the High Commissioner for Human Rights (OHCHR).

Ohlson, E. L., & Wilson, M. (1974). Differentiating female homosexuals from female heterosexuals by use of the MMPI. *The Journal of Sex Research, 10*(4), 308–315. https://doi.org/10.1080/00224497409550864

Otto, D. (2015). Queering gender [identity] in international law. *Nordic Journal of Human Rights, 33*(4), 299–318. https://doi.org/10.1080/18918131.2016.1123474

Pierce, D. M. (1973). Test and nontest correlates of active and situational homosexuality. *Psychology: A Journal of Human Behavior, 10*(4), 23–26.

Rangaswami, K. (1982). Difficulties in arousing and increasing heterosexual responsiveness in a homosexual: A case report. *Indian Journal of Clinical Psychology, 9,* 147–151.

Sandfort, T. G. (2003). Studying sexual orientation change: A methodological review of the Spitzer study,"Can some gay men and lesbians change their sexual orientation? *Journal of Gay & Lesbian Psychotherapy, 7*(3), 15–29. https://doi.org/10.1300/J236v07n03_02

Schroeder, M., & Shidlo, A. (2001). Ethical issues in sexual orientation conversion therapies: An empirical study of consumers. *Journal of Gay & Lesbian Mental Health, 5*(3), 131–166. https://doi.org/10.1080/19359705.2001.9962289

Shidlo, A., & Schroeder, M. (2002). Changing sexual orientation: A consumers' report. *Professional Psychology: Research and Practice, 33*(3), 249–259. https://doi.org/10.1037/0735-7028.33.3.249

Shively, M. G., & De Cecco, J. P. (1977). Components of sexual identity. *Journal of Homosexuality, 3*(1), 41–48.

Siegelman, M. (1974). Parental background of male homosexuals and heterosexuals. *Archives of Sexual Behavior, 3*(1), 3–18. https://doi.org/10.1007/BF01541038

Silverstein, C. (1977). Homosexuality and the ethics of behavioral intervention: Paper 2. *Journal of Homosexuality, 2*(3), 205–211. https://doi.org/10.1300/J082v02n03_02

Silverstein, C. (1991). Psychological and medical treatments of homosexuality. In J. C. Gonsiorek, & J. Weinrich (Eds.), *Homosexuality: Research implications for public policy* (pp. 101–114). Sage.

Silverstein, C. (2007). Wearing two hats: The psychologist as activist and therapist. *Journal of Gay & Lesbian Psychotherapy, 11*(3–4), 9–35. https://doi.org/10.1300/J236v11n03_02

Smith, G., Bartlett, A., & King, M. (2004). Treatments of homosexuality in Britain since the 1950s-an oral history: the experience of patients. *BMJ (Clinical Research ed.), 328*(7437), 427. https://doi.org/10.1136/bmj.37984.442419.EE

Socarides, C. W. (1968). *The overt homosexual.* Grune & Stratton.

Spitzer, R. L. (2003). Can some gay men and lesbians change their sexual orientation? 200 participants reporting a change from homosexual to heterosexual orientation. *Archives of Sexual Behavior, 32*(5), 403–417.

Spitzer, R. L. (2012). Spitzer reassesses his 2003 study of reparative therapy of homosexuality. *Archives of Sexual Behavior, 41*(4), 757–757. https://doi.org/10.1007/s10508-012-9966-y

Storms, M. D. (1980). Theories of sexual orientation. *Journal of Personality and Social Psychology, 38*(5), 783–792. https://doi.org/10.1037/0022-3514.38.5.783

Thompson, N. L., McCandless, B. R., & Strickland, B. (1971). Personal adjustment of male and female homosexuals and heterosexuals. *Journal of Abnormal Psychology, 78*(2), 237–240.

Tozer, E. E., & McClanahan, M. K. (1999). Treating the purple menace: Ethical considerations of conversion therapy and affirmative alternatives. *The Counseling Psychologist, 27*(5), 722–742. https://doi.org/10.1177/0011000099275006

Turner, R., Pielmaier, H., James, S., & Orwin, A. (1974). Personality characteristics of male homosexuals referred for aversion therapy: A comparative study. *The British Journal of Psychiatry: The Journal of Mental Science, 125*(588), 447–449.

UN. (1948). *Universal declaration of human rights.* U. N. G. Assembly.

UN. (1966). *International covenant on civil and political rights (ICCPR).* UN.

UN. (1969). *American convention on human rights* (Vol. 1144, p. 123). UN.

UN. (1979). *Convention on the elimination of all forms of discrimination against women.* U. N. G. Assembly.

UN. (1984). *Convention against torture and other cruel, inhuman or degrading treatment or punishment* (Vol. 1465, p. 85). UN.

Waldron, J. (2010). *Torture, terror, and trade-offs: Philosophy for the White House.* Oxford University Press.

Wareham, J. (2020, March 8). This is where LGBTQ 'conversion therapy' is illegal. *Forbes.*

Whitman, J. S., Glosoff, H. L., Kocet, M. M., & Tarvydas, V. (2006). Exploring ethical issues related to conversion or reparative therapy. *Counseling Today, 49*(1), 14–15.

WHO. (2017). *International classification of diseases 11th revision.* WHO.

Zucker, K. J. (2008). Reflections on the relation between sex-typed behavior in childhood and sexual orientation in adulthood. *Journal of Gay & Lesbian Mental Health, 12*(1/2), 29–59.

Exploring How Gender and Sex Are Measured in Criminology and Victimology: Are we Measuring What we Say we Are Measuring?

Courtney A. Crittenden, Hannah C. Gateley, Christina N. Policastro, and Karen McGuffee

ABSTRACT

Throughout the years, there have been sustained and increasing calls for criminology to become more inclusive in its research and measurements with the purpose of improving our knowledge of crime and victimization. The current study examined articles published in the past five years in a mainstream criminological journal and a well-respected victimization journal to explore the inclusion and operationalization of gender and sex. Findings indicate that measures of gender and sex were included more in the diversity-focused victimization journal compared to the mainstream criminological journal. In both journals, however, conceptualizations and operationalizations of these constructs rarely fell outside of a binary measure, which suggests the measurement and inclusion of gender are still lacking, and oftentimes when we say we are measuring gender we are actually still measuring sex.

It has often been stipulated that criminology is the study of male crime by male academics and that gender was historically only discussed with regards to men (Cook, 2016; Franklin, 2008). From its inception, the criminological theory was often based on male-only findings, with research on females either not occurring or being excluded from theoretical advancements, even though time after time gender has been noted as one of the greatest predictors of crime (Belknap, 2015; Cook, 2016; Franklin, 2008). When women were included in theoretical explanations of crime, it was often from a sexist perspective (e.g., early biological explanations were used even though they had fallen out of favor for explaining the crimes of men). Females were not widely introduced to criminology as participants and researchers until the second wave of the feminist movement (Burgess-Proctor, 2006; Franklin, 2008).

Feminist and queer criminology have introduced and expanded the study of gender and gender minorities (e.g., non-male, non-cis-gendered) and how they are measured within the field (e.g., how gender is conceptualized and operationalized, including gender minorities and their lived experiences in research), although, simultaneously allowing and encouraging female-authored publications. Women's primary authorship of such work, however, may also serve as a barrier in the progression of research on gender. The discussion of gender almost exclusively in specialty journals, often by female authors, allows such topics to be avoided by mainstream criminology, historically dominated with male authors (Eigenberg & Whalley, 2015). It may also further the notion that gender is strictly a female issue and not a concern for everyone. Although the creation and standing of specialty journals is progressive, it does not equate to an advance in the acceptance and inclusion of gender, racial, and sexual minorities within the field of criminology (Crow & Smykla, 2015; Eigenberg & Whalley, 2015). In fact, calls influenced by feminist and queer criminology have noted that inclusive conceptualizations of gender still need to be incorporated in the literature with greater frequency (Belknap, 2015; Woods, 2014).

The current study examines whether criminologists have begun to heed these calls for more expansive conceptualizations and operationalizations of gender along with comparing work in more criminological versus victimization focused research. Specifically, recent publications from two well-respected journals in both criminology and victimology research are evaluated to explore the inclusion of gender both within the articles and as variables. Additionally, presumed author gender is explored in order to determine its potential influence on the likelihood of publication in mainstream criminological and victimization journals and inclusion and measurement of gender within the articles.

REVIEW OF THE LITERATURE

Gender in Criminology and Victimology

Criminology is and has long been a male-dominated field, designed by heterosexual men to punish and treat other men (Belknap, 2015; Cook, 2016; Franklin, 2008). Despite the fact that analyses have, since the beginning of criminological research, suggested that sex and/or gender discrepancies might exist, gendered patterns of offending were often disregarded as concepts to be studied and criminological theory was, therefore, not designed with the intent to explain gendered patterns of offending (Cook, 2016; Franklin, 2008). Even more, contemporary control theories and life course theories fail to explore nuances in acknowledged gender discrepancies, and until the 21st century, critical criminology avoided analyzing gender-based power dynamics (Cook, 2016). Mainstream criminology reflects this disinterest in gendered analyses, often limiting the study of gender to a control variable (Sharp & Hefley, 2007) and often conceptualizing and operationalizing it as a binary measure (e.g., male/female). Instead of investigating gender differences, criminologists have consistently and typically incorrectly asserted that research on predominately male or all-male subjects can be broadly applied to females as well (Cook, 2016). Research on male-only subjects is often overgeneralized to apply to everyone without concern for whether the implications will hold true for females, and what little research exists on female-only subjects narrowly limits the generalizability of their findings (Cook, 2016; Hannon & Dufour, 1998).

Historically, when criminology did include females in analysis, Franklin (2008) argues it was only to impose female gender roles, penalizing women whose behavior falls outside of female gender expectations. Following the chivalry hypothesis, women are seen as weak and passive and the criminal justice system, as a patriarchal institution, shows females leniency as a way to protect them (Franklin, 2008). However, women who do not express feminine traits or who do not fall into traditional female roles are treated more harshly (Belknap, 2001; Franklin, 2008; Rafter, 1990). Further, according to the *evil woman* thesis, women who are convicted of more stereotypically masculine offenses receive harsher punishment than women convicted of stereotypically feminine offenses (Albonetti, 1988; Franklin, 2008; Koons-Witt, 2002; Kruttschnitt, 1984; Nagel & Hagan, 1983; Spohn & Spears, 1997). Any woman's betrayal of her socially prescribed gender role was historically seen as a threat to the male-dominated power structure and punished accordingly (Franklin, 2008).

Knowing that gender and sex differences have historically been ignored by criminologists and that criminology has long been a male-dominated field, it is unsurprising that women are more often the authors of empirical studies exploring these differences (Eigenberg & Whalley, 2015). Women dominate feminist criminological journals yet make up a disproportionately small percentage of authors in mainstream journals (Eigenberg & Whalley, 2015), even though more females than males are currently entering the field of criminal justice after earning their doctoral degrees (Crow & Smykla, 2015). Some scholars have expressed surprise that women are interested in entering the field at all given the "rampant sexism" that pervades the history of criminology (Renzetti, 1993, p. 226), and that "one cannot expect that the first generation of new scholars will be confident or sure-footed after centuries of exclusion from the academy" (Burgess-Proctor, 2006; Daly & Chesney-Lind, 1988, p. 506). Female criminologists may be slow to enter the field, testing the waters to determine whether they are welcome and where. Additionally, they may be more apt to conduct and publish research in subfields of criminology such as gender studies and sexuality studies. This may lead to women within criminal justice studying the victimization of these populations as well.

Victimology, the sociological field dedicated to studying victims, offenders, and society, has, unlike criminology, historically highlighted sex differences (Wallace & Roberson, 2011). Specifically, females were historically thought to be weaker and therefore more likely to be victimized. In his early victimology work, von Hentig 1948 reiterated this weakness, classifying females as a distinct subset of the weak victim. Although von Hentig's classification and theory have largely been abandoned, the remnants of gendered views of victimization have still been evident throughout victimology's history (Wallace & Roberson, 2011). In addition to pinpointing what predisposes an individual to victimization and how that predisposition may differ for males and females, research suggests that pathways to offending are different for males versus females and may overlap with their victimization (Franklin, 2008; Gottfredson, 1981; Jennings et al., 2010; Lauritsen et al., 1991; Mustaine & Tewksbury, 2000). This victim-offender overlap is clearly seen within the context of women's pathways to offending and has been highlighted by feminist criminologists. Female offenders of all ages report high levels of victimization, particularly at the hands of males, either as intimate partners or relatives (Franklin, 2008). Although victimology has brought light to domestic and sexual abuse of females, the same acts, when used to victimize males are often overlooked (Karmen, 2013; Tewksbury, 2009; Tewksbury & Mustaine, 2001). Although a growing body of literature has emerged focusing on the nature of IPV and sexual violence among male victims (e.g., Smith et al., 2018), the research on male victims pales in comparison to the large body of scholarship that makes up the "violence against women" subfield.

Conflation of Gender and Sex in Scientific Research

As highlighted in the previous sections, often when gender and/or sex are discussed in criminology or victimology they are discussed as a binary construct (e.g., male, female), and are often used interchangeably. However, researchers from medical science to psychology to education note that although there should be a difference in the research between sex and gender, there is not necessarily one standard. For instance, Noel and Lutz (2020) explored how sex, gender, and sexual orientation were measured in a variety of medical surveys by asking participants which of the questions measuring these characteristics that they preferred and concluded that, there was no clear standard for measurement. However, they did note that over 1/3 of their participants preferred being asked about their "sex at birth" for sex and "are you male, female, or transgender?" for gender (Noel & Lutz, 2020). In the simplest terms, across disciplines, sex is typically conceptualized as biological differences, whereas, gender is typically conceptualized as social differences (Anderson & Fine, 2017; Carl, 2012; Gentile, 1993; Tseng, 2008). Again, using broad strokes, masculinity and femininity represent gender (Carl, 2012; Gentile, 1993; Lesko, 2010) whereas, male and female represent sex differences (Carl, 2012; Gentile, 1993). Anderson and Fine (2017) argue that oftentimes, cultural and social differences used to distinguish gender between males and females tend to highlight male attributes, which often hold greater status and power—this can be referred to as hegemonic masculinity.

Researchers have noted that across the social sciences, not just in criminology or victimology, sex and gender are often used interchangeably in research (Gentile, 1993). However, more recently, researchers have made a point to note the differences between sex and gender. These claims function to highlight the idea that even though these concepts are distinct, they are also highly related. For instance, research shows that "popular beliefs attribute differences between males and females to biology, but bodily processes are objects of social practice" (Lesko, 2010, p. 393). Moreover, individuals are treated and socialized differently due to the sex they are assigned at birth, with research in education highlighting that boys and girls are treated differently by their teachers, with boys often receiving more attention from teachers and being allowed to speak more (Lesko, 2010). Additionally, society often creates narratives such as "boys are good at math" or "boys are more intelligent," and "girls are more emotional" (Lesko, 2010), which may become self-fulfilling prophesies (Carl, 2012). Interestingly, statistics show that the majority of bachelor and associate degrees in the U.S. are earned by women (Carl, 2012). Still, even though women make up the majority of those earning degrees, these degrees are most often in art, music, and social sciences—disciplines that are often considered more feminine or more acceptable fields for women to enter—rather than chemistry, engineering, or medicine, fields which are still highly dominated by men (Carl, 2012). This, indeed, maybe why we see an increase in women entering the academic side of criminal justice more so than the practitioner side—it is deemed as more acceptable for women.

Another issue highlighted in the conflation of sex and gender occurs within research studies themselves. Although Gentile (1993) noted in the early 1990s that sex and gender were often used as synonyms in social science research, he indicated that it was the 1960s when the use of gender as a synonym for sex occurred in the social science research literature. This leads to a conflation of the two terms and results in a loss of specificity and clarity in meaning when this occurs in research (Gentile, 1993). It is important that our conceptualizations of terms match our operationalizations of these terms. If we say we are looking at gender, then we need to be measuring gender. However, for the last several decades of our social science research history, we have not been matching our conceptualizations and operationalizations. Or at the very least, we have been using sex and, more often, gender incorrectly.

For instance, surveys often ask respondents to identify their gender but are given attributes of biological sex (i.e., male, female) to choose from instead of gendered attributes (Gentile, 1993). Indeed, Anderson and Fine (2017) note that research on gender has been shaped by social, political, and historical contexts and that "scientific inquiry on gender has been situated within—and has often reproduced and legitimized—racial and (dis)ability hierarchies, religious and moral paradigms, hetero- and cis-normativity, and deceptively simple gender categories and binaries" (p. 1416). Therefore, when social science research utilizes binary sex categories as the exhaustive and mutually exclusive attributes of gender, it reinforces sex and gender binaries (Anderson & Fine, 2017) and continues the conflation of the two terms. Such conflation may leave social sciences in a standstill where binaries are reified, and research does not move forward examining the variety of gender differences on the spectrum. This conflation and maintenance of binary sex and gender categories have not only suppressed gender minorities, it has also suppressed sexual minorities by imposing heterosexuality as the normal and appropriate form of sexuality (Anderson & Fine, 2017).

Notably, despite the advances of gender studies in the social sciences, Anderson and Fine (2017) note that these studies have often focused on cisgender women, specifically cisgender, privileged, white women. It is imperative to note that the newest research and perspectives indicate that gender, in particular, is not a binary measure. It is not dichotomous as so many studies have measured it. Rather, gender is fluid, dynamic, and situated on a continuum of masculine and feminine traits (Anderson & Fine, 2017). A person may be more masculine on one day or in one specific situation but more feminine another day or in another situation. Additionally, the definitions and characteristics of femininity and masculinity are socially constructed and vary across space and time. When we limit gender to binary sex categories, we are suppressing and marginalizing transgender, genderqueer, and non-conforming individuals (Anderson & Fine, 2017). Curtin and Okuyan (2017) note that in psychology, researchers are increasingly including nonbinary measures to enhance the validity of their measures. Studies in feminist and queer criminology have noted that there is a need in criminology to be more inclusive with research measures.

Calls for Inclusive Research

In the past, researchers and activists seeking to expand the scholarship on these issues have created new and specialized areas in the field to highlight the importance of studying these topics that have long been ignored by mainstream criminology (Woods, 2014). The recent emergence of queer and feminist criminology is due in large part as a response to calls that have been made over the years to include these marginalized populations in criminological research particularly gender and sexual minorities (Ball, 2014; Cook, 2016; Renzetti, 1993). Belknap (2015), in her presidential address to the American Society of Criminology, emphasized the need for all areas of criminology to become more inclusive—not just specialized fields. Belknap (2015) notes the "heightened responsibility" that criminologists have in dealing with marginalized populations, due to advantages in privilege, knowledge, and ultimately, power as criminologists are largely financially capable and well-informed university faculty members, quite familiar with the shortcomings of the justice system (p. 4). Belknap (2015) emphasized the need to redefine the damaging perceptions of sexual and gender minorities as deviants–a label attached by criminologists many years ago—both in the classroom and in criminological scholarship. Belknap's (2015) call echoes similar concerns voiced throughout criminology's history and those found in other disciplines across both social science and hard sciences.

Current Study

As noted, the inclusion of gender has been slow in criminological literature and sex and gender are often used interchangeably. Although incorporation by victimization studies might be more progressive, much of its history was sexist and men still are understudied as victims of rape and intimate partner violence. The current study explores the inclusion of gender in journals from the fields of criminology and victimology by examining articles in *Criminology* and the *Journal of Interpersonal Violence*. We are guided by the following research questions:

1. To what extent is gender included in criminological and victimization articles?
2. How is gender operationalized in criminological articles and victimization articles, and are there major differences across the disciplines?
3. What, if any, relationship exists between the presumed gender of the author(s) and the inclusion of gender?

METHODS

In order to answer our research questions, the current study employed content analysis to unobtrusively measure the "identification, organization, description, and quantification of text" in a systematic way (Berg, 2004; Garland et al., 2016, p. 54; Hesse-Biber & Leavy, 2006; Kraska & Neuman, 2011), although, also allowing for a certain richness of detail that might otherwise not be possible (Gray & Densten, 1998).

Data and Sample

The content analysis performed in this study analyzed two preeminent journals from 2015–2019 in the field of victimology and criminology to measure the inclusion of gender: *Criminology* and *Journal of Interpersonal Violence (JIV)*. *Criminology* is a mainstream and well-respected journal within the field of criminology with an impact factor of 3.879. It is also the flagship journal for the leading American criminological association, The American Society of Criminology (ASC), whose website notes that in the most recent rankings by the Institute for Scientific information, *Criminology* was ranked as the leading professional criminal justice journal (ASC, 2020). *JIV* is an interdisciplinary journal focusing on interpersonal violence with an impact factor of 3.573. It is also the first scholarly journal requiring the inclusion of diversity, evident as a component of *JIV*'s reviewer form[1] (SAGE, 2020). Both journals are marketed as "interdisciplinary" publication outlets and produce articles focused on a board range of topics. Although *Criminology* is geared toward crime/deviance-based research, *JIV* has a focus on both victims and offenders as part of its aims and scope. Moreover, the current study opted to focus on broad, interdisciplinary journals rather than specialty journals, in order to gauge if and how gender is measured across these types of outlets which are accessed by a broader audience.

Although all articles published in *Criminology* between 2015–2019 were analyzed ($n = 139$), a random sample of articles were selected for analysis from *JIV* to match the number of pieces published in *Criminology* during that same time period, due to the vast difference in the number of published pieces from each journal. In order to create equal sample sizes for comparison from each journal, a stratified random sampling technique was designed to select articles from *JIV*. For *JIV*, strata were created for each year from 2015–2019. Within the strata, all *JIV* articles from the specified year were listed in order of publication and assigned numbers. For each stratum, a random number generator was used to select an equal number of *JIV* articles as were published that year in *Criminology*. For instance, 30 articles were analyzed from 2015, 25 from 2016, 32 from 2017, 26 from 2018, and 26 from 2019. Across all five years, 139 articles were analyzed from both the *Journal of Interpersonal Violence* and *Criminology*, for a total of 278 articles analyzed.

Coding Technique

Two trained coders scored the articles from *Criminology* and *JIV*, one coder scored *Criminology* and the other coder scored *JIV*. Both coders followed a code sheet that analyzed each section of a journal article separately (e.g., title, keywords, abstract, introduction/literature review, methods, findings, and discussion/conclusion) along with examining if gender and/or sex was used as a variable, and if so what type of variable and how it was conceptualized were noted. The majority of this analysis required manifest coding (Gray & Densten, 1998; Payne et al., 2005, p. 34). Specifically, researchers searched the text for words indicative of gender and/or sex being discussed (i.e., "male," "femininity," "genderqueer," etc.). All attributes were measured as yes/no indicators of whether gender and sex were included in the various sections of the articles or as variables. Some latent coding was required, primarily to determine if gender and/or sex could be considered themes of the literature review or discussion/conclusion or if they were simply mentioned. In order to be considered a theme in either the literature review or the discussion/conclusion, concepts had to be included as a heading/subheading or had to be discussed throughout a substantial portion of the literature review or discussion/conclusion, as determined by the coder. In order to heighten reliability, both coders discussed and came to a consensus about what constituted a theme for the literature review and conclusion sections of an article before

---

[1]*JIV*'s submission guidelines specifically require "a discussion of diversity as it applies to the reviewed research," and its website defines diversity as "human differences such as socioeconomic status, race, ethnicity, language, nationality, sex, gender identity, sexual orientation, religion, geography, ability, age, and culture" (SAGE, 2020).

Table 1. Characteristics of sample.

Variable	% Yes (*n*)/Mean (SD; Range)
Journal	
Criminology	50.0 (139)
JIV	50.0 (139)
Gender of authors	
Male	19.8 (55)
Female	25.5 (71)
Both	42.4 (118)
Undeterminable	12.2 (34)
Type of article	
Empirical	91.7 (255)
Other	8.3 (23)
Gender	3.78 (2.04; 0–7)
Any mention	93.2 (260)
Title	24.5 (68)
Abstract	43.5 (121)
Keyword	14.4 (40)
Variable	63.3 (176)
Control variable	43.9 (122)
Independent variable	20.9 (58)
Dependent variable	3.6 (10)
Non-binary operationalization	1.1 (3)
Literature Review	76.6 (213)
Theme	40.3 (112)
Mention	36.7 (102)
Methods	80.9 (225)
Analysis/results	73.0 (203)
Discussion/conclusion	64.4 (179)
Theme	38.8 (108)
Mention	25.5 (71)

n = 278.

coding began[2]. Additionally, after all the articles had been coded, 20% of the articles (*n* = 56) coded by coder 1 were randomly selected and coded by coder 2 and vice versa resulting in a coder agreement rate of 96.91%[3].

Measures

Gender/Sex

The variable of interest in this study was gender and/or sex. There were several measures utilized to explore gender and/or sex in the articles. First, *inclusion* was explored by determining if gender and/or sex was included in the article's title, abstract, keywords, literature review (as a theme or simply mentioned), methods, analysis and findings, and discussion and conclusion (as a theme or simply mentioned). Second, how gender and/or sex was used as a *variable* was identified: dependent, independent, or control. Finally, the *operationalization* of the variable was recorded on the code sheet. Overall, gender was included an average of 3.78 of the article sections per article measured and was mentioned in about 93% of the articles examined, as shown in Table 1. Additionally, gender and/or sex was used as a variable in 63.3% of the articles examined, with the largest percentage of articles using it as a control measure (43.9%), followed by independent (20.9%), and dependent variable (3.6%). Regarding the operationalization of gender, it was only operationalized as a non-binary measure in 3 of the articles examined.

---

[2]When questions arose about a specific case, both coders would examine the article and come to a unanimous decision.
[3]The most common disagreement was whether gender as a "mention" or "theme." If coder 1 marked it as a theme and coder 2 marked it as a mention this counted as two differences (not just one).

Independent Variables

The two primary independent variables in this study were *journal type* (criminological or victimology) and *author gender*. Author gender was determined by the gendered pronouns (i.e., s/he, her/his) in author biographies at the end of each article. Authors who were referenced without gendered pronouns or with formal names instead of pronouns were coded as gender "not specified." After each author's gender was coded, the author gender was analyzed as (all) male author(s), (all) female author(s), male and female authors, or not (all) specified[4]. As shown in Table 1, the largest percentage of author teams were mixed-gender teams (42.4%), followed by all-female teams, (25.5%), and all-male teams (19.8%). In 12.2% of articles, the gender of all the authors in the author team could not be determined.

Control Variables

As part of the content analysis, each piece was coded for publication information, such as the year of publication, volume, number, and title, in addition to the independent variable, journal type. Coders also determined whether the article was empirical or if it was another type of publication (i.e., speeches, book reviews, and essays). Indeed, the vast majority of the articles were empirical (91.7%). Lastly, there was a section for additional comments at the end of every code sheet, which allowed coders to note nuance in measurements and any other relevant information.

ANALYSIS AND FINDINGS

In order to adequately analyze the data both univariate and bivariate analyses were employed. Specifically, due to the categorical nature of the data, chi-square analysis was utilized (Gau, 2019). Because this study was exploratory in nature, multivariate analysis was not used. Table 1 contains the results of a univariate analysis, which describes all variables individually.

As mentioned previously, over 9 out of every 10 articles included gender and/or sex in at least one section. Gender and/or sex was most commonly mentioned in the methods section (80.9%) followed by the literature review (76.6%) and the analysis/results section (73.0%). Notably, close to one-fourth of the articles mentioned gender and/or sex in the title (24.5%) and over 43% mentioned it in the abstract, however, it was only a keyword in about 14% of articles. When mentioned in the literature review, a greater percentage of articles used it as a theme (40.3%) than simply mentioning it (36.7%). Additionally, gender and/or sex was included in the discussions/conclusion sections of 64.4% articles, again with a higher percentage including it as a theme (38.8%) than simply mentioning it (25.5%).

As mentioned prior, gender was more commonly used as a control variable and was measured as a binary measure in almost all articles. These binary measures were commonly operationalized as male/other; male/female; female/other. The non-binary measures of gender were male/female/transgender female, female/male/male, and female/other/"it depends"/neither female nor male, and masculine (male)/feminine (female)/gender non-conformity. It should be noted that there was at least one other operationalization (transgender men/transgender women) that, although, indicative of greater inclusivity than the traditional gender binary, was still technically a binary measure.

Table 2 depicts the crosstab results of the bivariate analysis of journal type and gender inclusion overall and in each section of an article. Several significant relationships were found among article sections and journal titles. First, any inclusion of sex and/or gender at all was significant by journal type, with all but one article in *JIV* (99.3%) mentioning gender at some point in the article compared to about 88% of articles in *Criminology*. A significant association was found

---

[4]Author gender was deemed undeterminable if gender could not be assumed for all authors of a piece. If the gender was known for all but one author, that article was still coded as undeterminable author gender.

Table 2. Gender inclusion by journal type.

	Criminology %Yes (n)	JIV % Yes (n)	χ^2
Any mention	87.8% (122)	99.3% (138)	15.207***
Title	12.2% (17)	36.7% (51)	22.505***
Abstract	20.1% (28)	66.9% (93)	61.828***
Keyword	9.4% (13)	19.4% (27)	5.724*
Literature review	65.5% (91)	87.8% (122)	19.296***
Theme	17.3% (24)	63.3% (88)	61.246***
Mentioned	48.9% (68)	24.5% (34)	17.902***
Methods	74.1% (103)	87.8% (122)	8.416**
Analysis/Results	65.5% (91)	80.6% (112)	8.052**
Conclusion	48.2% (67)	80.6% (112)	31.767***
Theme	15.8% (22)	61.9% (86)	62.020***
Mentioned	32.4% (45)	18.7% (26)	6.828**

$*p < 0.05$; $**p < 0.01$; $***p < 0.001$.

Table 3. Gender variables by journal type.

	Criminology	JIV	χ^2
Gender	61.2% (85)	65.5% (91)	0.557
Control variable	51.1% (71)	36.7% (51)	5.843*
Independent variable	12.9% (18)	28.8% (40)	10.545**
Dependent variable	1.4% (2)	5.8% (8)	3.734
Non-binary operationalization	0.7% (1)	1.4% (2)	0.669

$*p < 0.05$; $**p < 0.01$.

between the journal type and article title, abstract, and keywords as well. Specifically, *JIV* included gender significantly more in titles (36.7%), abstracts (66.9%), and keywords (19.4%), as compared to *Criminology* (12.2, 20.1, and 9.4, respectively). A statistically significant relationship was also found between journal type and the inclusion of gender in the literature review, both overall, and as both themes and mentions. Again, more *JIV* articles (87.8%) included gender in the literature review, compared to *Criminology* articles (65.5%). Notably, significantly more articles in *Criminology* mentioned gender and/or sex, whereas, significantly more articles in *JIV* used it as a theme. A statistically significant relationship was also found between journal type and both methods and analysis/results, with a significantly greater percentage of *JIV* articles including gender in both the methods (87.8%) and analysis/results sections (80.6%), as compared to *Criminology* articles (74.1% and 65.5%, respectively). Statistically significant relationships were also found for gender inclusion in the discussion and conclusion section overall, as themes and as mentions. Specifically, *JIV* had a greater percentage of articles that included gender in the conclusion overall (80.6%) and as a theme (61.9%), as compared to *Criminology* (48.2 and 15.8%, respectively). Again, more *Criminology* articles simply mentioned it (32.4%) than *JIV* articles (18.7%).

Regarding the inclusion of gender and/or sex as variables, a couple of statistically significant associations were found, as shown in Table 3: journal type and control variable and journal type and independent variable. Specifically, a greater percentage of *Criminology* articles included gender as a control variable (51.1%) than *JIV* articles (36.7%). However, a significantly larger amount of *JIV* articles included gender as an independent variable (28.8%) as compared to *Criminology* (12.9%).

The bivariate analysis also revealed a statistically significant relationship between journal type and assumed author gender. More articles with all-male (33.8%) and mixed-gender (43.2%) author teams were published by *Criminology*, whereas more articles with all-female (33.8%) and undeterminable (18.7%) author teams were published by *JIV*. *Criminology* (43.2%) and *JIV* (41.7%) both published more mixed-gender authored articles than any other kind. Alternatively, the fewest number of *JIV* articles were authored by all-male teams (5.8%) and the fewest number of *Criminology* articles were published by gender-undeterminable author teams (5.8%) (Table 4).

Table 4. Author gender by journal type.

	All male	All female	Both	Undeterminable
Criminology	33.8% (47)	17.3% (24)	43.2% (60)	5.8% (8)
JIV	5.8% (8)	33.8% (47)	41.7% (58)	18.7% (26)
χ^2	44.669***			

***$p < 0.001$.

Table 5. Inclusion of any gender in journal by author team.

	All male	All female	Mixed gender	χ^2
Criminology	78.7% (37)	100.0% (24)	91.7% (55)	8.992*
JIV	100.0% (8)	100.0% (47)	98.3% (57)	1.407

*$p < 0.05$.

A bivariate analysis of the inclusion of gender by the gender composition of the author team was also conducted, layered by journal type, as depicted in Table 5. Specifically, chi-square analysis revealed a statistically significant relationship between author gender and the mention of gender at any point in *Criminology* articles. Although that relationship was the only statistically significant one found with bivariate analysis, the frequencies revealed through a univariate analysis were telling. Within *Criminology*, all-male author teams included gender in 78.7% of articles, compared to all-female author teams, who included gender in 100.0% of articles. Mixed-gender author teams, or teams that included at least one female and one male, included gender in 91.7% of *Criminology* articles. Within *JIV*, 100.0% of articles authored by all-male author teams, 100.0% of articles authored by all-female teams, and 98.3% of articles authored by mixed-gender author teams included the construct gender at some point.

DISCUSSION AND CONCLUSION

The primary purpose of this study was to analyze the inclusion of gender and/or sex in current *Criminology* and *JIV* articles. This study was founded upon a series of historic calls for greater inclusion of gender and gender minorities, namely Belknap's (2015) call for inclusion within the field of criminology during her presentation to the members of the American Society of Criminology. In an effort to determine if this and other calls for diversity calls were heeded, and to compare victimization and criminological research, this study examined the inclusion of gender and/or sex from both a mainstream criminological and diversity-focused, interdisciplinary victimization journal from 2015 to the present. The findings of this study bring to light some notable takeaways.

Overall, gender was included in significantly more *JIV* than *Criminology* articles. Although this inclusion could range from a single mention at one point in an article to the inclusion of gender as a theme of the article, a significantly greater percentage of *JIV* articles included gender and/or sex. When looking at themes found within the literature reviews of articles, over three times as many *JIV* articles included gender as a theme compared to *Criminology* articles. This is surprising because when looking at gender and/or sex as variables—arguably the most telling measure of inclusion—gender was included as a variable in a majority of both *JIV* and *Criminology* articles. However, gender was most commonly used as a control variable rather than an independent or dependent variable, which might explain the variation in its use as a theme. This finding fits the extant research which suggests that topics surrounding gender and gender minorities are reserved more for journals with a particular focus on inclusivity (Crow & Smykla, 2015; Eigenberg & Whalley, 2015). The dismissal of such topics by mainstream criminology journals was an unintended result of feminist and queer criminology's creation of academic journals uniquely designed to broach subjects of gender (Eigenberg & Whalley, 2015). Although specialty journals have done well, they allow the exclusion of otherwise necessary discussion of gender and sexuality in mainstream criminology, reflected in these findings.

Despite recognition of the problematic nature inherent in the dichotomizing of gender and sex (Callis, 2014; Collins, 1990), in the articles examined, only the gender was measured outside of a binary, and only in 3 of the articles examined. Although there were limitations even in non-binary operationalizations of these constructs, the fact that the vast majority of articles measuring either gender and/or sex operationalized their variables as binary measures seems to be indicative of a limited operationalization of the constructs of gender, which are often currently conceptualized as spectrum-type measures by society. To limit gender to binary measures such as male/female operationalizations not only fails to keep up with society's modern perspective, but it fails to account for a significant demographic of individuals.

Again, throughout the articles examined, sex and gender were both commonly measured as a binary sex measure: male or female. Therefore, because the inclusion of gender and sex in criminology and victimization journals is high—so is the conflation of the terms gender and sex. These terms are often used interchangeably. Researchers have noted that prior to the introduction of the term "gender" during the feminist movement of the 1960s and 1970s, the term sex was used to measure what we often refer to as "biological sex." It seems that Gentile's (1993) argument may still be particularly relevant to criminal justice and victimization studies: gender is used as a more "politically correct" term, even though we are commonly measuring sex assigned at birth. This has the unintended consequence of conflating sex and gender and reifying binary measures of both gender and sex. If criminologists continue to conflate sex and gender and measure these with binary attributes (that are presumably mutually exclusive and exhaustive), we will continue to marginalize and lose data on many vulnerable populations within our society. Additionally, these measures continue to legitimize hetero- and cis-normativity in our field. Other social sciences such as psychology have begun to use more inclusive measures for gender and sex; criminology needs to follow suit.

As stated in the findings, the relationship between the mention of gender in *Criminology* articles by author gender was found to be significant. All-male and mixed-gender author teams (teams which included at least one male) were the only author teams of *Criminology* articles not to mention gender at all. However, it should be noted that this was only the case in nine articles, some of which focused on topics not directly relevant to the measurement of gender, such as criminal hot spots. Every all-female author team of criminological articles mentioned gender at some point in their publication. Similarly, among *JIV* articles analyzed, every article authored by an all-female author team mentioned gender, as did every article authored by all-male author teams. Notably, when compared to *Criminology*, *JIV* had a greater percentage of articles that mentioned gender at any point, for authors' teams of all gender compositions.

These findings fit the context of the larger literature suggesting that females may not be welcomed into mainstream journals and are, therefore, relegated to journals that are more inclusive of gender diversity issues (Crow & Smykla, 2015; Eigenberg & Whalley, 2015). Eigenberg and Whalley (2015) noted that female authors who have often been relegated to feminist criminology journals are those discussing gender and sexuality in the literature. The current study's finding that *Criminology* publications had almost twice as many all-male author teams as all-female author teams, whereas *JIV* had just over six times as many all-female teams to all-male teams, supports previous stipulations that females may not be welcomed into mainstream criminology journals. Alternatively, our findings may indicate that women and all-female author teams are electively choosing not to submit their manuscripts for publication in more mainstream outlets (e.g., broad, criminological journals with higher impact factors) and are instead choosing to publish in journals with an intentional focus on diversity. Indeed, more current researchers have argued that it may be preferable to avoid mainstream journals, particularly regarding issues of queer criminology such as gender and sexuality, because it may limit the potential of knowledge

(Ball, 2014). The consequence, either way, may still be that their work, because it is not being published in more mainstream criminological outlets, may be easily ignored by numerous researchers and publications. Therefore, they may not be reaching the largest possible audience.

Among the significant findings of this study, a single conclusion stands out: the calls for inclusivity and activism have not been met, at least not entirely. Although progress has been made, it is slow, and there is still a noticeable gap between the inclusion of broad, inclusive conceptualization and operationalization of gender in mainstream and diversity-focused, interdisciplinary journals, with mainstream criminological journals, in particular, failing to heed the call. Even the more inclusive publications of diversity-focused journals have yet to match the nuance observed in the conceptualization and operationalization of gender among society at large, a concerning realization for a field rooted in sociology and the study of individual behavior. Renzetti (1993) once said: "My task, as I stated at the outset, was to develop an argument for greater emphasis on feminist analyses in criminal justice curricula. But as I completed this article, I found myself asking 'Why should I have to make this case *again*?'" emphasizing the redundant nature of these calls for inclusion and activism (p. 232). This lag in criminological research has contributed to an "epistemological blind spot" in criminological theory (Cook, 2016, p. 342; Flavin, 2001), that appears to still exist in varying forms today.

Limitations

Although there are some clear takeaways, there are also a few noteworthy limitations due to the exploratory nature of this study. Perhaps the most notable limitation is the narrow scope used in terms of journals. Although *Criminology* is a mainstream, interdisciplinary criminological journal and *JIV* is a diversity-focused, interdisciplinary journal, they are only two of the many academic journals in publication today. Therefore, although they are reflective of a portion of publications, the findings ascertained herein cannot be fairly generalized to make assumptions of *all* criminology and victimization journals. Further, because both coders in this study were trained and worked collaboratively to resolve questions and concerns of coding and the reliability check of randomly selected articles indicated a high inter-coder agreement, the reliability of the research method could have been strengthened by requiring multiple coders for each article, particularly in the analysis of latent content, which is where the most disagreement between coders was shown. The measurement of author gender as an assumption based on gendered pronouns is also somewhat limited because some authors did not use gendered pronouns in their biographies. We are unable to determine if they excluded pronouns incidentally or purposefully. Lastly, the analyses run in this study did not lend themselves to causal findings. It cannot definitively be said whether, for example, female authors include sexuality in a greater percentage of articles due to their gender. We were also not able to procure enough non-binary measurements to determine the results of a chi-square analysis on the relationship between author gender, journal type, and non-binary operationalization of variables.

Future research

In an effort to resolve some of the limitations of this study, future research should include the analysis of articles from other criminological journals to determine if similar results are found. Researchers should also take a partner approach to coding in order to ensure that judgment on the inclusion of these constructs is consistent. This work could also be strengthened by objectively determining author gender through author surveys, which would also allow future studies to eliminate the "undeterminable" gender category altogether. Additionally, if the author gender is determined by self-identification by the authors, gender conceptualization could be expanded as appropriate to include transgender and gender non-conforming gender identities.

Future research should also work on teasing out the differences between gender and sex and ensuring that the researcher is measuring what they intend to measure. Often researchers indicated they were measuring gender but in fact, were measuring sex assigned at birth—and doing so with a binary measure. As previously stated, this works to silence marginalized individuals who work within or come into contact with the criminal justice system. In order to fully understand crime and victimization, we must fully conceptualize gender and sex, as well as operationalize them accordingly. Moreover, researchers have highlighted the importance of examining intersecting identities such as race and gender. Future research should explore the degree to which the extant literature has examined the combined marginalization factors of race, sexuality, and gender in order to get a better understanding not only of how these characteristics are measured, but how they interplay with one another, and if research is highlighting these interactions.

REFERENCES

Albonetti, C. (1988). The role of gender and departures in the sentencing of defendants convicted of a white-collar offense under the federal sentencing guidelines. *Sociology of Crime, Law, and Deviance, 1,* 3–48.

Anderson, S. M., & Fine, M. (2017). Research: Overview. In K. L. Nadal (Ed.), *The SAGE encyclopedia of psychology and gender* (pp. 1416–1422). SAGE Publications, Inc.

ASC. (2020). *Publications.* American Society of Criminology.

Ball, M. (2014). What's queer about queer criminology? In D. Peterson & V. R. Panfil (Eds.), *Handbook of LGBT communities, crime, and justice* (pp. 531–555). Springer.

Belknap, J. (2001). *The invisible woman: Gender, crime, and justice* (2nd ed.). Wadsworth/Thompson.

Belknap, J. (2015). Activist criminology: Criminologists' responsibility to advocate for social and legal justice. *Criminology, 53*(1), 1–22. https://doi.org/10.1111/1745-9125.12063

Berg, B. L. (2004). *Qualitative research methods for the social sciences* (Vol. 5). Pearson.

Burgess-Proctor, A. (2006). Intersections of race, class, gender, and crime: Future directions for feminist criminology. *Feminist Criminology, 1*(1), 27–47. https://doi.org/10.1177/1557085105282899

Callis, A. S. (2014). Bisexual, pansexual, queer: Non-binary identities and the sexual borderlands. *Sexualities, 17*(1–2), 63–80. https://doi.org/10.1177/1363460713511094

Carl, J. (2012). Gender vs. sex: What's the difference? *Montessori Life, 24*(1), 26–30.

Collins, P. H. (1990). *Black feminist thought.* Routledge.

Cook, K. J. (2016). Has criminology awakended from its "androcentric slumber"? *Feminist Criminology, 11*(4), 334–353. https://doi.org/10.1177/1557085116660437

Crow, M. S., & Smykla, J. O. (2015). An examination of author characteristics in national and regional criminology and criminal justice journals, 2008-2010: Are female scholars changing the nature of publishing in criminology and criminal justice? *American Journal of Criminal Justice, 40*(2), 441–455. https://doi.org/10.1007/s12103-014-9250-x

Curtin, N., & Okuyan, M. (2017). Research methodology and gender. In K. L. Nadal (Ed.), *The SAGE encyclopedia of psychology and gender* (pp. 1423–1424). Sage Publications, Inc.

Daly, K., & Chesney-Lind, M. (1988). Feminism and criminology. *Justice Quarterly, 5*(4), 497–538. https://doi.org/10.1080/07418828800089871

Eigenberg, H. M., & Whalley, E. (2015). Gender and publication patterns: Female authorship is increasing, but is there gender parity? *Women & Criminal Justice, 25*(1–2), 130–144.

Flavin, J. (2001). Feminism for the mainstream criminologist: An invitation. *Journal of Criminal Justice, 29*(4), 271–285. https://doi.org/10.1016/S0047-2352(01)00093-9

Franklin, C. A. (2008). Women offenders, disparate treatment, and criminal justice: A theoretical, historical, and contemporary overview. *Criminal Justice Studies, 21*(4), 341–360. https://doi.org/10.1080/14786010802554238

Garland, T. S., Branch, K. A., & Grimes, M. (2016). Blurring the lines: Reinforcing rape myths in comic books. *Feminist Criminology, 11*(1), 48–68. https://doi.org/10.1177/1557085115576386

Gau, J. M. (2019). *Statistics for criminology and criminal justice* (3rd ed.). SAGE Publications, Inc.

Gentile, D. A. (1993). Just what are sex and gender, anyway?: A call for a new terminological standard. *Psychological Science, 4*(2), 120–122. https://doi.org/10.1111/j.1467-9280.1993.tb00472.x

Gottfredson, M. R. (1981). On the etiology of criminal victimization. The Journal of Criminal Law and Criminology, *72*(2), 714–726. https://doi.org/10.2307/1143011

Gray, J. H., & Densten, I. L. (1998). Integrating quantitative and qualitative analysis using latent and manifest variables. *Quality & Quantity, 32,* 419–431.

Hannon, L., & Dufour, L. R. (1998). Still just the study of men and crime? A content analysis. *Sex Roles, 38*(1–2), 63–71. https://doi.org/10.1023/A:1018712511855

Hesse-Biber, S. N., & Leavy, P. (2006). *Emergent methods in social research.* SAGE.

Jennings, W. G., Higgins, G. E., Tewksbury, R., Gover, A. R., & Piquero, A. R. (2010). A longitudinal assessment of the victim-offender overlap. *Journal of Interpersonal Violence, 25*(12), 2147–2174. https://doi.org/10.1177/0886260509354888

Karmen, A. (2013). *Crime victims: An introduction to victimology* (8th ed.). Wadsworth Cengage Learning.

Koons-Witt, B. (2002). The effect of gender on the decision to incarcerate before and after the introduction of sentencing guidelines. *Criminology, 40*(2), 297–327. https://doi.org/10.1111/j.1745-9125.2002.tb00958.x

Kraska, P. B., & Neuman, W. L. (2011). *Criminal justice and criminological research methods.* Pearson.

Kruttschnitt, C. (1984). Sex and criminal court dispositions: The unresolved controversy. *Journal of Research in Crime and Delinquency, 21*(3), 213–232. https://doi.org/10.1177/0022427884021003003

Lauritsen, J. L., Sampson, R. J., & Laub, J. H. (1991). The link between offending and victimization among adolescents. *Criminology, 29*(2), 265–292. https://doi.org/10.1111/j.1745-9125.1991.tb01067.x

Lesko, N. (2010). Gender research. In C. A. Kridel (Ed.), *Encyclopedia of curriculum studies* (pp. 393–397). Sage Publications, Inc.

Mustaine, E. E., & Tewksbury, R. (2000). Comparing the lifestyles of victims, offenders, and victim-offenders: A routine activity theory assessment of similarities and differences for criminal incident participants. *Sociological Focus, 33*(3), 339–362. https://doi.org/10.1080/00380237.2000.10571174

Nagel, I. H., & Hagan, J. (1983). Gender and crime: Offense patterns and criminal court sanctions. *Crime and Justice, 4*, 91–144. https://doi.org/10.1086/449087

Noel, J. K., & Lutz, T. M. (2020). Measuring sex, gender, and sexual orientation in national disease surveillance systems: A pilot study. *The Journal of Sex Research.* https://doi.org/10.1080/00224499.2020.1745740

Payne, B. K., Berg, B. L., & Sun, I. Y. (2005). Policing in small town America: Dogs, drunks, disorder, and dysfunction. *Journal of Criminal Justice, 33*(1), 31–41. https://doi.org/10.1016/j.jcrimjus.2004.10.006

Rafter, N. (1990). *Partial justice: Women, prisons, and social control* (2nd ed.). Transaction.

Renzetti, C. M. (1993). On the margins of the malestream (or, they still don't get it, do they?): Feminist analyses in criminal justice education. *Journal of Criminal Justice Education, 4*(2), 219–234. https://doi.org/10.1080/10511259300086111

SAGE. (2020). *Journal of Interpersonal Violence.* https://us.sagepub.com/en-us/nam/journal-of-interpersonal-violence/journal200855#submission-guidelines

Sharp, S. F., Hefley, K. (2007). This is a man's world… or at least that's how it looks in the journals. *Critical Criminology, 15*(1), 3–18. https://doi.org/10.1007/s10612-006-9016-y

Smith, S. G., Zhang, X., Basile, K. C., Merrick, M. T., Wang, J., Kresnow, M. J., & Chen, J. (2018). *The national intimate partner and sexual violence survey: 2015 data brief-updated release.* National Center for Injury Prevention and Control, Centers for Disease Control and Prevention. https://www.cdc.gov/violenceprevention/pdf/2015data-brief508.pdf

Spohn, C. C., & Spears, J. W. (1997). Gender and case processing decisions: A comparison of case outcomes for male and female defendants charged with violent felonies. *Women & Criminal Justice, 8*(3), 29–59.

Tewksbury, R. (2009). Male rape. In J. Wilson (Ed.), *The Praeger handbook of victimology* (pp. 161–163). Praeger.

Tewksbury, R., & Mustaine, E. E. (2001). Lifestyle factors associated with the sexual assault of men: A routine activity theory analysis. *The Journal of Men's Studies, 9*(2), 153–182. https://doi.org/10.3149/jms.0902.153

Tseng, J. (2008). Sex, gender, and why the differences matter. *The Virtual Mentor, 10*(7), 427–428. https://doi.org/10.1001/virtualmentor.2008.10.7.fred1-0807

von Hentig, H. (1948). *The criminal and his victim.* Yale University Press.

Wallace, H., & Roberson, C. (2011). *Victimology: Legal, psychological, and social perspectives* (3rd ed.). Allyn and Bacon.

Woods, J. B. (2014). "Queering criminology": Overview of the state of the field. In D. P. V. R. Panfil (Ed.), *Handbook of LGBT communities, crime, and justice* (pp. 15–41). Springer.

∂ OPEN ACCESS

Comparing the Gay and Trans Panic Defenses

W. Carsten Andresen

ABSTRACT
During the past fifty years, scholars have identified the following four ways that criminal defendants in the United States have used gay and trans panic defenses in murder cases involving victims who were gay men and transgender women: (1) insanity, (2) diminished capacity, (3) provocation, and (4) self-defense. While scholars have studied the first three defenses for gay men, little scholarship exists about the gay panic cases involving claims of self-defense. Additionally, there is a paucity of research regarding the trans panic defense. To address these empirical gaps, this research note uses open-source methods to study similarities between 99 homicide cases that occurred in the United States where criminal defendants made a gay or trans panic argument.

INTRODUCTION

During the past 30 years, the federal government has increasingly focused law enforcement attention toward offenders who, motivated by homophobia or transphobia, commit hate crimes targeting Lesbian, Gay, Bi-Sexual, Transgender, and Queer (LGBTQ+) victims.[1] In 1990, Congress passed and President George H.W. Bush signed into law the Hate Crime Statistics Act that required the United States Attorney General to track and report annually on "crimes that manifest evidence of prejudice based on race, religion, sexual orientation, or ethnicity" in the Federal Bureau of Investigation's (FBI) Uniform Crime Reports (Federal Bureau of Investigation, 2011). In 2009, Congress and President Barack H. Obama took additional action to protect people based on race, religion, sexual orientation, and ethnicity with the Matthew Shepard and James Byrd, Jr. Hate Crimes Prevention Act (Boven, 2009). Co-named after Matthew Shepard, a Wyoming college student murdered for being gay in 1998, this law focused on increasing prosecutions and enhancing punishments of defendants who killed people based on bias or hate.

Yet gay men and trans women still remain vulnerable to fatal violence because of the gay and trans panic defenses.[2] The gay and trans panic defenses are courtroom "defense strategies that rely on the notion that a criminal defendant should be excused or justified" if he kills a gay man or transgender woman in response to a sexual advance (Lee, 2008, p. 475). In most of the United States, defendants who kill gay men and trans women can currently raise one of the four gay or trans panic defenses (Capers, 2011; Comstock, 1992; Harvard Law Review, 1989; Lee, 2003, 2008, 2014, 2019; Lee and Kwan, 2014; Lippman, 2018; Nicolas, 2003; Patel, 2019; Suffredini, 2001; Tomei and Cramer, 2016; Woods et al., 2016). The first three defenses are excuse defenses, which focus on the defendant's state of mind at the time of the crime, and include insanity, diminished

This is an Open Access article distributed under the terms of the Creative Commons Attribution-NonCommercial-NoDerivatives License (http://creativecommons.org/licenses/by-nc-nd/4.0/), which permits non-commercial re-use, distribution, and reproduction in any medium, provided the original work is properly cited, and is not altered, transformed, or built upon in any way.

capacity, and provocation. The final panic defense is that of self-defense, where the defendant seeks to justify his use of deadly force by claiming he was defending his life from an attempted sexual assault. The gay and trans panic defenses include both excuse and justification defenses.

The gay and trans panic defenses are at odds with hate crime legislation in at least three ways (Tomei and Cramer, 2016). While hate crime legislation seeks to enhance the prosecution of bias and hate crimes, the gay and trans panic defenses conversely seek to (1) excuse or justify the use of violence against gay men and transgender women and (2) reduce the punishment of male defendants who kill gay men and trans women. To have hate crime legislation, but then to allow defendants to use gay and trans panic defenses to judges and juries projects contradictory messages "to society and victimized groups" (Tomei and Cramer, 2016, p. 228).

In response to several high-profile cases where homicide defendants used gay or trans panic defenses, fifteen states and Washington DC have passed legislation that bans most gay and trans panic defenses (LGBT Bar, n.d.).[3] California (2014) was the first state to pass anti–panic defense legislation and Oregon (2021) is the most recent. Under anti–panic defense legislation, murder defendants are prohibited from arguing that they killed a gay man or a trans woman as a result of insanity, diminished capacity, or provocation.[4]

Yet the legislation banning the gay and transgender panic defenses can still have one loophole for murder defendants. Even in states with anti–panic defense legislation, defense attorneys are still allowed to argue that a male defendant killed a gay man or transgender woman in self-defense from an attempted sexual assault. For example, in California in 2018, Gage McCartney strangled a man he worked with and claimed he was defending himself from a sexual assault. McCartney received a lenient plea deal in 2019—manslaughter and a 12-year prison sentence—despite the legislation in California prohibiting gay panic defenses (Salonga, 2019).

This research note focuses on the use of the gay and trans panic defenses. I have collected 191 homicides, committed by 223 offenders who entered gay or trans panic defenses, which claimed the lives of 205 victims from 1970–2019 in the United States.[5] This research note reports on a subset of these data (100 victims killed between from 2000–2019) to analyze differences between the murders of 68 gay men and 32 trans women. This note presents a literature review, methodology, findings, and conclusion.

LITERATURE REVIEW

The origins of the gay panic defense date back to 1920, when Yale University Psychiatrist Edward Kempf conceived of a psychopathology he referred to as "homosexual panic" (Lee, 2008).[6] Kempf applied a diagnosis of homosexual panic to patients who, after having experienced a same sex attraction to another person, found themselves becoming so anxious about their interest in that person that their attempts to repress those feelings resulted in profound psychological discord (Kempf, 1920, p. 477–479). For these patients, the experience of being in close contact with the people they were attracted to, such as living together in a military barracks, could exacerbate the psychological stress, and even cause hallucinations and psychotic episodes in the form of "visions, voices," and complaints of "'dopy' feelings, 'poison' and 'filth' in the food" (Kempf, 1920, p. 514). Much of the anxiety in homosexual panic probably derived from the early twentieth century conception of homosexuality as a pathology—something deviant—by the American medical profession (Polchin, 2019). A century ago, people attracted to members of the same sex also had to grapple with the realization that acting on those feelings could result in serious legal consequences, as intimate homosexual activities were felonies throughout the United States (Polchin, 2019). Homosexual panic as originally conceived in the 1920s referred to a psychiatric diagnosis for someone anxious about their own attraction to a person of the same sex, rather than a potential legal defense theory that a killer might raise in court in an attempt to excuse or justify the killing of someone perceived to be gay or transgender.

There is an additional distinction between the 1920s psychological concept of homosexual panic and the contemporary legal defense of gay panic. During the 1920s, Kempf characterized people suffering from homosexual panic as neurotic, but he was mindful to point out that they were rarely violent. In *Psychopathology* (1920), Kempf chronicles the histories of 18 male case studies and makes it clear that none of these patients were violent (Comstock, 1992; Kempf, 1920). For those individuals who found homosexual panic intolerable, Kempf also clarifies that they directed any aggression they felt inward, which sometimes manifested in "suicides" that involved "cutting the throat, hanging, or plunging on the head" (Kempf, 1920, p. 491). So how did the contemporary gay panic defense (a legal strategy that has arisen to excuse or justify homicidal violence) arise from the 1920s conception of homosexual panic (a diagnosis for patients who were neurotic, but nonviolent)?

During the 1960s, criminal defendants transplanted the concept of homosexual panic from the field of psychiatry into the courtroom. Defendants turned to homosexual panic, initially a psychiatric diagnosis, as a new option to draw upon for use in mounting the insanity defense in the courtroom. During this era, defendants charged with murder would sometimes raise an insanity defense that argued that they (the defendants) were suffering from homosexual panic at the time that they committed their homicide, and that this homosexual panic had prevented them from formulating the necessary *mens rea* to be held criminally responsible. Under the *M'Naghten* test (one of three ways that the courts measure a defendant's sanity in the courtroom) a defendant was assessed as mentally ill if he met one of following two prongs: "at the time" of the act, the defendant (1) "did not know the quality and nature of the act" or (2) "he did not know that what he was doing ... was wrong" (Patel, 2019, p. 120). Using a theory of homosexual panic, the defense counsel would try to prove in court that encountering someone who was gay drove the defendant into a state of insanity that prevented him from knowing what he was doing (i.e. he was unaware of his actions) or that prevented him from knowing that his actions were wrong (i.e. he was unaware that his actions were immoral or illegal). In the current Model Penal Code standard for measuring sanity, to be found insane by the fact-finder a defendant must be "found to lack substantial capacity to either appreciate the criminality of his conduct or to conform to the conduct required by law" (Patel, 2019, p. 120). The final test the courts can use is the federal standard that requires that "the defendant be unable to appreciate the criminality of his act" (Patel, 2019, p. 120). Whatever the legal test for sanity, to raise an insanity defense, the defendant had to have an expert mental health professional testify that he was suffering from homosexual panic at the time of the murder.

From the very beginning, the use of homosexual panic as an insanity defense was often unsuccessful in the courtroom. The outcome of *People v Rodriguez*, which legal scholars have identified as the first murder case to bring homosexual panic into the courtroom, foretold of the difficulties of raising homosexual panic as an insanity defense before a jury [(*People v Rodriguez*, 256 Cal.App.2d 663 (1967); Lee, 2008; Patel, 2019)]. In this case, 17-year-old teenager Joseph Rodriguez, intoxicated and out with his friends, picked up a large branch from the ground and bludgeoned an elderly man to death. Rodriguez was charged with second degree murder. Rodriguez's attorney raised an insanity defense. The defense called a psychologist, who testified that Rodriguez was urinating in an alley when the elderly man (the murder victim) grabbed him from behind. According to the psychologist, as a result of this action from the murder victim, Rodriguez experienced "an acute homosexual panic brought on him by the fear that the victim was molesting him sexually" and that Rodriguez "did not know the nature and quality of his act at the time of the attack" (*People v. Rodriguez*, 256 Cal.App.2d 663, 667 (1967)). Ultimately, Rodriguez's homosexual panic defense was unsuccessful; he was convicted of second-degree homicide and his appeal of his conviction was unsuccessful.

In the years following this case, a growing number of male defendants drew on the homosexual panic theory with a similar lack of success at trial and on appeal (Lee, 2008; Patel, 2019). In case after case, defendants and the mental health professionals who testified on their behalf, failed to prove to juries and appeal courts that homosexual panic was a reason for insanity. For example, in *People v. Parisie* (1972), the appellate court informed the defendant that they agreed with the jury that homosexual panic was not a mental illness that lent itself to an insanity or diminished capacity defense. In *State v. Thornton* (1975), the appellate court again upheld the jury decision; despite the testimony of two psychiatrists called by the defense, the jury and later the appellate court did not agree that homosexual panic was "a mental disease or defect excluding responsibility for" the defendant's conduct. In *Commonwealth v. Shelley* (1978), an appellate court again sided with a jury, who found the defendant guilty of murder after listening to psychiatrists testify on behalf of the defense and prosecution. In 1973, in the same decade as these criminal trials, the utility of using homosexual panic as a source from which to build an insanity defense was hampered by the American Psychiatric Association's removal of homosexuality from the second edition of their Diagnostic Statistical Manual of Mental Disorder (Lee, 2008; Patel, 2019). After the medical profession ruled that homosexuality was not a psychological pathology, "the gay panic defense vis-à-vis insanity … became moot from a medical perspective," making it become even harder for defendants to argue that homosexual panic should excuse their homicidal violence (Patel, 2019, p. 122).

Stymied in using an insanity defense, some defendants' attorneys began to raise diminished capacity as an affirmative defense in an attempt to mitigate their clients' charges in court. For diminished capacity, the defense must show that the defendant "was acting under the influence of a mental disease or defect which affected his capacity to premeditate and deliberate or form the requisite intent to kill" (Lee, 2008; p. 494). When successful, the defense could use diminished capacity to argue for a reduction in a defendant's criminal charges. One infamous case involving a diminished capacity defense occurred in 1995 when Jonathan Schmitz, a Michigan resident, agreed to travel to Chicago to appear as a guest on the daytime television talk show, The Jenny Jones Show (Lee, 2008). On the specific episode, entitled *Secret Admirers*, Jenny Jones invited the guests, including Schmitz, to learn on national television the identity of someone in their life who secretly had a romantic crush on them. On the show, Schmitz was surprised to learn that the person who had a crush on him was a man, rather than a woman, named Scott Amedure. In response to learning Amedure's identity, Schmitz appeared to take the news in stride, as evidenced by him smiling and hugging Amedure, and then telling him in a graceful way that the feeling was not mutual because he was straight. Three days after the filming, Schmitz purchased a shotgun, drove to Amedure's apartment, and killed Amedure by shooting him twice. Initially, Schmitz faced first-degree murder charges because his homicidal actions involved premeditation and deliberation. Schmitz had engaged in purposeful steps—he drove to his bank, took out cash, and then bought a shotgun—that suggested that he had planned, in advance, to kill Amedure.

During the trial, however, Schmitz entered a diminished capacity defense, claiming that he was humiliated and traumatized by his appearance on The Jenny Jones Show. Schmitz was successful in raising the diminished capacity defense; the jury convicted him of a lesser criminal charge of second-degree murder instead of first-degree murder. Although Schmitz received a conviction for a lower charge, he still was still sentenced to a lengthy prison term, and spent almost 22 years behind bars, before being released on parole in 2017.

The provocation defense, the final affirmative defense that a defendant seeking to excuse his conduct may raise, is a legal defense strategy used in an attempt to mitigate criminal charges. Defendants whose attorneys raise the provocation defense allege that a gay man or trans woman murder victim—through their own nonviolent behavior toward the defendant—played a role in their own murder. In states that rely on a common law standard, the defendant raising a provocation defense must prove three things in court: (1) that there was an "adequate" provocation from the victim, (2) that the defendant acted in the heat of passion before his "passion" could "cool," and (3) that "a causal connection" exists "between the alleged provocation, the claimed passion, and the act which led to the victim's death" (Patel, 2019, p. 123). In states that rely on the Model Penal Code, the defendant raising the provocation must satisfy a two-prong criteria. First, the defendant must prove that he was "under extreme emotional disturbance at the time of the killing" (Patel, 2019, p. 122). Second, the defendant must also prove that "there was a reasonable explanation" for his "emotional disturbance, based on the viewpoint of a person in the defendant's situation, under the circumstances as the defendant believed them to be" (Patel, 2019, p. 122). Ultimately, a defense attorney who raises the provocation defense, whether in states that use common law or the Model Penal Code, argues that the behavior of the gay or trans woman victim proved so upsetting to the defendant that the defendant should be partially excused for reacting to it with deadly violence.

This defense is controversial because a defense attorney, in arguing that a murder victim's behavior provoked the defendant, draws on the defendant's own subjective perspective rather than on an objective standard (Patel, 2019). In a 1999 trial, defense counsel for defendant Aaron McKinney raised a defense that McKinney killed his victim, Mathew Shepard, because Shepard had openly flirted with McKinney in front of a people in a crowded bar; Shepard's flirting was so provocative that it resulted in McKinney losing control of himself and committing murder (Lee, 2008, p. 510).[7] While McKinney's defense was unsuccessful, other defendants have successfully partially mitigated their murder charges through the use of the provocation defense. In Indiana, Timothy Schick, who was charged with murder for killing Stephen Lamie in 1991, raised a provocation defense alleging that Lamie, who had propositioned Schick and attempted to touch Schick's penis, had engaged in such upsetting behavior that Schick's homicidal actions should be partially excused (Lee, 2008). The jury seemed to agree with Schick's defense of provocation, as they convicted him of the lesser crime of manslaughter. In a similar case from North Carolina, David Mills, who in 1974 killed a man and stole his jewelry and automobile, also successfully raised a provocation defense, resulting in a conviction for manslaughter rather than second-degree murder (Lee, 2008). Ultimately, when it comes to raising a provocation defense, the act of assessing a nonviolent behavior as a "legally adequate provocation" for homicide is a "term of art" rather than a science (Lee, 2019, p. 1425).

Criminal defendants who kill trans women often enter provocation defenses in an attempt to mitigate their criminal charges. Indeed, the following definition of the trans panic defense incorporates the provocation defense: "a male defendant charged with murdering a male-to-female transgender person claims he was provoked into a heat of passion upon discovering that the person with whom he had sexual relations was biologically male rather than female" (Lee, 2008; p. 513). At trial, many defendants suggest that the "discovery" that the person with whom they were sexually interested is transgender (or "biologically male," to use Lee's term) is so startling, so aberrant and provocative, that the fatal violence is a natural outcome, an involuntary reflexive action to a specific stimulus. For example, in New York City in 2013, James Dixon beat Islan Nettles to death on the street after his friends taunted him for flirting with a trans woman (Lee, 2019). In a statement to the police, Dixon raised a sort of pretrial provocation defense, stating: "I don't care about what they do. I just don't wanna' be fooled. My pride is at stake" (Lang, 2016). In the end, Dixon entered into a plea deal where he pled guilty to manslaughter and was sentenced to twelve years in prison. Many other criminal defendants have raised similar arguments, suggesting that trans women, by existing as trans women, were actively engaged in deceit, trying to trick cisgender men into having sex with them. In California in 2002, Michael Magidson and Jose Merel killed Gwen Araujo, a trans woman, after discovering that she was transgender (Lee, 2008). During their trials, their defense used provocation arguments that Araujo had deceived them and that their violence was in response to this deception (Lee, 2008, pp. 513–517). The jury from their first trial deadlocked, resulting in a mistrial. A second jury convicted both men of second-degree murder, rather than manslaughter, with a juror from the second trial stating that the defendants had "no basis … for beating and murder" (quote cited by Lee, 2008, p. 517;

Lee, 2005). Across the country, several defendants have killed trans women and raised nearly identical provocation defenses, alleging the trans woman deliberately set out to fool the murder defendants into having sex (Lee, 2008; Wodda and Panfil, 2015).

In some of these cases, criminal defendants have also suggested that trans women, by expressing a romantic interest in them, behaved so inappropriately that their homicidal actions should be partially excused (Lee, 2008). In 2008 in California, Brandon McInerney, a fourteen-year-old boy, killed a classmate, Larry King, for giving him a Valentine. King wanted a change of name to Leticia, sometimes used cosmetics and wore women's clothing, and was infatuated with McInerney. Because McInerney was embarrassed about being the object of such a crush, he brought a gun to school and killed King. During the first trial, the jurors could not agree whether to convict McInerney of murder or manslaughter, and the proceedings ended in a mistrial. Some of the jury believed that King, because King wore make-up and women's clothing, had engaged in unseemly and provocative behavior. These jurors expressed blame for the juveniles' school for letting the victim "defy sex and gender norms" during the school day (Strader et al., 2015, p. 1477). One juror even wrote to the District Attorney to state that King "had a long history of deviant behavior" and had "bullied" and sexually harassed McInerney (Letter from Juror 11 to District Attorney Gregory D. Totten, excerpted in Lee, 2019, p. 1432). Prior to another trial, McInerney entered into a plea deal, pleading guilty to second-degree murder and manslaughter (and a firearm charge), for which he was sentenced to 21 years in prison (Lee, 2008)

Criminal defendants who kill gay men or trans women may also raise a self-defense argument, seeking to justify their violent actions in court and to mitigate their criminal charges. To enter a self-defense argument, the defendant must prove several elements in court to demonstrate that he "honestly and reasonably believed deadly force was necessary to protect against an imminent threat of death or serious bodily injury" (Lee, 2008, p. 518). In states that rely on a common law standard, the defendant must prove in his self-defense argument that "he was threatened with imminent force, that belief was objectively reasonable, and with respect to the force he was threatened with, that would justify the force he used in response (i.e. deadly force only to repeal deadly force)" (Patel, 2019, p. 125). In states that rely on the Model Penal Code, the defendant must raise a self-defense argument that proves that at the "time of the incident" he "reasonably believed such deadly force was immediately necessary for the purpose of protecting himself against the use of unlawful force by such other person on that present occasion" (Patel, 2019, p. 125). In cases involving homicidal violence against gay men or trans women, male defendants have generally raised self-defense arguments in court alleging that their victims tried to sexually assault them. In raising a self-defense argument, these defendants seek to prove each element of this defense to show that they killed the victims to defend themselves from a sexual assault, and because of this, their violence was justified rather than a crime. Unlike like the affirmative excuse defenses, the defendants in these cases differ from defendants raising excuse defense in that they are making the arguments that because their actions were justified, the jury should completely acquit them of their charges in court.

A defendant, in raising a self-defense argument in court, has to prove several elements, such as whether he faced imminent harm from the victim and whether he responded with force that was proportional to the alleged aggressive actions of the victim. A controversial element of these self-defense cases is that there is only one party in the original dispute, the defendant, alive to provide an account of what happened; this account often takes the form of a self-defense argument. In at least three cases involving claims of self-defense, juries acquitted defendants who brutally killed their victims:

- Georgia 2001: Defendant Roderiqus Reshad Reed hit victim Ahmed Dabarran more than a dozen times in the head as Dabarran was sleeping.
- Texas 2005: Defendant Joshua Abbott stabbed victim David Morrison more than 38 times.

- Illinois 2008: Defendant Joseph Biedermann stabbed victim Terrance Michael Hauser more than 60 times.

Although self-defense is premised on the notion that a defendant faced an immediate threat of violence, Comstock (1992) found that in many cases involving a gay panic self-defense argument, it is often the defendants who "overpower and use excessive force against their victims, rather than vice-versa" (p. 96). Indeed, defendants in gay or trans panic defense cases have used several weapons against unarmed victims: "guns; steel-tipped boots, a log, and sledgehammer; a tire jack; a hatchet; knives; mace; and fire" (Comstock, 1992, p. 96).

Defendants raising self-defense gay or trans panic arguments to justify the murder of their victims often flip the traditional scripted roles of the courtroom and direct suspicion toward the victims (Lee, 2008). Yet while some defendants allege that they should be acquitted for killing their victims because they were under attack, the substance of their arguments focus on the sexual orientation or sexual identity of their victims (Comstock, 1992, p. 97). In many gay panic cases involving arguments of self-defense, the defendants portray their victims as sexual predators who sought to corrupt their heterosexuality. This is common in cases where the defendants are in their teens or twenties (Lee, 2008). An example of this involving the gay panic defense occurred during a murder trial in Denton, Texas in 2005, when jurors acquitted Joshua Abboutt, a 19-year-old defendant who stabbed a 40-year-old man 38 times (McNary, 2007). Female jurors who participated in this trial stated in later interviews that they felt concern for the defendant because they had sons the same age (McNary, 2007). A similar case also occurred in Hawaii in the 1997 murder of Kenneth Brewer by Stephen Bright (Lee, 2008, pp. 518–521). In this murder, 30-year-old Bright bludgeoned 58-year-old Brewer, and then entered a claim of self-defense to justify this violence. Bright claimed that he was straight and committed murder in self-defense because Brewer attempted to assault him. Bright's defense was ultimately successful in that it resulted in a conviction for a lesser charge, third-degree assault; Bright was released from jail for time served on the day of the verdict and sentenced to only 400 hours of community service.

The cultural historian James Polchin, who brings another perspective to the study of gay and trans panic defenses, has explored how preexisting biases in society against gay men contributes to the ability of defendants to raise these defenses.[8] In *Indecent Advances* Polchin (2019) focused on how defendants raised and wielded the gay panic defense from the 1920s–1960s. During that time, society criminalized gay men and viewed homosexuality as a disease that some could catch through exposure to a same-sex sexual advance. If a defendant in this time used violence to repel a gay advance, society viewed him as protecting himself from the "disease" of homosexuality—from being "turned gay" (Polchin, 2019). Defense attorneys during the mid–twentieth century did not have to be masters of persuasion to successfully use panic defenses to convince a jury to show leniency. Another study that focuses on present day society also suggests that bias against gay men and trans women continues to influence the decision-making of juries. Specifically, Tomei et al. (2017) found that a jury's political beliefs and views about homosexuality impact their willingness to accept the gay panic defense. Politically conservative jurors generally support guilty verdicts and more severe punishments, except when the victim is gay. When a murder or violent crime victim is gay, conservatives support more lenient verdicts and punishments compared to other jurors. Tomei et al. suggests that gay panic defenses might "represent an area in which legalized discrimination can occur without societal repercussions" (Tomei et al., 2017, p. 17).

Social science researchers have also provided broader perspective of violent crimes and bias crimes committed against gay men and trans women.[9] The research by these scholars differs from studies involving the gay and trans panic defense by focusing on the role of bias in violent crimes committed against victims. In one of the first studies to examine lethal violence against gay men, Miller and Humphreys (1980) used official police records and interview data to study

52 gay men murdered from 1973–1977. Among their findings was that these gay men were killed in brutal ways that seemed to indicate homophobia. Gruenewald and coauthors, analyzing a dataset of 121 LGBTQ+ individuals murdered between 1990–2008, explicated the unique dangers that the LGBTQ+community faces (Gruenewald, 2012; Gruenewald and Kelley, 2014; Kelley and Gruenewald, 2015). Consistent with Miller and Humphreys (1980), Gruenewald found that the murders of LGBTQ+individuals differ from the murders of "straight" people and involve increased violence and the use of weapons that involve close contact with the victim, such as knives, hands, and heavy objects.

Consistent and often overlapping with research about the use of gay and trans panic defenses, the murders of LGBTQ+people also frequently follow scripts that involve prejudice, crises of masculinity, and predatory property crimes (Kelley and Gruenewald, 2015). In an analysis of 121 homicides of LGBTQ+people, Gruenewald and Kelley (2014) identified two broad categories—predatory and responsive—that constitute pathways toward bias homicides. Two of these pathways closely relate to gay and trans panic homicides. In one common scenario, a defendant acts in a predatory manner and plans to attack a LGBTQ+individual to commit a robbery and steal cash or property. In another common scenario (often committed by juveniles or youth), a defendant responds with violence to an undesired romantic or sexual advance.

The present research note reports on how my larger ongoing study seeks to synthesize these similar but distinct research areas—legal and socio-historical research with social science studies of bias crimes against gay men and trans women. At the same time, this research note also reports on how the larger study is seeking to create an ongoing dataset that scholars and agencies can use to research bias crimes and gay and trans panic defenses.

METHODS

This study, which began in June 2018, focuses on homicide cases where murder defendants used a gay or trans panic defense to excuse or justify their lethal violence. For gay panic cases, it is worth stating that although many defendants premised their defense on the notion that the victim was gay, this study purposefully refrains from attempting to determine the sexual orientation of the victim or defendant. This study captured instances where murder defendants raised a gay panic defense and whether this impacted the legal outcomes in the courts. This study never tried to ascertain sexual orientation because definitively identifying a person's sexual orientation is a challenge, even when interviewing someone is possible.[10] I was unaware of how to distinguish between a murder victim's isolated or habitual instances of same-sex sexual behavior. This study also recognizes that a person's sexual preference or sexual identity, which might be anywhere on various continuums, can be fluid and open to different interpretations (Comstock, 1992).

My larger ongoing study draws on open-source data to identify a sample of homicides in the United States where the defendant ultimately advanced a gay or trans panic defense in court. It was necessary to use open-source data, which is defined in the next paragraph, because, at present, there are no official data sources that report on the murders of gay men or trans women. The FBI collects only limited information about the sexual orientation of homicide victims in its Uniform Crime Reports (UCR) or Supplementary Homicide Reports (SHR). Although the FBI captures data about bias crimes committed against people who are gay men or trans women (in addition to collecting information about bias crimes based on race-ethnicity and religion), these numbers are often underreported, which makes it difficult to identify the actual numbers of gay men and trans women murder victims (Gruenewald and Kelley, 2014). While the SHR captures information about the relationships between the homicide offender and victim (i.e. SHR captures "homosexual" relationships), this is also too little information to study information about bias crimes committed against gay or trans victims. According to Wirtz et al. (2018), it is also particularly difficult to accurately count the murders of people who are transgender because "there are no national surveillance systems that track murders of trans people and … trans victims of violence are often misgendered" (Wirtz et al., 2018 as cited by Lee, 2019, p. 1420, note 49). Finally, there is also limited information about the number of times each year that defendants advance gay or trans panic defenses. There do not appear to be any federal or state agencies that track the use of gay and trans panic defenses introduced by defendants.

Therefore, to investigate gay and trans panic defenses, this study relies on open-source data to collect and analyze a sample of cases—a time-consuming process. Open-source data refers to "media articles, legal transcripts, and academic writings" that the general public can access for free or for a reasonable price (Parkin and Gruenewald, 2017, p. 2694). A benefit of using open-source data is that this sometimes allows researchers to capture more detail about the circumstances and dynamics of a criminal homicide with a comparable level of accuracy to official records (Parkin and Gruenewald, 2017). This is especially important when identifying the murders of gay and trans victims, which are basically invisible in the SHR. The limitations in the SHR data present challenges in both identifying homicides that involved gay and trans victims, and also present challenges in examining similarities and differences between the murders of gay and trans victims. Yet the methodology used to collect open-source data becomes especially important because there is no official gatekeeper for these data, and no previously articulated quality control standard for maintaining the integrity of these data.

To ensure scientific rigor, this study developed a three-prong methodology (1) to identify potential cases, (2) to decide on whether to include or exclude these cases from the study sample, and (2) to analyze each case. The first prong of the methodology involved finding candidates for possible inclusion in this study. At the beginning of my study, I searched for cases in an informal way, typing search terms and phrases ("gay-panic," "homosexual," "sexual assault," and "self–defense") into various internet search engines hoping to locate possible cases, which is, difficult to replicate for future researchers (I did keep a log of most of the search terms that I used for these keyword searchers).[11] I also identified prospective cases through conversations with people employed in advocacy or legal professions.[12]

By the end of the first six months of the study, I had developed a more systematic approach to identify potential cases. Specifically, I had identified specific sources on the internet for identifying and researching cases (see Figure 1). To identify potential cases, I searched through the following data and media sources:

- *Preexisting Lists or Databases Focused on LGBTQ± Murders*: I identified potential cases through three lists that enumerated gay and/or trans murder victims and an extract from a database that collected open source data about bias crimes. First, I used The Transgender Day of Remembrance website, created by Gwendolyn Ann Smith, that includes an annual list of transgender individuals killed in instances of transphobic violence from 1970–2019 (Smith, 2020). Second, I used a database published by The Coloradoan that focused on Lesbian, Gay, Bi-Sexual and Transgender victims killed between 1998–2018 (Marmaduke and Hindi, 2018). Third, I used a list that appeared in Wikipedia under the topics "Gay Panic Defense" that included potential gay and trans panic defense cases. Finally, I requested (and received) a list of cases from the Bias Homicide Database (maintained by the Terrorism Research Center (TRC) at the University of Arkansas) that contained gay and trans murder victims killed by defendants who raised panic defenses (Terrorism Research Center, 2020).
- *Advocacy Research and Reports*: I identified potential cases by reading through reports from the Human Rights Campaign (a nonprofit group) from 2013–2019 and the Williams Institute (a think tank at the University of California in Los Angeles).
- *Legal and Social Science Articles*: I read through legal articles and social science studies and marked any potential gay and trans panic cases with a highlighter.

A. **Pre-Existing Lists or Databases Focused on LGBTQ+ Murders**:

    1. The Transgender Day of Remembrance website: transgender individuals killed by transphobic violence from 1970–2019 (Gwendolyn Ann Smith), https://tdor.info/

    2. The Coloradoan (2018) Lesbian, Gay, Bi-Sexual and Transgender victims killed between 1998–2018 (Marmaduke and Hindi, 2018), https://www.coloradoan.com/story/news/2018/10/31/more-than-600-lgbtq-people-killed-us-past-two-decades-since-matthew-shepard-murder/1670264002/

    3. List of cases in Wikipedia under the search term "Gay Panic Defense", https://en.wikipedia.org/wiki/Gay_panic_defense

    4. Data Extract from Bias Homicide Database (Terrorism Research Center at the University of Arkansas): Gay and trans murder victims killed by defendants who raised panic defenses.

B. **Advocacy Research and Reports:**

    1. Human Rights Campaign (a non-profit group) reports from 2013–2019

    2. The Williams Institute (University of California in Los Angeles) Reports

C. **Legal and Social Science Articles**

D. **Specific Internet Searches / Search Engines**

    1. Criminal Legal Appeals
       - Justia, https://www.justia.com
       - Google Scholar, https://scholar.google.com

    2. Recent Cases Reported in the News
       - Google Alert: News/media stories with "Gay Panic" forwarded to my email
       - The New York Times, https://www.nytimescom
       - Google News, https://news.google.com
       - Lexis/Nexis, https://www.lexisnexis.com
       - https://www.newspapers.com

    3. Official Government Documents and Data for Cross-Reference and Verification:

Figure 1. Methodology: finding potential cases.

- *Official Government Documents and Data for Cross-Reference and Verification*: I also searched for court documents (i.e. charging documents, legal appeals, trial transcripts) whenever possible to confirm the criminal court charges, the legal outcome of court cases, and, if there was a conviction, the criminal sentences attached to the court case. If the defendant appealed his sentence, I also used the legal appeal to cross reference and verify information about a case. If the defendant did not appeal his sentence, I looked up his court case in two other places. First, I looked up each case in the county where it was processed by the criminal justice system, and using the criminal court case look-up feature (the majority of counties have websites that allow people to look up the criminal charges from a criminal case) to confirm the defendant's criminal charge(s), court outcomes, and if applicable, his court sentence. Second, I used official government websites for state prisons and I looked up the defendant to confirm his criminal charge(s) and sentence.

These strategies generated a list of cases to screen for potential inclusion in my study sample.

The second prong of my methodology involved deciding which cases should be included or excluded from the study sample. This study created a set of criteria for determining which cases to include and which cases to reject. To create these criteria, this study drew on legal scholarship and social science to identify the legal and empirical elements that indicate that a defendant raised a gay or trans panic defense. This study also drew on the codebooks from two official databases that focus, in part of in whole, on crimes committed against the LGBTQ + community. First, I examined the Bias Homicide Database (BHDB) Manual and Codebook from the Terrorism Research Center at the University of Arkansas (Terrorism Research Center, 2020). The BHDB, as described in the BHDB Manual and Codebook, "is an open-source database containing offender, victim, and incident-level data on all bias homicides occurring in the U.S. since 1990" (p. 1). Researchers have used data in the BHDB database, which includes crimes committed against the LGBTQ + community, for several research articles about bias crimes against the LGBTQ + community. Second, I also studied the codebook from the National GLBT Homicide Dataset at the Center for Homicide Research (Center for Homicide Research, 2015).

Ultimately, for the second prong, this study devised the following criteria to decide which cases to include in the analysis:

- the crime had to take place between 1 January 1965 and 31 December 2020,
- the case had to include at least one known defendant and victim (the police have yet to identify suspects in several of the murders of trans women),
- the criminal defendant has to articulate a gay or trans panic argument (i.e. insanity, diminished capacity, provocation, self-defense) to either the police or the courts (there are eight pretrial cases where defendants are awaiting trial),
- the case remained in the analysis even if the defendant was acquitted or had the charges against him dropped.

This study also devised the following criteria to exclude cases from inclusion in the analysis sample:

- the defendant killed a victim during a stalking situation,
- the defendant killed the victim as a result of intimate partner violence within the context of a dating or romantic relationship,
- the victim survived the violence committed against him or her,
- the defendant killed the victim defending himself from a clear-cut sexual-assault (e.g. there were cases in prison settings, where defendants appeared to be acting in actual self-defense).[13,14]

From these criteria, I identified a sample of cases of defendants who had killed people and then raised a gay or trans-panic defense.

The third prong of the methodology focused on developing strategies the would allow me to analyze these cases in different ways. For the third prong, I prepared each case for entry into a digital archive library. Specifically, I created a digital file folder, named for the victim in each case, where I stored information about the case (legal documents and news media cases, most often newspaper stories, about the victim and defendant). Next, I entered information about each case into a large SPSS database for the purposes of conducting a variety of analyses of these cases. For the design of this database, I again drew on the work of two established databases, reviewing the codebooks from the BHBD (Terrorism Research Center, 2020) and the National GLBT Homicide Dataset (Center for Homicide Research, 2015). The database allows me to easily run informal statistics on my sample. When I observe interesting things, it is easy to return to the data that I collected and stored in each folder to go deeper in my research.

In entering the case information into this database, I cross-referenced the information from the various documents in each victim folder in the digital archive-library to ensure accuracy. Yet while official court documents (i.e. charging documents, legal appeals, trial transcripts) are the gold standard for deriving accurate information about court cases and outcomes, these documents are sometimes non-existent or difficult to obtain. If a defendant is acquitted of criminal charges or enters into a plea bargain agreement, it may be challenging to access useful sources of legal information about the criminal case. Indeed, Lee (2019) has written that the majority of "successful gay panic cases… are not likely to be in published court opinions" because the defendant is "not likely to appeal" and "the government is also unlikely to appeal because the double jeopardy clause prohibits the government from retrying a defendant for the same offense" (p. 1428). Even if the defendant is convicted of a criminal charge by a judge or jury, a researcher may still have difficulty obtaining legal documents if the defendant does not file an appeal, as the courts are reluctant to spend the time and money to create a trial transcript.

FINDINGS

My research note analyzes 99 cases where criminal defendants killed 100 gay men or trans women and raised panic defenses between 2000–2019. Before discussing the 100 victims, it is important to examine the specific panic defenses raised by the 101 defendants identified for this study (eight defendants, who had pending cases, were omitted from this analysis). Specifically, 42 defendants raised provocation defenses and 59 defendants raised self-defense arguments (see Table 1). While there is at least one defendant who was diagnosed as suffering from a mental illness, there were no cases where a defendant raised insanity or diminished capacity panic defenses. It is, however, highly probable that a defendant who has not yet been identified used this defense

Table 1. Gay and trans panic defenses: provocation vs. self-defense.

	Provocation N = 42		Self-defense N = 59		Total N = 101	
Highest charge in case						
Murder	38	90.48%	55	93.22%	93	92.08%
Manslaughter	3	7.14%	4	6.78%	7	6.93%
Other	1	2.38%	0	–	1	0.99%
Charge reduction						
Any reduction in severity/charges	10	23.81%	20	33.90%	30	29.70%
Murder dropped to Manslaughter	4	9.52%	8	13.56%	12	11.88%
Murder dropper to Other	1	2.38%	3	5.09%	4	3.96%
Legal outcomes						
Acquittal	1	2.38%	5	8.47%	6	5.94%
Pled guilty in plea deal	15	35.71%	20	33.90%	35	34.65%
Jury/judge find guilty	25	59.52%	33	55.93%	58	57.43%
Other	1	2.38%	1	1.69%	2	1.98%
Legal appeals filed (post-outcome)	20	47.62%	27	45.76%	47	46.53%
Outcome from legal appeal	N = 20		N = 27		N = 47	
Judgment affirmed	19		25		44	
Remanded	1		2		3	

Notes:
1. The unit of analysis for this table is the defendant. There are 109 defendants in this study, but this table excludes 8 defendants with pending cases (1 Provocation Defense and 7 Self-Defense Cases). These cases have yet to go to court.
2. Under **Charge Reduction**, the first category "Any Reduction in Severity/Charges" includes cases that had any type of reduction in charge (i.e. degrees in murder). The second and third categories, "Murder dropped to Manslaughter" and "Murder dropped to Other," are subsets of the first category "Any Reduction in Severity/Charges." The category of "Other," which is also a subset refers to charges changed to criminal charges that are murder or manslaughter.
3. Under **Highest Charge** in Case, the "Other" category captures a defendant who was charged with Arson.
4. Under **Legal Outcomes**, the "Other" Category refers to cases where the Judge refused the charge and the defendant was unindicted. There was evidence that showed the defendant committed the murder, but specific situations in each case that led to these rare outcomes.

between 2000–2019. It is complicated to identify the universe of defendants who raised gay panic defenses because they are not tracked by the government and when they are successful, "acquittals are not appealed" (Pinello, 2003, p. 164). The dearth of insanity and diminished capacity defenses in this sample is consistent with prior research that suggests that "male defendants charged with murdering gay" and trans victims "tend to assert the defense of provocation... claiming that they were provoked into a heat of passion by the victim's... advance" or to assert self-defense (Lee, 2008, p. 499).

In examining the provocation and self-defense cases, prosecutors often charged defendants with murder (92.08%), rather than manslaughter (6.93%). During the court process, though, the initial charges against the defendants were reduced. In some instances, when the defendant faced multiple charges, a charge or charges might be dropped or replaced with a less serious charge. Scholars have identified that defendants raising provocation defenses are often trying to mitigate their murder charges to get them reduced to manslaughter (Lee, 2008; Patel, 2019). In the preliminary analysis of the cases in this study, 12 defendants (11.88%) facing murder charges received a reduction in their charges from murder to manslaughter. Future analysis of this sample will try to pinpoint what role the gay or trans panic defense played in the reduction of charges in these cases.

An analysis of the legal outcomes found that few defendants who raised gay or trans panic defenses were acquitted of their charges. Specifically, only one of the defendants who raised a provocation defense and five of the defendants who raised self-defense arguments were acquitted. Of the defendants who raised these defenses, 35 (34.65%) pleaded guilty, rather than going to trial. Finally, most defendants opted to take their cases to trial, and the majority of these defendants were found guilty. For the provocation defense, 25 out of 42 defendants (59.52%) were found guilty by a jury. Of those who raised a self-defense argument in court, 33 out of 59 defendants (55.93%) were found guilty by a jury.

Finally, this study examined how many of the defendants in this sample filed appeals after their convictions. For this part of my analysis, I checked all of the defendants with convictions. None of the defendants who entered a guilty plea filed an appeal. This is consistent with research that suggests that people who enter into plea deals are less likely to have grounds for an appeal (Lee, 2008). Most of the defendants who were convicted in court by a jury, however, went on to file legal appeals seeking to challenge their guilty verdicts. Specifically, I found that 47 of the 58 people convicted in a trial filed appeals. For this study, I read through each of the appeals, which I will focus on in a future analysis. The courts affirmed the original verdict from the trial in 44 of the 47 appeals. For the three defendants who filed appeals where the courts ruled in their favor:

- One defendant received two new trials (but was convicted again in each trial)
- One defendant had his life sentence vacated, but then, the lower court resentenced him to life in prison
- One defendant had two charges dropped (but his life sentence in prison was unaffected)

Ultimately, most of the defendants who raised gay or trans panic defenses were charged and convicted of murder. Nevertheless, it is striking how frequently gay men and trans women are killed and how frequently gay and trans panic defenses are raised in court.

Next, my ongoing study focuses on the 99 cases where criminal defendants killed 100 gay men ($N = 68$) or trans women ($N = 32$) and raised panic defenses (Tables 2 and 3). Organizing this analysis by victim (gay men vs. trans women) provides the opportunity to identify the similarities and differences between these murders. In comparing the gay men and trans women victims, the first noteworthy difference involves demographic differences in the race-ethnicity between these victims groups. Of the 31 trans women where race/ethnicity information is available, the majority

Table 2. Gay men victims 2000–2019 (N = 68).

Average age	43.91	
Average age of Offender (N = 70)	26.09	
Weapons		
Multiple weapons	15	22.05%
Firearm	11	16.18%
Knife	29	42.65%
Hands	24	35.29%
Objects	15	22.06%
Multiple stabbings (out of 29 total stabbings)	25	86.21%
Five or more stab wounds (out of 29 total stabbings)	20	68.97%
Events with robbery / theft involvement	25	36.77%
Motivation		
Provocation	11	16.18%
Self-Defense	57	83.82%

Note:
1. Missing race/ethnicity for 1 victim.
2. Missing stabbing data for 3 victims (though some cases noted "multiple" stab wounds).
3. Under **Weapons**, the specific categories (i.e. Firearm, Knife) are not mutually exclusive.

Table 3. Trans women victims 2000–2019 (N = 32).

Average age	26.07	
Average age of Offender (N = 39)	24.92	
Victim Race/Ethnicity (N = 31)		
African-American	21	67.74%
Caucasian	2	6.45%
Latinx	7	22.58%
Native American	1	3.23%
Victim involved in Prostitution	11	34.38%
Weapons		
Multiple weapons	2	6.25%
Firearm	16	50.00%
Knife	9	28.13%
Hands	7	21.88%
Objects	3	9.38%
Multiple stabbings (out of 9 total stabbings)	6	66.66%
Five or more stab wounds (out of 9 total stabbings)	4	44.44%
Events with robbery / theft involvement	2	6.25%
Motivation		
Provocation	24	75.00%
Self-Defense	8	25.00%

Note:.
1. Missing race/ethnicity for 1 victim.
2. Missing stabbing data for 2 victims (though some cases noted "multiple" stab wounds).
3. Under **Weapons**, the specific categories (i.e. Firearm, Knife) are not mutually exclusive.

were people of color, with 21 (67.74%) of the victims African-American and 2 (6.45%) Caucasian. While this study is still working on confirming and finalizing the race-ethnicity of the gay victims, the majority of them are Caucasian. This finding is consistent with prior research findings that the majority of gay men who are selected and killed for discriminatory reasons are Caucasian (Gruenewald and Kelley, 2014).

This study also found differences in the average ages of the trans women and gay men victims. The average age of the trans women victims was 26.07 years of age, while the average age of the gay victims was just over 17 years higher at 43.91 years of age. The age of the two groups of offenders, however, was nearly identical with the average ages of the men who killed trans women and the men who killed gay men, respectively, averaging 24.92 and 26.09 years of age. Ultimately, then, this research suggests that gay men were killed by offenders who were on average 18 years younger than them. While the finding that gay men are often killed by younger men is consistent with prior research, the symmetry between the average age of the trans women and their killers warrants additional consideration in future studies.

This analysis also found that most of the homicide defendants in this study sought out the trans women for sexual activity, which might explain why the victims were younger and closer in age to the defendants (in comparison to the defendants who killed gay men, who had a variety of different relationships—acquaintance, coworker, friend, neighbor, potential romantic partner— with their victims). Indeed, in 24 cases, the murder defendants stated that they had killed the trans women in response to discovering that they were transgender. In 11 cases, the trans women were involved in prostitution, and the men who killed them had sought them out for commercial sex. It is worth remarking that the trans women involved in prostitution faced considerable economic challenges. Perhaps if these trans women were raised in middle-income households, they would have had more access to gender affirming surgeries, and more access to the stability (i.e. housing, higher education at liberal arts colleges, professional employment opportunities) that is conferred upon those with financial privilege, which could have protected them from these violent men.

These preliminary findings also lend support to prior research that documents some of the unique risks that gay men face in the United States. A consistent pattern that runs through the literature involves younger men targeting older gay men for theft or robbery (Gruenewald and Kelley, 2014). The homicides of gay men in this study follows the distinct pathway identified by prior research, with 25 (36.77%) of the 68 murders of gay men also including robbery or theft from the victim. Yet in regards to trans women victims, the murder defendants seemed motivated by a desire to commit expressive violence. Indeed, in this research, there were only 2 of the 32 murders of trans women where offenders stole property from their victims.

This analysis of the 68 gay men also provides additional empirical support for the findings from Miller and Humphreys (1980) and Gruenewald and Kelley (2014) that the murders of gay men often involve extreme brutality. The defendants in this analysis who killed the 68 gay men in this study used multiple weapons 22.05% of the time, which often resulted in a serious mutilation of their victims' bodies. These defendants were also more likely to inflict lethal violence on their gay victims using weapons that involved close and personal contact, such as knives (42.65%), hands (35.29%), and/or objects (22.06%) such as crow bars, hammers, and tire jacks. For the 29 homicides of gay men that involved a knife, 25 out of 29 of the victims were stabbed multiple times; and at least 20 of these 29 victims were stabbed five or more times. In comparison, the defendants who killed the 32 trans women in this analysis primarily used a single weapon (93.75%) rather than multiple weapons (6.25%). The men who murdered trans women were also more likely to use firearms (50.00%), followed by knives (28.13%), hands (21.88%), and/or objects (9.38%).

By raising the gay or trans panic self-defense, these defendants, whether consciously or unconsciously, link homosexuality or transgender identity with criminality. The pairing of sexual orientation or gender identity with an allegation of sexual assault contributes to a discriminatory narrative that implies that these victims, who were gay or transgender, were sexual predators rather than victims. In the future, this study plans to probe these cases to examine the role that the defendant, and possibly the justice workers and legal professionals, played in creating these gay and trans panic narratives, especially in regards to provocation and self-defense. Within the study data, there are at least two cases where defendants initially reported to police that the victims merely made passes at them; after meeting with their lawyers, the defendants then later alleged that victims had engaged in attempted sexual assaults. In the future, it will be important to analyze a variety of legal documents, especially trial transcripts, to analyze what was actually said in the courtroom. Additionally, it will be important to examine how traditional media and social media sources reported on these cases. Specifically, researchers should examine the reach of the gay and trans panic defense beyond the courtroom. Even in cases where a jury rejects this defense, the toxic message of a gay or trans panic defense can still negatively influence public opinion about gay men and trans women.

Some defendants also raised self-defense claims that alleged that their victims were HIV positive to argue that they killed to protect themselves from sexual assaults and potential HIV infections. In three homicides cases in 2005, 2014, and 2016, defense attorneys stated that the victims were HIV positive, and claimed that being HIV positive was equivalent to carrying a lethal weapon. It is noteworthy that these cases happened between 2005–2016, 15–20 years after the initial public hysteria around AIDS in the United States. From a legal perspective, these defendants are entitled to make this self-defense argument. Indeed, several states have laws that prohibit people who are HIV positive, from knowingly engaging in unprotected sex or from threatening to assault people with their bodily fluids (saliva, blood). In Texas in 2002, for example, a jail inmate suffering from HIV was charged with assault with a deadly weapon for biting a nurse (*Degrate v. State*, 2005 Tex. App. LEXIS 547). The courts, however, are inconsistent about finding that a person's HIV status is a potential lethal weapon. In Maryland in 1993, a man who was HIV-positive robbed and sexually assaulted three women without using a condom; this man was convicted for attempted murder (because he was HIV positive), sexual assault, and robbery (*Smallwood v. State*, 680 A.2d 512 Md. 1996). However, on appeal, the State repealed the charge for attempted murder, arguing that the defendant's" actions are wholly explained by an intent to commit rape and armed robbery, the crimes for which he has already pled guilty ... " but "that his actions fail to provide evidence that he also had an intent to kill" (*Smallwood v. State*, 2006, p. 9)

Examining the three cases where these defendant raised self-defense claims that posited they were defending themselves from potential HIV infections suggests that these defenses are more problematic than they might at first appear (see Table 4). In Denton, Texas, in 1995, one defendant, Joshua Abbott, argued that he killed the victim, David Morrison, to protect himself from a potential sexual assault that might infect him with HIV. Yet Abbott, who was supposedly trying to protect himself from HIV, stabbed Morrision at least 38 times. Abbott directed the majority of these stabbings to Morrison's throat and face, which resulted in large quantities of blood splashing Abbott in the face (Unequal Justice Joshua Abbott, 2008); Abbott also stabbed Morrison with such force that blood flew over him and saturated the back of his shirt (McNary, 2007). Why would Abbott, if he believed that Morrison was HIV positive, choose to kill Morrision in such a bloody manner that would be more likely to expose Abbott to HIV?

Another case that involved a defendant alleging self-defense from HIV involved two victims. In Bakersfield, California, in 2014, Joaquin Balassa, a former Mixed Martial Arts fighter, invited three people—a close friend and two older men who were a romantic couple—to his apartment. After a night of heavy drinking Balassa, killed the two gay men. At trial, Balassa raised a self-defense argument, alleging that he woke up to the two men sexually assaulting him; fearing that they had HIV, he proceeded to kill them. Similar to the other cases with victims alleged to be HIV positive, Balassa killed these men in a close and personal way, with his hands, in a manner that resulted in considerable bloodshed. Indeed, in his legal appeal, the appellate court judges make note of the scene that the police encountered when they went to his apartment: "One of officers told the other that when defendant opened the door, she saw broken glass and what appeared to be a large amount of blood in the entryway, leading her to believe someone inside was either seriously injured or dead" (*People v Balassa*, 2020). The appeal also details how when the police entered the apartment, they "described the scene as very bloody" If Balassa was concerned about being exposed to HIV, why would he kill his victims in such an intimate way that resulted in so much bloodshed and could have exposed him to the virus? Additionally, according to the appeal, neither of the defendant's victims was in fact HIV-positive.

In El Paso, Texas, in 2016, a defendant, Anthony Bowden, made a similar self-defense argument claiming that he killed Erykah Tijerina to protect himself from being raped by someone with HIV. Yet Bowden was unable to prove his self-defense argument in court. A weakness in his

Table 4. Extract of gay and trans panic defenses, alphabetized by defendant last name.

Trial	Case	Court	Location	Defendant	Victim	Defense	Outcome
2006	State v Abbott	158th Judicial District Court	Denton, Texas	Abbott, Joshua Aaron	Morrison, David	Gay Panic, Self-Defense	Acquitted,1st Degree Murder
2019	State v Bowden	384th District Court	El Paso, Texas	Bowden, Anthony Michael	Tijereinta, Erykah	Trans Panic, Self-Defense	Convicted, 1st Degree Murder and Sentenced to 35 years
2014	People v Balassa	Superior Court of Kern County in California	Bakersfield, California	Balassa, Joaquin Miguel	Fajardo, Jose Antonio and Koukal, Guy Richard	Gay Panic, Self-Defense	Convicted, 1st Degree Murder Sentenced to Life without Parole
2019	People v Harris	9th Judicial District Court	Alexandria, Louisiana	Harris, Desmond	McGlory, Jaylow	Trans Panic, Self-Defense	Acquitted, 2nd Degree Murder
2015	State v James	Superior Court of Dougherty County	Albany, Georgia	James, Kuyaunnis	Johnson, Shatoya	Trans Panic, Self-Defense	Grand Jury did not indict for Voluntary Manslaughter, pled guilty to Pandering (Misdemeanor). Sentence Unknown
2006	People v Kyles	[unable to find court name]	Dotham, Alabama	Kyles, Steven	Nickson, Ashley	Trans Panic, Self-Defense	Convicted Felony Murder, Sentenced to Life
2018	State v Lewis	187th District Court	San Antonio, Texas	Lewis, Mark Daniel	McFadden, Kenne	Trans Panic, Self-Defense	Judge Dismissed Manslaughter
2018	State v Miller	450th District Court	Austin, Texas	Miller, James Robert	Spencer, Daniel	Gay Panic, Self-Defense	Convicted, Criminally Negligent Homicide, 6 months jail and 10 years probation
2017	State v Rowell	299th District Criminal Court	Austin, Texas	Rowell, Jon Casey	Loera, Monica	Trans Panic, Self-Defense	Convicted, 1st Degree Murder and Sentenced to 20 years
2019	State v Twyne	147th District Court	Austin, Texas	Twyne, Justin	Short, James	Gay Panic, Self-Defense	Convicted, 1st Degree Murder and Sentenced to 40 years
Pending	State v Weathers	3rd Judicial Circuit of Michigan	Detroit, Michigan	Weathers, Albert	Stough, Kelly	Trans Panic, Self-Defense	Pending

self-defense argument was that he was missing a critical element to prove self-defense–imminent danger. Specifically, Bowden exited the victim's apartment and was standing alone outside. Tijerina did not follow him out into the parking lot of her apartment complex. Therefore, Bowden did not face immediate danger from Tijerina when he decided to walk over to his car, open the trunk, take out a chisel, and return to her apartment, where he proceeded to stab her to death 24 times. Ultimately, the jury seemed unpersuaded by his claim of self-defense, convicting him of first-degree murder; the court sentenced him to 35 years in prison.

At the same time, defense attorneys, in raising self-defense arguments on behalf of their clients, have attempted to prove a gay or trans panic affirmative defense by suggesting that the act of homicide is so extreme that the motive for the defendants could only be self-defense. In one case, a defense attorney in 2018 so stated: "It was so uncharacteristic of (him) that for him to engage in this behavior clearly had to be an act of self-defense" (Powell, 2018). In this case just described, defendant James Miller in Texas in 2015, chased the victim around his own apartment, pulled the victim out from underneath a table where he was hiding, stabbed the victim four times (including once in the back), cleaned up the apartment, returned to his home, and showered and changed his clothes before he called the police. In another case from 2019 in Texas, a defense attorney stated that the defendant, Justin Twyne, is "either a serial killer or there's some horrible triggering event, and there's nothing that you've seen to indicate he's a serial killer" (Kamath et al., 2020). In this case, the defendant, who portrayed himself as a sex worker to gain entry to the victim's house, tied up the victim (a man in his 70s), burned him with a lighter, stabbed him 28 times, and tied a plastic bag around his head to asphyxiate him. The defendant then stole cash, property, and an automobile from the victim.

The defendants in my study argued self-defense in six cases with transgender women victims. In two of those cases, defendants were looking to purchase sex, then killed the victims with firearms and later claimed the victims had tried to rob them. These claims of robbery represent a new type of trans panic legal self-defense strategy for men accused of killing transgender women. In these two cases, the men shot the victims and left them to die; one defendant, Albert Weathers in Michigan in 2018, called the police an hour later to report an attempted robbery and the other defendant, Jon Casey Rowell in Texas in 2016, fled the scene without calling the police. Each of the victims were portrayed as attacking the defendant with a deadly weapon (sharp metal object, baseball bat), even though there was no evidence of these weapons, much less an attack.

In two other cases involving transgender victims, defendants claimed that the victims, who they had sex with, had tried to sexually assault them. In one case, a defendant, Desmond Harris in 2019 in Louisiana, who had previously had sex with the victim, stated in court that the victim had tried to sexually penetrate him before he murdered her in 2017. This defendant, who was called to testify, made certain that the jury knew that he was the one who had penetrated the victim in their past sexual encounters, and not vice versa. In the second case where the defendant, Michael Bowden in Texas in 2019, claimed to be fighting back against an attempted sexual assault from a transgender woman, the defense attorney stated that the victim was a predator who had raped the defendant previously and was attempting to rape the victim again. Additionally, the defense attorney misgendered the victim as male and alleged that she had HIV and was therefore attempting to use deadly force on the defendant.

Similar to the cases involving gay panic, defendants sought to denigrate the transgender women victims, and in two cases, their attorneys misgendered the victims by referring to them as males. Perhaps these defense attorneys were reluctant to refer to the victims as women because it would emphasize that these cases involved "gender violence" against women (Lee and Kwan, 2014, p. 82). The issue of gender pronouns, and the language that legal professionals use to refer to people who are LGBTQ+, is an especially timely issue given a recent court case decision from the United States Court of Appeals for the Fifth Circuit, *United States v. Varner* (2020), which denied the motion of an inmate, who identifies as a trans woman, to change the name on her judgment of committal to a female name. This decision, which was controversial (Hyer, 2020; Millhiser, 2020), asserted three points: (1) that there was no legal precedent or legislation for this request, (2) that the use of pronouns that match a person's gender identity could call the court's impartiality into question, and that (3) the use of gender pronouns is sometimes more complicated than merely using the opposite pronoun (i.e. some prefer gender neutral pronouns).

While *Varner* seems to indicate that legal professionals are under no obligation to use the gender pronoun that reflects the individual's gender identity, it is worth noting how legal professionals involved in the cases in this study addressed issues of gender pronouns in regards to the trans women victims. The Texas First Court of Appeals in Rowell v. *State* (2019) refers to the victim, a trans woman, as Monica Loera, the name that matches her gender identity. The California Court of Appeals in People v. *Scott* (2003) explicitly addresses the victim's gender by stating: "The victim, Alina Barrigan, was a 19-year-old man. From an early age, Alina had identified as a female, and her family accepted her as such. Alina dressed in female clothing and adopted a female name." In *People v. Merel* (2009), the California Court of Appeal seems to address some of the concerns (in 2009) raised by *United States v. Varner* (about how using preferred pronouns may "be more complex than at first it might appear"). Specifically, the Court states that the victim "had dressed and presented herself as a female since she was 14 years old, and was also known by the name Gwen." In a footnote in the same opinion, the Court clarifies that it will refer to the victim as Lida "[b]ecause defendants knew Araujo as Lida at all times relevant to this case," but clarify that they "intend no disrespect by this designation." Finally, the Court states: "We shall refer to Edward/Lida/Gwen Araujo as 'she' because it is clear the victim self-identified as female." In responding to these appeals, the courts involved seems to be attempting to communicate in a manner that is respectful to the defendant and sensitive to the victim (and the victim's friends and family)—the judges, in their response to these appeals, do not seem to be attempting to engage in activism on behalf of the LGBTQ + community. At no point does it appear that the Courts, in their sensitive and precise language, are trying to stack the deck against the cisgender male defendants in order to confer benefits or advantages upon these transgender victims. In the criminal cases that preceded these legal appeals, the victims died in terrible ways, and the justices writing these opinions seem to be attempting to conduct themselves in a manner that is sensitive to the victims and their families. American society is changing quickly in regards to how the government, including the criminal justice system, treats people who identify as transgender or non-binary, and what is and is not good manners when referring to a transgender's name or pronouns. The Fifth Circuit's *Varner* decision (2020) is not the final word on the civil rights that are to be extended toward people who are transgender or non-binary.

CONCLUSION

This research note reports on an ongoing study of 100 homicide victims from 2000–2019 with defendants who raised a gay or trans panic argument alleging that their homicidal actions should be excused or justified. This ongoing study builds on two prior research areas that include studies of the gay and trans panic defense and studies about bias crimes committed against the LGBTQ + community. This ongoing study also builds on prior studies that have started to collect and analyze caseloads of gay and trans victims.

Research focused on the gay and trans panic defense has the potential to benefit many different stakeholders. This research enables scholars to communicate the importance of gay and trans lives, through the rigor of their methods and the strength of their findings. Even in the year 2021, trans women and gay men experience discrimination and violence trying to openly live their lives. Focusing on the gay and trans panic defense provides researchers the opportunity to help dismantle at least a century of propaganda that has led generations of Americans to believe that they can harm and kill gay men or trans women with impunity.

Research about the gay and trans panic defense benefits scholars and researchers who are interested in identifying the gay men and transgender women who were killed by defendants who raised a panic defense. Policymakers can use these data to learn about the people who were killed to appreciate the stakes of this issue. Policymakers can also examine specific instances of how defendants raised these defenses and identify the different themes in these defenses. For researchers, studies about the gay and trans panic defenses also contribute to studies of other legal defense theories that seek to justify a private citizen's use of force against another person, such as the Stand Your Ground self-defense laws in several states. Research about the gay and trans panic defense adds to the research about how gender, sex, race-ethnicity, and other types of identity impact the legal defenses of excused and justified homicides.

This ongoing study has several limitations. One limitation is that this study is a long way from identifying all homicide cases where a defendant relied on a gay or trans panic defense argument. Researchers trying to identify these cases by searching for legal appeals will miss cases that were acquitted or ended in plea deals. At the same time, researchers trying to find these cases in newspaper archives face challenges in that there is no standard language over the decades to identify these cases, which means it is easy to miss instances in the past involving the gay and panic defense. Another challenge of using the media to identify gay and trans panic cases is that the public and thus the media have not always prioritized these cases. Prior to 1969, several media sources could only report about LGBTQ + issues generally and gay and trans panic defenses specifically in coded ways; they were prevented from directly discussing same-sex relationships and sexual identity (Polchin, 2019). Some newspapers may continue to have editorial policies that prefer to ignore or minimize discussion of LGBQT + legal issues (Polchin, 2019). Finally, sometimes there was also limited information about specific cases in newspapers, which made it difficult to examine what had transpired in these cases.

NOTES

1. A prior reader of this article made an important comment that the Lesbian, Gay, Bi-Sexual, Transgender, and Queer (LGBTQ+) community is not one community. Specifically, according to this reader, each of the individuals who are LGBTQ + are different. Additionally, people who commit bias or hate crimes against victims who are LGBTQ + are targeting specific individuals for specific reasons. Yet, this study sometimes uses inclusivity, and the term LGBQT + community, because bias seems to target the entire community, whether it is violence, the protesting of same sex marriage, or legislation allowing businesses to deny services to individuals based on their sexual orientation or sexual identity.
2. Recently, the LGBT Bar, a section of the American Bar Association, has begun to use the phrase "LGBTQ + panic defenses" to refer to the gay and trans panic defenses (LGBT Bar, n.d.). This research note, however, focuses on gay men and trans women, as these are the majority of the victims in these cases. There are, however, outliers. One outlier case occurred in 1988, when Stephen Roy Carr shot two women multiple times, killing one, at an Appalachian campsite (Lee, 2003). During Carr's murder trial, Carr's defense attorney raised a gay panic defense, claiming that the romantic relationship between the two women had driven Carr into a state of temporary insanity. Carr was found guilty and sentenced to life in prison. I have not located any cases where a female murder defendant used a gay or trans panic defense.
3. The districts and states with anti–panic legislation are: California (2014), Colorado (2020), Connecticut (2019), District of Columbia (2020), Hawaii (2019), Illinois (2017), Maine (2019), Maryland (2021), Nevada (2019), New York (2019), New Jersey (2020), Oregon (2021), Rhode Island (2018), Vermont (2021), Virginia (2021) Washington (2020) (LGBT Bar, n.d.).
4. While several legal organizations, such as the LGBT Bar, have celebrated anti-panic defense legislation, not everyone welcomes these changes. Criminal defense attorneys have pushed back against anti-panic defense legislation, arguing that it interferes with their ability to provide a vigorous defense of their clients, and have threatened to challenge this legislation in court in an attempt to get these laws overturned (Kamins, 2019).
5. I have collected gay and trans panic cases dating back to 1970. Ultimately, I want to count as many of these cases as I can from 1970 to the present. The reason I had originally selected 1970 as my starting point was that is the year after the Stonewall Riots (28 June–3 July 1969) and three years after what is

considered the first legally recognized use of the gay panic defense in 1967 (People v Rodriguez, 256 Cal.App.2d 663). This seems like an intersection of increased civil riots for the LGBTQ + community and the rise of a legal defense that signals out individuals who are LGBTQ+. For this analysis, I focus on 2000–2019, because I am prioritizing the most recent cases, with the notion that it is important to study what is happening now (in the more recent cases) to best address the contemporary manifestations of this problematic defense strategy.

6. This review of the legal history of the gay and trans panic defense is heavily influenced by Cynthia Lee, who has written extensively about the development of these affirmative defenses (Lee, 2003, 2008, 2014, 2019; Lee and Kwan, 2014). This review also draws heavily on Patel's (2019) review of the gay panic defense.

7. While the judge presiding over Mathew Sheppard's murder trial prohibited the use of a gay panic defense, the defendant Aaron McKinney found a way to introduce the provocation defense (Lee, 2008). His defense counsel painted Sheppard as a gay predator by introducing two witnesses who told of Sheppard sexually propositioning them in an overt, almost aggressive manner. The judge allowed this testimony, not recognizing this as a form of a gay panic defense. As a result, the defense was allowed to suggest that Sheppard encouraged the fatal violence directed at him. In the end, the jury acquitted McKinney of the more serious charge of 1st degree murder, convicting him instead of felony murder (Lee, 2008).

8. It is important to note that beginning in the 1970s, LGBTQ + activists began to openly report on violence in LGBTQ + newspapers and leveraged this reporting to provide evidence to mainstream society of the violence that they confronted trying to live their lives (Polchin, 2019). The legacy of these efforts has continued today with annual reports of violence against LGBTQ + people as well as special projects that focus on collecting cases for a set period of time. For example, The Coloradoan newspaper published a dataset of over 600 violent deaths of LGBTQ + people in America between 1998 and 2018 (Marmaduke and Hindi, 2018).

9. Studies of the gay and trans panic defense focus on how gay and trans panic defenses are raised, and the impacts these defenses have on prosecutors, judges, and juries. By contrast, studies of violent crimes are focused on offenses committed against LGBTQ + victims. For these latter studies, researchers take steps to verify the sexual orientation or gender identity of the victims.

10. Possible questions regarding the assessment of sexual orientation in no particular order: Does the person have to self-identify? Does the person have to have some prior same-sex sexual experience? What if there is prior heterosexual experience? What if the person has never engaged in same-sex sexual experience? What if the person engaging in a same-sex sexual experience is only experimenting? What if the person has never engaged in any same-sex sexual experience and everyone "knows" that person is heterosexual?

11. When I began this research, I had to experiment with various search terms. Entering the search term "gay panic" can generate many different types of hits depending on the search engine and the time period searched.

12. Reaching out to people (face-to-face conversations, telephone calls, emails) resulted in approximately 10 additional cases that did not show up in my initial reading or search engine research.

13. In examining cases, this study occasionally came across homicides that arose from domestic violence. These cases had several kinds of evidence that suggested that the homicide was an instance that may well have truly justified lethal self-defense, such as a history of stalking, accounts of prior violence, and accounts of a troubled relationship between the parties involved.

14. This study carefully evaluated alleged self-defense murders that occurred in correctional settings, as the remedies to protect one's self from sexual assault are limited in prison (Levan Miller, 2010; Rowell-Cunsolo et al., 2014).

REFERENCES

Boven, J. (2009). Matthew Shepard Hate crimes act passes despite GOP opposition. *The Colorado Independent*, October 9. https://www.coloradoindependent.com/2009/10/09/matthew-shepard-hate-crimes-act-passes-despite-gop-opposition/.

Capers, B. (2011). Real rape too. *California Law Review*, 99(5), 1259–1307. https://doi.org/10.15779/Z38570D

Center for Homicide Research. (2015). *National GLBT Homicide Dataset Codebook*. 2015 Access Version. Center for Homicide Research 2006-2015, Minneapolis, Minnesota.

Comstock, G. D. (1992). Dismantling the homosexual panic defense. *Law & Sexuality: A Review of Lesbian and Gay Legal Issues*, 2, 81–102.

Degrate v. State. (2005). No. 05-04-00218-CR (Tex. App. Jan. 26, 2005).

Federal Bureau of Investigation. (2011). *Hate Crime Statistics. Crime in the United States, 2010.* Retrieved July 13, 2020, from https://ucr.fbi.gov/hate-crime/2010/resources/hate-crime-2010-about-hate-crime.

Gruenewald, J. (2012). Are anti-LGBT homicides in the United States unique? *Journal of Interpersonal Violence, 27*(18), 3601–3623. https://doi.org/10.1177/0886260512462301

Gruenewald, J., & Kelley, K. (2014). Exploring anti–LGBT homicide by mode of victim selection. *Criminal Justice and Behavior, 41*(9), 1130–1152. https://doi.org/10.1177/0093854814541259

Harvard Law Review. (1989). Developments in the law: Sexual orientation and the law. *Harvard Law Review, 102*(7), 1508–1671. https://doi.org/10.2307/1341338

Hyer, J. L. (2020). *Sherry Levin Wallach and Kristen Prata Browde. "Examining Judicial Civility in New York Courts for Transgender Persons in the Wake of United States v. Varner" New York State Bar Association, 18 August 2020.* https://nysba.org/examining-judicial-civility-in-new-york-courts-for-transgender-persons-in-the-wake-of-united-states-v-varner-2/

Kamins, B. (2019). New York Eliminates a Criminal Defense: A Due Process Violation? *Law.com New York Law Journal,* 2 August. https://www.law.com/newyorklawjournal/2019/08/02/new-york-eliminates-a-criminal-defense-a-due-process-violation/#.

Kamath, T., Falcon, R., Glas, B. (2020). *Man found guilty of killing attorney, stabbing him 28 times. KXAN,* March 11, 2019. Retrieved July 13, from https://www.kxan.com/news/local/austin/man-found-guilty-of-killing-attorney-stabbing-him-28-times/amp/

Kelley, K., & Gruenewald, J. (2015). Accomplishing masculinity through Anti–Lesbian, Gay, Bisexual, and Transgender Homicide: A comparative case study approach. *Men and Masculinities, 18*(1), 3–29. https://doi.org/10.1177/1097184X14551204

Kempf, E. J. (1920). *Psychopathology.* C. V. Mosby Company.

Lang, N. (2016). James Dixon pleads guilty in death of Islan Nettles. *Advocate,* April 5. Accessed June 28, 2021 from https://www.advocate.com/transgender/2016/4/05/james-dixon-pleads-guilty-death-black-trans-woman-islan-nettles

Lee, C. (2003). *Murder and the reasonable man passion and fear in the criminal courtroom.* New York University Press.

Lee, C. (2008). The gay panic defense. *U.C. Davis Law Review, 42*(2), 471–566.

Lee, C. (2014). Masculinity on trial: Gay panic in the criminal courtroom. *Southwestern Law Review, 42*(4), 817–831.

Lee, C. (2019). 57 AM. CRIM. L. REV. 1411 (2020); GWU Law School Public Law Research Paper No. 2019-63; GWU Legal Studies Research Paper No. 2019-63. https://ssrn.com/abstract=3481295

Lee, C., & Kwan, P. K. Y. (2014). The trans panic defense: Masculinity, heteronormativity, and the murder of transgender women. *Hastings Law Journal, 66*(1), 77–132.

Lee, H. K. (2005). Manslaughter Ruled Out, Araujo Juror Says, S.F. CHRON., Sept. 14, 2005, at B1.

Levan Miller, K. (2010). The darkest figure of crime: Perceptions of reasons for male inmates to not report sexual assault. *Justice Quarterly, 27*(5), 692–712. https://doi.org/10.1080/07418820903292284

The LGBT Bar. (n.d.). LGBTQ+ 'panic' defense. Retrieved May 29, 2020, from https://lgbtbar.org/programs/advocacy/gay-trans-panic-defense/.

Lippman, M. (2018). Part 2, criminal and regulatory laws, 2.9 crimes against the person: The 'gay panic' defense. In *Striking the balance: Debating criminal justice and law* (pp. 85–92). SAGE.

Marmaduke, J., Hindi, S. (2018). Suffering in the shadows: More than 600 LGBTQ people killed in the US in past two decades. *The Coloradoan,* 31 October. https://www.coloradoan.com/story/news/2018/10/31/more-than-600-lgbtq-people-killed-us-past-two-decades-since-matthew-shepard-murder/1670264002/

McNary, C. (2007). DA's Burden: Sympathy for a Killer. *The Dallas Morning News,* 11 November. Retrieved July 13, 2020, from https://www.dallasnews.com/news/investigations/2007/11/11/da-s-burden-sympathy-for-a-killer/

Millhiser, I. (2020, January 17). Trump judge lashes out at a transgender litigant in a surprisingly cruel opinion: Judge Kyle Duncan was a prominent anti-LGBTQ lawyer before joining the bench. *Vox.* Retrieved June 24, 2021, from https://www.vox.com/2020/1/17/21067634/trump-judge-transgender-cruel-kyle-duncan-united-states-varner

Miller, B., & Humphreys, L. (1980). Lifestyles and violence: Homosexual victims of assault and murder. *Qualitative Sociology, 3*(3), 169–185. https://doi.org/10.1007/BF00987134

Nicolas, P. (2003). They say he's gay': The admissibility of evidence of sexual orientation. *Georgia Law Review, 37*(3), 793–892.

Parkin, W. S., & Gruenewald, J. (2017). Open-source data and the study of homicide. *Journal of Interpersonal Violence, 32*(18), 2693–2723. https://doi.org/10.1177/0886260515596145

Patel, D. N. (2019). The indefensible "gay panic defense. *Journal of Legislation, 46*(1), 114–133.

People v. Balassa. (2020) No. F073733. Court of Appeals, Fifth District. February 20, 2020.

Pinello, D. R. (2003). *Gay rights and American law.* Cambridge University Press.

Polchin, J. (2019). *Indecent advances: A hidden history of true crime and prejudice before stonewall.* Icon Books.

Powell, J. (2018, April 26). After using rare 'gay panic' legal defense, Austin man avoids prison time. *KXAN*. Accessed July 13, 2020, from https://www.kxan.com/news/local/austin/after-using-rare-gay-panic-legal-defense-austin-man-avoids-prison-time/1141686601/

Rowell-Cunsolo, T. L., Harrison, R. J., & Haile Rowell-Cunsolo, R. (2014). Exposure to prison sexual assault among incarcerated Black men. *Journal of African American Studies, 18*(1), 54–62. https://doi.org/10.1007/s12111-013-9253-6

Salonga, R. (2019, December 22). "Man who killed popular south bay safeway butcher takes plea deal." *The Mercury News.* https://www.mercurynews.com/2019/12/06/man-who-killed-popular-south-bay-butcher-takes-manslaughter-plea/

Smith, G. A. (2020). *The transgender day of remembrance website.* Accessed April 29, Transgender Day of Remembrance | Honoring those lost to anti-transgender violence (tdor.info).

Strader, K., Selvin, M., & Hay, L. (2015). Gay panic, gay victims, and the case for gay shield laws. *Cardozo Law Review, 36*(4), 1473–1531.

Suffredini, K. S. (2001). Pride and prejudice: The homosexual panic defense. *Boston College Third World Law Journal, 21*(2), 279–314.

Terrorism Research Center. (2020). *Bias Homicide Database (BHDB) Manual and Codebook.* University of Arkansas.

Tomei, J., Cramer, R. J., Boccaccini, M. T., & Panza, N. R. (2017). The gay panic defense: Legal defense strategy or reinforcement of homophobia in court? *Journal of Interpersonal Violence, 32*(1), 1–23. https://doi.org/10.1177/0886260517713713

Tomei, J., & Cramer, R. J. (2016). Legal policies in conflict: The gay panic defense and hate crime legislation. *Journal of Forensic Psychology Practice, 16*(4), 217–235. https://doi.org/10.1080/15228932.2016.1192331

Unequal Justice Joshua Abbott. (2008, March 6). Young man stabs an older man in his neck and face repeatedly for trying to kiss him. [Video]. YouTube. https://www.youtube.com/watch?v=e2AEa8loV5c

Wirtz, A. L., Poteat, T. C., Malik, M., & Glass, N. (2018). Gender-based violence against transgender people in the United States: A call for research and programming. *Trauma, Violence & Abuse, 21*(2), 227–241. https://doi.org/10.1177/1524838018757749

Wodda, A., & Panfil, V. R. (2015). Don't talk to me about deception': The necessary erosion of the trans-panic defense. *Albany Law Review, 78*(3), 927–972.

Woods, J. B., Sears, B., Mallory, C. (2016). Model legislation for eliminating the gay and trans panic defenses. *The Williams Institute.* Retrieved July 13, 2020, from https://escholarship.org/uc/item/391006hj

Legal cases cited

Commonwealth v. Shelley. (1978). 373 N.E.2d 951, 956 (Mass. App. Ct. 1978).

People v. Merel. (2009). Court of Appeals of California, First Appellate District, Division Four. May 12, 2009. Unpublished Opinion

People v. Parisie. (1972). 287 N.E.2d 310, 329 (Ill. App. Ct. 1972).

People v. Rodriguez. (1967).64 Cal. Rptr. 253, 255 (Cal. Ct. App. 1967).

People v. Scott. (2003). California Court of Appeal. Mar. 27, 2003. Unpublished opinion.

Rowell v. State. (2019). NO. 01-18-00064-CR (Tex. App. Feb. 21, 2019).

Smallwood v. State. (1996). 680 A.2d 512 (Md. 1996).

State v. Thornton. (1975). 532 S.W.2d 37, 44 (Mo. Ct. App. 1975).

United States v. Varner. (2020). No. 19-40016 (5th Cir. 2020).

Index

Taylor & Francis eBooks

www.taylorfrancis.com

A single destination for eBooks from Taylor & Francis with increased functionality and an improved user experience to meet the needs of our customers.

90,000+ eBooks of award-winning academic content in Humanities, Social Science, Science, Technology, Engineering, and Medical written by a global network of editors and authors.

TAYLOR & FRANCIS EBOOKS OFFERS:

A streamlined experience for our library customers

A single point of discovery for all of our eBook content

Improved search and discovery of content at both book and chapter level

REQUEST A FREE TRIAL
support@taylorfrancis.com

 Routledge
Taylor & Francis Group

 CRC Press
Taylor & Francis Group